T0381792

The Dialogical Roots of Deduction

This comprehensive account of the concept and practices of deduction is the first to bring together perspectives from philosophy, history, psychology and cognitive science, and mathematical practice. Catarina Dutilh Novaes draws on all of these perspectives to argue for an overarching conceptualization of deduction as a dialogical practice: deduction has dialogical roots, and these dialogical roots are still largely present both in theories and in practices of deduction. Dutilh Novaes' account also highlights the deeply human and in fact *social* nature of deduction, as embedded in actual human practices; as such, it presents a highly innovative account of deduction. The book will be of interest to a wide range of readers, from advanced students to senior scholars, and from philosophers to mathematicians and cognitive scientists.

Catarina Dutilh Novaes is Professor of Philosophy and University Research Chair at Vrije Universiteit Amsterdam, and Professorial Fellow at Arché (University of St Andrews). She is the author of *Formalizing Medieval Logical Theories* (2007) and *Formal Languages in Logic* (Cambridge University Press, 2012), and co-editor of *The Cambridge Companion to Medieval Logic* (with Stephen Read, Cambridge University Press, 2016).

The Dialogical Roots of Deduction

Historical, Cognitive, and Philosophical Perspectives on Reasoning

Catarina Dutilh Novaes

Vrije Universiteit Amsterdam and University of St Andrews

CAMBRIDGE
UNIVERSITY PRESS

University Printing House, Cambridge CB2 8BS, United Kingdom

One Liberty Plaza, 20th Floor, New York, NY 10006, USA

477 Williamstown Road, Port Melbourne, VIC 3207, Australia

314–321, 3rd Floor, Plot 3, Splendor Forum, Jasola District Centre,
New Delhi – 110025, India

79 Anson Road, #06–04/06, Singapore 079906

Cambridge University Press is part of the University of Cambridge.

It furthers the University's mission by disseminating knowledge in the pursuit of
education, learning, and research at the highest international levels of excellence.

www.cambridge.org
Information on this title: www.cambridge.org/9781108479882
DOI: 10.1017/9781108800792

First published 2021

A catalogue record for this publication is available from the British Library.

Library of Congress Cataloging-in-Publication Data
Names: Novaes, Catarina Dutilh, author.
Title: The dialogical roots of deduction : historical, cognitive, and philosophical
perspectives on reasoning / Catarina Dutilh Novaes, VU Amsterdam and
University of St Andrews.
Description: Cambridge, United Kingdom ; New York, NY, USA : Cambridge
University Press, 2021. | Includes bibliographical references and index.
Identifiers: LCCN 2020035672 (print) | LCCN 2020035673 (ebook) | ISBN
9781108479882 (hardback) | ISBN 9781108800792 (ebook)
Subjects: LCSH: Logic.
Classification: LCC BC71 .N69 2021 (print) | LCC BC71 (ebook) | DDC
162–dc23
LC record available at https://lccn.loc.gov/2020035672
LC ebook record available at https://lccn.loc.gov/2020035673

ISBN 978-1-108-47988-2 Hardback

Contents

Contents   vii

Figures

Preface

This book has been in the making for over ten years or, to put it differently, I have been thinking about deduction from a dialogical perspective for over ten years. In February 2010, I submitted the grant proposal "The Roots of Deduction" to the Netherlands Organisation for Scientific Research (NWO) (VIDI 720225), which I had been working on for at least six months before that. At the time, I did not yet have a permanent academic position, and securing this grant was of vital importance for my career, as it would put me in a strong position to negotiate a permanent position somewhere (such is the system in the Netherlands, for better or worse). On October 7, 2010 (I remember the exact date, as it also happens to be the birthday of my older daughter), I received the happy news that my application had been successful. I could finally relax, knowing that my future in academia was more or less guaranteed from then on. I was then offered a permanent position at the Philosophy Faculty of the University of Groningen, where I started running the project in July 2011.

Ten years may sound like a long time for a book to be written, and indeed it should have been completed years ago (roughly coinciding with the end of the project funding in 2016). But life interfered with my plans, as it usually does (though these were particularly challenging years on the personal front for me). Still, late or not, here it is, finally; I owe it to the world (not to mention the funding agencies that generously supported me with taxpayer money) to share what I take to be the important findings presented here.

The main hypothesis defended throughout the book is the idea that deduction has dialogical roots, and that these dialogical roots are still largely present both in theories and in practices where deduction features prominently. Of course, this claim can be understood in many ways. The original inspiration for this approach came from the history of deduction, in particular the emergence of deduction in Ancient Greek philosophy and mathematics (discussed in Chapters 5 and 6). Defying the perils of the genetic fallacy, I hypothesized that these historical roots would still be present in current instantiations of conceptualizations and practices of deduction, albeit enmeshed with non-dialogical components picked up along the way. Thus, it seemed to me that the dialogical perspective would allow for a unified account of deductive theories and practices, which would explain at one stroke some puzzling and apparently disconnected features of the phenomena in question.

In the past years, I have published a number of papers where the dialogical hypothesis is applied to specific issues; however, the whole story requires a book-length treatment to bring all these different pieces together. Indeed, individually each of these findings only offers limited evidential support to the dialogical hypothesis; it is only when put together side by side that the strength of the dialogical account truly emerges. Put differently, the argumentative structure of this book can be described as an inference to the best explanation: the dialogical hypothesis is the best way to make sense of the variety of manifestations of deductive reasoning and argumentation across time and across domains – but, again, never forgetting the non-dialogical components picked up along the way.

To produce this grand dialogical narrative, I adopted the integrative methodology that I have deployed in most of my career (and which is described in detail in the conclusion of my monograph *Formal Languages in Logic*, Dutilh Novaes, 2012a). I had to approach deduction from a number of different angles, each of them requiring specific methods, such as 'traditional' philosophical conceptual analysis, historical analysis (mostly of philosophical texts, but also taking into account sociocultural and political factors), and empirically informed philosophical analysis, with extensive engagement with adjacent (empirical) disciplines including cognitive science, psychology, and education studies. (A fourth methodology, not extensively deployed in this book but present in some of the articles with related material, is philosophical analysis aided by formal tools.) Another term that I recently adopted to describe the kind of philosophy that I practice is 'synthetic philosophy' (Schliesser, 2019), which reflects the thought that philosophers are ideally placed to bring together findings from a number of disciplines that normally do not engage with each other much.

Accordingly, the book is divided into three main parts. Part I (Chapters 1 to 4) presents the philosophical roots of deduction, relying predominantly on conceptual analysis and engagement with previous authors who have addressed similar issues. Part II (Chapters 5 to 7) is dedicated to the historical roots of deduction, and there the main method used is traditional textual analysis of philosophical texts of the past. (In the future, I would like to add techniques from digital humanities to my toolkit as a historian of philosophy.) Part III (Chapters 8 to 11) focuses on the cognitive roots of deduction, deploying the method of empirically informed philosophical analysis by engaging extensively with findings from cognitive science and mathematical education studies, as well as quasi-sociological observations on the practices of mathematicians.

Chapter 1 starts by defining the explanandum of the whole book, i.e. the phenomenon (or phenomena) that it is about. There, I introduce deduction as having three main characteristics: necessary truth-preservation (which is perhaps the most central one, distinguishing deduction from other forms of inference and argument such as induction and abduction), perspicuity, and belief-bracketing. I also discuss a number of puzzling features of deduction, i.e. philosophical issues pertaining to deduction that remain open questions, as they have not yet been adequately 'solved.' In other words, there *is* a problem (rather a number of problems) with deduction, which justifies a book-length treatment of the topic such as this one. In Chapter 2, I argue that what is needed is a 'roots' approach, and briefly present the four main senses in which deduction has dialogical roots treated in this book: philosophically, historically, cognitively, and pertaining to mathematical practices. In Chapter 3, I discuss the prominent dialogical accounts of deduction and deduction proposed by Paul Lorenzen, Jaakko Hintikka, and Imre Lakatos. This discussion then allows me to offer a precise formulation of the dialogical model that I defend, the *Prover–Skeptic model*. In Chapter 4, I present a dialogical rationale based on the Prover–Skeptic model for the three main features of deduction identified in Chapter 1, and address a number of ongoing debates in the philosophy of logic – the normativity of logic, logical pluralism, logical paradoxes, and logical consequence. I argue that the Prover–Skeptic model sheds new light on these debates.

Part II starts with Chapter 5, where I turn to the historical roots of deduction in Ancient Greek philosophy and mathematics. I rely extensively on the work of G.E.R. Lloyd and Reviel Netz to argue that dialogical, debating practices in a democratic city-state like Athens were causally instrumental for the emergence of the axiomatic-deductive method in mathematics. The same sociocultural political background was decisive for the emergence of practices of *dialectic*, the kinds of dialogical interactions famously portrayed in Plato's dialogues. In turn, dialectic provided the background for the emergence of the first fully-fledged theory of deduction in history (that we know of at this point, at least), namely Aristotle's syllogistic. In Chapter 6, I turn to Aristotle and argue that syllogistic did indeed emerge from the dialectical matrix as well as from considerations pertaining to scientific demonstration and demonstration in mathematics. This means that, even early on, non-dialogical components motivated and were integrated into practices and theory of deduction. Chapter 6 also briefly discusses two other formidable ancient intellectual traditions, namely the Indian tradition and the Chinese tradition. It is argued that, while these were indeed highly sophisticated, fully-fledged theories of deduction are not to be found in them (in the early stages, at least; later developments in India may well count as theories of deduction). Finally, Chapter 7 retraces the genealogical development of deduction from the Ancient Greeks (unfortunately, not covering the late antiquity period – a regrettable lacuna) in the Latin and Arabic medieval traditions, in the early modern period, and finally with the emergence of mathematical logic in the nineteenth century. This chapter thus explains why we (i.e. twenty-first century philosophers) have by and large forgotten the dialogical roots of deduction, as mentalistic conceptions of logic and deduction became increasingly prominent.

Part III focuses on deduction in human cognition. It starts in Chapter 8 with a review of experimental work on deductive reasoning, which has shown that human reasoners do not seem to reason spontaneously according to the deduction canons. However, there are also experimental results suggesting that, when tackling deductive tasks in groups, performance comes much closer to these canons. These findings already offer a partial vindication of the dialogical conception of deduction insofar as they show that, when given the opportunity to engage in dialogues with others, humans become better deductive reasoners. In Chapter 9, I look at the three main features of deduction defined in Chapter 1 from a cognitive, empirically informed perspective. I discuss experimental findings that lend support to the dialogical conceptualization of these three features presented in Chapter 4. I also discuss the notion of internalization formulated by Vygotsky, which allows for an explanation of how deductive practices can also take place in purely mono-agent situations: as an intrapersonal enactment of interpersonal dialogues. The upshot of Chapter 9 is that framing deductive practices dialogically provides cognitive scaffolding that facilitates the ontogenetic development of deductive reasoning in an individual. Chapter 10 in turns focuses on the 'phylogeny' of deduction, i.e. how deductive reasoning may have emerged given the genetically endowed cognitive apparatus of humans. I argue that the emergence of deduction should not be viewed as genetically encoded, but rather as a product of cultural processes. Finally, Chapter 11 may seem a bit of an outlier in Part III, but it investigates deductive practices in (what I take to be) their main current instantiations, namely practices of mathematical proofs. Here again the dialogical hypothesis delivers a compelling account of a number of features of these practices; as it turns out, the fictive characters Prover and Skeptic are in fact instantiated by real-life mathematicians, e.g. referees for journals acting as Skeptics.

This book is the result of countless 'dialogues' I've engaged in over the years, so there are many people to thank for their contributions of different kinds. First of all, I want to thank the funding agencies that made this research possible, in particular NWO, but also the European Research Council by awarding me a Consolidator Grant for the project "The Social Epistemology of Argumentation" (SEA) (ERC-17-CoG 771074) in 2017, which has allowed me to dedicate more time to research since the project started in July 2018, and thus to complete this book. I am also grateful for the trust and appreciation that Cambridge University Press, in particular Hilary Gaskin, continues to place in my work.

Other than institutions, the humans who most contributed to the findings reported in this book are undoubtedly the members of the "Roots of Deduction" team in Groningen: the official ones, Leon Geerdink, Matthew Duncombe, and Rohan French, and the unofficial ones, Erik Krabbe (I cannot emphasize enough what a privilege it has been to be able to count on Erik's expertise and infinite knowledge on all matters pertaining to Aristotle's logic, argumentation theory, dialogical logic, etc.), my Ph.D. students Job de Grefte, Herman Veluwenkamp, Bianca Bosman, and César Frederico dos Santos, and various colleagues at the Faculty of Philosophy in Groningen, Jan Albert van Laar and Barteld Kooi in particular. Other colleagues in Groningen have contributed more indirectly but equally importantly, in particular Martin Lenz, Leah Henderson, and Jan-Willem Romeijn. Thanks also to my new colleagues at Vrije Universiteit Amsterdam, who since July 2018 have provided an inspiring philosophical environment and a warm welcome. Thanks especially to my new SEA team, Hein Duijf, Merel Talbi, and Elias Anttila, who fortunately also enjoy my communal style of doing philosophy.

A number of people have read drafts of chapters and offered insightful comments, in particular Matthew Duncombe, Leon Geerdink, Marije Martijn, Fenner Tanswell, Line Andersen, Benoît Castelnérac, Tushar Irani, Koji Tanaka, Andrew Buskell, and Keith Stenning. (Of course, the remaining shortcomings are all my own.) Drafts of chapters were also fruitfully discussed in seminars at a number of places: Bristol, ANU, and VU Amsterdam. I thank those who participated in these sessions for their comments. I've also benefited tremendously from sustained engagement with readers of my blog posts at NewAPPS and M-Phi between 2010 and 2016; it is a shame that the 'golden age' of philosophical blogging seems to have come to an end, but I am grateful to have been part of it.

Of course, there is also life outside philosophy, and many people have inspired me and given meaning to my life in these ten years. My daughters, Sophie and Marie, remain the main energy-drainers in my life, while also inspiring me and giving me joy every single day. I consider it my biggest accomplishment that they are becoming strong, loud feminist ladies who think that the sky is the limit for their ambitions and plans. A number of other people – friends, family, partners – have been in my life and supported me in different ways over the last ten years: Stephen Read, Ole Hjortland, Richard Pettigrew, Florian Steinberger, Marije Martijn, and Eric Schliesser; my mother, Maria, and my brother, Frederico; Reinout, Izaak, and Jan Roel.

Just as it takes a village to raise a child, it takes a village – more like a mid-sized city, really – to write a book.

Part I

The Philosophy of Deduction

1   The Trouble with Deduction

1.1   Introduction

From the observation that all dogs are animals, and that Fido is a dog, I may conclude with absolute certainty, without the shadow of a doubt, that Fido is an animal (i.e., provided that all dogs are indeed animals and that Fido is indeed a dog and not a cleverly disguised automaton, for example). Inferences where the truth of the premise(s) guarantees the truth of the conclusion(s)[1] are known as *deductive inferences*;[2] these are usually contrasted with *inductive* and *abductive* inferences, which do not have the property of necessary truth-preservation. In other words, in an inductive or abductive inference, the premises may be true while the conclusion is not (though the truth of the premises should make the conclusion more *likely* to be true), whereas the very definition of a deductive argument rules out this possibility. Another prominent concept used to bring out the contrast between deductive reasoning and other kinds of reasoning is that of (in)defeasibility; defeasible reasoning, as characterized in the seminal work of John Pollock (Pollock, 1974, 1987) and further studied in philosophy, artificial intelligence, and other fields of inquiry, is the kind of reasoning where premises do confer justification and support to a conclusion (prima facie reasons), but the argument in question may be defeated by new incoming information.

---

[1] Traditionally, a deductive argument is conceived as having one or more premises (though in certain cases, such as with Aristotelian syllogistic, there is a requirement for multiple premises) and one conclusion. The idea of multiple-conclusion arguments has its proponents (Restall, 2005), but is not unanimously accepted (Caret & Hjortland, 2015). At this point, it makes sense to keep things as general as possible, and thus not to make any restrictions on the number of either premises or conclusions involved in a given argument. However, more often than not, I will speak of premises in the plural and conclusion in the singular, as this reflects the more traditional understanding of a deductive argument throughout history (e.g. Aristotelian syllogistic).

[2] Initially, I will use 'inference' and 'argument' interchangeably, but later on it will be important to discuss the differences between the two notions. In particular, 'inference' is usually associated with mono-agent situations of mental, epistemic acts, whereas 'argument' is often (though not always) used in multi-agent contexts of argumentation. Thus arguments are typically viewed as linguistic entities, whereas inferences are also used in the sense of mental entities.

3

Simple examples such as Fido's above may seem to suggest that deduction is not a particularly powerful or interesting reasoning tool, one that only allows for the derivation of rather trivial conclusions. But this is not what the history of mathematics, science, and philosophy suggests: for millennia, deductive argumentation has occupied a crucial role in various areas of intellectual inquiry. Originally, the two canonical presentations of what could be described as the 'deductive method,'[3] that is, the method of inquiry where deductive argumentation occupies pride of place, are Euclid's *Elements* and Aristotle's *Posterior Analytics*. In both cases, one begins with a few purportedly self-evident truths – axioms – and then derives further truths from them in a stepwise manner by means of deductive inferences, in what is also known as the *axiomatic-deductive method*. These two models, the Euclidean model for mathematics and the Aristotelian model for the (empirical) sciences, remained influential for millennia, and still represent what could be described as the classical conception of mathematics and science (de Jong & Betti, 2010). In philosophy, influential authors adopted the Euclidean *more geometrico* for the development and presentation of their philosophical systems, most notably Baruch Spinoza (Spinoza, 1985). More recently, Carl Hempel and Paul Oppenheim's deductive-nomological model of scientific inquiry (Hempel & Oppenheim, 1948) is another example of deduction presented as a quintessential component of scientific inquiry.

Indeed, it is not surprising that philosophers, mathematicians, and scientists would be impressed by the deductive method, with its allure of certainty and its promise of unshakable foundations. But doubts concerning the reliability and applicability of deductive reasoning as a method of inquiry have also been raised, including ancient Skeptic criticism, distaste for 'the logic of the schools' (Descartes, 1985), and, more recently, worries concerning the non-ampliative, non-informative nature of deductive reasoning (Hintikka, 1973). In fact, the very notion of deduction raises a number of issues that, despite having received sustained attention from philosophers, remain puzzling.

In this chapter, I bring to the fore and further clarify these issues. Before addressing them, I present the three key features of deductive reasoning that will act as the cornerstones for the analysis throughout the book.

1.2   What Is a Deductive Argument?

Despite considerable variation in its numerous manifestations, three core features of deductive reasoning seem to stand out. They are aptly captured in the following definition of a mathematical proof, taken from the 1989 guideline of the National Council of Teachers of Mathematics (and quoted in Balacheff,

---

[3] Though this is probably more of a cluster of methods than a unified method as such.

1991, p. 177): a mathematical proof is "a careful sequence of steps with each step following logically from an assumed or previously proved statement and from previous steps." So, a deductive argument is (i) a stepwise process, (ii) where each step 'follows logically' (iii) from assumed or previously established statements. In the remainder of this book, it will be further argued that focusing on these three aspects offers an adequate vantage point to investigate deduction in its many facets. Here, they are presented in decreasing order of general recognition of their centrality for the notion of deduction.[4]

1.2.1 Necessary Truth-Preservation

Recall the example above: if Fido is a dog and all dogs are animals, then it is *necessarily* the case that Fido is an animal; things just couldn't possibly be any other way, if the premises are true. This property is typically referred to as the property of *necessary truth-preservation*, and is usually thought to be what distinguishes deductive arguments from inductive and abductive arguments (Douven, 2011), or deductive from defeasible arguments (Pollock, 1987). Indeed, this is what distinguishes deductive reasoning from other modes of reasoning – a necessary, constitutive property for any argument to count as deductively valid (though it may not be *sufficient* for deductive validity).

   Another property that is closely related to necessary truth-preservation is the property of *monotonicity*: if an inference from A and B to C is valid, then adding any arbitrary premise D will not block the inference to the conclusion C from A, B, and D. Monotonicity follows quite straightforwardly from necessary truth-preservation in the following way: what necessary truth-preservation ensures is that in all situations where A and B are the case, C will also be the case. Now, this includes all situations where A, B, and D are the case, for any arbitrary D, since these constitute a subclass (proper or not) of the class of situations where A and B are the case. And thus, the addition of a premise will only restrict (or keep unchanged) the class of situations under consideration, which will then still satisfy C. In effect, inductive, abductive, and more generally defeasible inferences, which lack the property of necessary truth-preservation, also lack the property of monotonicity (Koons, 2013).

---

[4] It might be thought that necessary truth-preservation alone constitutes the true core of deduction, as a necessary as well as sufficient condition for a reasoning to count as a deduction, and that the other two requirements, especially perspicuity, in fact define what counts as a 'good' deduction rather than deduction tout court. To some extent, this is merely a terminological matter; but my choice to include these two other features of deduction as what constitutes its core reflects the functionalist commitment that underpins this investigation. I am not only interested in what a deduction is in some abstract, freestanding sense; I am mostly interested in what deduction can do for us, and thus in those instances that fulfill the roles attributed to a deductive argument in, for example, mathematical practice.

Notice, however, that there are examples of deductive systems that lack the property of monotonicity, in particular, relevant logics, which require that there be a relation of relevance between premises and conclusion and thus restrict the addition of arbitrary premises to a given (relevantly valid) argument. These systems will have necessary truth-preservation as a necessary but not as a sufficient condition for deductive validity. (Classical logic is what is obtained if necessary truth-preservation is viewed as both necessary *and* sufficient for validity, at least if we restrict ourselves to bivalent systems.)

Once deductive validity is defined as having necessary truth-preservation as a necessary condition, what it takes to show that an argument or inference is deductively *in*valid is to show that it is possible for the premises to be true while the conclusion(s) is (are) not, usually by describing a situation where this is the case. These situations are typically referred to as *counterexamples*. What a counterexample shows is that the truth of the premise(s) does not necessitate the truth of the conclusion, and instead is compatible with the non-truth of the conclusion (it may in fact be compatible both with its truth and with its non-truth).

This may all seem quite straightforward at first sight, but the nature of the necessity relating premises to conclusions in deductively valid inferences/arguments is perhaps one of the most mysterious features of deduction. What kind of necessity is this? Is it metaphysical? Semantic/linguistic? Logical? This question will be discussed in more detail in Section 1.3.2 below.

1.2.2 Stepwise Structure: Perspicuity

However, necessary truth-preservation is not the whole story. Take for example Fermat's last theorem, which was proved in the 1990s by Andrew Wiles after having defied mathematicians for centuries. (Wiles' proof is exceedingly complex and long.) Now imagine that I state the axioms of Peano Arithmetic and then in one step, with no intermediaries, conclude Fermat's last theorem. This 'argument' is truth-preserving, and indeed necessarily so (as we now know); no counterexample can be provided. And yet, such a one-step 'argument' will not be deemed satisfactory by anyone minimally acquainted with the deductive method. This is because something else is required of a good deductive argument other than necessary truth-preservation: it must somehow make clear what the connection is between premises and conclusion such that the truth of the premise(s) guarantees the truth of the conclusion(s). In other words, a deductive inference/argument, especially when formulated publicly (i.e. not 'mentally' by a given individual), must fulfill an *epistemic function* (more on which soon), and so each step must be individually perspicuous and the whole still comprehensible.[5]

Notice that for individual inferential steps to be properly chained, obtaining the desired effect of leading from premises to conclusion(s) in a deductive argument, the property of *transitivity* must be in place. That is, if A implies B and B implies C, this entails that A implies C. Transitivity is usually taken to be a rather straightforward principle, as indeed the very possibility of a multiple-step deductive argument seems to hinge on it. But it has been contested in recent work, especially with respect to the sorites paradox (Zardini, 2008; Fjellstad, 2016).

Indeed, a deductive argument, say a mathematical proof, will typically contain numerous steps, each of which may be individually simple and thus individually not very informative, but by chaining such steps in a suitable way we may derive non-trivial conclusions from the given premises. And thus, the interesting, informative deductive arguments are typically those with a fair number of steps, precisely because it is a desirable feature of a deductive inference that it be compelling – that each of its steps be at least to some extent self-evident, or in any case that they be suitably *justified*. Importantly, the level of granularity required for a deductive argument to be considered adequate will vary according to context; for example, a mathematical proof presented in a journal for professional mathematicians will typically be more 'dense,' i.e. less detailed, than a proof presented in an introductory textbook for students (Schiller, 2013).

Consider for instance proofs in Euclid's *Elements*, where the steps are often justified in terms of the postulates presented at the very beginning of the work, or else by other theorems previously proved. The balance between perspicuity and informativeness is thus achieved by chaining a significant number of individually evident one-step inferences. (Notice, though, that a very long proof, with a very large number of steps, which can no longer be easily surveyed by a human at a glance, is often thought to lack perspicuity [Bassler, 2006]. Indeed, mathematics educators observe that there is often a tension between local and global understanding of proofs [Alibert & Thomas, 1991].)

1.2.3   Bracketing Belief

Perhaps the least recognized of the three key components of deductive reasoning as described here is what we might refer to as the *bracketing belief* requirement. In its basic form, the game of deduction requires the reasoner to take the premises at face value, no questions asked: the focus is exclusively on

---

[5] Wittgenstein speaks of the *Übersichtlichkeit* or 'surveyability' of proofs (Marion, 2011), which is sometimes interpreted as an objection to very long mathematical proofs, but more generally simply amounts to a recognition of the essential epistemic import of proofs.

the *connection* between premises and conclusions, not on the nature or plausibility of the premises or conclusions. (However, this is not the case for Aristotle's theory of science in the *Posterior Analytics* and the axiomatic method more generally, where a number of requirements are placed on acceptable premises.)

For those suitably 'indoctrinated' in the game of deduction, this feature may appear to be unproblematic or even trivial, but this is in fact not the case. Try to explain to a group of uninitiated, logically naïve interlocutors (say, high-school students) that 'All cows are blue, and all blue things are made of stone, so all cows are made of stone' is a perfectly fine deductive inference. In most cases, the reaction will be of mild indignation that such a strange argument can be deemed 'good' in any sense whatsoever, given the absurdity of the sentences involved. (In more technical terms: the distinction between the soundness and the validity of an argument is usually not grasped by those not having received some kind of training in logic, mathematics, or philosophy.)

What is required of the reasoner is that she put her own beliefs about premises and conclusions aside in order to focus exclusively on the *connection* between premises and conclusions. As it happens, this is a cognitively demanding task, as the extensive literature on the so-called belief bias effect illustrates: despite being told to focus solely on the validity of arguments, participants often let their judgments of validity be influenced by the (un)believability of the sentences involved (Markovits & Nantel, 1989; Evans, 2016) (see Chapter 8). Typically, arguments with believable conclusions will be deemed valid, whereas arguments with unbelievable conclusions will be deemed invalid, regardless of their actual validity (though validity also has an effect, as, within each of these two believability classes, valid arguments are more often deemed valid than invalid ones).

In fact, it has been observed that, in reasoning experiments, participants with little or no formal schooling often resist the very idea of reasoning on the basis of premises that they have no knowledge of. In the 1930s, the Russian psychologist Alexander Luria conducted reasoning experiments with unschooled peasants in the then-Soviet republic of Uzbekistan, which showed that the unschooled participants did not spontaneously dissociate their beliefs in the premises from the reasoning itself (see Chapter 9). Here is a description of one of his experiments:

"In the Far North, where there is snow, all bears are white. Novaya Zemlya is in the Far North. What colour are bears there?" In response to this problem, [a given participant] protested: "You've seen them – you know. I haven't seen them, so how could I say!?" . . . the interviewer encouraged him to focus on the wording of the problem: "But on the basis of what I said, what do you think?" and re-stated the problem. This repetition met with the same refusal: "But I never saw them, so how could I say?" (Harris, 2000, p. 96)

Thus, it seems that inferring conclusions from premises while disregarding one's own doxastic attitudes toward premises and conclusions may require specific training. Yet, it is an integral component of deductive reasoning. Indeed, in mathematics it is very common to produce conditional proofs: 'If A and B are true, then so is C.' For example, the ABC conjecture, which, pending wide acceptance of the correctness of Shinichi Mochizuki's purported proof by the mathematical community, is still a conjecture (see Chapter 11), has been proved to imply a number of other interesting conjectures, such as Catalan's conjecture (Glivický & Kala, 2017). In such cases, the mathematician takes a conjecture as her starting point and goes on to investigate what follows from it even if she does not (yet) have a definite position on the conjecture itself.

These three features of deductive reasoning will provide the cornerstones for the analysis throughout the book. At this point, I have only presented each of them superficially, but we will see that each raises a number of puzzles and issues; none of them is either cognitively or philosophically straightforward. In Section 1.3, I present an overview of the main difficulties and issues pertaining to the concept of deductive reasoning as they have been discussed in the literature. We will see that the property of necessary truth-preservation has been quite extensively discussed and problematized, but the other two properties less so.

Before we move on, a few remarks are in order on a property that is typically associated with deduction, and yet is conspicuously absent from my list: the property of *formality*. According to a familiar story, deductive validity is a matter of *logical form*; an argument is valid if and only if it suitably instantiates one of the logical forms recognized as ensuring validity. Elsewhere, however, I have argued extensively against accounts of the nature of deductive validity in terms of logical form (Dutilh Novaes, 2012a, 2012b). Rather than being that in virtue of which an argument is deductively valid, logical forms/ schemata are in fact convenient devices that allow us to track deductive validity with less effort (though for a limited range of arguments). Philosophically, however, the doctrine of logical form fails to deliver a satisfactory account of validity (as also argued by authors such as John Etchemendy [1983] and Stephen Read [1994] before me). For this reason, the property of formality will not be considered among the key features of the notion of deduction in the present investigation, despite the widespread (but to my mind erroneous) belief that it is indeed one of its key features.

1.3   Issues

In this section, I present three philosophical questions pertaining to deductive reasoning which remain by and large unresolved. The point of this section is mainly to show that the puzzle of deduction has not yet been cracked, and thus that an extensive investigation on deductive reasoning and argumentation is still very much needed. These open questions will then be further addressed in later chapters.

1.3.1   Where Is Deduction to Be Found?

In much of the literature in philosophy of logic and on deductive reasoning more generally, it is often assumed that deduction is a widespread phenomenon. For example, according to Stewart Shapiro in his recent book *Varieties of Logic*, "logic is ubiquitous" (Shapiro, 2015, p. 209). In these discussions, it is customary to adduce armchair arguments on what 'people' do or do not conclude deductively in a number of scenarios; the presupposition seems to be that something like deductive competence (akin to Chomskian linguistic competence) is a given in humans (and perhaps even in some non-human animals).

But is it really so? The experimental literature in the psychology of reasoning seems to suggest that things are not so simple. (See Dutilh Novaes, 2012a, chapter 4 for a systematic survey of these findings, and Chapter 8 of this book.) Initially conducted against the background of a Piagetian (neo-Kantian) paradigm where the traditional canons of logic were thought to correspond to the basic building blocks of human cognition, since the 1960s experiments have shown time and again that participants typically perform 'poorly' in deductive reasoning tasks (at least in experimental settings) (Johnson-Laird, 2008). Deviations from the normative responses as dictated by the canons of deductive reasoning were robust, consistent, and systematic, but traditional logic (in particular, syllogistic and classical propositional logic) continued to provide the theoretical background for the formulation and interpretation of experiments for decades. It was only in the 1980s that some researchers (in particular Mike Oaksford and Nick Chater) began to question the adequacy of traditional logic as a theoretical framework for the investigation of human reasoning, and only in the 2000s that the idea that traditional deductive logic is not in any way an adequate descriptive model of human reasoning became more or less a consensus among psychologists of reasoning (Elqayam, 2018). Tellingly, a survey article by one of the leading researchers in the field, Jonathan Evans (2002), is informally known among psychologists as the 'death of deduction.'

Other than questioning the adequacy of logic as the right normative theoretical framework, a number of responses to the discrepancy between the deductive canons and these experimental findings have been formulated (Elio, 2002). One may, for example, maintain that the deductive canons do indeed define the ideal of rationality, and that the realization that human reasoners do not conform to these canons forces upon us the bitter conclusion that humans are irrational. One may also discount these discrepancies as a competence/

performance gap, similar to how generative grammar explains the fact that competent speakers regularly make grammatical mistakes.[6] Another response is to discredit the importance of these experimental findings in view of their presumed lack of ecological validity: what human reasoners do in the artificial experimental setting of these experiments is not illustrative of how they in fact reason in more realistic situations (Gigerenzer, 1996).

A view that has garnered much prominence in recent decades (though probably still not unanimously accepted) is that human reasoning has a very strong component of defeasibility, both in everyday life and in specific, specialized contexts such as legal argumentation and scientific reasoning (Pollock, 1987; Stenning & van Lambalgen, 2008; Oaksford & Chater, 2002; Koons, 2013). Defeasible reasoning can be defined in the following way: from premises A and B, the agent may reasonably conclude C. However, upon receiving new information, say D, C is no longer plausible to the agent, even if A and B still stand. In other words, the agent takes A and B to imply C, but not A, B, *and* D to imply C. Naturally, given that it has the properties of necessary truth-preservation and monotonicity as described above, deductive reasoning is fundamentally at odds with the principles of defeasible reasoning; indeed, it is *indefeasible*. How best to model defeasible reasoning formally (Bayesian probabilities, non-monotonic logics, etc.) is still a matter of contention, but it is clear that monotonic, indefeasible deductive logics are utterly inadequate for this job.

In sum, whether deductive reasoning is ubiquitous is by and large an empirical question, and the empirical data currently available suggest that it is not. So where is deduction to be found? Are we theorizing about a non-existent phenomenon, like seventeenth-century scientists who theorized about phlogiston? I submit that deductive reasoning is *not* like phlogiston; it may not be as widespread and ubiquitous as Shapiro and many others still surmise, but it *is* a thing. Indeed, as hinted at the beginning of this chapter, deductive reasoning is a central component of mathematical practice, both historically and in its current state, and is thus also present in fields where mathematics is widely used. Deduction is also present in a number of other areas of inquiry, in particular in philosophy.

Notice that not all reasoning in mathematics is deductive, strictly speaking (Aberdein, 2009), but much of it is: what counts as a mathematical proof is still by and large dictated by the canons established by Euclidean mathematics (even if there have been significant transformations across time – in particular, but not exclusively, pertaining to standards of rigor). Indeed, Euclid-style proofs are still a fundamental part of the mathematics curriculum, and any

---

[6] This response is from the start not very convincing, because the magnitude of deviation between competence and performance in the case of deductive reasoning appears to be much larger than in the case of language use.

trained mathematician recognizes Euclid's own proofs as 'proper proofs.' Similarly, in the empirical sciences, strictly deductive methods are but one of the tools in the scientist's toolkit, and it may be plausibly argued that scientists rely more heavily on inductive and abductive (inference to the best explanation) reasoning than on deduction. Still, deduction does seem to occur in the practices of scientists with considerable regularity (e.g. in theoretical physics).

In other words, one of the main claims of the present investigation is that deductive reasoning is hardly ever instantiated 'in the wild,' so to speak, as it is at odds with the strong component of defeasibility in everyday reasoning. In most everyday circumstances, deductive reasoning is overkill: the point is not to infer with absolute certainty what follows *necessarily* from the available information, but rather what is likely to happen given the available information and a number of background assumptions. In fact, deductive reasoning is usually quite 'costly': much is needed as input for meager output to come about, and in most cases the available information will underdetermine which conclusions can be drawn (deductively). Instead, deductive reasoning belongs in niches of specialists: mathematicians, scientists, and philosophers, and even in these niches it does not completely overpower other forms of reasoning. Indeed, for some specialist niches, where it might be thought that deduction should play a prominent role (e.g. legal argumentation), research shows that the incidence of deduction is very minimal indeed (e.g. non-monotonic reasoning in law; Bex & Verheij, 2013).

And so, given that the phenomenon we are interested in here, deductive reasoning, is predominantly instantiated in mathematics and in some other regimented contexts of argumentation, such as philosophy, it makes sense for us to focus on data coming specifically from these quarters. Indeed, I submit that it is the practice of *mathematical proof* that most clearly epitomizes the principles of deductive reasoning, and thus much of the material to be discussed in this book pertains, directly or indirectly, to mathematical proof.

1.3.2   What Is the Nature of Deductive Necessity?

As already mentioned in Section 1.2, the property of necessary truth-preservation, perhaps the most characteristic feature of deduction, has been extensively discussed in the literature on the philosophy of logic. In particular, the prolific debates on the concept of logical consequence (Shapiro, 2005; Caret & Hjortland, 2015)[7] can be viewed as essentially revolving around the issue of the nature of the necessity relation between antecedents and

---

[7] Logical consequence can be described as the relation that obtains between the premises and conclusion(s) of a deductively valid argument, which means that what is said in the literature about logical consequence ultimately concerns the phenomenon of deductive validity (hence the ease with which I will switch between the two concepts in what follows).

consequents, which correspond to premises and conclusions in a deductive argument. However, while much has been said, we do not seem to have come anywhere near an adequate understanding of the kind of necessity involved in a deductive argument.

Aristotle's definition of a *syllogismos* at the beginning of *Prior Analytics* (Aristotle, 2009),[8] arguably the first (and subsequently very influential) explicit definition of deductive validity in the history of logic, already contains a reference to a relation of necessity:

> A *syllogismos* is an argument in which, certain things being posited, something other than what was laid down *results by necessity* because these things are so. (24b18–20, emphasis added)

However, it is not clear what the notion of necessity alluded to here amounts to. Is it metaphysical necessity? Is it linguistic necessity? Is it epistemic necessity? In later developments, for example in medieval theories of consequence (Dutilh Novaes, 2016a), the necessity in question tended to be interpreted metaphysically, in terms of the impossibility of things being as the premises (antecedent) say they are and other than as the conclusion (consequent) says they are. But metaphysical necessity is obviously a rather murky notion, and so this characterization still calls for further clarification.

In *Remarks on the Foundations of Mathematics* (Wittgenstein, 1978), Ludwig Wittgenstein uses a particularly apt expression to describe this property: "the hardness of the logical must" (VI, 49). Much of his later work in the philosophy of mathematics and logic amounts to attempts to come to grips with this mysterious property, the 'compulsion' that seems to be associated with a deductive argument. It would seem that, upon being presented with premises, an agent is compelled, even forced, to accept their deductive conclusion, especially if each step is individually convincing. But Wittgenstein points out that it is also possible to balk at assenting to the conclusion, that is, to resist the force of the logical must. What he is problematizing is the presumed *normative* import of deductive necessity in connection with the rule-following problem: if I have granted the premises of a deductive argument, it seems that I *must*, on pain of irrationality or some other serious infraction, grant the conclusion, too. (For more on the normative import of deductive reasoning, see Section 1.3.3.) But how exactly the hardness of the logical must operates, and even *whether* it indeed operates, is not in any way obvious.

More recently, Shapiro (2005) has presented a survey of different views on the notion of deductive validity and logical consequence. He distinguishes four

---

[8] The Greek term *syllogismos*, as used by Aristotle, is tricky to translate, as it appears to be more general than what we now call syllogisms (arguments with two premises and one conclusion, all of which are of one of four propositional forms), but also less general than our notion of a deductive argument, since it excludes, for example, reflexive inferences of the form 'A implies A.'

main accounts of deductive necessity (the glosses are mine, partially borrowing from Shapiro's formulations):

- Metaphysical (modality): it is impossible for the premises to be true while the conclusion is not.
- Linguistic (semantics): the truth of the premises necessitates the truth of the conclusion in virtue of the meanings of the terms featured in them.
- Formal: the truth of the premises necessitates the truth of the conclusion in virtue of the meanings of the *logical* terms featured in them (their logical forms).
- Epistemic: anyone aware of the truth of the premises will recognize the truth of the conclusion.

Each of these proposals seems to bring a host of issues, and each of them on its own does not seem to capture the full breadth of the notion of deductive necessity. This leads Shapiro to conclude that the notion of logical consequence/deductive validity is multifaceted, and that each of these accounts captures only some of these facets. He may well be right, but such an answer seems to represent an invitation to further reflection rather than a definitive answer; it basically amounts to saying that 'it's complicated.'

The question of the primacy of one of these conceptions over the others raises a related question, namely which formal framework is best suited to capture the 'right' notion of deductive necessity. Here, the main contenders in recent decades have been *model theory* – which is usually viewed as related to the metaphysical understanding of necessity, that is, to situations that make propositions true or false – and *proof theory* – which focuses on the necessity that seems to emerge in virtue of the very meaning of the sentences involved, often also having a strong epistemic component (such as in Prawitz, 2005). Both traditions emerged in the 1930s, in the works of Alfred Tarski and Gerhard Gentzen, respectively. Tarski (2002) famously introduced the notion of a *model* in order to formulate a reductionist account of the necessity involved in the relation of logical consequence: in all models where the premises (antecedent) are true, so is the conclusion (consequent). The goal was to tame the notoriously thorny modal notion of necessity in terms of a more manageable notion, that of models. This approach remained influential for decades, but was later challenged by Etchemendy (1990), thus giving rise to lively debates on the pros and cons of the Tarskian approach (see Caret & Hjortland, 2015 for an overview).

A closely related technical framework often used to account for modalities in general, and for the necessity of the consequence relation in particular, is possible worlds semantics (Shapiro, 2005). The thought is that deductive validity can be adequately accounted for by means of quantification over possible worlds: an argument is deductively valid (or equivalently, the relation of consequence holds between its premises and conclusion) if and only if in all possible worlds in which the premises are true/hold, so is/does the conclusion. While there are some technical differences between the notion of models and the notion of possible worlds, for our purposes here the two accounts can be treated as equivalent insofar as they are based on quantification over mathematical, theoretical constructs (models, possible worlds).

The question is ultimately whether the modal necessity that seems inherent in deductive validity can be eliminated in the way that Tarski intended, in terms of more manageable devices such as quantification over models or possible worlds. As mentioned above, Etchemendy (1990) voiced serious doubts regarding the success of such reductionist programs, and a number of authors have found these arguments compelling (e.g. Read, 1994). In particular, Etchemendy notes that the Tarskian account relies crucially on the problematic distinction between logical and non-logical terminology in a language, and that it fails to capture the 'intuitive notion' of logical consequence. More recently, Otávio Bueno and Scott Shalkowski (2009) have argued that the necessity of logical consequence/deductive validity must be viewed as a primitive notion that is not to be further analyzed in terms of other notions such as models (a view they dub 'modalism').

On the proof-theoretical side of things, the founding figure is, as mentioned above, Gentzen, who in the 1930s developed a number of logical systems where the notion of proof occupies pride of place, in particular natural deduction and sequent calculus. But what exactly is *natural* about natural deduction? This is how Gentzen motivates the system:

My starting point was this: The formalization of logical deduction, especially as it has been developed by Frege, Russell, and Hilbert, is rather far removed from the forms of deduction used in practice *in mathematical proofs*. Considerable formal advantages are achieved in return. In contrast, I intended first to set up a system which comes as close as possible to actual reasoning. (Gentzen, 1969, p. 68, emphasis added)

So the naturalness in question does not refer to reasoning or argumentation as conducted in everyday life, but rather specifically to the argumentative flow of mathematical proofs. The significance of this observation cannot be emphasized enough; much philosophical confusion arises from a misapprehension of what Gentzen's target phenomenon was when developing the system of natural deduction.

As quintessential deductive arguments, mathematical proofs display the three main features described in Section 1.2: all inferential steps are truth-preserving; the argument must proceed in a stepwise manner so as to obtain the desired epistemic effect; the argument starts with assumptions and concessions which function as premises. In particular with respect to the latter point, Gentzen is keenly aware of the importance of the role of assumptions, and this is one of his main criticisms of previous axiomatic systems such as David Hilbert's (Pelletier, 1999).

Regarding the necessity of deductive arguments, while the model-theoretical approach seeks to capture this feature in terms of quantification over models (or possible worlds), the proof-theoretical approach reduces it to conformity to previously established self-evident *rules* recognized within a given system. To justify these rules, proof-theorists often resort to epistemic and/or linguistic arguments: it is self-evident that these rules are correct; the correctness of these rules emerges from the very meaning of the (logical) terms involved (Prawitz, 2005). And so, within proof theory, the necessity of deductive arguments is not viewed as an essentially metaphysical notion; instead, the key concept is that of *rules of inference* and conformity to these rules. It is sometimes said that these rules, rather than being truth-preserving, are above all *meaning-preserving*.

But just as the model-theoretical approach must deal with challenges pertaining to whether the necessity in question can be reduced to quantification over models or possible worlds, the proof-theoretical approach faces its own challenges. In particular, what constrains the introduction of rules within a system? As famously shown by Arthur Prior's *tonk* connective (Prior, 1960), it is not the case that any more or less arbitrary collection of rules will yield a system with desirable properties: *tonk*, which has the introduction rule of the classical disjunction (from P to 'P *tonk* Q') and the elimination rule of the classical conjunction (from 'P *tonk* Q' to Q), trivializes the system, given that from any P, any Q will follow (by two successive applications of the connective). However, the formulation of constraints and criteria of adequacy for a system of inference rules in a non-ad hoc way is a complex issue. (See Caret & Hjortland, 2015 for an overview of the options that have been explored.)

In sum, the two main proposals on the table both seem to face a number of challenges in their attempts to offer formal as well as philosophical accounts of the property of necessary truth-preservation. Moreover, each of them seems to capture only part of the story; it is often remarked that the proof-theoretical approach is better equipped to deal with the notion of validity (the existence of a proof going from premises to conclusions), while the model-theoretical approach has better resources to deal with the notion of *in*validity (the existence of a counterexample, i.e. a situation where the premises obtain but the conclusion does not).[9] The bottom line is that, at this point, the nature of deductive necessity remains elusive.

---

[9] Notice that the practices of logicians seem to confirm the observation that both perspectives are needed. The 'standard' way to go about is to define a consequence relation syntactically (i.e. by means of rules) and semantically (i.e. by means of models), and then go on to prove that they agree in their judgments of validity and invalidity – i.e. are sound and complete with respect to each other (Dummett, 1978).

It has also been suggested that what is preserved in a deductive argument is in fact not truth at all. This may seem rather surprising at first sight, given that necessary truth-preservation has been at the heart of the concept of deductive validity in virtually all its historical instantiations. Some of those who reject the truth-preservation account do so on the basis of paradox-related considerations (Beall, 2007; Field, 2008). Others have suggested that what is preserved in the transition from premises to conclusions of individual inferential steps is *warrant or assertibility* rather than truth (Restall, 2004): if I am warranted in my belief that P, and P implies Q, then I am warranted in my belief that Q. Yet others, such as proponents of preservationist approaches to paraconsistent logic, posit that what is preserved by the consequence relation is the coherence, or incoherence, of a set of premises (Schotch et al., 2009).

We may never come to a fully convincing account of the necessity involved in deductive arguments. For instance, it is not clear what can count as evidence for or against the different proposals, or which methods should be adopted to make progress on this issue. Given the apparent impasse, one may, for example, take the necessity in question as a primitive, non-analyzable notion (as in Bueno & Shalkowski, 2009). Alternatively, one may adopt a practice-based, functionalist perspective (roughly as Wittgenstein does), and investigate what, if anything, the property of necessary truth-preservation *means* for those who engage in the practice of deductive reasoning. Why is it of use to them? Of course, prima facie this property offers the promise of a high degree of certainty, but in most cases (i.e. in most relevant real-life situations), so much certainty may well be superfluous. Thus, also from a functionalist perspective, no obvious answer is immediately forthcoming, as I argue in Section 1.3.3.

1.3.3   What Is the Point of Deduction?

This brings us to the question, what is the point of deduction? What does it do for us? Why is it viewed as an important component of our cognitive lives? There may be multiple such 'points,' but presumably there must be some sort of rationale behind the practice (as for all human practices) so as to motivate humans to engage in it. More generally, arguments and reasoning of different kinds, not only deductive arguments, are commonly thought to have the function of allowing us to infer new information from the information we already possess; in other words, arguments and reasoning are expected to have an ampliative effect so as to be informative. But then, we immediately seem to run into new issues: if the truth of the premises necessitates the truth of the conclusion, then isn't the content of the conclusion already somehow contained in the content of the premises? In what sense is a deductive argument informative?

These worries go as far back as Greek antiquity. The Skeptic philosopher Sextus Empiricus (second century AD) formulated sustained objections concerning the usefulness of deductive reasoning precisely along these lines in his *Outlines of Pyrrhonism* (Book II, 137–203).[10] Sextus' skeptical point was, of course, that *all* reasoning is suspicious, not only deductive reasoning, but the arguments he adduces against deduction specifically get to the crux of what is puzzling about deductive arguments: how can they at once be valid (given that necessary truth-preservation is a constitutive feature of deduction) and informative?

This problem has been variously described as 'the paradox of inference' (Cohen & Nagel, 1934) or 'the scandal of deduction' (Hintikka, 1973). In 'The Justification of Deduction,' Michael Dummett describes it in the following terms:

For [deduction] to be legitimate, the process of recognising the premisses as true must already have accomplished whatever is needed for the recognition of the truth of the conclusion; for it to be useful, a recognition of its truth need not actually have been accorded to the conclusion when it was accorded to the premisses. (Dummett, 1978, p. 297)

In other words, there seems to be an inherent tension between the *justification* and the *usefulness* of a deduction, given that its very core, necessary truth-preservation, is what makes it ultimately non-informative and thus (purportedly) useless. Another prominent critic of deduction in its scholastic variation, namely René Descartes, makes a similar point when commenting on how the education of a young pupil should proceed:

After that, he should study logic. I do not mean the logic of the Schools, for this is strictly speaking nothing but a dialectic which teaches *ways of expounding to others what one already knows* or even of holding forth without judgment about things one does not know. Such logic corrupts good sense rather than increasing it. I mean instead the kind of logic which teaches us to direct our reason with a view to *discovering the truths of which we are ignorant*. (Preface to the French edition of *Principles of Philosophy*, Descartes, 1985, p. 186; emphasis added)

We here encounter again the theme of the lack of informativeness of logical, deductive reasoning, now with the charge that deduction is powerless when it comes to discovering the truths of which we are ignorant. (Naturally, being the great mathematician that he was, Descartes made extensive use of deductive arguments in his mathematical work; here, he speaks specifically of scholastic logic, not of deductive reasoning as a whole, but the point is the same one that Sextus Empiricus and Dummett seem to make about deduction in general.)

---

[10] Epicureans, Cyrenaics, and Cynics also expressed doubts about the value of *dialektike*, which included deductive logic (see Barnes, 2008, p. 68).

There have been a number of responses to this problem, including a fair amount of technical work on the putative information gain afforded by a deductive inference, despite the appearance of no gain. Much recent work on the issue is explicitly a response to Jaakko Hintikka's formulation of the scandal of deduction (e.g., Sequoyah-Grayson, 2008; D'Agostino & Floridi, 2009; Jago, 2013). However, the scandal is persistent, and the threat of uselessness still looms large as long as the presupposition that the foremost purpose of an inference, including a deductive inference, is to be informative (and thus produce information gain) is in place.

In fact, even if it were possible to formulate a satisfactory account of the (putative) information gain of a deductive inference, reasoning deductively would still remain costly: because in a deductive argument the premises must rule out completely the non-truth of the conclusion, typically a large amount of informational input is required for a small amount of informational output. In many cases, the available information will not be sufficient for the derivation of a deductive conclusion. Indeed, in most practical real-life situations, the high degree of certainty afforded by deductive reasoning is not needed; in these situations, what we need to know is what is *likely* to follow from the available information, given some background assumptions, such as that nothing abnormal is going on (the basic principle of some well-known non-monotonic logics [Stenning & van Lambalgen, 2008] and default reasoning).

If deductive reasoning is not particularly suitable for obtaining new information and discovering new truths (as also argued in Mercier & Sperber, 2017), what other purposes might it have? A common leitmotif is that the deductive canons embody ideals of rationality, of what it means to think correctly; this is usually described as the issue of the *normativity of (deductive) logic* (Steinberger, 2017).

That there must be a tight connection between deductive logic and the canons of rationality is at least presupposed, even if not always explicitly stated, in the importance accorded to logical principles within scientific methodology and intellectual inquiry since Greek antiquity (as described above). Recall that Aristotle's theory of scientific method, presented in the *Posterior Analytics*, is crucially based on syllogistic arguments. Indeed, logic maintained its foundational role in the millennia-long Aristotelian tradition, alongside the equally quintessentially deductive Euclidean *more geometrico*.

However, the idea that deductive logic provides the canons for human agents (including outside of scientific contexts) to manage their cognitive lives arguably only became fully articulated in the work of Immanuel Kant, in the *Critique of Pure Reason* (Kant, 1998). To be sure, the details of how exactly Kant conceived of the normative role of logic for thought are intricate (Tolley, 2012). But when he claims that (general) logic deals with "the absolutely necessary rules of thought without which there can be no employment whatsoever of the understanding" (KrV: A52/B76), it is clear that we are entering normative territory (even if the normative import may derive from a descriptive approach to the very structure of the understanding, as in Clinton Tolley's reading of Kant). Kantian views on logic remained influential throughout the nineteenth and twentieth centuries, and the work of seminal authors such as Gottlob Frege (Steinberger, 2017) illustrates the strength of the association between logic and correct thinking: the laws of logic "are the most general laws, which prescribe universally the way in which one ought to think if one is to think at all" (Frege, 1967, p. 12).

Prima facie, the idea that one is to follow the principles of deductive logic "if one is to think at all" may seem plausible. Take modus ponens, for example: if I believe p, and p implies q (perhaps it may also be required that *I believe* that p implies q), then I should believe q. This may well be an utterly uninformative inference, but at the very least I must not violate it. (Note that the presumed uninformativeness of a deductive inference does not directly affect its presumed normative status, given that adhering to the deductive canons may be construed as a minimal requirement for rationality.)

However, even a minimal construal of deduction as a requirement for rational thought has come under attack, in particular in the work of Gilbert Harman (1986, 2009). He argued that deductive logic is not a sensible normative guide for managing our cognitive lives, for a number of reasons. The main claim is that "logic is neither a normative nor a psychological theory and, although immediate implication and inconsistency may play a role in reasoning, there is nothing special about logic in this connection" (Harman, 2009, p. 333). Logic would be the study of truth-preserving patterns of implication, and by claiming that logic does not have normative import for reasoning, Harman seems to be severing the link between a normative conception of rationality and the concept of necessary truth-preservation. In other words, according to Harman, necessary truth-preservation would not be an adequate norm for the regulation of one's thoughts and beliefs. He offers a number of arguments to support this claim, such as the principle of 'clutter-avoidance' (one should not clutter one's mind with irrelevant and uninformative consequences of one's beliefs, especially in view of the infinite number of deductive consequences of any sentence), and the observation that, faced with the derivation of a highly counterintuitive belief p, the best course of action may well be to revise the beliefs leading to p as a conclusion rather than simply accepting p.

In an unpublished but widely read manuscript (MacFarlane, 2004), John MacFarlane further tackles the issue of the presumed normative import of logic for thought by means of the concept of bridge principles. These are conditionals that have a relation of logical consequence between propositions on one side, and a statement of normative relations between beliefs on the other side. Much of the recent literature on the issue focuses on different formulations of bridge principles (Dutilh Novaes, 2015a; Steinberger, 2016), but the upshot for now seems to be that no bridge principle connecting the relation of logical conse-quence and normative statements concerning beliefs in the propositions involved is fully satisfactory.[11]

And thus, two of the presumed main rationales for deductive logic, both construed in terms of thinking and reasoning (understood as processes belong-ing to the internal, mental realm), do not seem very compelling. Deduction does not seem to be a particularly suitable way to produce new information, given that it is non-ampliative,[12] and it does not seem to be a reasonable guide for managing our beliefs and thoughts either (at least not on its own, as per Harman's arguments). What, then, if anything, is the 'point' of deduction? In order to address this and other questions adequately, I will argue that we must go back to the 'roots of deduction.'

1.4   Conclusion

In this chapter, I first introduced the three key features of deduction that will provide the conceptual foundations for the inquiry in the rest of the book: necessary truth-preservation, perspicuity, and belief-bracketing. I then dis-cussed three unresolved philosophical issues pertaining to deduction: the range and scope of deductive reasoning, the nature of deductive necessity, and the function(s) of deduction. The fact that these three issues continue to puzzle and mesmerize us illustrates the need for a wide-ranging investigation of deductive reasoning, which is what is offered in this book.

---

[11] Elsewhere (Dutilh Novaes, 2015a), I have argued that this deadlock arises from a misconception of what deductive logic is normative *for*; rather than thought and beliefs, its normative import pertains to specific dialogical interactions. This idea will be further discussed in Chapter 4.

[12] Notice, however, that some authors contest the attribution of non-ampliativeness to deductive reasoning. Frege, for example, viewed certain proofs, despite their being strictly deductive, as also constituting a real extension of our knowledge, and so as ampliative rather than merely explicative (Macbeth, 2012). Moreover, even if deductive reasoning is not logically or epistem-ically ampliative, it may still be psychologically ampliative, in the sense that the information contained in the premises needs to be 'unpacked' by a deduction in order to become available to the reasoner.

2   Back to the Roots of Deduction

2.1   Introduction

In Chapter 1, I argued that deduction remains a puzzling phenomenon. While a number of accounts have been proposed, none of them is entirely satisfactory. Given the deadlock we seem to find ourselves in, which approach(es) can we adopt if we are to make progress in understanding the nature of deduction? In the literature, one sees extensive use of formal analysis for the study of the basic properties of deduction, and in the formulation of different technical renditions of the deductive canons. There is also much reliance on what can be described as 'traditional' conceptual analysis, for example, through attempts to isolate necessary and sufficient conditions for what is to count as a deductively valid argument, or recourse to so-called intuitive notions of logical consequence and deductive reasoning (Etchemendy, 1990). (From what was said in Chapter 1, the reader may – correctly – infer that I have a number of reservations regarding the very existence of a 'commonsense,' 'pre-theoretical,' 'intuitive' concept of deduction; it is, I believe, a term of art that has no immediate counterpart outside circles of specialists.)

Now, while the present investigation certainly relies on a fair amount of conceptual analysis of this kind as well, a more encompassing perspective seems to be required; the stalemate is to a great extent due, I submit, to the somewhat restricted range of methodological approaches being deployed. As I described elsewhere (Dutilh Novaes, 2012a, Conclusion), I favor what I call an *integrative methodology*, where different approaches and angles are brought together in the hope that this will shed new light on the topics under investigation. (More recently, I have been using the term 'synthetic philosophy' [Schliesser, 2019] to describe this approach.)

In particular, the key idea of the project culminating in this book was to go back to the roots of deduction. It is obviously inspired by Quine's classic *The Roots of Reference* (Quine, 1974), but the way in which I conceive of the roots in question is broader in scope than Quine's. Indeed, while Quine is primarily interested in how language is learned by a particular individual – that is, the developmental, ontogenetic roots of language use through the pivotal concept of reference – I here bring in another perspective, which I take to be equally significant: the roots of practices of deductive reasoning and argumentation across time. In other words, I am interested in how deductive reasoning skills may arise in a particular individual and in how these skills and practices developed over time across generations.

For the ontogenetic question, sustained engagement with the empirical literature in psychology, cognitive science, and education sciences is required, resulting in what can be described as empirically informed philosophy (see Chapters 8 and 9). For the cross-temporal question, there are two timescales to be considered: the phylogenetic timescale pertaining to the evolutionary development of the human species; and the historical timescale that covers the cultural development of ideas and methods that are transmitted to the next generations by cultural learning. Of these two timescales, the historical one is the more relevant in the present context (given the claim that deduction emerged primarily as a cultural product, not as an 'instinct' in humans), and so it will be treated in detail in Chapters 5–7. The methodology to be used is the analysis of historical texts, that is, the 'usual' methodology of the historian of philosophy, but combined with a broader historical perspective taking into account developments outside philosophy as far as possible (e.g. the work of historians such as Reviel Netz [1999]). The phylogenetic timescale, where the question of the evolutionary roots of deductive reasoning is addressed, will be treated briefly in the present chapter, and more extensively in Chapter 10.

In this chapter, I start by clarifying the different meanings of the expression 'roots of deduction' and why the roots approach is fruitful. Next, the main hypothesis of the present investigation, namely that deduction is an inherently *dialogical* notion, is presented in some detail. I then briefly introduce the four main senses in which deduction may be said to be dialogical: historical, philosophical, psychological/cognitive, and with respect to mathematical practices.

2.2   The Different Roots of Deduction

2.2.1   *Phylogeny, History, and Ontogeny*

In evolutionary biology, ontogeny refers primarily to the embryonic development of a living being, whereas phylogeny pertains to the history of the biological evolution of a species (Gould, 1977). Ontogeny is also used to refer to the post-birth maturation and development of individuals within a species. Phylogeny and ontogeny are two distinct and prima facie unrelated phenomena, but they became closely associated in virtue of the by now largely discredited *theory of recapitulation*, according to which the (embryo to adult) development of an individual retraces the evolutionary development of a species. In other words, the thought is that in developing from embryo to adult (ontogeny), living beings go through stages resembling or representing successive stages in the evolution of their remote ancestors (phylogeny). In a slogan: 'Ontogeny recapitulates phylogeny.'[1]

The general principle connecting phylogenetic and ontogenetic development is potentially applicable to a number of features in humans other than genetic encoding, including the origins of language, cognitive development, and learning. While with respect to biological development the recapitulation principle is now viewed as largely refuted, this does not mean that it is completely implausible in other realms. In particular, with respect to learning, the principle yields the prediction that a child's cognitive development (roughly) follows the historical stages of the cognitive and cultural development of the human species, as registered in the archeological and historical record. If this is correct, then we may learn something about these historical developments by focusing on ontogenetic development (which is presumably empirically more accessible), and, conversely, we may improve our conception of cognitive development and education by relying on archeology and cultural history. This general approach has been described as 'cultural recapitulation' (Egan, 1997).[2]

For deductive reasoning specifically, we can distinguish the ontogenetic level of how deductive reasoning skills emerge in a particular (human) individual from the phylogenetic level of how the practices of deductive reasoning emerged and evolved across generations of reasoners (including what can be described as 'proto-deduction'). As to whether there may be interesting points of contact between phylogenetic and ontogenetic development with respect to deduction, the first issue to be addressed is whether deductive reasoning is to be seen as emerging from our genetically encoded endowment, such as, for example, bipedal walking, or instead if it is to be seen as fundamentally tied to contingent cultural practices emerging in specific circumstances, for example, writing (and thus not corresponding to genetic changes across generations). If deduction has a genetic basis, given the well-founded and compelling criticism that recapitulation theory has received in the biological realm (Gould, 1977), then we should not expect deductive phylogeny and ontogeny to have much in common. If, however, deductive reasoning is more akin to writing than to bipedal walking, i.e. if it is by and large a product of cultural rather than genetic processes, then perhaps a case can be made for some form of 'cultural recapitulation' (Egan, 1997) with respect to deductive reasoning. In this case, one suggestion might be that retracing the phylogenetic and historical

---

[1] Originally formulated by the nineteenth-century biologist Ernst Haeckel.
[2] Kieran Egan is heavily influenced by the Soviet psychologist Lev Vygotsky, whose work is also relevant for the present investigation (see especially Chapter 9).

development of deductive practices may give us clues on how best to elicit the emergence of deductive reasoning in the individual reasoner.

What evidence do we have to adjudicate between the two options, i.e. whether the emergence and development of deductive reasoning is by and large a matter of genetic evolutionary processes or, alternatively, of cultural processes? Recall that in Chapter 1 it was argued that deductive reasoning is by no means a ubiquitous phenomenon among humans, which prima facie suggests that the second option is more plausible.

Yet, evolutionary accounts of deductive reasoning have enjoyed some popularity in recent decades (Cooper, 2003; Maddy, 2002; Schechter, 2013). The basic idea is that an explanation for why we have developed the ability to reason deductively (*if* indeed we have developed this ability, which is precisely one of the pressing open questions) is that it conferred a survival advantage to those individuals among our ancestors who possessed it. These in turn were reproductively more successful than the individuals in the ancestral population who did not possess this ability, in the absence of the genetic encoding required for deductive reasoning to emerge. In other words, deductive reasoning would have arisen as an *adaptation* in humans (and, possibly, in some non-human animals too – see Chapter 10).

Attractive though it may seem at first sight, this approach faces numerous difficulties. Firstly, it is not clear that deductive reasoning abilities in fact confer survival advantages on those individuals. As noted in Chapter 1, deductive reasoning is costly and typically underdetermines the conclusions that can be drawn; presumably, it is not of much use in situations where quick decisions need to be made on the basis of scarce information. Moreover, evolutionary (adaptationist) accounts of deductive reasoning seem to suffer from a lack of evidential support. For deductive reasoning to be an adaptation, first of all it would have to be a trait widely present in the population in question, namely humans. It would be necessary not only that humans have the *capacity* for deductive reasoning, but also that this capacity be regularly and systematically deployed (otherwise, it would not confer an evolutionary advantage on those possessing the trait). Do human reasoners indeed exhibit the trait of successfully performing deductive reasoning? According to a large body of literature in experimental psychology (see Chapter 8), they do not, as can be inferred from results in well-known reasoning tasks such as the Wason selection task, syllogistic reasoning, and so on.

Joshua Schechter (2013, footnote 14) is aware of these results, but suggests that this discrepancy still does not affect his thesis because it arises from a performance/competence discrepancy. However, even if human reasoners have the capacity to reason deductively but in fact rarely deploy it, it is still unclear how a capacity that is rarely used could confer an evolutionary advantage over individuals in the ancestral population not having this capacity so as to be selected for. (One might conjecture that our ancestors made more extensive use of deductive reasoning than we now do, and thus that we still have an ability which was selected for but is now rarely used. But why would such a change have occurred? This seems implausible.)[3]

All things considered, it is not at all clear how an account of deductive reasoning as an evolutionary genetic adaptation can be reconciled with the observation that human reasoners do not seem very proficient in deductive reasoning (which does not mean that human reasoners cannot *learn* to reason deductively). And so, the alternative hypothesis, namely that the emergence of deductive reasoning in humans is *not* a genetically encoded evolutionary story, seems better supported by the available data.

One criterion often used to distinguish the genetic from the cultural is prevalence and universality in the population in question; traits that are universally present in a genetically homogeneous population, despite important geographical and environmental differences, are more plausibly associated with genetic endowment (though universality does not necessarily entail that the trait is a direct product of genetic processes of natural selection; Heyes, 2018). For humans, bipedal walking and speech are quintessential examples of universally present traits, which thus seem more amenable to genetic, evolutionary explanations. In contrast, literacy, for example, is not a species universal. The technology of literacy clearly emerged as a cultural phenomenon; it appeared independently only at three (maybe four, with Egypt) different times/places in human history – Mesopotamia, China, Mexico – and then spread out to much (though not all) of the rest of the world (Schmandt-Besserat, 1996). Ontogenetically, literacy is typically (though not exclusively) tightly connected to formal education and schooling, usually not emerging from sole exposure, unlike speech. Naturally, there must be a cognitive basis in our genetic endowment that makes reading and writing possible at all for creatures such as ourselves. (The work of Stanislas Dehaene [2009], among others, addresses precisely this question.) And so, all neurologically typical humans have in principle the *capacity* to learn how to read and write, but it is not a universally instantiated feature in the human species; indeed, even now there remain a significant number of non-literate cultures in the world.[4]

The claim is thus that deductive reasoning emerged as a cognitive technology (though arguably, it remains restricted to circles of specialists), in a way similar to literacy. And so, we end up with three (kinds of) questions. (1) The phylogenetic question: what is the genetically encoded cognitive basis that supports deductive reasoning? (2) The historical question: which cultural processes gave rise to the emergence of deductive reasoning? (3) The ontogenetic question: how do

---

[3] See Stanovich, 2003 for a related analysis.
[4] See Krämer, 2003 and Menary, 2007 for writing as a technology.

deductive reasoning skills arise in a given individual? The fact that deductive reasoning is not ubiquitous, either across time or across cultures, and not even among highly educated populations (e.g. the typical undergraduate who participates in psychological experiments does not seem to be a proficient deductive reasoner), suggests that the ontogenetic story will be fundamentally connected to specific social and cultural practices of learning.

Notice, though, that the cultural perspective still does not entail that there will be significant convergence between phylogenetic, historical, and ontogenetic development in different domains and for different skills. To go back to literacy, it is not plausible at all that the best way to teach a child how to read and write is to retrace the steps of the historical development of writing – among other reasons, because an evolving technology is to a great extent a matter of 'trial and error' until it acquires the desirable characteristics that make it useful. However, as I will argue, in the case of deductive reasoning specifically, when it comes to fostering the emergence of such skills in an individual, it does pay off to 'recapitulate' to some extent the historical development of such practices.

And thus, just as historians and archeologists trace the historical emergence and development of different cultural technologies such as, for example, literacy, I here present the outlines of the emergence and development of deductive reasoning, drawing on the history of logic and mathematics (Chapters 5 and 6). And just as developmental psychologists and educators investigate, for example, the emergence of literacy in individuals, I here survey the main findings on how deductive reasoning skills emerge and develop in individuals, drawing in particular from the literature on the psychology of reasoning and on mathematics education (Chapters 8 and 9). Inspired by the dialogical historical origins of deduction, it will be argued that adopting a dialogical perspective for teaching purposes tends to lead to better learning outcomes than the focus on individualistic conceptions of, say, mathematical proofs or deductive arguments in general. And so, the conclusion will be that, specifically with respect to deductive reasoning, there is an interesting sense in which ontogeny may (culturally) recapitulate 'phylogeny,'[5] or in this case cultural history.[6]

---

[5] Insofar as deductive reasoning emerges from dialogical practices (as I claim here), and insofar as dialogical practices presuppose the development of certain forms of sociality in the human species (as argued in Chapter 10), then presumably there are also some parallels between phylogenetic and ontogenetic development. But we will not pursue this question further and will instead focus on how the ontogenetic emergence of deductive reasoning may fruitfully mirror the relevant historical developments.

[6] Incidentally, the general idea of recapitulation for mathematical cognition has had some illustrious proponents: "Zoologists maintain that the embryonic development of an animal recapitulates in brief the whole history of its ancestors throughout geologic time. It seems it is the same in the development of minds ... For this reason, the history of science should be our first guide" (Poincaré, 1946, p. 437). "The history of mathematics and the logic of mathematical discovery, i.e. the phylogenesis and the ontogenesis of mathematical thought ..." (Lakatos, 1976, p. 4). In

2.2.2   Why Adopt a 'Roots' Perspective?

The reader may be wondering: but what justifies the 'roots' approach with respect to deductive reasoning? Can a historical investigation of the concept of deduction tell us something *philosophically* relevant about current instantiations of the concept? As suggested above, deduction is not only a cultural product; more specifically, it is a technical/theoretical concept (a term of art), restricted to circles of specialists (philosophers, logicians, mathematicians).[7] And so, the development of practices and conceptualizations of deduction is arguably chiefly a *theoretical* development. If this is right, then the methodology of *conceptual genealogy*, which I have previously presented in detail (2015b), seems to offer a suitable viewpoint not only for a historical analysis of the concept of deduction, but also for a systematic, philosophical investigation (see Chapter 5 on this methodology).

The underlying conception of (philosophical) concepts is historicist and functionalist, positing that at each stage of development a particular concept would have been embedded in a set of practices that were meaningful to those engaged in these practices at that point. And thus, rather than viewing philosophical concepts as ahistorical, non-situated, disembodied entities, I consider them within a larger context of practices and general cultural background. A genealogical analysis focuses on the successive stages of development of the concept under investigation, discerning both what does and what does not change in the transitions from one stage to another. Thus, this approach focuses both on *continuity* and on *discontinuity* in the historical development of a concept, specifically with respect to the function(s) the concept is expected to fulfill at different stages. Philosophical concepts then turn out to be multi-layered entities, where new layers of functions and meanings are imposed while older layers do not disappear completely.[8]

One might object that it seems problematic to infer (uncritically at least) current function or meaning from ancestral function or meaning. Such inferences can be described as instantiations of *genetic reasoning*: "any attempt to support or to discredit a belief, statement, position or argument based upon its causal or historical genesis, or more broadly, the way in which it was formed" (Klement,

---

Proofs and Refutations, Imre Lakatos has his characters retrace in a dialogical manner the historical steps in the development of mathematical theories on the properties of polyhedra, i.e. three-dimensional geometrical entities (solids), thus presenting a version of the recapitulation principle. Lakatos also maintains that the history of mathematics is an indispensable component of the philosophy of mathematics. (More on Lakatos in Chapter 3.)

[7] Smiley, 1988 and Smith, 2011 hold a similar view with respect to the closely related notion of logical consequence.

[8] This is the methodology that I have deployed to investigate the concept of logical form (Dutilh Novaes, 2012b, 2012c). I have argued that the concept of logical form maintains traces of its metaphysical origins (Aristotelian hylomorphism) even when transposed to a different domain, namely logic.

2002, p. 384). It is often thought that genetic reasoning is always fallacious, as it amounts to confusing the origins of a concept or belief with the question of its correctness and justification. One reason to think that such inferences are indeed fallacious is the observation that past instantiations of a given phenomenon may be so fundamentally different from its current instantiations that reference to the former can in no way serve as justification, explanation, or critique of the latter. Even if at each transition something of the previous instantiation remains present, after a long series of transitions there may not be anything left in common between ancestral instantiations and current instantiations (as in a sorites series).

The concept of genetic fallacy suggests that going back to the 'roots' of a phenomenon or concept may not be a suitable approach to investigate its current instantiations, and in some cases, indeed, it is not. However, as I will argue throughout the book, current conceptions of deduction still maintain much of their (dialogical) origins; thus, to truly comprehend the nature of deduction, going back to its historical origins is in fact indispensable. But, naturally, the proof will be in the pudding, i.e. in how much mileage we can get out of the (historically inspired) main hypothesis of the book – that deduction is essentially a dialogical notion – when addressing the puzzles and questions pertaining to deduction that still loom large. In other words, I do not take the 'roots' approach to be automatically suitable in all cases. It is, however, a particularly suitable approach to investigate the concept of deduction specifically, as I hope will become evident as we proceed.

2.3   Deduction as a Dialogical Notion

With these methodological considerations in place, I now introduce the main hypothesis of the present investigation: deductive reasoning is essentially a dialogical phenomenon. It is this hypothesis that will be further investigated in subsequent chapters; it will receive corroboration insofar as it is able to shed new light and explain a number of otherwise puzzling properties of the concept and practices of deduction, at different levels. The overall argumentative structure of this book can be described as *abductive*: it is by showing that the dialogical account is able to explain a wide range of apparently unrelated phenomena pertaining to deduction that an 'inference to the best explanation' – deduction as a dialogical notion – presents itself. The project is an instantiation of the method of *synthetic philosophy* (Schliesser, 2019), where findings from different areas are brought together by means of a unifying hypothesis.[9]

---

[9] The work of Kim Sterelny is a quintessential example of synthetic philosophy in this sense. "The essay is an essay in philosophy in part because it depends primarily on the cognitive toolbox of philosophers: it is work of synthesis and argument, integrating ideas and suggestions from many different research traditions. No one science monopolizes this broad project though many

Importantly, there are different, largely independent ways in which the dialogical nature of deduction can be understood, which means that the dialogical hypothesis being plausible in one of these senses does not entail that it will be plausible in the other senses. And yet, the claim to be defended here is that the dialogical hypothesis is plausible in a number of different senses, and each of them will be presented in detail in different chapters of the book.

2.3.1   Historical Perspective

As already mentioned, the initial motivation for the present investigation was provided by the historical development of deduction, in particular its birth in Ancient Greek philosophy and mathematics. As detailed by Benoît Castelnérac and Mathieu Marion (2009) for philosophy and by Reviel Netz (1999) for mathematics, the emergence of deductive reasoning in both fields was very strongly influenced by contexts of argumentation and debate. G.E.R. Lloyd (1996) further discusses the social and political background that paved the way for these developments, in particular the structure of Athenian democracy where argumentation and persuasion occupied pride of place. As aptly described by Netz:

> Greek mathematics reflects the importance of persuasion. It reflects the role of orality, in the use of formulae, in the structure of proofs ... But this orality is regimented into a written form, where vocabulary is limited, presentations follow a relatively rigid pattern ... It is at once oral and written (Netz, 1999, pp. 297–298)

The idea is thus that deductive proofs emerged initially as a means of persuasion in a multi-agent, dynamical setting – the famous proof of the duplication of the square in Plato's *Meno*, conducted as a dialogue between Socrates and a young slave (82b–d), would be an example of how these oral proofs would have been conducted (see Chapter 5). As indicated by Netz's passage above, when these oral proofs became regimented in written form, their dialogical origins were no longer immediately apparent, but dialogical traces remained. This is why Netz says (and this slogan truly summarizes the gist of the present proposal) that deductive arguments such as mathematical proofs are "at once oral and written." A deductive argument both is and is not a dialogue, as it is a mixture of dialogical features inherited from its origins with non-dialogical features picked up along the way.

The dialogical component is also at the core of the art and practice of *dialectic*. Dialectic is the game of questions and answers, as illustrated in Plato's dialogues and regimented in Aristotle's *Topics*, where participants test

contribute to it. So I exploit and depend on data, but do not provide new data" (Sterelny, 2012, p. xi).

the coherence of each other's views by eliciting discursive commitments and drawing further implications from them. In turn, it is against the background of dialectical practices that logic, in particular Aristotelian logic, has emerged (Duncombe & Dutilh Novaes, 2016). And so, just as for mathematics, with respect to logic, too, the historical 'roots of deduction' appear to be essentially dialogical, as will be discussed in detail in Chapters 5 and 6.

2.3.2   *Philosophical Perspective*

These historical observations then lead to the formulation of a philosophical account of the nature of deductive argumentation and deductive reasoning, resulting in what can be described as a *rational reconstruction* – a methodology deployed by Rudolf Carnap, among others (see Carus, 2008, chapter 6). A rational reconstruction is an idealization that presents the outlines of a phenomenon in a rigorous but simplified form, where some of the aspects of the phenomenon are disregarded. But the overall result is expected to provide an accurate picture of its main structural features, and thus to allow for systematic investigation.

Inspired by the historical developments briefly described above, we arrive at a conceptualization of deductive arguments in terms of semi-adversarial dialogues involving two (fictive, idealized) participants, referred to as *Prover* and *Skeptic*, or as *Proponent* and *Opponent*. (I favor Prover and Skeptic, a terminology borrowed from Sørensen & Urzyczyn, 2006, as these terms outline the functional nature of these two roles.) At a lower level, it may seem that the participants have opposite goals: Prover wants to establish a given conclusion from given premises, and Skeptic wants to block the establishment of the conclusion – hence the adversariality component. But at a higher level, they are actually also cooperating, hence the qualification *semi-adversarial*; they do not only seek to 'crush' their interlocutor no matter what. Prover seeks not only to establish the conclusion, but to do so in a way that is convincing and explanatory for Skeptic; Skeptic will not obstruct Prover's argument at all costs, but will ask for clarification when needed and thus will help Prover produce a more perspicuous, persuasive, and explanatory argument that is immune to counterexamples. Without this cooperative component, the strong epistemic import of deductive arguments is hard to make sense of.

The dialogue starts with Prover asking Skeptic to grant certain premises.[10] Once these are in place, Prover puts forward further statements which she claims follow necessarily from what Skeptic has already granted, thus

---

[10] Alternatively, it may start with a statement of the thesis to be proved, as in a typical mathematical proof.

uncovering what else Skeptic is committed to after having made certain concessions. (Prover may ask for additional premises along the way.) Skeptic's main moves are:

(1) To grant premises, or to reject the proposed premises.
(2) To provide counterexamples, i.e. situations in which the premises obtain but the conclusion does not, thus showing that the inference does not have the property of necessary truth-preservation. (A counterexample can be local, i.e. aiming at a specific step in the argument, or global, aiming at the overall premises and conclusion of the argument; Lakatos, 1976.)
(3) To ask for further clarification when a particular inferential step is not sufficiently clear/convincing/perspicuous. Prover is thus invited to reformulate the argument with more convincing inferential steps.

The three key properties of a deductive argument described in Chapter 1 can then all be given a natural dialogical explanation in this rational reconstruction. Firstly, the property of necessary truth-preservation can be given a *strategic* rationale: if each step is necessarily truth-preserving, the whole argument will be immune to objections from Skeptic. In this respect, what stands out is the adversarial component of these dialogues. Accounting for necessary truth-preservation in terms of the game-theoretical concept of a *winning strategy* is an idea present in other prominent dialogical, game-theoretical approaches to logic, such as Paul Lorenzen's dialogical logic (Keiff, 2009) or Jaakko Hintikka's game-theoretical semantics (Hintikka & Sandu, 1997). This idea is to some extent incorporated in the present account, but with some important modifications (see Chapter 3 for a comparison between these two earlier approaches and my proposal).

By contrast, the property of perspicuity – the idea that each step in a deductive argument must be clear and convincing – speaks directly to the strong *cooperative* component of such games. Indeed, this is perhaps the most prominent difference between my approach and other dialogical, game-theoretical approaches, namely the fact that I emphasize cooperative components alongside adversarial components, whereas these other approaches tend to focus mostly or even exclusively on adversarial components (see Chapter 3). If Prover wants not only to force Skeptic to grant the conclusion but also to obtain an explanatory effect, then it is incumbent on her (Prover) to formulate the argument with steps that Skeptic will find persuasive and explanatory.

Finally, the requirement of premise acceptance is understood in terms of speech acts of proposing and granting. The proverbial 'granting for the sake of the argument' allows for a dissociation of one's actual beliefs from what one grants in the specific dialogical, argumentative situation. (As noted in Chapter 1, this dissociation in mono-agent contexts is cognitively demanding.) This idea gives rise to the technical notion of 'supposition' or 'assumption' in the context of a proof (Jaskowski, 1967), which is different from a categorical assertion in that it can be discharged by the introduction of a conditional where the antecedent is the proposition supposed and the consequent the conclusion arrived at. Importantly, in a dialogical context, it is possible and in fact quite natural to draw conclusions from an interlocutor's commitments without having to endorse them oneself (this is particularly noticeable with *reductio ad absurdum* arguments; Dutilh Novaes, 2016b). And thus, in these dialogical situations, drawing conclusions from premises one does not in fact believe to be true is a rather natural activity, whereas doing so in mono-agent situations is cognitively challenging for untrained reasoners.

2.3.3   *Cognitive Perspective*

As already mentioned, from a cognitive perspective, too, deductive reasoning is best understood from a dialogical perspective (or so I claim). This is a normative rather than a descriptive claim; as a matter of fact, deduction is typically *not* conceptualized or presented as a dialogical notion by most researchers and educators. This is partly what explains the difficulties that students tend to have with the technique of mathematical proof (Robert & Schwarzenberger, 1991; Gilmore et al., 2018), as well as the difficulties that participants have in performing simple deductive tasks in experiments when reasoning on their own – performance tends to improve significantly when participants tackle these tasks in groups (Moshman & Geil, 1998; Trouche et al., 2014. Mercier and Sperber, 2017 go a step beyond this to claim that *all* reasoning, not only deductive reasoning, has a dialogical, interactionist basis – see Chapter 10). In other words, the claim is that deductive reasoning should be conceptualized as dialogical also at a cognitive level, and this conceptualization would lead to better learning outcomes.

Another indication of the dialogical nature of deductive reasoning is what may be described as the 'phenomenology of mathematical proof,' i.e. what it 'feels like' to produce a mathematical proof. Although typically not explicitly taught to think of proofs dialogically, expert mathematicians often describe the process of producing a proof as a role-switching process, where they alternate the roles of trying to prove the conclusion and of playing the 'stubborn proponent' (a term coined by the mathematician Mark Kac; Fisher, 1989, p. 50) who is not easily convinced.

In fact, the deduction-as-dialogical claim is a special case of a more general conceptualization of human cognition as essentially social, where the Vygotskian concept of *internalization* plays a prominent role (Vygotsky, 1978). While on the Vygotskian story the so-called 'higher functions of the mind' all have a social genesis (Vygotsky, 1931), it will be argued in Chapter 9 that this is especially the case with respect to deductive reasoning. In this chapter, I discuss the research in mathematics education that indicates that a dialogical approach yields promising results when it comes to teaching the technique of mathematical proofs. The general idea is actually quite simple: if students are explicitly told what the rationale for a deductive proof is – it is a piece of discourse intended to persuade a putative target audience in an explanatory way – then they are more likely to internalize and successfully apply the technique subsequently.

Further evidence for the dialogical hypothesis is to be found in the work of linguist Esther Pascual, who introduced the concept of *fictive interaction* (Pascual & Oakley, 2017). The claim is that there is a conversational basis permeating all of language, including discourse that is not obviously dialogical, which serves to structure cognition, discourse, and grammar. This observation has implications for thought (conceived of as 'talking to oneself'), for discourse organization (e.g. monologues structured as dialogues), and for central features of language use (e.g. rhetorical questions). If this is right, then it is in fact not very surprising that a mathematical proof, too, would have a conversational (dialogical) basis. My main contribution here is to spell out in more detail the specific kind of conversation that a mathematical proof reenacts: semi-adversarial dialogues following fairly strict rules, involving the fictive participants Prover and Skeptic.

2.3.4   *Mathematical Practices*

The fourth sense in which deduction is dialogical to be investigated pertains to mathematical practices and the 'sociology' of mathematical proof. The thought is that the social dynamics of proof in mathematics communities roughly follow the dialectic of proofs and refutations as described by Lakatos (Lakatos, 1976), and are thus essentially dialogical. When a mathematician announces a new proof, especially when it is an important result and she has a good standing in the community, then the community as a whole takes it upon itself to play the role of Skeptic by checking the correctness of the proof. (For actual examples of community checking in mathematics and computer science, see MacKenzie, 2001 and Martin & Pease, 2013. The latter covers some of the ways in which recent community checking is changing thanks to new technologies and the Internet.) In this process, mistakes may be found, which will force the original Prover to go back to the proof in the hope of fixing the mistake – as happened with Andrew Wiles after he announced the first version of his proof of Fermat's Last Theorem. He then had to spend another year on fixing the mistake (in collaboration with Richard Taylor) so that the proof could finally receive the seal of approval from the mathematics community as a whole (Taylor & Wiles, 1995) (see Chapter 11).

More recently, the saga of Shinichi Mochizuki's (purported) proof of the ABC conjecture reveals some of the complexities of the Prover–Skeptic dynamics (see Chapter 11). The proof remains impenetrable for the mathematics community at large, as it relies on techniques and concepts that Mochizuki (a highly regarded mathematician) developed in isolation for more than a decade (Castelvecchi, 2015). And so, it remains in a limbo; meanwhile, a number of mathematicians are working hard to familiarize themselves with the novel techniques introduced by Mochizuki in order to be able to ascertain whether the proof is correct or not. At this point, the jury is still out (Roberts, 2019).

Moreover, practices of journal peer review in mathematics (which is, of course, also a form of community checking, but in a more regimented context and 'behind the scenes') also reveal key details of these mathematical 'conversations.' Indeed, a referee for a mathematical paper basically adopts the role of Skeptic, asking 'why?' questions and producing counterexamples (when available) and objections (Andersen, 2017).

Another aspect of mathematical practice that brings out the dialogical nature of deductive proofs is what has been described as the varying *levels of granularity* of a proof presentation, depending on the context (Schiller, 2013). For instance, in an introductory textbook, proofs will typically be very detailed, as the intended audience (undergraduates) is not expected to be able to follow the argument unless it is presented in detail. In a professional mathematics journal, by contrast, proofs will typically be presented in a rather contrived, abbreviated way, as the presupposition is that the intended audience, expert mathematicians, will be able to reconstruct the full argument on their own. In fact, professional proofs often contain intentional 'gaps' (Fallis, 2003). The moral is that there is always an intended audience the proof aims at: a mathematical proof is discourse that is never produced in a vacuum.

Furthermore, the suspicion that most mathematicians still harbor toward certain kinds of proofs, in particular computer-assisted and probabilistic proofs, can also be explained from a dialogical perspective. If these proofs fail to convince a relevant expert of the truth of the conclusion of the proof just by consideration of each of the steps in the proof – which Kenny Easwaran (2009) dubs the property of *transferability* – then they fail to perform the function of explanatory persuasion that is typically associated with deductive proofs. However, it may well be that these proofs will in the long run force us to revise the very concept of what a proof is. The concept of a mathematical proof is ultimately an open-textured one, which may have to be revised if the relevant practices undergo substantive modifications. But for now, it seems that what can be described as the 'classical,' Euclidean conception of a deductive mathematical proof requires the property of transferability, which in turn is essentially dialogical.

2.4   Conclusion

In this chapter, I presented and defended the 'roots' approach to be adopted in the book. As the 'roots' in question can be understood in different ways – historically, philosophically, cognitively – what is required is a multi-disciplinary, integrative approach. I also briefly introduced the four ways in which the hypothesis that deduction is a dialogical notion will be investigated in the coming chapters: philosophically, historically, cognitively, and in terms of mathematical practices.

Throughout the book, a number of interesting and often puzzling features of deductive reasoning will be discussed; it will be argued that they become less puzzling if considered from the vantage point of the dialogical hypothesis. Some of these issues are: Why does it seem to be so difficult for untrained human reasoners to reason deductively? How can the teaching of the technique of mathematical proofs be improved? What are the main transitions in the history of logic/deduction? Which side offers the best account of the notion of logical consequence, model theory or proof theory? What happens when a purported mathematical proof is proposed but no one in the mathematics community is able to understand it?

At first sight, these may appear to be unrelated questions coming from different fields of inquiry. And yet, through the unifying power of the dialogical hypothesis, they can all be addressed in a synthetic way. In turn, if the hypothesis delivers explanatory success for a wide range of different questions and puzzles, then collectively this will constitute compelling evidence for the main thesis of the book: deduction has dialogical roots and retains much of its dialogical origins.

3   The Prover–Skeptic Dialogues

3.1   Introduction

In this chapter and the next, I investigate the philosophical roots of deduction as a dialogical notion. Even though the initial inspiration for this hypothesis comes from the historical developments to be described in Chapter 5, it seems more appropriate not to follow this 'order of discovery' for the presentation of the material here, as the philosophical concepts introduced here and in Chapter 4 will then support the historical analysis in Chapters 5, 6, and 7. Thus, I start with the philosophical foundations, including a detailed presentation of the rational reconstruction of deduction as corresponding to Prover–Skeptic dialogues (briefly presented in Chapter 2).

This chapter is organized as follows. I start with a discussion of the relations between logic, games, and dialogues, elaborating on two prominent earlier dialogical proposals by Paul Lorenzen and Jaakko Hintikka, respectively. I then present in detail the rational reconstruction of Prover–Skeptic dialogues and discuss the complex interplay between cooperation and adversariality in these games (thus emphasizing what is distinctive about my proposal with respect to earlier proposals).

3.2   Earlier Dialogical Proposals

That there are interesting connections between logic and multi-agent situations, in particular dialogical interactions, is not in any way a new idea. It is in fact a very old one, dating back to a number of ancient logical traditions (Chapters 5 and 6). However, starting in the post-medieval period in Europe, dialogical conceptions of logic as well as dialogical practices in connection with logic began to lose prominence (see Dutilh Novaes, 2017a and Chapter 7). As a result, the historical dialogical roots of logic and deduction remained by and large forgotten for centuries.

In the mid-twentieth century, however, logic and the idea of multi-agent dialogical interactions were reunited to some extent. One important factor in these events was the development of game theory as a mathematical theory.[1] (And of course the fact that, since the nineteenth century, logic had become closely associated with mathematics – see Chapter 7.) From the 1960s onwards, a number of mathematical and logical theories were developed in terms of games between (typically two) players. As presented by Wilfrid Hodges (2013), a range of different games were introduced, such as semantic games used to define truth, back-and-forth games used to compare (model-theoretical) structures, and dialogue games representing formal (deductive) proofs. In most of these cases, the idea of games features primarily as a metaphor, or as a convenient abstract device to investigate mathematical concepts or structures; usually, no deeper account of *why* we should think about these concepts in terms of multi-agent games is provided. This may be perfectly fine in the context of mathematics or mathematical logic, but it raises a number of philosophical questions as to why the game perspective is suitable for these investigations. As well put by Mathieu Marion (2009), the question is: why play logical games at all?

The two most comprehensive accounts of the philosophical foundations for game-based approaches to logic and deduction were both initially formulated in the 1960s and further developed in the following decades: Lorenzen's dialogical logic program (Keiff, 2009; Lorenzen & Lorenz, 1978; Rahman et al., 2018) and Hintikka's game-theoretical semantics (Hintikka, 1973; Hintikka & Sandu, 1997). These two accounts are now well known among logicians and philosophers, but have not enjoyed much uptake outside of specific circles. Indeed, the received view is by and large still based on mono-agent, mentalistic ideas. Moreover, they have also been criticized *qua* dialogical foundations for logic; it has been argued that, while having promising ideas as their starting points, they ultimately fail to deliver convincing dialogical, game-based accounts of logic and deduction (Hodges, 2001, 2013; Marion, 2009, 2006; Trafford, 2017).[2]

I first present a brief description of each of these two research programs, and later explain how my account differs from Lorenzen's and Hintikka's. The differences are in part motivated by the criticisms voiced by Hodges and Marion (among others), but also due to some general shortcomings that (in my opinion) remain in these earlier accounts, especially their neglect of the cooperative components of such games. (The analysis here will remain essentially philosophical, and so no special attention will be paid to the more technical aspects of these frameworks.)

[1] It is not a coincidence that logicians such as Lorenzen and Leon Henkin became interested in game-theoretical concepts in the late 1950s: they were both at the Princeton Institute for Advanced Study at the same time as John von Neumann and Oskar Morgenstern, two game-theory pioneers. For Lorenzen in particular, there seem to be no obvious traces in his earlier writings of the dialogical, multi-agent conception of logic that he went on to develop.
[2] As will become clear, I rely substantially on earlier work by Hodges and Marion for this section, as well as on work by Erik Krabbe for dialogical logic.

3.2.1   Lorenzen's Dialogical Logic

The first detailed modern dialogical account of logic is due to the German mathematician Paul Lorenzen, inspired by what he described as the 'agonistic' origins of logic in Ancient Greece (Lorenzen, 1960). (In practice, he offered only some brief remarks on this historical source of inspiration; see Krabbe, 2006 for a more detailed discussion of the presumed historical sources for dialogical logic.) *Agon* in Ancient Greek refers to contests of different kinds between different participants: athletics, music, poetry. It is a key concept in Ancient Greek theater (drama), where it refers to a contest or debate between two characters: the prot*agonist* and the ant*agonist*. As such, the 'struggles' in these performances bear similarities to dialectical dialogues (see Chapter 5). Indeed, when Lorenzen spoke of the agonistic origins of logic, it is Ancient Greek dialectic that he seemed to have in mind, in particular the more competitive forms of dialectical dialogues.

Thus, two central components of Lorenzen's agonistic conception of logic are that it is (i) a *multi-agent* and, indeed, (ii) a *competitive* activity, where one participant will win while other(s) will lose. Notice that these two components are mutually independent: an activity can be multi-agent without being competitive (say, cooperative children's games such as skipping rope), and it can be competitive without being multi-agent (say, a game of solitaire). But for Lorenzen, these two components seem intrinsically connected, probably as a result of the influence of game-theoretical ideas.[3]

Lorenzen's chief concern when formulating dialogical logic seems to have been, in the context of key developments in the first half of the twentieth century (the work of David Hilbert, Kurt Gödel, Alfred Tarski, etc.), with the foundations of mathematics. In this context, a preoccupation with the semantics of logical connectives took central stage, given the goal of formulating axiomatic systems that would allow for the rigorous derivation of mathematical truths. Lorenzen thought that a Tarskian approach to the semantics of connectives was rather dissatisfying: if the meaning of the conjunction is defined as '$A \& B$ is true if and only if A is true *and* B is true' and '$A \& B$ is false if and only if A is false *or* B is false,' this presupposes the availability of the metalinguistic *and or* (Marion, 2009, p. 9), and so only seems to push the problem one level up. Thus, a different way to define the semantics of the connectives, one that would avoid the apparent circularity of defining the semantics of $\&$ in terms of its metalinguistic counterpart *and* and so forth, would be a highly desirable

---

[3] Besides these historical considerations, Lorenzen also held philosophical views on how logic was ultimately to be grounded in our practical non-verbal activities (*die Praxis unseres sprach-freien Handelns*) and our prelogical speech practices (*vorlogische Redepraxis*) (Marion, 2009, p. 12). These ideas were further developed in what is known as the Erlanger Program (Krabbe, 2001). However, as argued by Marion, 2009, Lorenzen's reliance on the concept of prelogical speech practices to ground dialogical logic is ultimately untenable.

result. Lorenzen's key idea was to define the meanings of logical connectives in terms of moves by players in dialogical games, thus articulating a non-circular foundational bedrock for the connectives. Moreover, he was not neutral with respect to the different proposals for the foundations of mathematics available at the time; he favored a constructive, intuitionistic approach, and believed that his dialogical system would unequivocally vindicate constructivism (Krabbe, 2006, section 3.2).

In sum, Lorenzen's approach to the general project of providing solid foundations for mathematics, in particular by grounding the semantics of logical connectives in a non-circular way, was to turn to game-theoretical ideas (alongside historical inspiration from the Ancient Greek *agon*) in order to develop a dialogical account of the connectives by means of competitive, zero-sum dialogical games of perfect information. (The first complete presentation of the system of dialogical logic is to be found in Kuno Lorenz's 1961 dissertation, supervised by Lorenzen.) The two participants are called 'Proponent' and 'Opponent,' and their moves in the game are presented as 'attacks' and 'defenses,' thus stressing the adversarial, competitive nature of these games.

The game starts with Proponent stating a complex formula, which Proponent claims to be a valid formula (a theorem of the system). Thus, Proponent wants to establish the validity of the formula stated, while Opponent wants to show that the formula is not valid: they have opposite goals, and only one of them can win. What the players then in fact proceed to do is to *decompose* the complex formula into atomic formulas according to the rules determining the valid moves for each player at each point (akin to tableaux proof systems; Keiff, 2009, section 2.2.1).[4]

While at the start of the game Proponent takes on a defensive position and Opponent is the attacker, these roles can change along the way. This happens especially with an occurrence of the negation, which in effect functions as a role-switching device: if Proponent states not-ϕ, then Opponent states ϕ as an attack; the game then continues with Opponent defending ϕ, and thus with Proponent attacking ϕ. The rule for the conjunction states that it can be attacked in two ways, namely by challenging the left conjunct or challenging the right conjunct. It is the player who attacks the conjunction who gets to pick which one, under the assumption that the player defending a conjunction must have a defense for each conjunct. The game then proceeds with the formula chosen by the attacker (one of the two conjuncts). A disjunction, in turn, can only be challenged as a whole, and it is then up to the defender to pick one of the two

---

[4] It is perhaps worth noting explicitly that a game that starts with a complex formula, which is then decomposed through the moves of the players, bears no real resemblance to the Ancient Greek dialectical dialogues that Lorenzen claims are one of his main inspirations.

disjuncts for the game to continue, under the assumption that it is sufficient to have a defense for only one of the disjuncts for the disjunction to be defensible. Similar rules are defined for the quantifiers (Krabbe, 2006, p. 677).

The game ends when one of the players has made a move and there are no available moves left for the other player; the last player to have made a move wins the game. (If the game does not end in a finite number of steps, it is a win for Opponent.) If Proponent is the last player to have made a move, then she wins the game, which means that the initial formula stated by Proponent is valid. If Opponent is the last player to play, he wins the game, which means that the initial formula is not valid. Against this background, an explicit connection between the notion of validity and plays of these games is drawn: if Proponent has a *winning strategy* in this game, one for which each play is a win for her no matter what Opponent does, then there is a proof for the formula in question, which is thus valid. To be sure, there are a number of technical complications regarding how the game is defined, including different structural rules determining its procedural aspects (see Krabbe, 2006; Keiff, 2009), but for the present purposes this brief presentation should suffice. So, let us now take a look at a concrete example.

Consider the law of the excluded middle, ϕ *or not*-ϕ, which is classically valid but is intuitionistically invalid. (The example is taken from Marion, 2009, p. 14.) To which dialogue(s) does it correspond? Before considering the dialogues specifically, it is worth stating explicitly two structural/procedural rules, one for intuitionistic dialogues and one for classical ones.

- **Intuitionistic Rule**: Each player can either attack a (complex) formula asserted by one's adversary or defend oneself against the last attack that has not yet been answered.
- **Classical Rule**: Each player can either attack a (complex) formula asserted by one's adversary or defend oneself against any attack, including those already defended.

In other words, the Intuitionistic Rule restricts the possibility of defense to the last attack not yet defended, whereas the Classical Rule imposes no such restriction. The corresponding dialogues for $\phi \vee \neg\phi$ then become:

P: $\phi \vee \neg\phi$	P: $\phi \vee \neg\phi$	1
O: ?	O: ?	2
P: $\neg\phi$	P: $\neg\phi$	3
O: ϕ	O: ϕ	4
	P: ϕ	5

In the intuitionistic game (left), after O asserts ϕ in line 4, there is no move left for P, and so O wins the game; this means that there is no (intuitionistic) defense for the initial formula. In the classical game (right), P can reply again to the first challenge (the first move by O, marked as ? in line 2) in line 5, which she had initially replied to with ¬φ in line 3. Now that O has stated φ in line 4 as an attack to P's move of stating ¬φ, P can avail herself of φ, because it has been previously stated by O.[5] But now there is no move available to O, which means he loses the game; P wins, and the formula is thus shown to be classically valid.

But what is the rationale for the Intuitionistic Rule, which restricts responses to the latest pending challenge? Why should it be 'better' or more natural than the Classical Rule? While Lorenzen and others ultimately sought to establish the superiority of intuitionistic/constructive approaches and thus had reasons to prefer the Intuitionistic Rule, the requirement of only responding to the latest pending challenge does not seem to reflect anything 'natural' about dialogues in general, at least not any more than the Classical Rule does. We postpone a more detailed critical evaluation of Lorenzen's dialogical games for later, but let us keep this issue in mind.

It is worth noting that, in recent decades, the original framework formulated by Lorenzen and Lorenz has been further developed by a number of different researchers, in particular by the Lille group of Shahid Rahman and collaborators (Rahman et al., 2018). The framework has also received a number of different applications beyond its original purpose of providing constructive foundations for mathematics (Keiff, 2009; Krabbe, 2006). In recent work, Rahman and collaborators emphasize the importance of the *play level* over the *strategy level* of analysis for such games, while also highlighting their cooperative components. This is an important departure from the original dialogical logic framework, and in this respect there is some convergence between their proposal and my own (more on which shortly).

3.2.2   *Hintikka: Game-Theoretical Semantics*

Another philosophically sophisticated dialogical account of logic and deduction is Game-Theoretical Semantics (GTS) for quantifiers, initially introduced by Leon Henkin (1961) but later further developed in particular by Hintikka and colleagues (Hintikka & Sandu, 1997).[6] While Lorenzen drew philosophical and historical inspiration from Ancient Greek dialectic, Hintikka's main philosophical inspiration comes from Ludwig Wittgenstein's notion of 'language games' (Hintikka, 1973, 1996; Marion, 2006). Unlike Lorenzen, Hintikka's starting point was not a concern with the foundations of mathematics (though he does

---

[5] These games usually follow the 'formal rule,' according to which P may not assert an atomic sentence unless it has been previously asserted by O. As noted by James Trafford (2017, p. 85), this principle introduces an important asymmetry between the players.

[6] Other authors have developed game-based accounts of the semantics of quantifiers and other logical particles, but it is fair to say that Hintikka's version has become the most influential. Moreover, to my knowledge, it is the only one that comes equipped with a detailed (though ultimately unconvincing) philosophical story for its foundations.

extend his approach to mathematics in Hintikka, 1996); his main focus was the phenomenon of linguistic meaning as such, both in the 'vertical' sense of the connections between language and reality, and in the 'horizontal' sense of how different moves in language games are related to each other.

Hintikka's GTS focuses chiefly on quantifiers, in particular the classical universal and existential quantifiers. A formula such as

$$(*) \quad \forall x \; \exists y \; P(x,y)$$

states that each object in the relevant domain is paired with a different object (or possibly with itself) by means of relation P. Hintikka proposes an account of the meaning of this formula (and other formulas involving quantifiers) in terms of games involving two participants: $\forall$, also referred to as 'Nature,' 'initial falsifier,' and 'Abelard'; and $\exists$, also referred to as 'Myself,' 'initial verifier,' and 'Eloise.' The meaning of (*) thus corresponds to a game where Myself wants to establish the truth of (*) while Nature (presumably) wants to falsify (*). (Whether one can attribute intent and agency to Nature is one of the philosophical challenges for the framework – see Hodges, 2013.) In this case, Nature makes the first move, as a universal quantifier requires that the claim hold for *all* objects in the domain, and so it is up to the falsifier to pick a witness (object) that will not be particularly advantageous for the verifier (who might otherwise want to 'cherry-pick' her witness). Once Nature picks an object a, now it is the turn of the other player, Myself, to pick an object that will satisfy relation P with the object previously picked by Nature, as now we have an existential quantifier which corresponds to a move for the verifier. (It is sufficient that *one* object satisfy the property in question, so it can be picked by the player seeking to verify the formula. If instead we had two universal quantifiers, then Nature would pick the witness twice.) If Myself is able to find a suitable object b that entertains relation P with the object a picked by Nature, then Myself has won the particular play, given that Myself will then be in a position to assert an atomic formula that is true in the relevant model – $P(a, b)$ in this case. (Correctly asserting a true atomic formula counts as a win in these games.)

However, to establish that the initial quantified formula is true, what Myself needs is a *winning strategy* such that, for *any* witness that Nature may pick in the first round, Myself will be able to pair it with an object from the domain satisfying relation P. In this particular case, a winning strategy corresponds to the availability of a Skolem function that will deliver a suitable object to Myself for every object picked by Nature (Marion, 2006). Notice that, thus described, there are some relevant similarities with Lorenzen's dialogues, in particular the fact that the game starts with a complex formula which is decomposed by means of moves by the players.

This game-based conception of quantifiers is in many senses ingenious and aesthetically pleasing, but it gives rise to a number of philosophical questions. For starters, who are these players, and what are these games they are playing? As mentioned above, Hintikka here turns to Wittgenstein's notion of language games, and more specifically to what he (Hintikka) calls 'games of seeking and finding.' Hintikka suggests that, when Nature and Myself are 'picking objects' as described above, they are engaging in a (language-)game of seeking and finding.

One 'language-game' in which quantifiers can naturally occur is what I shall call the language-game of seeking and finding; and it seems to me that this is by far the most important kind of language-game in which they can occur. (Hintikka, 1973, p. 59)

Because Hintikka is interested in the 'vertical' relation between language and reality (and ultimately seeks to defend a realist conception of meaning), the connection with objects in seeking-and-finding games is crucial. In the spirit of Wittgenstein's notion of language games as embedded in more general (extra-) linguistic, social practices in a given environment ('forms of life'), these games are presented not as frivolous activities but rather as part and parcel of the fabric of (human) life.

We thus have a very different philosophical story when compared to Lorenzen's agonistic dialogues. Wittgenstein's language games are essentially multi-agent activities, but they are not intrinsically adversarial-competitive. Indeed, most of Wittgenstein's own examples are more accurately described as cooperative games of coordination, for example the builder's language game (Wittgenstein, 1953, § 2), where a builder and his assistant use exactly four words to coordinate their activities. On the diverse list of language games formulated by Wittgenstein in the *Investigations* (Wittgenstein, 1953, § 23), none of the items mentioned appears to be a straightforwardly competitive activity. So-called games of seeking and finding are not on the list either (though this is not in itself an argument against Hintikka, as he openly acknowledges that the notion of games of seeking and finding is his and not Wittgenstein's).[7] One could perhaps imagine a situation where a teacher says to a class, "How disappointing that *none* of you did your homework!" – a claim that would be disproved by a student who is able to show she has in fact done her homework. But does it make sense to view these seeking-and-finding games as *essentially* adversarial? One could certainly come up with examples where this is the case, perhaps the case of the angry teacher just described, or children playing hide-and-seek. But it seems quite implausible, and positively un-Wittgensteinian, to view adversarial instantiations of such games as paradigmatic.

---

[7] He does claim that the notion is very much *in the spirit* of Wittgensteinian language games, but to engage in exegetical work at this point is not a reasonable goal for the present investigation. See Marion, 2006 for some considerations on this issue.

True enough, Hintikka does not set up these seeking-and-finding games as explicitly adversarial (unlike Lorenzen's agonistic dialogues). However, their structure and texture are clearly adversarial; for example, the very idea that universal quantification corresponds to a move for Nature/falsifier presupposes an uncooperative player, who will choose the least advantageous witness (object) for Myself/verifier to continue the game with. The very terms 'verifier' and 'falsifier' suggest that players have opposite goals, and indeed these games are presented as zero-sum games. Why? Perhaps the goal is to allow for the incorporation of powerful game-theoretical concepts into the framework, in particular the concept of a winning strategy, which (as argued above) is essential to ground the truth of a quantified formula in plays of such games (mere wins are not enough). But the resulting story is simply not very convincing, in particular when Nature is portrayed as a somewhat hostile player seeking to falsify Myself's statements.[8]

In sum, Hintikka's GTS is characterized by a focus on quantifiers, even if the main idea can be generalized to other connectives. Moreover, although he superficially does not emphasize adversariality as much as Lorenzen does (in GTS, players' moves are not described as 'attacks' and 'defenses'), ultimately GTS remains intrinsically tied to adversarial zero-sum games. References to Wittgenstein's notion of language games are meant to provide philosophical foundations for GTS, but there seem to be a number of discrepancies between the nuts and bolts of the theory as it is in fact developed and its alleged Wittgensteinian background.

3.2.3   The Dawkins Question

Thus, despite containing a wide range of brilliant ideas as well as sophisticated technical solutions to logical issues, Lorenzen's dialogical logic and Hintikka's GTS both rest on rather flimsy philosophical grounds. This general point has been convincingly made before by Hodges and Marion in a number of writings, and I essentially concur with their critical arguments (while also believing that at least some of the issues they raise might be remedied by extensions of the systems, as proposed in Krabbe, 2001 and Rahman et al., 2018). Importantly, both frameworks seem to fail to offer a satisfactory answer to what Hodges dubs the Dawkins question, in reference to the evolutionary biologist Richard Dawkins:

If we want $\exists$'s motivation in a game G to have any explanatory value, then we need to understand what is achieved if $\exists$ does win. In particular we should be able to tell

---

[8] "In the corresponding logical games one should think of $\exists$ as Myself and $\forall$ as a hostile Nature who can never be relied on to present the object I want; so to be sure of finding it, I need a winning strategy. This story was never very convincing; the motivation of Nature is irrelevant, and nothing in the logical game corresponds to seeking" (Hodges, 2013, section 3).

a realistic story of a situation in which some agent called $\exists$ is trying to do something intelligible, and doing it is the same thing as winning in the game. (Hodges, 2013, section 2)

In other words, turning to game-related concepts when providing an account of logic and deduction is a move that will only have true explanatory value insofar as plausible stories for such games can be told – that is, if these stories rely on practices and activities that the agents in question (most plausibly, but not necessarily, human agents) would have good reasons to engage in. In the case of Lorenzen's dialogues, a fair amount of bending and shaping seems to be required in order to obtain the desired technical results – in particular, given the goal of establishing intuitionistic-constructive foundations for mathematics. (Recall the absence of motivation for the Intuitionistic Rule over the Classical Rule, as described above.) The result is by and large a game that is not likely to entice many potential players, as it does not latch on to any remotely realistic situation (despite Lorenzen's references to "prelogical speech practices" and to the agonistic origins of logic in Ancient Greek dialectic.). As for Hintikka, the plausibility of such games as reasonable, realistic activities is equally questionable, and no amount of lip service to Wittgensteinian language games seems to offer enough remedy.

Thus, one important desideratum for any dialogical, game-based, multi-agent account of logic and deduction is that it should offer an adequate answer to the so-called Dawkins question. In Section 3.3, I introduce in more detail the Prover–Skeptic dialogue that I claim is in a better position to explain the nature of logic and deduction from a dialogical, multi-agent perspective than the two earlier accounts just discussed.

3.3   The Prover–Skeptic Games

Among other proposals in the literature, the one that comes closest in spirit to the present proposal is Imre Lakatos' account of mathematical practice in terms of the dialectic of *Proofs and Refutations* (Lakatos, 1976).[9] The main text consists of a classroom dialogue between a teacher and students named after letters of the Greek alphabet, discussing various (attempted) proofs of Euler's conjecture for polyhedra, which links the vertices (V), edges (E), and faces (F) through the formula $V - E + F = 2$. The dialogue is presented as a rational reconstruction of the actual historical development of (attempted) proofs for

---

[9] Lakatos' work did not provide initial inspiration for my dialogical account of deduction, which was in fact mainly inspired by the historical emergence of deduction in Ancient Greece (both in logic and in mathematics). But there are some important similarities, as will become clear in what follows, and indeed engagement with Lakatos' ideas while working on the 'The Roots of Deduction' project helped me clarify a number of aspects of my proposal. There are also some relevant differences, though, which will be discussed below.

the conjecture and their refutations; the different students are portrayed as representing the various positions and reactions.[10]

The dialogue starts with the teacher presenting an argument (due to the nineteenth-century mathematician Augustin-Louis Cauchy) supporting the conjecture, which the students then go on to scrutinize and criticize for various reasons. At each objection, the proof is modified so as to withstand the force of the objection, for example, by restricting the relevant definition so that the counterexample produced is now excluded from the range of the hypothesis/conjecture. Through this process, it becomes clear that many of the key concepts involved (e.g. the concept of a polyhedron itself) were in fact vague and poorly understood at the starting point, and through the dialectic of proofs and refutations these concepts become sharpened and clarified (Tanswell, 2017, section 3.3).

As the discussion progresses, the method of proofs and refutations is described in the following terms:

- Rule 1. If you have a conjecture, set out to prove it and to refute it. Inspect the proof carefully to prepare a list of non-trivial lemmas (proof-analysis); find counterexamples both to the conjecture (global counterexamples) and to the suspect lemmas (local counterexamples) (Lakatos, 1976, p. 50).
- Rule 2. If you have a global counterexample, discard your conjecture, add to your proof-analysis a suitable lemma that will be refuted by the counter-example, and replace the discarded conjecture by an improved one that incorporates that lemma as a condition. Do not allow a refutation to be dismissed as a monster. Try to make all hidden lemmas explicit (Lakatos, 1976, p. 50).
- Rule 3. If you have a local counterexample, check to see whether it is not also a global counterexample. If it is, you can easily apply Rule 2 (Lakatos, 1976, p. 50).
- Rule 4. If you have a counterexample which is local but not global, try to improve your proof-analysis by replacing the refuted lemma by an unfalsified one (Lakatos, 1976, p. 58).

Counterexamples thus play a key role in the dialectic of proofs and refutations, and can be of two sorts: local counterexamples to specific steps in the proof (lemmas), or global counterexamples that affect the whole conjecture. In the case of local counterexamples, the conjecture itself may still hold up, but cannot be shown to be true by that very proof. Global counterexamples, in turn, require a more serious modification of the initial conjecture, as described in Rule 2.[11]

---

[10] Notice, though, that the historical accuracy of this rational reconstruction has been contested (Musgrave & Pigden, 2016, section 3.1).

[11] See Easwaran, 2015 on the two kinds of counterexamples in terms of rebutting and undercutting defeaters.

Lakatos had grand philosophical ambitions when developing the dialectic of proofs and refutations. Indeed, he sought to establish the superiority of dialectical philosophy of mathematics over other philosophical accounts of mathematics, especially those that emphasized formality and infallibility in mathematical proofs (Larvor, 2001; Tanswell, 2017). Notice though that 'dialectical' here does not refer to ancient dialectic. Instead, the relevant reference is Hegelian dialectic (Larvor, 2001). The general idea seems to be that a clash of contraries – proofs and refutations – gives rise to a third 'thing' which represents a synthesis of the two contraries.

It is far from certain that Lakatos' dialectical picture as a whole offers a suitable philosophical account of mathematics, either descriptively or normatively.[12] Nevertheless, the crucial idea of a constant interplay between proofs and counterexamples (refutations) does seem to capture something deeply true about mathematical practices (as I will further argue in Chapter 11).

Interestingly, and despite the fact that *Proofs and Refutations* is written in dialogue form, Lakatos' dialectical philosophy of mathematics is not particularly *dialogical*. Indeed, notice that the rules stated above do not make explicit reference to multi-agent situations at all. One might speculate that this feature is somehow related to a Hegelian disregard for specific agents, given that the objective *Geist* should transcend the individual's subjective mind. Be that as it may, if the dialogical, multi-agent component is indeed not fundamental to Lakatos' overall account after all, then this is a significant dissimilarity between the Lakatosian picture and the present proposal, in which agents and their interactions play a fundamental role.

While Lakatos himself does not speak of specific characters carrying out proofs and refutations, we may well think of these two sides of the practice as two functional roles, which can be associated to participants in dialogical games. We may thus introduce two fictive characters, Prover and Refuter, each performing one of the two crucial features in the dialectic of proofs and refutations.[13] Notice, though, that these Lakatosian dialogues would not obviously correspond to typical zero-sum games with losers and winners, and indeed there does not seem to be any counterpart to the notion of a winning strategy in these dialogues (Lakatos defends the controversial view that there is no end point for a proof). He does seem to suggest at times that interlocutors are 'opponents' to each other, and debates in *Proofs and Refutations* can get quite heated, but the ultimate goal of the 'game' is the higher-order (cooperative?)

---

[12] Indeed, it has been argued that the dynamics described in *Proofs and Refutations* can be observed in only a handful of actual case studies from the history of mathematics (Koetsier, 1991), or in recent mathematical developments (Tanswell, 2017, section 3.3).

[13] Trafford (2017, pp. 88–94) explicitly introduces these two 'players' when discussing Lakatos. Before that, Prover–Refuter games were widely used and studied in the computer science literature on theorem-proving.

purpose of improving the conjecture–proof pair.[14] As somewhat dramatically put by one of the characters in the dialogue:

Then not only do refutations act as fermenting agents for proof-analysis, but proof-analysis may act as a fermenting agent for refutations! What an unholy alliance between seeming enemies! (Lakatos, 1976, p. 48)

However, thus described, the role of Refuter, restricted to the search for counterexamples, appears to be rather limited. In reality, someone at the receiving end of an argument such as a mathematical proof (or perhaps a philosophical argument) is likely to be interested in a number of other features of the proof. Does it start from plausible, potentially fruitful premises?[15] Is the argument as a whole illuminating, i.e. does it improve one's understanding of the issue? Are the individual inferential steps compelling? In other words, there is much more to being at the receiving end of a mathematical proof than merely looking for counterexamples. Indeed, as suggested by Alison Pease and colleagues, these dialogues appear to be essentially of the *persuasive* kind:

Lakatos describes the interactions of mathematicians, when aiming to prove the conjecture, in the way that is the most closely related to the concept of persuasion dialogue, and in particular its "conflict resolution" subtype. Persuasion dialogue is triggered by a difference of opinion between participants, each of them aims to persuade each other and the main goal of the conversation is to achieve the resolution of the conflict. (Pease et al., p. 187)

I want to suggest, however, that the putative audience for a mathematical proof does *not* start out with the conviction that the proof is incorrect, or that there must be a mistake in it (which would count as a more straightforward 'difference of opinion'). Instead, it seems more plausible that the audience initially adopts an agnostic, neutral position, but that the bar for persuasion is set quite high. Douglas Walton and Erik Krabbe (whose classification Pease et al. rely on) recognize this possibility and classify it as a subclass of persuasive dialogues:

Every persuasion dialogue is based on an initial conflict of opinions, but these conflicts can be of various types. In a simple conflict, only one party has a positive thesis to defend, the other party being merely a critical doubter or questioner, with no expressed positive viewpoint of his own. (Walton & Krabbe, 1995, p. 118)

This appears to be an accurate description of how the two interlocutors position themselves in such dialogues. The receiver of a mathematical proof (or other kinds of deductive arguments) will look critically at it, searching, indeed, for counterexamples and other imperfections, but not with the goal of refuting the

---

[14] A formal reconstruction of these Lakatosian dialogues is to be found in Pease et al., 2017.

[15] "We may still reasonably enquire how the premises for proofs are chosen. Why should mathematicians explore the deductive closure of *this* set of axioms rather than *that?*" (Larvor, 2001, p. 214).

proof at all costs. The audience functions rather as an examiner, who will not allow Prover to produce sloppy arguments, but who is not in the business of knocking down the proof no matter what. A good proof is one that convinces a fair but 'tough' opponent; as (allegedly) noted by the mathematician Mark Kac, "the beauty of a mathematical proof is that it convinces even a stubborn proponent" (Fisher, 1989, p. 50).

In view of these considerations, I submit that the 'stubborn proponent' (or better put, stubborn interlocutor) is better described as a *skeptic* rather than as a refuter. A skeptic is simply someone who is not easily convinced, not someone who from the beginning has a different opinion and who will dog-matically hold on to it. What characterizes a skeptic is a general questioning attitude and the tendency to withhold judgment unless there is strong evidence that a given belief is well-founded. Indeed, the Greek terms at the origin of the term 'skeptic,' namely σκεπτικός and σκέψις, mean 'inquirer' and 'inquiry': the skeptic is one who inquires, one who asks for (further) clarification. When presented with sufficiently persuasive argumentation, a skeptic may well become convinced of a conclusion, but this will not constitute any kind of 'loss' for him. In other words, a skeptic is not actively trying to disprove the arguer, but he[16] will only become convinced of the conclusion if the argument is strongly persuasive.[17]

And thus, instead of Prover–Refuter games, the practice of mathematical proofs (and deductive arguments more generally) viewed from a dialogical perspective is perhaps best described in terms of Prover–Skeptic games. Games with these players have been deployed and studied in the theoretical computer science and mathematics literature (Moore & Mertens, 2011, chapter 8), including games of information-hiding (Kolata, 1986; Wayner, 2009), though not nearly as extensively as Prover–Refuter games. The presentation of Prover–Skeptic games that comes closest to what we are after here is to be found in the work of Morten Sørensen and Paweł Urzyczyn (2006), where these games are described as a dialogue between a Prover, who is to produce a construction (proof) for a formula, and a Skeptic, who doubts that the construction (proof) exists and thus must be persuaded that it does (Sørensen & Urzyczyn, 2006, p. 89). Notice, though, that while Sørensen and Urzyczyn often use zero-sum concepts such as winning strategy, it is not clear that such dialogues are indeed best viewed as games with winners and losers (more on cooperation and adversariality in Section 3.4).

Going back to Pease et al.'s characterization, mentioned above, of Lakatosian games as dialogical games of persuasion, the framing of such

---

[16] I generally use feminine pronouns for Prover and masculine pronouns for Skeptic.

[17] The notion of 'organized skepticism' is presented as one of the pillars of modern science in Robert Merton's influential 1942 book *The Sociology of Science* (Merton, 1942).

games in terms of Prover and Skeptic allows us to see that these are *asymmetric* persuasion games: Prover wants to persuade Skeptic that there is a proof for a given conclusion from given premises, but Skeptic does not have a particular stake in convincing Prover that there is no such proof (or more precisely, that the particular proof proposed by Prover is not valid). The game is also asymmetric in terms of the moves available to each player, thus being a variant of what Walton and Krabbe describe as Rigorous Persuasion Dialogue (RPD):

> Whereas PPD [Permissive Persuasion Dialogue] was symmetric in that both players made the same kinds of moves RPD is asymmetry. One player plays a positive role of proponent, while the other plays a negative or questioning role of opponent.[18] (Walton & Krabbe, 1995, p. 154)

Prover (proponent, in Walton and Krabbe's terminology) seeks to persuade Skeptic (opponent, in Walton and Krabbe's terminology) of the correctness and cogency of her proof, while Skeptic raises objections but also specifies what it would take for him to become convinced – for example by pointing out inferential steps that aren't sufficiently compelling to him, even if he does not have a knock-down counterexample. After all, absence of counterexamples is not sufficient for a proof to count as genuinely persuasive; witness proofs that are considered correct by the mathematics community, but which somehow fail to be persuasive (such as Stephen Smale's proof of the eversion of the sphere, discussed in Dutilh Novaes, 2018a).

There are a number of significant discrepancies between the Prover–Skeptic games presented here and the Lakatosian picture. An important one seems to be that, on the Lakatosian picture, Prover first fully formulates a proof, in all its steps, which is then scrutinized by Refuter, who may come up with counterexamples (be they global or local), thus forcing Prover to revise the original proof. On the current picture, by contrast, Prover and Skeptic interact during the very production/presentation of the proof; even when Skeptic has no objection to raise, he is tacitly agreeing and endorsing the steps of the proof. This is thus a component of Prover–Skeptic games that they share with Lorenzen's dialogical logic and Hintikka's GTS: participants take turns in making moves at each inferential step of the proof. Moreover, notice that such dialogues do not correspond to the 'context of discovery' of a proof: when starting one such dialogue, Prover already has a plan for how to persuade Skeptic that the conclusion follows from the premises. As aptly described by Descartes in the *Principles of Philosophy* (see Chapter 1, Section 1.3.3), a deductive argument is predominantly a "way of expounding to others what

---

[18] I do not endorse the use of the terms 'positive' and 'negative' to describe the moves by each player, as Skeptic is not only making a negative contribution, so to speak. But, otherwise, the general idea is clear, and in the spirit of the present proposal.

one already knows."[19] Skeptic, in turn, is effectively acting as a proof checker, and if a mistake is found, then Prover's 'plan' has to be revised or abandoned.

What does it take for Skeptic to become persuaded by a proof? Formulating a satisfactory answer to this question at a suitable level of abstraction and generality is not an easy task, given that persuasion is obviously an agent-relative, contextual notion. However, we may formulate a few minimal conditions:

- To become convinced of the conclusion of a proof, Skeptic must accept its premises. Alternatively, if he only expects conditional persuasion (*if* the premises are true, *then* the conclusion must be true), he must at the very least be persuaded that the particular set of premises in question is relevant and interesting enough such that establishing what follows from it is not a futile endeavor.
- He must not be in possession of counterexamples, either global or local.
- He must also deem each step in the proof/argument to be individually perspicuous and convincing. As already noted, an inferential step may be unconvincing even if Skeptic cannot immediately find a counterexample; in such cases, he is still entitled to request further clarification, for example, that the step be broken down into smaller, more perspicuous steps.

And thus, these three components seem to be necessary (though they may not be sufficient, for example, in very long, unsurveyable proofs) for Skeptic to become persuaded by the proof. Consequently, for each of these components, there must be moves available to Skeptic to ensure that persuasion (or refutation, as the case may be) occurs. On the basis of these considerations, we can now return to the brief presentation of the Prover–Skeptic games sketched in Chapter 2, but now the rationale for each of the features of the game should emerge more clearly.

To recapitulate: a Prover–Skeptic dialogue that corresponds to a mathematical proof begins with Prover stating explicitly the conjecture to be proved and then requesting Skeptic's endorsement of certain premises. At this point, Skeptic has the option of refusing to endorse one or more of the premises, perhaps because he thinks they are problematic or unwarranted. In this case, and if Prover cannot provide alternative premises from which she can also derive the desired conclusion and which would meet with Skeptic's

---

[19] In other words, how a mathematician comes up with the idea for a proof (its 'context of discovery') is not registered in these dialogues, given that their main goal is to produce persuasion. (This is a small difference with respect to Lakatos, who is also interested in how the dialectic of proofs and refutations track heuristics and contexts of discovery.) However, once the mathematician has had the idea in question, she still needs to formulate an argument for public consumption, and at that point she will be entertaining a dialogue with her own inner Skeptic (more on the internalization of Skeptic in Chapter 4). Moreover, insofar as the original proof is modified in response to Skeptic's objections, there is a sense in which the dialogue can also be a process of joint discovery for Prover and Skeptic.

approval, then the dialogue halts. Another way in which the dialogue can be aborted early on is if Skeptic can provide a global counterexample, that is, a situation where the premises just requested hold but the conjecture just stated does not. But assuming Skeptic does grant the premises proposed by Prover and no global counterexample is found, then Prover proceeds to put forward a sequence of further statements that she claims follow necessarily from what Skeptic has already granted. If Prover is right that these statements follow necessarily from what has been granted, then Skeptic is indeed committed to them (in the sense of Brandom's notion of discursive commitment; Brandom, 1994) and thus may not refuse to grant them. Prover may also perform *imperative* speech acts, whereby Skeptic is instructed to execute a given operation or construction that is required for him to become convinced of the conclusion, given the premises (Tanswell, 2020).

At this point, there are three possible moves for Skeptic: (i) the 'null move,' which means that he does nothing explicitly, simply because he accepts the inferential moves proposed by Prover so far as legitimate; (ii) proposing a local counterexample to a specific inferential step; (iii) asking for further clarification if a particular inferential step is not sufficiently convincing and perspicuous (he may simply ask, 'why does this follow?') In response to (ii), Prover may withdraw or modify that particular inferential step, but may still want to pursue the proof as a whole by taking a different route. In response to (iii), Prover may maintain the same route, but she must provide further clarification and motivation for the particular step just questioned. (See Figure 3.1 for a tree that represents these dialogues.)

If eventually the intended conclusion is reached through successive inferential steps that were not questioned or refuted by Skeptic, or if Skeptic's objections and requests for clarification have been dealt with satisfactorily, then Prover will have succeeded in her goal of persuading Skeptic of the conclusion. Otherwise, if pending challenges have not been dealt with, and in particular if Skeptic has provided conclusive counterexamples, then Prover will not have succeeded in persuading. Notice, however, that the second outcome does not necessarily count as a 'win' for Skeptic, as his goal was not to block the establishment of the conclusion at all costs; his goal was merely to ensure that Prover's attempted proof is indeed valid and persuasive, and, if not, to show what is wrong with it (which can be a very valuable outcome for Prover, too). We will turn to the cooperative and adversarial components of these dialogues in more detail in Section 3.4, but for now it is important to note that the concepts of 'winning and losing conditions,' in particular the idea that a win for one participant will necessarily entail a loss for the other, do not apply here in any straightforward way.

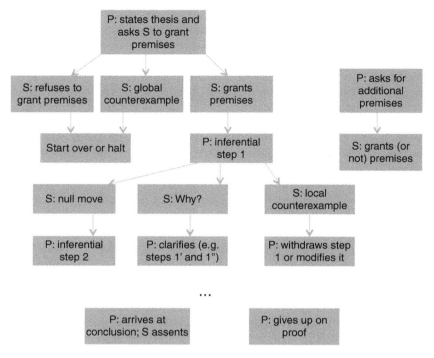

Figure 3.1 A tree for Prover–Skeptic dialogues

3.4   Cooperation and Adversariality

As discussed above, both Lorenzen's dialogical logic and Hintikka's GTS are presented as based on adversarial, zero-sum games. Of course, a minimal amount of cooperation among the players is required for them to accept entering the game and playing it by the agreed-upon rules. But, otherwise, the games are presented as adversarial in that players have opposite goals, and a win for one of them entails a loss for the other. I conjectured that the primacy of adversarial games in these frameworks is motivated by a reliance on useful game-theoretical notions, in particular the concept of a winning strategy, which presuppose adversarial games.

However, both in Lorenzen's dialogical logic and in Hintikka's GTS, the adversarial component of these games quickly becomes strained. Hodges points this out when discussing dialogical logic, but the objection applies to GTS as well:

If P claims A&B, then O chooses one of A and B and requires P to claim the chosen sentence. As before, if P is serious about claiming A&B then she probably has defences of both A and B up her sleeve. This 'attack' by O invites her to start on one of these defences. In fact it releases her from her obligation to defend the other sentence; so it is more of a help than an attack. (Hodges, 2001, pp. 23–24)

In other words, many of the moves defined by the rules of the game do not fit neatly into the categories of 'attack' and 'defense' and in fact hint at a hidden layer of cooperation in these games. This suggests that Lorenzen and Hintikka overlook potential cooperative components by overemphasizing adversarial components. However, if these games are no longer viewed as strictly competitive games, then it is not clear whether Lorenzen and Hintikka can avail themselves of the notion of a winning strategy, which is, however, essential to define validity in game-theoretical terms within their frameworks.

More generally, if Lorenzen and Hintikka want to claim that their games are somehow grounded in 'ordinary' linguistic practices (and they both seem to suggest this much), then their exclusively adversarial focus is only defensible if the majority of conversations involving multiple participants are indeed essentially adversarial. However, this does not seem to correspond to the reality of social interactions. Indeed, a number of influential theoretical frameworks that investigate linguistic interactions, such as Gricean theories of conversation (Wilson & Sperber, 1981), Michael Tomasello's work on social cognition (Tomasello, 2014), and in fact most theories of dialogue (Ginzburg, 2016) focus on cooperative dialogues. There are, of course, a number of situations where dialogue is overtly non-cooperative (e.g. political debates), but, while obviously important, non-cooperative dialogues seem to be a less frequent phenomenon than cooperative ones (though this is ultimately an empirical question).

Importantly, our Prover–Skeptic games are not 'ordinary,' everyday dialogues: they are very specific kinds of dialogues reserved for a niche of specialists (as argued in Chapter 1 and Chapters 8 and 9). When presenting the outlines of the game in Section 3.3, I indicated that it has adversarial as well as cooperative components, but this hybrid status can be cashed out in different ways. Here are four possible scenarios:

(1) Prover and Skeptic have a common goal, that of establishing the validity or invalidity of proofs, and no (conflicting) individual goals (they either win or lose together). They each perform a different task, but in view of a common interest (or converging individual interests). This is a purely cooperative, division-of-labor game, where neither player can 'win' alone; both players will benefit from achieving the overall goal of correctly identifying (in)validity.

(2) Prover wants her proof to go through no matter what (as this counts as a win for her), regardless of whether it is a valid proof or not. Skeptic, by contrast,

wants valid proofs to go through and invalid ones to be refuted, and is neutral with respect to 'pay-offs' of the game for him (no win or loss). Here, Prover can win or lose the game, and Skeptic can neither win nor lose (the outcome is neutral for him).

(3) Skeptic wants to block (refute) the proof no matter what (as this counts as a win for him), regardless of whether it is a valid proof or not. Prover, by contrast, wants valid proofs to go through and invalid ones to be refuted, and is neutral with respect to 'pay-offs' of the game for her (no win or loss). Here, Skeptic can win or lose the game, and Prover can neither win nor lose (the outcome is neutral for her).

(4) At a lower level, the game is a classical adversarial, zero-sum game: Prover wins if the proof goes through, Skeptic wins if the proof is refuted or otherwise blocked. But, at a higher level, they are in fact cooperating to establish whether a proof is valid or not.[20]

Games such as those in (2) and (3) are known as partial-conflict-of-interest games (Zollman et al., 2013). These two kinds of games may be described as semi-adversarial, non-zero-sum games, given that a legitimate win for Prover (the proof is valid) does not necessarily constitute a loss for Skeptic in (2), and a legitimate win for Skeptic (the proof is invalid) does not necessarily constitute a loss for Prover in (3). The game described in (1) is purely cooperative, with no adversarial component at all. The other three games feature different combinations of cooperation and adversariality: unilateral cooperation/adversariality in games (2) and (3), or lower-level adversariality combined with higher-level cooperation in game (4).[21]

While all four scenarios are prima facie plausible, I submit that scenario (2) comes closest to the actual 'game of proof' in mathematical practice, for the following reason: a mathematician's reputation is very strongly connected to her ability to produce interesting proofs (as famously argued in Jaffe & Quinn, 1993), but rewards for finding mistakes in proofs are considerably less significant (though some counterexamples and refutations become famous in themselves). For this reason, scenario (3) is, in fact, less plausible. There is thus a motivational asymmetry between the roles of Prover and Skeptic, even if we optimistically prefer to believe that mathematicians, Provers and Skeptics alike, are ultimately moved by the pursuit of mathematical knowledge.[22]

---

[20] An analogy with adversarial judicial systems may be helpful here: at a lower level, defense and prosecution are competing, and only one of them can win, but at a higher level, they are both pursuing the ultimate goal of achieving justice.

[21] To be sure, there are many ways in which cooperation and competition can interact in games (see Brandenburger & Nalebuff, 1996 for a popular account), so I do not claim to have exhausted the possible combinations with this list.

[22] Lakatos' dialectic of proofs and refutations does not seem to recognize a motivational asymmetry, and thus seems to fall within scenario (4), though it could also plausibly be construed as falling within scenario (1).

At any rate, distinguishing these four scenarios constitutes an improvement over previous proposals, which had uncritically adopted a model of exclusively adversarial, zero-sum games. To be fair to these previous authors, in the early days of game theory, adversarial, zero-sum games represented the dominant model, and so it is not surprising that this was the theoretical framework they relied on. But game theory has developed in a number of different directions since, and so now we are better equipped to formulate a more sophisticated game-theoretical account of deductive arguments as characterized by a subtle interplay between adversariality and cooperation.

Another way in which the complex interplay between cooperation and adversariality in these games may be spelled out is by distinguishing explicitly the play level from the strategy level, and emphasizing the (ontological and logical) primacy of the play level, as suggested by Rahman and colleagues (Rahman et al., 2018, section XI.2). On Rahman et al.'s account, at the play level participants in these dialogues do not set out to 'beat' their interlocutors no matter what; instead, they are essentially engaging in the game of giving and asking for reasons (in the terminology deployed in Brandom, 1994): "accepting or contesting a local reason is a process by means of which players cooperate in order to determine the meaning associated to the action-schema at stake" (Rahman et al., 2018, pp. 226–227). The strategy level allows for the comparison of different plays for the same thesis, without necessarily attributing strategic intentions to the players themselves: "*strategies* are not actually carried out by the players, they are only a *perspective* on the possible plays for a given thesis" (p. 59). The perspective in question seems to be an external perspective that seeks to determine whether a given thesis is a valid formula in the framework (i.e. if there is a winning strategy for it which allows its proponent to 'win' in each play), not the perspective of either one of the players. It is thus possible to retain the theoretical benefits of the concept of a winning strategy without presupposing that the plays themselves are adversarial, or, equivalently, that the participants in question adopt a competitive attitude. This proposal seems to fall roughly within scenario (1) as described above, but with the addition of the higher-level, external strategic perspective.

Before closing this section, a few comments are in order concerning potential abuses of the rules of the game by different participants. This becomes a significant issue in particular with respect to games where the participants have asymmetric motivations, such as (2) and (3), as the participant with a higher stake in the game is more likely to engage in deviant behavior. (In games such as (1), none of the participants is likely to 'cheat,' and in (4) they should keep each other in check, since they both want to win.)

In games such as (2), Prover may want to deploy a number of strategies to confuse Skeptic, which nevertheless technically do not represent infringements of the rules of the game (Krabbe, 2008). For example, in its minimal version, the game does not feature restrictions on relevance regarding the premises that Prover asks Skeptic to grant. So Prover may ask for premises she will in fact not use in the deduction, in order to produce an 'information overload' effect in Skeptic (who needs to keep track of all the concessions he has made so far), and thus hinder his ability to survey the correctness of the proof.[23]

In a similar vein, in games such as (3), where Skeptic seeks to block the deduction at all costs, there are a few 'tricks' he may turn to: he may, for example, refuse to grant any premise and thus obstruct the dialogue from the get-go. Alternatively, he may make excessive use of the 'why does it follow?' move, obtusely refusing to be convinced by even the most obvious, self-evident inferential step. This uncooperative Skeptic (in Aristotle's terms, a 'cantankerous opponent' – see Chapter 5) is impeccably personified in the figure of the Tortoise in Lewis Carroll's famous fable (Carroll, 1895). The Tortoise refuses to be persuaded by simple instantiations of modus ponens, and forces Achilles to write down an endless number of additional premises in his notebook, thereby blocking the deductive argument in question.[24]

Does the possibility of such abuses count as an argument against the present account? I do not think so, given that virtually every interesting enough game is liable to some form of misuse or abuse of its rules. What these observations suggest, however, is that the game is not deterministic, and this plasticity leaves room for extreme uses of the moves that are not conducive to a fruitful unfolding of the dialogue (even if not explicitly banned by its rules). More restrictive versions of Prover–Skeptic games may include provisions to avoid such pitfalls, such as restrictions related to relevance imposed on Prover's requested premises, or a foundation of agreed-upon valid inferential moves that Skeptic cannot legitimately question (i.e. an underlying formal inferential system that both participants agree upon). But at this stage, we seek to describe the game in its most general formulation, and leave discussion of such restrictions for later.

Before closing this chapter, let me add a few words on feminist critiques of adversariality in argumentation and its implications for logic. A number of feminist thinkers have condemned the inherent adversarial component of argumentation as a crystallization of gendered categories of aggressiveness and violence, typically viewed as masculine traits (Hundleby, forthcoming). Insofar as a certain degree of adversariality underpins deductive logic (even if modulated by a fair amount of cooperation, as in the Prover–Skeptic model), and insofar as adversariality is necessarily a masculine-coded tool of oppression, some thinkers have concluded that deductive logic should be entirely rejected (Nye, 1990). Others propose instead a substantive reformulation of the deductive canons in order to purge it from oppressive tendencies (Plumwood, 1993).

---

[23] See Dutilh Novaes & French, 2018 and Chapter 4 on relevance as a cooperative desideratum.
[24] See Scotto di Luzio, 2000 on this problem.

Feminist critiques of deductive logic raise a number of crucial points, in particular as they indicate the perils of failing to contextualize theories within their social and political backgrounds and implications. In this sense, the 'human, all too human' focus of the present investigation shares some of the commitments of these critiques. Where we part ways, however, is in our conceptualizations of adversariality. While many feminist thinkers seem to maintain that all forms of adversariality are masculine-coded forms of oppression, I here develop a more sympathetic account of adversariality, which allows for the possibility of productive forms of adversariality.

3.5   Conclusion

In this chapter, I have presented and critically assessed a number of earlier dialogical accounts of logic and deductive reasoning: Lorenzen's dialogical logic, Hintikka's GTS, and Lakatos' dialectic of proofs and refutations. Against the background of these earlier accounts, I have described a distinctive dialogical game, Prover–Skeptic dialogues, which I claim captures more accurately the ebb and flow of deductive reasoning and argumentation than the alternatives. In particular, I have argued that Prover–Skeptic games feature a complex combination of cooperation and adversariality.

To close, let me return to Hodges' Dawkins question, discussed in Section 3.2.3. Do the Prover–Skeptic games pass the Dawkins test? In other words, are Prover and Skeptic trying to do something intelligible, and is doing it the same thing as winning in the game? Insofar as these are persuasion dialogues, and given that persuasion dialogues are very natural kinds of dialogues for humans, then there is a straightforward story for why they engage in these dialogues. But we may want to ask ourselves whether it makes sense for participants to engage in *this* specific kind of persuasion game.

If I am right in claiming that Prover–Skeptic dialogues reflect the basic features of the practice of producing and consuming mathematical proofs (and other deductive arguments) as engaged in by mathematicians, scientists, students, teachers, etc., then this game is de facto regularly played by a sizable number of actual humans, and so the desideratum of a realistic component is undoubtedly met. The main motivation to engage in the game seems to be that of exchanging epistemic resources, as suggested by Kenny Easwaran's account of (classical) mathematical proofs in terms of transferability (2009, p. 343): "the basic idea is that a proof must be such that a relevant expert will become convinced of the truth of the conclusion of the proof just by consideration of each of the steps in the proof." Prover must provide Skeptic (or any other putative audience) with the necessary ingredients and instructions on how to put them together, so that the persuasive force of the proof is transferred from Prover to Skeptic.

Moreover, I submit that variations of Prover–Skeptic games are also played in contexts other than mathematics, specifically in regimented intellectual contexts such as philosophical discussions. As long as participants are motivated to exchange epistemic resources such as arguments, objections, and reasons, Prover–Skeptic games offer a suitable platform for such exchanges. From these observations I tentatively conclude that the Prover–Skeptic games do pass the Dawkins test as formulated by Hodges, but further corroboration for this claim will be offered throughout the book.

4 Deduction as a Dialogical Notion

4.1 Introduction

Having introduced the Prover–Skeptic dialogues in Chapter 3, in this chapter I first turn to the three main features of deductive reasoning identified in Chapter 1 – necessary truth-preservation, perspicuity, and belief-bracketing – and provide a dialogical rationale for each of them. I then discuss the process of internalization of Skeptic, which is the reason why a deduction superficially does not look like a dialogue. In the final section, I look at four pressing issues in the philosophy of logic that have received much attention in recent years, but now from the dialogical perspective defended here: logical consequence, the normativity of logic, paradoxes and structural rules, and logical pluralism. I argue that there are substantive theoretical benefits to be obtained from examining these issues with dialogical lenses.

4.2 Dialogical Interpretations of Three Key Features of Deduction

Let us now return to the three main characteristics of deductive reasoning and argumentation introduced in Chapter 1. If it can be shown that all three features can be motivated and explained in terms of their dialogical roles, then this will lend strong support to the overall claim that deduction is best understood as a dialogical notion. In the final part of this section, I explain why a deduction does not appear to correspond to a dialogue in any obvious way, at least superficially; this is due to a process of *internalization* of Skeptic into the very method of deduction.

4.2.1 *Necessary Truth-Preservation: Adversariality*

Let us start with necessary truth-preservation, which is usually viewed as the most distinctive feature of a deductive argument (as classically construed at least). A piece of reasoning with this property is usually described as *indefeasible*: if A and B deductively imply C, then the addition of any premise

D whatsoever will not invalidate drawing conclusion C. The connection between necessary truth-preservation and indefeasibility is rather straightforward: if C is true in every single situation in which A and B are true, then it will be true also in the situations where A, B, and D are true, since this class will be a subclass (proper or not) of the class of situations in which A and B are true. Arguments having this property are quite powerful persuasive tools, as they cannot be defeated by incoming information or counterexamples.

As discussed in Chapters 1 and 8, and argued elsewhere by a number of influential authors, 'ordinary' human reasoning seems to be very strongly defeasible; necessary truth-preservation is in fact a cognitive oddity. This observation suggests that there must be special circumstances under which deductive, indefeasible reasoning would make sense. The suggestion here is that it is in specific *argumentative situations* where an interlocutor is not to be easily convinced that necessary truth-preservation becomes a sensible property for a piece of reasoning to have. In other, more mundane conversational situations, when the interlocutor is not so hard to please/convince, necessary truth-preservation is superfluous, and defeasible arguments suffice (see Chapter 9).

As discussed in Chapter 3, earlier dialogical accounts of logic and deduction posited a strong connection between the concepts of necessary truth-preservation and of winning strategy: an argument with the necessary truth-preservation property corresponds to a winning strategy for its proponent, as an interlocutor cannot defeat it with additional premises. In this sense, necessary truth-preservation seems inherently tied to the *adversarial* component of such games.

When describing Prover–Skeptic games, I argued that we should move away from a strictly adversarial, zero-sum conception of these deductive dialogues. This may seem to imply that the purported connection between necessary truth-preservation and adversarial discourse should be entirely discarded; however, this more extreme conclusion can be avoided. It does seem overly restrictive to account for necessary truth-preservation strictly in terms of the concept of a winning strategy (as traditionally construed, at least), given that such an account would in principle only apply to strictly adversarial, zero-sum games. Yet, there is something very compelling about the idea that a necessarily truth-preserving argument is indefeasible, and thus particularly suitable to *persuade* someone who is not initially favorably inclined toward the thesis to be argued for. Cognitive scientist Keith Stenning captures this idea in the following terms:

What *follows* in deduction is anything that is true in *all* interpretations of the premises – that is the definition of logically valid inference. Our job, as speaker or hearer of a discourse that purports to be a deduction, is to test the drawing of inferences to destruction, to ensure that what is inferred is true in *all* models of the premises, not just the intended one. It is in this technical sense that logic models adversarial discourse. We may actually be socially co-operating in testing a deduction for validity, and certainly we have to co-operate a great deal to be sure that we are assuming the same things about the range of interpretations which are intended, but there is a core of seeking out all possible assignments of things, not simply finding one intended one. This is perhaps not accidentally related to the fact that logic arose as a model of legal and political debate. (Stenning, 2002, p. 138)

Thus seen, the key difference between indefeasible (monotonic, deductive) reasoning and defeasible (non-monotonic, non-deductive) reasoning can be cashed out in terms of the *range* of models of the premises under consideration. In deductive reasoning, *all* models of the premises must be taken into account, and the conclusion must hold in all of them. By contrast, defeasible reasoning typically requires that only a proper subset of the models of the premises, perhaps even only one (the unique intended model), be taken into account. Computer scientist Yoav Shoham introduced the very useful concept of 'preferred models' to capture the idea that non-monotonic, defeasible reasoning does not require all models of the premises to be considered: only the preferred models of the premises, that is those that seem most 'normal' to the agent (i.e. in accordance with her general prior beliefs), need to be considered (Shoham, 1987; Dutilh Novaes & Veluwenkamp, 2017).

From this point of view, it is quite reasonable to view deductive reasoning in somewhat adversarial terms: to consider *all* models of the premises is particularly useful in the context of having to anticipate objections from a 'stubborn,' skeptical (or downright hostile) interlocutor. Defeasible reasoning, by contrast, would more naturally correspond to a situation of the agent reasoning by herself and considering only her most preferred models, or to cooperative situations where the goal is to establish jointly the preferred models for certain premises (see Chapter 9).

In other words, we need not fully take on board the notion of a winning strategy in zero-sum games to still benefit from the idea that necessary truth-preservation has an adversarial, or at least *goal-oriented* component. Indeed, if Prover has the goal of persuading Skeptic, it is clear that indefeasible, deductive arguments will be particularly suitable to achieve this goal, even if this will not necessarily constitute a win for Prover or a loss for Skeptic. (To be clear, we are here at play level in Rahman et al.'s terminology.) In other words, relying on deductive arguments is typically strategically advantageous in a persuasive dialogue, given that these arguments cannot easily be defeated by objections, counterexamples, or additional premises. In this sense, it still makes sense to view necessary truth-preservation as a somewhat adversarial component of deductive reasoning, even when not assuming full-blown competitive situations.[1] The corresponding

---

[1] This suggestion is thus different from Rahman et al.'s proposal discussed in Chapter 3, as they seem to describe fully cooperative games at the play level. It is only at the strategy level, and from an external perspective, that the competitive component is introduced in their account. By contrast, on my account, there is a modicum of competition also at the play level, in any case

move that allows Skeptic to ensure that Prover's inferential steps are necessarily truth-preserving is the possibility of presenting a counterexample (either local or global) when necessary truth-preservation fails.

What might be an alternative, non-dialogical rationale for necessary truth-preservation in reasoning contexts, given that it seems to be a cognitive oddity in most ordinary, everyday contexts? One might endorse a purely epistemological account, for example in terms of the high degree of certainty afforded by arguments having this property. However, for reasons presented in Chapter 1 (and in Dutilh Novaes, 2015a, relying on Harman, 1986), I very much doubt that a credible purely epistemological story on the rationale(s) for necessary truth-preservation can be told. By contrast, a dialogical rationale for necessary truth-preservation as a tool for persuasion, especially in discussions with skeptical interlocutors, seems quite plausible.

4.2.2   Perspicuity: Cooperation

The second feature of deductive reasoning introduced in Chapter 1 is its stepwise, procedural character, where individually self-evident inferential steps are chained together so as to constitute a longer argument from premises A, B, C, ... to final conclusion Z through intermediate conclusions (lemmas).[2] An ordinary mathematical proof, for example, is a careful sequence of basic mathematical inferences, where a basic mathematical inference is one that is "accepted by the mathematical community as usable in proof without any further need of argument" (Fallis, 2003, pp. 49–50). As noted in Section 1.2.2 of Chapter 1, this feature presupposes that a deductive argument has the property of transitivity (if A implies B and B implies C, then A implies C). A sufficiently detailed argument, where all logical connections and steps are made explicit, can be described as suitably *perspicuous*. (The property of perspicuity can be attributed both to individual inferential steps in an argument and to the argument as a whole.) Typically, the argument as a whole will be perspicuous if each of its steps is so, though it may happen that a long proof composed of individually perspicuous steps is itself not perspicuous.[3]

---

insofar as Prover wants to achieve her goal of obtaining persuasion and Skeptic will not let her achieve this goal too easily.

[2] It might be thought that this property is a corollary of the property of necessary truth-preservation, rather than an independent feature of deduction. But to see that this is not the case, it suffices to note that, while necessary truth-preservation is a quasi-metaphysical notion, perspicuity is an inherently *epistemic* notion. An argument may have the property of necessary truth-preservation and yet fail to have the property of perspicuity, for example a one-step 'argument' from the axioms of number theory directly to Fermat's Last Theorem.

[3] Indeed, there is the risk of missing the forest for the trees, as it were: in a very detailed proof, each step may be individually perspicuous, but the general idea of the proof may become obscured, thus interfering with the understanding of the proof as a whole (Detlefsen, 2008, section 4). Mathematics educators are well aware of this problem (Alibert & Thomas, 1991).

The property (or desideratum) of perspicuity in a deduction is very naturally understood in dialogical terms; dialogue itself is a stepwise, dynamic process, where parties typically take turns in making contributions to the conversation as reactions to what has been said previously – be it by making assertions, asking questions, raising objections, expressing doubt, issuing imperatives, etc. In the Prover–Skeptic dialogues understood as asymmetric persuasive dialogues, Prover must offer perspicuous arguments that will obtain the desired effect of epistemic transfer, so that Skeptic can become convinced of the cogency of the argument and thus of the truth of its conclusion himself (Easwaran, 2009).

Thus understood, perspicuity is clearly a cooperative component of such dialogues, as ideally Prover seeks not only to force Skeptic to grant the conclusion but to produce true understanding/enlightenment: Prover seeks to establish not only *that* the conclusion follows but also *why* it follows (hence the desideratum that proofs be explanatory (Dutilh Novaes, 2018a)). Through this process, Prover is transmitting something epistemically valuable to Skeptic, namely solid grounds upon which Skeptic can draw the conclusion himself. Conversely, Skeptic is cooperating with Prover when he points out which steps of the proof are not yet sufficiently convincing and perspicuous by asking appropriate 'why does this follow?' questions. Such challenges, which are often described as *attacks* (e.g. in Paul Lorenzen's approach), in fact correspond to *cooperative* gestures from Skeptic toward Prover. Moreover, by inviting Prover to unpack inferential steps, it may transpire that there is a stealthy reliance on hidden premises, which should then be made explicit. Furthermore, when an inferential step is unpacked, a (local) counterexample may emerge which wasn't immediately obvious prior to unpacking, thus exposing that the step in question is not necessarily truth-preserving after all.

Typically (though perhaps not always), such challenges are addressed at inferential steps that are too much of a 'leap' for Skeptic to follow (e.g. 'gaps' in a mathematical proof; Fallis, 2003), and which can presumably be broken down into a number of intermediate, more perspicuous steps. This means that, often, the adequate response to a 'why does this follow?' question from Skeptic is for Prover to make explicit the 'hidden' inferential steps (e.g., in the case of enthymematic gaps, in Fallis' terminology) and thus introduce a finer-grained series of steps (which in turn can be accepted, questioned, or refuted by Skeptic). This idea is nicely captured in the following passage (interestingly, an earlier use of the prover–skeptic terminology):

When the skeptic then reiterates his challenge, directing it now to these particular steps, the prover interprets this as a request for a *more detailed* proof in which the inferences in the original proof are replaced by a series of finer-grained ones. The prover does *not* interpret this as a request for some sort of direct justification of the original steps themselves. Even if the prover believes her original steps to be valid . . ., she nonetheless assumes that it would be inappropriate to defend the original proof "as is," and that the skeptic's challenge (whatever it may be) is better met by providing a proof with a finer grain. Why might this be so? Perhaps it is generally easier to see the validity of finer-grained transitions, and hence the skeptic's challenge might be adequately met by providing a sufficiently detailed proof. (Scotto di Luzio, 2000, p. 120)

Can this process go on indefinitely? In Section 4.2.1, I discussed the possibility of Skeptic acting in bad faith by repeatedly asking 'why' questions and thus deliberately blocking progress toward the conclusion – even when the inferential steps proposed by Prover already display the level of perspicuity appropriate for the circumstances (Carroll's Tortoise being the embodiment of such an obstructive Skeptic). But it is not only in virtue of bad faith that a regress may ensue (Rescorla, 2009). Indeed, what counts as basic inferential steps that must not be questioned is one of the most vexed questions in philosophy of logic and epistemology (Boghossian, 2008). The development of formal systems where basic inferences are made explicit and taken to constitute rock bottom is, arguably at least, to some extent motivated by the need to avoid such regresses, both in dialogical and monological situations (Scotto di Luzio, 2000). But, of course, even a formal system can be made as fine-grained and detailed as one wishes; an inferential rule that counts as basic in, say, first-order logic, may correspond to a number of inferential steps in a more fine-grained system, for example lambda calculus.

What the risk of dialogical regress suggests, though, is that for such a dialogue to progress smoothly, a significant degree of agreement between the parties must be in place (either explicitly or implicitly) on what counts as a legitimate, sufficiently perspicuous inferential step that should not be contested by Skeptic – for example, conventions on what counts as a basic mathematical inference in the mathematical community (Fallis, 2003). How detailed a deductive argument such as a mathematical proof must be to fulfill its persuasive function is by and large a contextual matter, as different audiences will require different levels of granularity (Schiller, 2013). Indeed, even the community of professional mathematicians is not homogeneous in this respect, and the kinds of gaps that are acceptable in a mathematical proof may vary, depending, for example, on the mathematical sub-area (Andersen, 2018). This audience-relativity is yet another reason to view the perspicuity of deductive arguments as a dialogical feature: what counts as perspicuous and explanatory depends on who you are talking to (Dutilh Novaes, 2018a). (More on granularity and 'gaps' in proofs in Chapter 11.)

Could there be alternative, non-dialogical explanations for perspicuity in deductive reasoning? As in the case of necessary truth-preservation, a contender might be a purely epistemic, mono-agent explanation, for example in terms of epistemic justification. Indeed, internalist accounts of epistemic justification also emphasize the need for reasoning to be broken down into individually perspicuous steps that wear their justification on their sleeves, as it were, so that the relevant justificatory structure is evident to the agent. (By contrast, in externalist accounts, this kind of evidential perspicuity is not crucial for justification.) At this point, I concede that a purely epistemic rationale for perspicuity, in particular in terms of an internalist account of justification, is not necessarily less plausible than the dialogical rationale developed here (though the phenomenon of audience-relativity seems to speak in favor of the dialogical proposal). But, at the very least, I claim to have established that a dialogical rationale for perspicuity in deductive reasoning as a cooperative component in Prover–Skeptic dialogues is quite compelling and sensible.

4.2.3   Belief-Bracketing: Perspective Shift

The third feature of deductive reasoning discussed in Chapter 1 is the requirement of belief-bracketing with respect to premises and conclusions. What this means in practice is that, to reason deductively, one is not required to truly assent to the premises, doxastically/epistemically speaking; one may draw deductive conclusions even from premises one disbelieves. What's more, in many cases, one is positively discouraged from attending to one's real doxastic attitudes regarding the premises, and instead is encouraged to take them at face value and focus only on the logical connections between premises and conclusions (a task that participants in reasoning experiments tend to perceive as difficult; Evans, 2016). The key point here is that, in its minimal version at least (but not, for example, in Aristotle's theory of demonstration or Frege's account of the foundations of mathematics), the deductive method is only concerned with logical *connections* between premises and conclusions, not with their actual truth-values or believability taken in isolation.

One way to further explicate this general point is to conceptualize deductive reasoning as essentially *hypothetical* as opposed to categorical (Schroeder-Heister, 2012). Hypothetical reasoning does not require assertions or categorical truths as its starting point, as it proceeds from *hypotheses*.[4] Premises may be merely assumed or supposed for deductive reasoning to take place. (Of course, deductive reasoning can also take place *with* categorical assertions as its starting point, but these are the special cases rather than the general ones.) In fact, one may take as a hypothesis even a proposition that one actually disbelieves, and then reason toward its consequences while not changing one's

---

[4] Thus understood, hypothetical reasoning is related to what is known as *counterfactual reasoning*, that is, the cognitive task of creating alternative scenarios to reality, usually pertaining to past events. However, it seems that it is only with respect to specific counterfactual propositions that people spontaneously imagine alternatives: exceptional events, controllable rather than uncontrollable events, actions rather than inactions (Byrne, 2018). So counterfactual reasoning does not constitute a fully general mechanism to reason with premises one knows not to be true.

doxastic position with respect to the hypothesis (though this may happen at a later stage). But this approach raises the question of what kind of (mental or speech) act an assumption or supposition is, as opposed to a more straightforward assertion/endorsement (Schroeder-Heister, 2016).

Moreover, in Chapter 1, I have argued (on the basis of empirical findings pertaining to the so-called belief bias phenomenon as well as experimental data on reasoning experiments with unschooled participants) that bracketing belief when reasoning is, cognitively speaking, a demanding task (more on this in Chapters 8 and 9). The cognitive oddity of bracketing belief when reasoning becomes particularly conspicuous in *reductio ad absurdum* reasoning, that is, the form of reasoning where one supposes (assumes) something precisely in order to conclude soon thereafter that it is untenable (because it implies something absurd, as the name has it). Reductio reasoning is a fundamental component of the deductive method, and can be found in seminal texts such as Aristotle's *Prior Analytics* and Euclid's *Elements*. Schematically, it can be represented as follows:

Square brackets are used to indicate that the initial proposition A is not asserted but merely assumed as a hypothesis. B and C represent additional premises used to derive the absurdity together with the assumption. (The set of auxiliary premises plus initial assumption is assumed to be consistent.) Now, while the speech act of assuming a hypothesis without actually asserting it is already somewhat puzzling, such a speech act becomes particularly puzzling when an assumption is made precisely with the goal of refuting it soon after; this seems to amount to a form of pragmatic incoherence that many reasoners express discomfort with when formulating or consuming reductio proofs (Antonini & Mariotti, 2008). In the (somewhat dramatic, but illuminating) words of mathematics educator Uri Leron:

> We begin the proof with a declaration that we are about to enter a false, impossible world, and all our subsequent efforts are directed towards 'destroying' this world, proving it is indeed false and impossible. (Leron, 1985, p. 323)

As I have argued in more detail elsewhere (Dutilh Novaes, 2016b), the apparent pragmatic incoherence of the first speech act in a reductio argument is dissolved if one adopts a dialogical interpretation of the background situation. (More precisely, I argued that reductio arguments are closely related to the Ancient Greek dialectical notion of an *elenchus*, to be discussed in Chapter 5.) In a mono-agent setting, one and the same agent has to formulate the initial hypothesis and then lead the hypothesis to destruction via an absurdity. By contrast, in a dialogical setting, what Prover does is to get *Skeptic* to commit to an initial statement rather than to commit to this statement herself, and then show that this commitment by Skeptic (with auxiliary premises) will lead to absurdity, and thus must be rejected. In this way, there is a division of labor between the agent who commits to the premises (albeit perhaps merely for the sake of the argument) and the agent who draws inferences from these premises to absurdity without having committed to them herself.

Now, if the dialogical story works for reductio arguments insofar as it circumvents the apparent pragmatic incoherence of the first speech act of positing a hypothesis (only to go on and destroy it), then a similar dialogical story should apply to instances of proofs starting with hypotheses in general, not only reductio proofs. Indeed, my claim is that the requirement of belief-bracketing in deductive reasoning is best explained by the observation that deduction is essentially hypothetical reasoning, which in turn is best explained in dialogical, multi-agent terms. In other words, I am here proposing an inference to the best explanation: the best way to account for this somewhat odd feature of deductive reasoning, namely its indifference to the doxastic states toward the propositions involved, is by reference to the practice of drawing conclusions from one's interlocutor's commitments in a dialogical situation.[5]

When reasoning deductively in a dialogical setting, it is crucial to be able to draw deductive consequences from one's own discursive commitments (which presumably reflect, at least to some extent, one's doxastic commitments) as well as the deductive consequences of one's *interlocutor's* discursive commitments, which may be very different from one's own. Then, from the practice of drawing inferences from the commitments of a specific interlocutor (other than oneself) to the practice of drawing inferences without the requirement of explicit endorsement of the premises by any specific agent is a fairly natural step (though in no way trivial – see Chapter 9). To make an assumption is thus to consider the possibility that *someone* (actual or fictive) in fact makes that particular discursive commitment in a dialogical situation, and then see what else she would be committed to (as discursive commitment is closed under entailment).

---

[5] "Another framework would be the dialogical or game-theoretical approach to semantics, in which the duality of assumptions and assertions is reflected by the roles of the two players of a game, which means that the primacy of the hypothetical is built into the framework from the very beginning" (Schroeder-Heister, 2012, p. 940).

4.2.4   Internalization of Skeptic

One obvious objection to the claim that deduction is essentially a dialogical notion is the observation that deductive arguments typically do not display an explicit dialogical structure, at least not if dialogues are understood in the usual sense of discursive interactions involving at least two participants,[6] who take turns making contributions to the conversation. By contrast, a deductive argument such as a mathematical proof is typically presented in written form, and only one 'voice' is in fact heard, namely Prover's. Where is the dialogue? Where are these alleged interlocutors? To defend the claim that deduction is by and large a dialogical notion after all, we need an explanation for why a typical deductive argument seems to lack a dialogical structure, at least superficially.

To respond to this explanatory challenge, I rely on the idea of the *internalization of Skeptic* into the deductive method itself. Skeptic becomes an *implicit interlocutor*, as it were, given that his main roles in Prover–Skeptic dialogues become constitutive of the deductive method as such.[7] We no longer hear the voice of Skeptic because, if all goes well and the proof is correctly formulated according to the precepts of the deductive method, there is no need for Skeptic to interject. Indeed, in such a proof, every step is not only necessarily truth-preserving (and thus immune to local counterexamples) but also sufficiently perspicuous/explanatory; an actual, physical Skeptic would not have had much to do other than to endorse each move by Prover by means of the silent null move.

In other words, a proof in its worked-out, final form is one where all 'imperfections' have already been weeded out, and all that is left for Skeptic to do is to acquiesce by means of repeated instances of the null move. (Recall the three basic moves available to Skeptic beside granting premises: producing a counterexample, asking why-questions, and the null move of endorsement.) In terms of the tree defining the different moves available to each participant presented in Chapter 3, such a 'purified' proof corresponds to a path where all moves by Skeptic are null moves (except for granting the premises/assumptions at the beginning). Importantly, the null move is a *silent* move, which explains (even if somewhat metaphorically, perhaps) why we do not hear the voice of Skeptic in a 'clean' proof. In fact, however, such a 'clean' proof is often the result of a previous (probably 'messy') process of 'proofs and

---

[6] The prefix 'dia-' suggests exactly two participants, but the term is used more generally, covering interactions with more than two participants as well. Moreover, the audience may also play a key role, for example, in political debates where different candidates are not aiming at convincing their interlocutors but rather members of the audience. In the case of mathematical proofs, the audience is the whole mathematical community, and thus an essential component of the system.

[7] However, in Chapter 11, I argue that the Skeptic is in fact alive and kicking in mathematical practice: the Skeptic is also the referee who evaluates article submissions to professional journals, as suggested by the work of Line Andersen interviewing mathematicians on their refereeing practices (Andersen, 2018).

refutations.' (Incidentally, it is for this reason that Lakatos objects to standard practices of proof presentation, which 'hide' the history of a proof's discovery and thus make the choice of lemmas and definitions seem quite arbitrary and opaque; Lakatos, 1976.)

The key observation here is the idea that Skeptic's active role in Prover–Skeptic dialogues has become *constitutive* of the deductive method as such: the method has a *built-in Skeptic*, as it were.[8] In particular, necessary truth-preservation, which is in the first instance strategically advantageous for a persuader but not a mandatory property for inferential steps in dialogues more generally (not even argumentative ones), becomes a constitutive feature of an argument that purports to be deductively valid. In other words, a recommendation on how to play the game *well* becomes a condition of playing the (new) game *at all*. Moreover, while non-deductive dialogues can rely on implicitly shared background knowledge among the participants, in a strictly deductive dialogue all premises need to be made explicit, and only what follows from explicitly stated premises counts as a valid conclusion.

Perspicuity, in turn, arises from internalizing the desideratum that each inferential step be sufficiently evident, such that the proof as a whole will be persuasive to its intended audience. But notice that this desideratum does not become fully internalized, insofar as a deductive argument or proof will typically still display the appropriate level of granularity for its intended audience.[9] A specific implicit interlocutor remains present, which means that perspicuity remains a relative, contextual notion in the deductive method.

Finally, the need to draw inferences from one's interlocutor's beliefs and commitments leads to the hypothetical nature of deductive reasoning, where inferences can be drawn from premises regardless of the premises' truth-value or epistemic status to the agent. In other words, Skeptic's role of granting the initial premises is transformed into the more abstract property of hypothetical reasoning, which thus roughly corresponds to the idealization of a hypothetical Skeptic granting the premises in question (if only 'for the sake of the argument').

Indeed, the internalized Skeptic can be viewed as corresponding to a *universal* Skeptic: a deductive argument aims to be convincing and explanatory for the widest possible range of Skeptics (understood as those having the necessary epistemic credentials), and thus presupposes as little as possible that is specific to particular Skeptics (e.g. background knowledge, styles of

---

[8] In my earlier work, I used the term 'built-in Opponent' (Dutilh Novaes, 2012a, chapter 4), but later I moved away from the Proponent–Opponent terminology towards Prover–Skeptic.

[9] Compare discussions on intended and acceptable gaps in mathematical proofs (Andersen, 2018; Fallis, 2003; see Chapter 11).

argumentation).[10] It is, I submit, in this sense that a deductive argument such as a mathematical proof is "at once oral and written," as suggested by Reviel Netz (1999, p. 298). While not being explicitly a dialogue, it retains a number of dialogical features, in particular in virtue of the built-in Skeptic. Paul Ernest describes this process in the following terms:

> Mathematical proof is a special form of text, which since the time of the ancient Greeks, has been presented in monological form. This reflects the absolutist ideal that total precision, rigour and perfection are attainable in mathematics. Thus the monologicality of the concealed voice uttering a proof itself belies and denies the presence of the silent listener. But as it is an argument intended to convince, a listener is presupposed. The monologicality of proof tries to forestall the listener by anticipating all of his or her possible objections. So the dialectical response is condensed into the ideal perfection of a monologic argument, in which no sign of speaker or listener remains, except for the idealized and perfected utterance, the proof itself. (Ernest, 1994, p. 38)

In fact, the dialogical nature of a deductive argument is an instance of a more general phenomenon, namely what linguist Esther Pascual refers to as *fictive interaction*: the idea that human language in general rests on a conversational basis even in occurrences that appear to be strictly monological.

> Specifically, we present the premise that there is a conversational basis for language, which serves to partly structure cognition, discourse, and grammar. Stemming from this tenet, we discuss the notion of fictive interaction or 'FI,' namely the use of the template of face-to-face interaction as a cognitive domain that partially models: (i) thought (e.g. talking to oneself); (ii) the conceptualization of experience (e.g. 'A long walk is the answer to headache'); (iii) discourse organization (e.g. monologues structured as dialogues); and (iv) the language system and its use (e.g. rhetorical questions). (Pascual & Oakley, 2017, p. 348)

Given the observation that a deductive proof or argument is a (specific, regimented, and specialized) form of discourse, and the idea that interactive, conversational structures permeate what appears to be monological discourse at first sight, it is in fact not surprising that a deductive argument, too, would have a conversational (dialogical) basis. A deductive argument is a monologue that is structured as an implicit dialogue, with an internalized Skeptic. Similarly, a mono-agent mental occurrence of deductive reasoning is ultimately a form of inner dialogue. My main contribution here is to spell out in more detail the kind of conversation that mathematical proofs and other deductive arguments reenact: the dialogues that are rationally reconstructed here in the form of Prover–Skeptic dialogues.

---

[10] Compare the distinction between the concepts of a particular vs. a universal audience in the New Rhetoric framework of Perelman & Olbrechts-Tyteca, 1969. See Dufour, 2013 for an application of the New Rhetoric framework to mathematical argumentation.

4.3   Philosophical Issues Pertaining to Deduction

Equipped with the Prover–Skeptic framework, we can now revisit some of the open questions pertaining to logic and deduction introduced in Chapter 1, as well as some others not mentioned there. I argue that, for each of them, the dialogical perspective can deliver new insights, which in turn strengthens the case for the dialogical conception of deduction.

4.3.1   *Logical Consequence*

As discussed in Chapter 1 (Section 1.3.2), one of the most persistent debates in the philosophy of logic of the last decades has been on the nature of logical consequence (Shapiro, 2005; Caret & Hjortland, 2015). One of the main issues within these debates has been the 'dispute' between proof-theoretical and model-theoretical accounts of logical consequence. As the names suggest, the former gives pride of place to the concept of *proof*, while the second takes the notion of *model* as its primitive concept. What the dispute boils down to is the following question: Is logical consequence/deduction above all a matter of necessary truth-preservation – that is, that the conclusion be true in all models of the premises – or is it primarily a matter of the inferential steps that connect premises to conclusion in a stepwise manner?

On the account presented here, however, this is a false dichotomy. *Both* components are integral to the notion of deduction, which is reflected in the fact that each corresponds to one of Skeptic's key moves: to formulate (global or local) counterexamples and to ensure that the inferential chain of the argument is suitably perspicuous. (The third of Skeptic's moves, that of granting premises, is represented in both frameworks: a model of the premises represents the truth-conditions for Skeptic's commitments, and proof-theoretical frameworks such as natural deduction systems typically explicitly codify the hypothetical status of assumptions, for example by signaling it with square brackets.)

One might think (as I used to think) that a straightforward account of the model-theory/proof-theory divide within the Prover–Skeptic framework might be given in terms of the perspectives of each of the two players: proof theory would represent the perspective of Prover, while model theory would represent the perspective of Skeptic. However, this account would only be plausible if the main or perhaps even the only function of Skeptic in these dialogues were that of formulating counterexamples, either global or local. But as argued in Section 4.2.2 above, the 'why does it follow?' move by Skeptic is just as essential, both to Skeptic as a fictive character and to the dialogue as a whole. After all, Skeptic is not simply a Refuter, but truly an Inquirer. Conversely, Prover, who is indeed more naturally represented by the proof-theoretical perspective, must still ensure that all her inferential steps are necessarily truth-preserving, which suggests that some 'model-theoretical processing' must also be part of Prover's cognitive engagement in these dialogues. Thus, I submit that the suggestion of a neat division of labor between proof theory as representing Prover and model theory as representing Skeptic does not truly do justice to the intricacies of these dialogues. Instead, each of these two frameworks seems to correspond to a specific move by Skeptic: model theory for the formulation of counterexamples and proof theory for the 'why does it follow?' questions.

Nevertheless, what these two proposals (model theory and proof theory representing specific moves by Skeptic vs. representing the perspectives of each of the players) have in common is an underlying *conjunctive pluralism*. Shapiro (2005) proposes a form of *disjunctive pluralism* to reconcile the different and purportedly competing accounts of logical consequence; according to him, model theory and proof theory are not competitors after all but merely different, equally legitimate perspectives. For Shapiro, one can study the concept of logical consequence equally well *either* from a proof-theoretical *or* from a model-theoretical perspective. On the present account, however, *both* perspectives are required to do justice to the notion of logical consequence and deduction in all its intricacies.[11] In other words, what is required is a *conjunction* of these different perspectives, not a disjunction (as implied by Shapiro), and this is made particularly conspicuous within the Prover–Skeptic framework by giving equal weight to the different moves available to Skeptic.

Moreover, the dialogical perspective allows for a concrete account of the relations between a proof system and its semantics. If a proof system is sound and complete with respect to its intended semantics, what this means in dialogical terms is that, for each argument containing propositions of the relevant language, either there is a proof of it that Prover can produce, or there is a countermodel that Skeptic can produce where premises are true and conclusion is false. When a proof system is incomplete with respect to the relevant semantics, however, there will be arguments that neither correspond to a proof nor can be given a countermodel: these are arguments for which a dialogue between Prover and Skeptic would remain inconclusive.

4.3.2   The Normativity of Logic

As also noted in Chapter 1 (Section 1.3.3), another central debate in the philosophy of logic of the last decades has been on the issue of the (putative)

---

[11] Indeed, the dialogical framework presented here accommodates the three kinds of semantics pervasive in the literature: proof-theoretical, model-theoretical, and (for obvious reasons) game-theoretical semantics.

normative status of logic (Steinberger, 2017).[12] Harman's (1986) famous challenge to views attributing a normative import to logic for reasoning and thinking has given rise to vigorous reactions from those wishing to defend the status quo and preserve a normative remit for logic. However, these defenses have not been entirely successful (Dutilh Novaes, 2015a), and the question of how exactly logic has a normative import for thinking and reasoning (*if* it does) remains by and large unanswered (despite some progress made on how to frame the discussion in the first place, in particular with the introduction of the notion of bridge principles [MacFarlane, 2004]).

I have previously argued (Dutilh Novaes, 2015a) that much of the difficulty with making progress on the issue of the normativity of logic for thought, as discussed in the literature, stems from a misapprehension of what logic is normative *for*. Unsurprisingly (given the proposal that I have been developing so far), my claim is that (deductive) logic in fact comprises norms for quite specific situations of multi-agent dialogical interactions.[13] The dialogical perspective allows for the formulation of compelling bridge principles between the relation of logical consequence and dialogical normative principles, something that has remained challenging in mono-agent settings pertaining exclusively to thinking and belief.

To formulate bridge principles, John MacFarlane takes as his starting point the following schema:

If A, B $\Rightarrow$ C, then (normative claim about believing A, B, and C).

The instantiations of 'normative claim about believing A, B, and C' all take the form of conditionals where the antecedent concerns beliefs about A and B and the consequent concerns belief about C. From this general schema MacFarlane obtains thirty-six different bridge principles, by varying the kind of deontic operation (obligations [denoted by o], permissions [p], defeasible reasons [r]), polarity of believing (believe [+], disbelieve [−]), and the scope of the deontic operator in the embedded conditional stating the normative claim (the consequent only [C], the antecedent and the consequent [B], or the whole conditional [W]).

More concretely, some of the bridge principles he formulates are: if A, B $\Rightarrow$ C, then

- (Co−) if you believe A and you believe B, you ought not to disbelieve C.
- (Bp+) if you may believe A and believe B, you may believe C.

---

[12] This section is based on the results presented in Dutilh Novaes, 2015a, with some modifications. In particular, in this earlier paper I referred to the fictive participants in the dialogue as Proponent and Opponent (following Lorenzen's terminology).

[13] MacKenzie, 1989 and Dogramaci, 2015 have defended similar views; MacKenzie's views, especially, come very close to mine on a number of points. I will have more to say on their proposals shortly.

- (Wr+) you have reason to see to it that, if you believe A and you believe B, you believe C.

As it turns out, none of the thirty-six bridge principles generated by MacFarlane's schema succeeds in capturing the (presumed) normative import of logical consequence for reasoning (as recognized by MacFarlane himself and further discussed in Steinberger, 2016). My claim is that this stalemate stems from a mistaken conceptualization of the normative remit of logical consequence and deduction from the get-go: rather than normative for mono-agent processes of thought, logic's normative import pertains to multi-agent dialogical processes of debating, along the lines of the Prover–Skeptic dialogues. Indeed, in the Prover–Skeptic dialogical setting, compelling bridge principles can be easily formulated which successfully capture the normative import of the relation of logical consequence.

If A, B $\Rightarrow$ C, then

- (Wo + d_S) Skeptic ought to see to it that, if he has granted A and B and Prover puts forward C, then he will grant C.
- (Cp + d_P) if Skeptic has granted A and B, then Prover may put forward C (and require Skeptic to grant it).

('d' stands for 'dialogical' and the subscripts stand for the agent to whom the normative recommendation applies, i.e. Prover or Skeptic.) Why exactly these bridge principles and not others? Regarding the scope of the operator, in (Wo + d_S) it ranges over the whole conditional in order to allow for the commitment to A and B to be retracted (an equivalent disjunctive formulation which makes this possibility explicit will be discussed shortly). In (Cp + d_P) it ranges only over the consequent because the permission only affects Prover.

Why the positive polarity? What about 'not rejecting'? Not rejecting would also be compatible with suspending judgment about a given C, but, given the rules of the dialogical game, what is required from Skeptic is for him to explicitly grant C if it follows from his previous discursive commitments, and if C is proposed by Prover. So 'not rejecting' would not be strong enough.

Why 'ought' as the deontic operator in (Wo + d_S)? The point is precisely that Skeptic is in charge of ascertaining whether the statements put forward by Prover indeed follow necessarily from the previously granted statements. If they do, Skeptic ought to assent; he is compelled to grant C by the force of necessary truth-preservation. As for (Cp + d_P), here again the 'may' modality emerges straightforwardly from the rules of the dialogical game. Given premises A and B, typically there is a multitude of different Cs that Prover may put forward; she is not obliged to propose any particular C, but has permission to propose any (or at least most) of them (modulo perhaps considerations of relevance).

These bridge principles seem to circumvent the main objections raised against the mono-agent bridge principles. In particular, the mind-clutter objection does not affect (Wo + d_S), because Skeptic is only required to grant a sentence C *if it is explicitly proposed* by Prover.[14] In a dialogical setting such as the one described here, Skeptic must take a stance only with respect to the small, and in any case finite, number of sentences explicitly put forward by Prover. (MacKenzie, 1989, p. 104 makes a similar point.) One might think that the requirement of logical omniscience (Skeptic must grant everything that follows from his commitments, even very remote implications) remains a problem, but here again the fact that C is put forward by an agent with equally limited cognitive resources alleviates this worry, at least to some extent (again, something noted in MacKenzie, 1989, p. 105). In other words, it is the very concreteness of dialogical situations that make these two objections less threatening.[15]

What about the issue of retracting one's original beliefs rather than embracing an implausible conclusion, i.e. the possibility of revision/retraction? (The fact that logical frameworks cannot account for this possibility is one of Harman's main objections.) To make the possibility of retraction explicit, (Wo + d_S) can be given a straightforward disjunctive formulation (disjunction marked with 'V'):

- (Wo + d_SV) Skeptic ought to see to it that, if he has granted A and B and Prover puts forward C, then he will either grant C *or* retract his endorsement to A or B.

In practice, this formulation reflects the idea that, in such debates, Prover may intend to show the absurdities that follow from Skeptic's commitments in order to force Skeptic to revise these commitments (as in a typical *elenchus*, to be discussed in Chapter 5). This is particularly conspicuous in a reductio proof, as described in Section 4.2.3. It is precisely the dialogical setting that allows for the introduction of the speech act of retraction, something that a monological framework typically cannot easily accommodate.

---

[14] Recall that the mind-clutter objection pertains to the explosion of the class of sentences an agent is required to believe if she must believe everything that follows logically from her existing beliefs (such as, for each sentence A she believes, the potentially infinite collection of disjunctive sentences containing A as one of the disjuncts).

[15] Notice that (Wo + d_S) does seem to be contradicted by (a dialogical version of) the preface paradox, just as MacFarlane's (Wo−). I respond to this objection by noting an interesting dissimilarity between the epistemic context and the discursive context (Dutilh Novaes, 2015a, pp. 605–606). While deductive consistency seems not to be a reasonable requirement for ideal epistemic rationality (as recently argued by a number of authors who emphasize the primacy of *accuracy*), a stronger case can be made for the plausibility of deductive consistency as a norm within *discursive, dialogical contexts*. Indeed, it can be argued that consistency (as embodied by the principle of non-contraction) is originally and fundamentally a discursive, dialogical principle rather than an epistemic one, in which case a dialogical version of the preface paradox will be much less threatening than the epistemic version.

In sum, reframing the issue of the normativity of logic in dialogical terms seems to dissolve many of the difficulties that a purely mono-agent formulation of the issue appears inexorably saddled with. At the very least, it allows for the formulation of neat dialogical bridge principles capturing the normative effect of logical consequence on these dialogical situations.

Before closing this section, let me briefly comment on how my proposal is related to Sinan Dogramaci's account of deductive reasoning (Dogramaci, 2015), given that there are a number of commonalities between the two proposals. Dogramaci's starting point is very different from mine; he is interested in the question of what function(s) our uses of the term 'rational' could serve, predominantly from an epistemological perspective. This leads him to formulate a position dubbed *epistemic communism*, according to which epistemic evaluations serve first and foremost the purpose of promoting social coordination of our belief-forming rules, allowing us to pursue true belief as a team of parallel epistemic processors. Applied specifically to deductive reasoning as a putative canon for rationality, epistemic communism yields a conventional account of the rules of logic as geared toward social epistemic coordination. So Dogramaci's account shares with the present proposal an emphasis on the social role of logical rules for coordination of multi-agent situations (though in his case, these situations seem to correspond to a wider class than the Prover–Skeptic games being considered here), and an openly deflationary account of the normativity import of logic for thought (where there isn't more to logical rules as 'correct' or 'rational' than allowing for successful epistemic coordination). To be sure, Dogramaci's proposal remains essentially different from mine, in particular in that the questions he is addressing to start with are different from the ones I am addressing. Nevertheless, it is worth noting that we seem to converge on a number of conclusions, despite having quite dissimilar starting points.

4.3.3   Paradoxes and Structural Rules

The next issue to be approached with dialogical lenses here is one that is not explicitly discussed in Chapter 1, but has given rise to formidable debates throughout the history of logic: the semantic paradoxes.[16] It is well known that combining some apparently innocent principles of logic with apparently innocent predicates such as the truth predicate leads to an explosive mix. The Liar paradox is a quintessential example (Liar sentences can be shown to be both true and false), but there are other such paradoxes, some of which are even more recalcitrant (e.g. Curry's paradox). Since we can't have everything we want (the familiar principles of logic plus apparently intuitive semantic predicates such as 'is true') without heading straight into paradox, something has to

---

[16] This section summarizes the main results presented in Dutilh Novaes & French, 2018.

go. In recent decades, there has been much discussion on what might be the least damaging revisions, either to logical principles or to the semantics of certain predicates, so as to restore peace and shield us from paradoxes.

In recent years, substructural approaches to paradoxes have become particularly popular (Schroeder-Heister, 2012). The key idea is the following: rather than restricting the application or modifying the semantics of logical connectives such as the negation or the implication in order to block the derivation of paradoxes, a more promising avenue is to restrict the application of familiar *structural rules*, such as contraction or transitivity. These substructural approaches have delivered some interesting results, but have also been criticized on a number of grounds (see Rosenblatt, 2017 and Shapiro, 2016). It is clear, however, that whatever restrictions on structural rules we may want to enforce, it is crucial that such restrictions be accompanied by independent motivation, not directly related to paradoxes. Why is it that a particular structural rule, which has served us well for so long, is now singled out as the culprit? In order to offer motivations on why we should restrict (or altogether eliminate) any one of them, we must address the question of why they were viewed as plausible in the first place.

Moreover, by restricting or modifying structural rules, substructural solutions to paradoxes give rise to different logics; are these logics then all equally adequate? We thus end up with two very pressing questions: what (independent) motivations we have (if any) for restrictions on structural rules, and what to make of the plurality of new logics emerging from these restrictions, i.e. how to 'choose' among the different options.

In a recent paper, Rohan French and I (Dutilh Novaes & French, 2018) argue that dialogical interpretations of structural rules – that is, as rules determining specific structural properties of the dialogues in question – provide a conveniently neutral framework to adjudicate between the different substructural proposals that have been made in the literature on paradoxes.[17] In the paper, we discuss a number of structural rules and possible dialogical motivations to restrict or maintain them, thus coming to conclusions on which of these rules are more plausibly revisable; perhaps surprisingly, our conclusion is that reflexivity (the rule according to which A implies A, for any A) is the most plausible candidate for revision, from a dialogical perspective.

I now briefly present the dialogical interpretations of some of these rules (for a more detailed presentation, see Dutilh Novaes & French, 2018). Let us start with Left Weakening, which can be thus formulated in a simplified version:

$$\frac{A, B \;\Rightarrow\; C}{A, B, D \;\Rightarrow\; C}$$

---

[17] As discussed in Chapter 3, dialogical logics usually specify structural rules, which are meant to capture procedural aspects of the game, so this is a rather natural connection.

Informally, on a dialogical interpretation, Left Weakening says that, having granted A and B as premises, and then C as following necessarily from A and B, an interlocutor cannot retract commitment to C if she grants an additional D, for any D. The permissibility of Left Weakening follows straightforwardly from the property of necessary truth-preservation and its sibling, the property of monotonicity. Thus, prima facie, it seems that Left Weakening is irreproachable from the point of view of Prover–Skeptic dialogues: if Skeptic has granted A and B, and they together entail C, then no additional premise D will defeat his obligation to concede C. In other words, with respect to *Skeptic*'s moves, it seems that no restriction on Left Weakening can be justified.

But what about *Prover*? Can Prover avail herself of the possibilities offered by Left Weakening without restriction? At this point, we need to consider different dialogues that are to various degrees adversarial or cooperative. In purely adversarial dialogues, Prover seeks to force (coerce) Skeptic to grant the final conclusion at all costs, and this is the main or perhaps even the sole goal of such interactions (say, in antagonistic debating situations, where Prover may want to force Skeptic to grant something embarrassing for Skeptic). By contrast, in a more cooperative situation, Prover does not want Skeptic to be coerced into granting something, but for Skeptic to understand *why* the conclusion follows from the premises. In other words, in adversarial contexts Left Weakening can be strategically advantageous for Prover, as asking for irrelevant premises may confuse Skeptic by causing information overload. In turn, in more cooperative contexts, if the goal of such a dialogue is to produce explanatory persuasion for Skeptic, then the potential confusion caused by having irrelevant premises on the table is not a desirable effect.

Next is **Transitivity**, or **Cut**, which in simplified form says that if A entails B and B entails C, then A entails C:

$$\frac{A \Rightarrow B \qquad B \Rightarrow C}{A \Rightarrow C}$$

Essentially, Transitivity ensures that inferential steps can be concatenated such that one can derive a conclusion Z from a number of premises by means of intermediary inferential steps. The goal is that each step in the argument be individually perspicuous and convincing for the intended audience, and it is the very possibility of chaining such steps that allows for surprising results to come about while the argument remains convincing. It seems thus that significantly restricting Transitivity would fundamentally affect the very core function of a deductive argument as conceived here, that is, as intended to ensure explanatory persuasion. In other words, dialogical considerations clearly militate against revisions or restrictions on Transitivity.

Finally, what about **Reflexivity**? This rule simply states that, for any proposition A, it entails itself:

$$\frac{}{A \;\Rightarrow\; A}$$

This rule is at first glance irreproachable: what could possibly be more truth-preserving than an inference from A to A itself? Indeed, reflexivity appears to be as innocent as it gets, as far as structural rules go; for many of those engaged in developing substructural solutions to paradoxes, Reflexivity is the one rule that simple must stay put.

However, and perhaps surprisingly, from a dialogical perspective Reflexivity is not nearly as obvious or straightforward. Once we move to an explicitly multi-agent context such as Prover–Skeptic dialogues, Reflexivity amounts to Prover putting forward a proposition A for Skeptic to grant twice. Imagine the following dialogue:

PROVER: Do you grant me premise A?
SKEPTIC: Yes, I grant you A.
PROVER (victorious look): Right, gotcha! So now you also need to grant me A!
SKEPTIC (puzzled look): Are you kidding me? I just granted you A!

This is a somewhat exaggerated version of such a dialogue, but the main point should be clear: to 'force' Skeptic to grant A once he has already granted A is a rather pointless dialogical move, a violation of pragmatic conversational norms against redundant moves (indeed, a breach of the Gricean maxim of quantity). In an adversarial context, this move would most likely make Prover look silly rather than triumphant; in a cooperative context, this move would be utterly uninformative and superfluous.

The analysis of these three structural rules suggests a ranking among them, going from most plausibly revisable to least plausibly revisable, from a dialogical perspective.[18] This ranking thus defines an order in which substructural solutions to paradoxes are to be preferred over others, from a dialogical perspective:[19]

(1) Reflexivity
(2) Left Weakening
(3) Transitivity

---

[18] In Dutilh Novaes & French, 2018, we also discuss Left Contraction, which is a popular candidate for restriction in the literature on paradoxes (left out here for reasons of space). Left Contraction ends up third in our revisability ranking, between Left Weakening and Transitivity.

[19] Though notice that, to my knowledge, no one currently proposes restrictions on Left Weakening as a solution to paradoxes such as the Liar, Curry, etc. Restrictions on Left Weakening are often responses to concerns pertaining to relevance, such as in relevant logics.

Hence, dialogical interpretations of structural rules allow for the formulation of independent (i.e. not paradox-related) motivations to restrict or not restrict specific structural rules in attempts to 'tame' the semantic paradoxes. So yet again, the dialogical perspective sheds light on an important but recalcitrant debate in the philosophy of logic.

4.3.4   Logical Pluralism

The fourth and final key issue in the philosophy of logic to be discussed here is the debate between logical pluralists and logical monists. The debate was (re)ignited in the 2000s by J.C. Beall and Greg Restall's (2006) forceful defense of logical pluralism, which prompted logical monists such as Stephen Read and Graham Priest to defend their position against the pluralists, and others to seek more precise formulations of what logical pluralism in fact amounts to (Keefe, 2014).

> Logical pluralism is the thesis that there is more than one correct logic. The main opposing view, logical monism, is the thesis that there is only one. In fact there are many pairs of such opposed theses – and so, many different versions of the thesis of logical pluralism – corresponding to the different ways in which one can specify more carefully what a *logic* is, and what it would be for one to be *correct*.[20] (Russell, 2013)

More recently, Stewart Shapiro (2015) has defended logical pluralism inspired by the plurality of legitimate logical systems underpinning mathematical practice. He has also argued (with Teresa Kouri Kissel) that various logics are constitutive for thought within particular practices, but none is constitutive for thought as such, across the board (Kouri Kissel & Shapiro, 2020). This position seems to amount to what could be described as *global logical pluralism* paired with *local logical monism* (i.e., there is exactly one logic adequate for each practice).

A form of logical pluralism akin to Shapiro and Kouri Kissel's proposal emerges quite naturally from the dialogical conception of logic defended here, in terms of the different kinds of dialogues that one may want to engage in. The particular practices they refer to can naturally be construed more specifically as *dialogical* practices (though the range of practices they want to consider is apparently broader). For a form of logical pluralism to emerge along these lines, it is sufficient to recognize that there is a plurality of different kinds of dialogues that people may want to engage in (in different circumstances), and that different logics (corresponding to different agreements on what counts as

---

[20] Making sense of what 'correct' means naturally brings us back to the issue of the normativity of logic. Moreover, there are also obvious connections with the discussion on substructural approaches to paradoxes, given that 'tinkering' with different structural rules gives rise to different logical systems. This then naturally gives rise to the question of whether they are equally legitimate or whether there will ultimately be one single correct, optimal logical system emerging from these revisions.

valid moves in the dialogue) underpin each of these various kinds of dialogues. In other words, there isn't a general, all-purpose codification of dialogical rules of engagement; as Wittgenstein would put it, we play a large number of different language games, depending on the circumstances. However, given that participants in a dialogue must minimally agree on the rules of engagement, it seems that, at least at the level of specific conversations, a form of local monism emerges as well.

In particular, variations on the adversarial–cooperative parameter generate different kinds of dialogues; we've seen for example that the presence or absence of Left Weakening reflects how adversarial or cooperative a dialogue is, which is captured by relevance criteria. While the analyses in this chapter may seem to suggest that more cooperative dialogues are always to be preferred over more adversarial ones, this is actually not a view I endorse. Instead, I submit that a plethora of kinds of dialogues should be embraced, and insofar as different logical systems will correspond to different kinds of dialogues, we end up with different, equally legitimate logical systems. What defines which logic is the 'right one' are the motivations of participants when engaging in a given dialogical situation, and their mutual agreement in terms of the structural and logical features of that particular conversation.[21] (See French, 2015 and 2019 for detailed discussion of logical pluralism against the background of Prover–Skeptic games.)

There is still the issue of whether there will be exactly one logic defined for each dialogical situation (given the relevant motivations and agreements); there may well be none, or perhaps more than one logic suitable for a particular kind of dialogical situation. However, for one and the same conversation (i.e., one and the same 'play' of the game), if participants adopt different background logics, and thus follow different rules of engagement, they may well end up talking past each other. Similarly, if participants cannot agree (either tacitly or explicitly) on these rules of engagement, it may well be that the conversation is thereby rendered unviable. (It is a familiar point in argumentation theory that there must be a modicum of common ground for a dialogical interaction to be fruitful.) This means that, while there is no guarantee that a unique logic suitable for a given conversation will emerge, this is desirable if the dialogue is to progress smoothly. (Though it is conceivable that dialogues may occur somewhat successfully even when participants rely, tacitly or explicitly, on different logics.)

Notice that these considerations do not imply that any arbitrary tinkering with the rules of a logical system will deliver rules for viable dialogues; certain modifications will lead to rather dysfunctional 'dialogues' that no one is likely

---

[21] This position resembles that defended in Restall, 2004, where pluralism arises out of different argumentative concerns, in particular what the structure of a sequent is.

to want to engage in.[22] (This point is of course related to Hodges' Dawkins question, discussed in Chapter 3.) Rather than entailing an overly permissive 'anything goes' attitude, the dialogical perspective in fact allows for the formulation of restrictions on what can count as a legitimate logical system: one that corresponds to a plausible kind of dialogue that people may actually feel compelled to engage in (though, admittedly, much work remains to be done on specific criteria of adequacy for dialogical systems).

4.4   Conclusions

In this chapter, I have argued that the three key features of deductive reasoning presented in Chapter 1, which are to some extent cognitive oddities in mono-agent situations, can be given very natural dialogical rationales. Necessary truth-preservation may be seen as related to the desideratum of producing convincing arguments that are not easily defeated by objections; perspicuity may be seen as related to a deductive argument's function of enabling the transfer of epistemic resources so as to produce not only persuasion but also true understanding in its receiver; belief-bracketing may be seen as emerging from the need to draw inferences not only from one's own avowed beliefs, but also from the discursive commitments of one's interlocutors. These observations thus reinforce the hypothesis that deduction is fundamentally a dialogical notion, given that the hypothesis provides a rationale for features of deduction that are otherwise difficult to account for in purely mono-agent doxastic contexts.

Moreover, I have provided an explanation for why deductive proofs and arguments do not appear to be dialogical at first sight; this is due to a process of internalization of Skeptic, such that the only 'voice' heard in a worked-out proof is that of Prover. But this does not mean that a proof has lost its dialogical nature completely, given that Skeptic's role has been taken over by the method itself. A proof, thus, both is and is not a dialogue: it is not a dialogue properly speaking, but it retains key dialogical features.

Finally, I discussed four 'hot topics' in the philosophy of logic of the last decades against the background of the dialogical conception of logic and deduction presented earlier. I submit that the dialogical perspective allows for a welcome 'gestalt shift' in these debates, thus shedding new light on these much discussed but still unresolved issues. In turn, to the extent that this is indeed achieved, these analyses lend further support to the dialogical conception of deduction.

---

[22] For an example of a dysfunctional dialogical logic, see Uckelman, Alama, & Knoks, 2014.

Part II

The History of Deduction

5 Deduction in Mathematics and Dialectic in Ancient Greece

5.1 Introduction

In the next chapters, we turn to the historical roots of deduction. The goal is to describe the emergence of practices and theories of deduction as well as the main transformations for both through the centuries. To this end, I adopt a diachronic, *longue durée* perspective on these developments. The method adopted is the method of *conceptual genealogy*, inspired by Nietzschean genealogical analysis (described in detail in Dutilh Novaes, 2015b). Naturally, the survey to be presented here will be a very condensed, somewhat partial account of these developments; an entire library would be needed to cover them all thoroughly. Still, a conceptual genealogy of deduction is an essential piece of the puzzle, and a bird's-eye view is what is required for my overall argument at this point.

The main thesis defended in the next three chapters is that deduction emerged against the background of specific dialogical practices and retained many of the original dialogical components throughout the centuries. But the concept (and relevant practices) also underwent significant transformations motivated by non-dialogical factors, in particular but not exclusively related to the use of the written medium for the exposition and use of deductive theories (in mathematics as well as in logic). Another important trend in the development of the concept of deduction is a departure from embodied, situational elements of concrete dialogical situations, in particular specific interlocutors, toward more abstract, 'de-personalized' conceptualizations.[1] The result is a hybrid notion, featuring a mixture of dialogical and non-dialogical components.

---

[1] This observation echoes some aspects of the critique in Nye, 1990 of deductive logic as presenting itself as independent of concrete human relations. On my account, deduction started out as closely connected to specific concrete dialogical situations, but then quickly moved towards more (purportedly) impersonal forms of discourse. This being said, I disagree with Nye on the claim that this process of 'de-personalization' is inherently problematic.

In this chapter, I start with a brief presentation of the notion of conceptual genealogy (Section 5.2). I then turn to events in Ancient Greece as the first significant stage in the development of deduction, starting with a brief account of the relevant social and political context (Section 5.3). In Section 5.4, I discuss the emergence of the deductive method in Ancient Greek mathematics, relying primarily on the work of Reviel Netz (1999). In Section 5.5, I turn to the practice of *dialectic*, including the crucial notion of *elenchus* (refutation).

5.2   A Conceptual Genealogy of Deduction

Let us start with the very idea of a genealogy. Ideally, a genealogy is a narrative with no gaps: a person's genealogy is a detailed account of her ancestry, which specifies every relevant parent–offspring step in the chain. Typically, a genealogy may focus on the transmission of a family's surname through generations, thus indicating *continuity* (of positive value in particular, e.g. nobility). At the same time, a genealogy always contains elements of *transformation* as well, if nothing else because parents and offspring are by definition different individuals.

Of course, here we are not interested in genealogies of people; instead, the focus is on genealogies of (philosophical) *concepts* and their development through time.[2] The idea that thought itself is a historical phenomenon rather than immutable and atemporal can be traced back (at least) to the German historicist tradition that emerged in the eighteenth century (Beiser, 2011). Hegel's famous adage illustrates the key idea: "As far as the individual is concerned, each individual is in any case a child of his time, thus, philosophy, too, is its own time comprehended in thoughts" (Hegel, 1991, p. 21). Thus, different times and different (social, political, cultural) contexts will give rise to different instantiations of philosophical concepts. It follows that philosophical concepts themselves will change over time, following more global changes.

Hegel's conception of history in general, and of the history of concepts in particular, is *teleological*: things could not have taken a different turn, as temporal developments follow an inevitable path. In this sense, he differs from most historicists in the nineteenth century, who focused on the *contingency* of history (Beiser, 2011). Among those, Nietzsche is usually seen as the inaugurator of a new approach, which can be described as a *subversive* variant of historicist projects. In *On the Genealogy of Morality* (1887) (Nietzsche, 2007), he offers a genealogy of Christian morality that is meant to expose its 'shameful' origins. Rather than comprising eternal, immutable moral precepts, Christian morality (and the human practices associated with it) is in fact the

---

[2] The phenomenon of conceptual changes over time is also known as 'concept drift' (Betti & van den Berg, 2014).

product of *contingent* historical developments, more specifically a conjunction of various lines of events, none of which is particularly admirable (Geuss, 1994). Specifically, Christian morality arises from the resentment of slaves directed toward their masters, and thus has distinctively malevolent origins (while currently presenting itself as pure and magnanimous).

A key feature of Nietzsche's genealogy of Christianity for the present purposes is the idea of a *superimposition of layers* through processes of reinterpretation of previously existing practices, giving rise to new practices that nevertheless retain residual traces of their previous instantiations. The first significant step in this succession of reinterpretations is the influential conception of Christianity formulated by Saint Paul, which, however, represents a drastic departure from the way of life exemplified by Jesus himself:

Paul's 'interpretation' represents so drastic and crude a misinterpretation of Jesus' way of life that even at a distance of 2000 years we can see that wherever the Pauline reading gets the upper hand ... it transforms 'Christianity' ... into what is the exact reverse of anything Jesus himself would have practiced. (Geuss, 1994, p. 280)

However, such processes of reinterpretation never manage to quash entirely vestiges of previous practices:

Nietzsche thinks that such attempts to take over/reinterpret an existing set of practices or way of life will not in general be so fully successful that nothing of the original form of life remains, hence the continuing tension in post-Pauline Christianity between forms of acting, feeling, judging which still somehow eventually derive from aboriginal Christianity and Paul's theological dogmas. (Geuss, 1994, p. 281)

In other words, even when a particular new meaning manages to impose itself, the old meanings remain present, albeit in vestigial form, in the resulting complex. Indeed, this is arguably very much how the historical development of a philosophical concept unfolds: it undergoes modifications, but the super-imposition of layers of meaning typically retains traces of previous stages and instantiations, even within new meanings.

Nietzschean genealogy is thus characterized by constant interaction between continuity and change. (Indeed, how can we say that a genealogy is a genealogy *of X* if there is nothing permanent at all in the phenomenon in question over time?) Four components of the Nietzschean conception of genealogy are especially relevant for genealogies of philosophical concepts: a particular *historicist* conception of concepts and values, an emphasis on the *contingency* of the underlying historical developments, the involvement of *multiple lines of influence*, and the *superimposition of layers of meaning*, resulting in both change (the new meanings) and continuity (residual traces of the old meanings).

Applied to philosophical concepts (and I take deduction to be a quintessential philosophical concept, albeit one that reflects practices outside of philosophy, in particular in mathematics), a genealogy will most likely not deliver a neat, linear progression like a parent–offspring genealogy. Instead, different meanings associated with a given concept will typically coexist (with or without explicit interaction between them) at different stages. But we still often observe more or less coherent patterns, with new meanings becoming predominant while traces of earlier meanings remain. Equally important for this genealogical perspective is its *functionalist* component: philosophical concepts emerge as responses to particular functions, needs, practices, and goals, both within philosophical/intellectual practices and more generally against the background of cultural and societal factors. We must thus also consider these broader contexts when tracing the development of specific philosophical concepts.

For the birth of deduction, the relevant period roughly coincides with the period of the Athenian Democracy (508–322 BCE), and this is no coincidence. As argued by Lloyd (1990, 1996, 2013), a public domain revolving around *debates* provided the crucial background for scientific and intellectual activities in this period. Not coincidentally (given that my dialogical account of deduction was from the start inspired by the historical work of Netz and Lloyd), a number of key aspects of the present account can be traced back to the centrality of public debates in the relevant contexts: orality, persuasion, and adversariality.

At the same time, already during the early days of deduction in Ancient Greece, substantive transformations occurred, in particular with increased prominence of the written medium and a shift from concrete dialogical situations involving actual participants toward an abstract, impersonal approach, where (e.g.) all premises necessary to derive a conclusion must be made explicit (Malink, 2015). Indeed, as argued by Lloyd, the axiomatic-deductive model developed by mathematicians and philosophers "was a reaction against what were perceived as the merely persuasive modes cultivated by orators, sophists and politicians in the context of public debate" (Lloyd, 2013, p. 437). We may say, thus, that deduction emerges as a different, purportedly *better* response to similar needs and functions related to rational discourse and persuasion in public life.

In what follows, I examine how deduction emerges from the complex interaction between rejecting the *logos* of the sophists and yet maintaining a number of its key components, such as persuasion and adversariality (albeit modulated by cooperation). Indeed, what the thinkers who criticize and reject the sophist *logos* seek is a model of argumentation that will secure *incontrovertibility*, as opposed to the inherent defeasibility of mere persuasion. They seek a model of argumentation that will ensure the necessity (and thus acceptability) of a conclusion given certain premises, regardless of the particular interlocutor one is arguing with/against. It is in this sense that deduction is no longer strictly dialogical and yet retains important dialogical components – a clear instance of superimposition of layers of meaning, thus suitable for investigation from a genealogical perspective.[3]

5.3   Historical Background

Before we move on to developments in mathematics and logic/philosophy specifically, a brief recapitulation of the relevant historical background is required. The relevant period is that of the Athenian democracy (508 to 322 BCE). In the first half of this period (until the Peloponnesian Wars, 431–404 BCE), Athens became a superpower whose influence extended toward inland Greece as well as further into the Mediterranean basin, in what is known as the 'golden age' of Athenian democracy.

In Athenian democracy, all citizens could (in theory, at least) participate directly in decisions on matters pertaining to governance of the city (Hansen, 1991). (Of course, foreigners and slaves did not count as citizens, and female Athenian citizens had significantly less space for political participation, e.g. they could not be members of the political bodies.) The three main political bodies where citizens gathered were the *assembly* (with a quorum that could go up to 6,000 people), the *boule* (a council of 500 citizens having an advisory and administrative role, with little control over policy), and the *courts* (charged with enforcing Athens' intricate legal system). The meetings of the assembly were the main events in Athenian democracy, where decisions were taken on public matters such as deciding whether to go to war, elections of officials, and legislation. The standard format consisted in different speakers making speeches for and against a position on a given matter, after which those present would vote 'yes' or 'no' on the position in question (only those physically present could vote).

The courts also held significant political power, and were thought to represent the will of the people just like the assembly, because jurors were drawn from the same pool of citizens (with the difference that jurors were required to be 30 or older, whereas for the assembly the minimum age for participation was 20). The cases were typically presented by the litigants themselves (officially, there could be no paid lawyers to represent them), each of whom had a certain

---

[3] Notice that, while Nietzsche's genealogy of Christian morality is debunking – it presents itself as a critique of this moral system by exposing its shameful origins – the genealogy presented here is neither debunking nor vindicatory (i.e. meant to glorify its object by revealing its noble origins). Instead, it is meant to offer an *explanation* of how the concept of deduction developed: not only to demonstrate *that* the relevant practices or concepts are contingent and therefore could be otherwise, but also to show *how* those practices and concepts were shaped through a complex series of events (Dutilh Novaes, 2015b).

amount of time to speak. Decisions were then immediately reached by voting, with no further deliberation among the jurors, in a procedure structurally similar to that of assembly meetings. Plato's *Apology*, a dramatic rendition of Socrates' defense in his trial for impiety and corruption, is possibly the most famous description of the Athenian courts in action.

From this very brief description, it becomes immediately apparent that being a persuasive orator was of paramount importance for a citizen (both to obtain votes in the assembly and to argue for a legal case in court). As votes were immediately gathered after the speeches, these had to be effective and compelling. Another key feature of this mode of decision-making is the *adversarial* setup: arguments for and against a given position were offered by orators representing each of the two sides, and so these debates easily became competitions of persuasiveness, to be decided by public vote.

In this setting, those who could train citizens to become skilled orators had something immensely valuable to offer. Many of the well-known thinkers of this period were exactly that: itinerant professional teachers who became collectively known as the *sophists*, most famously Gorgias and Protagoras. Nominally, what they taught was virtue or excellence more generally (*aretē*), but in democratic Athens *aretē* became increasingly understood as the ability to influence fellow citizens in political gatherings through rhetorical persuasion. Citizens were reportedly prepared to pay lavish sums for the teachings of the sophists.

This social and political background had profound implications for the remarkable intellectual flourishing of this period. Netz aptly summarizes the main findings of Lloyd's extensive investigations of the connections between political and intellectual life in Athenian democracy, and Greece more generally:

Lloyd stresses the role of debate in Greek culture – the way in which *debate* was essentially *open* to participants and audience, and the way in which it was *radical* in its willingness to challenge everything. It is this polemical background which explains the role of forms of persuasion in Greek culture. One should stress also the orality of this setting. By 'orality' it should be understood not that the political life of the Greek *polis* was uninfluenced by literacy but that the characteristic mode of political debate – which is the background most important in this context – was oral. And indeed, as Lloyd shows, there are many intellectual domains where presentation is heavily influenced by the form of an *epideixis*, a public, oral presentation, akin in a sense to a political speech. (Netz, 1999, p. 292)

However, the so-called golden age of Athenian democracy, during which the statesman Pericles (495–429 BCE) was the most influential figure, ends with the Peloponnesian Wars (431–404 BCE) between the Delian league, led by Athens, and the Peloponnesian league, led by Sparta. Before the wars, Athens was the strongest city-state not only in Greece but also in the whole Mediterranean basin, but in the aftermath it was reduced to devastation. Sparta, the victor, emerged as the new leading power in the region.

These historical events must be kept in mind as we survey the intellectual developments of the period, as philosophical/intellectual developments were directly influenced by them. In particular, some viewed the catastrophic consequences of the Peloponnesian Wars for Athens as a sign of the failure of democracy as a political system, especially as the victor Sparta represented a competing political system, oligarchy. Indeed, much of Plato's criticism of democracy in the *Republic* and elsewhere may be seen as a response to the postwar state of affairs and the demise of Athens' prewar prosperity. (Plato was born around the time of the war's onset.) Moreover, his critique of the sophists as prototypical intellectuals, and his search for a new mode of argumentative engagement, may also be understood in this light: the sophists, with their exclusive focus on persuasion, represented all that is amiss with democracy. And thus, inasmuch as the deductive method emerged as a reaction to modes of arguing that aimed exclusively at persuasion, inasmuch as these modes of arguing were closely associated with democratic values and institutions, and inasmuch as democratic ideals were under attack during and in the aftermath of the Peloponnesian Wars, then these historical developments may well be viewed as one of the factors contributing to the emergence of deductive modes of reasoning and arguing.

Moreover, as argued by Netz (1999, chapter 7, section 3.1), beside the significance of public political speech as a mode of presentation also in nonpolitical, intellectual domains, *writing* became an important means of communication for intellectuals, because peers were often geographically separated (united in an international rather than local community). This observation entails that only an aristocratic elite could be part of this international 'conversation,' as literacy was then restricted to members of the elite. Thus, while a democratic structure in public life no doubt profoundly influenced developments in intellectual domains, it would be a mistake to conclude that social hierarchies among citizens played no role in intellectual domains.

5.4   Ancient Greek Mathematics

In this section, I briefly discuss the roots of deduction in Ancient Greek mathematics, as the portion of Ancient Greek mathematics that culminated in the systematization offered in Euclid's *Elements* (circa 300 BCE) is one of the two main loci for the regimentation of deductive reasoning (the other being Aristotelian logic).

There are a number of remarkable ancient mathematical traditions, such as the Egyptian, Babylonian, Indian, and Chinese traditions. There has been a regrettable tendency in historiography of mathematics to give pride of place to Ancient Greek mathematics at the expense of these other traditions, and to view the latter as 'primitive and rudimentary' when compared to their Greek counterpart (Charette, 2012). According to this view, Greek mathematics would be inherently superior, because, among other reasons, it contains abstract *proofs* (demonstrations), whereas these other traditions would remain at the level of calculations and algorithms to address concrete problems.

In recent years, historians of mathematics have done much to redress this oversimplified picture (Chemla, 2012). It has been shown that there is much mathematics in the Greek tradition, too, that does not conform to Euclidean deductive ideals of abstraction and generality (Lloyd, 2012). It has also been argued that, with a more encompassing notion of what counts as a mathematical proof, these other traditions do contain mathematical discourse that may well be viewed as instances of proof (albeit perhaps not in a strict Euclidean sense), for example in the Chinese tradition (Chemla, 2012a).

And yet, there is something quite unique about the specific approach to mathematics that emerged in Ancient Greece and led to mathematical proofs. Their two main features are *necessity* (given the truth of the premises, the conclusion *must* be true) and *generality* (particular arguments can establish the truth of claims holding of a very large, possibly infinite collection of items; Netz, 1999). In this context, arguments take as their starting points definitions, geometrical postulates, and axioms; conclusions are then derived by means of necessarily truth-preserving inferential steps, which allow for no exceptions or counterexamples. The emergence of the Greek axiomatic-deductive method thus understood is an extraordinary event in the global history of mathematics, quite unlike anything that can be found in other traditions around the same time.

One of the remarkable features of Euclidean mathematics is that the level of certainty ensured by a demonstration goes well beyond what is required for purely practical purposes.[4] Indeed, unlike much of the calculations and procedures motivated by practical problems such as land-surveying and division of goods (for which approximations typically suffice), Euclidean mathematics does not seem to be primarily motivated by such practical applications. Instead, Lloyd and Netz have argued that it is a response to the social and political environment of Athenian democracy just described, as it emerged as a mode of argumentation that both shares elements with and differs from political speech in public life.[5] Lloyd has further argued that it is the distinctiveness of this social and political context that (partially) explains the emergence of such a unique approach to mathematics, when compared to other ancient traditions (Lloyd, 1990, chapter

---

[4] I use here the term 'Euclidean mathematics' for simplicity. The tradition features a number of other prominent figures beside Euclid, in particular Archimedes and Apollonius.

[5] On the relevance of broader sociopolitical contexts for the history of mathematics, see Netz, 2003. For decades, the history of Ancient Greek mathematics had been studied nearly in complete isolation from the broader social contexts. A seminal paper by Sabetai Unguru (1975) represented a historiographical turning point, with its plea for historically contextualized analysis.

3). In particular, with respect to the Chinese tradition, Lloyd argued that the fact that argumentation in China was primarily directed toward people in positions of authority (rulers) entailed conditions that were not favorable for the emergence of the kind of argumentation that characterizes Euclidean mathematics (Lloyd, 2013).[6] By contrast, in the Greek context, argumentation was primarily directed toward equals, namely fellow citizens, and these were also often 'adversaries' in the sense of defending contrary positions. Against this background, the kind of argumentation that is *incontrovertible* and *indefeasible* is particularly valuable (though, of course, one should not expect these to be *sufficient* conditions for the emergence of these modes of argumentation either).

Netz estimates the formative period, when portions of Greek mathematics took a 'Euclidean turn,' as 440–360 BCE (440 BCE is a more speculative estimation; 360 BCE pertains to Aristotle's references to mathematical knowledge that is already by and large 'Euclidean'). There is an old debate on the primacy of mathematics vis-à-vis philosophy/dialectic or vice versa when it comes to historical origins: Árpád Szabó (1978) famously claimed that mathematics grew out of dialectic, but this view is not widely shared (see, for example, Mueller, 1974 for a different account). Fortunately, we need not take a position on this issue: what matters for our purposes is that mathematicians and philosophers/dialecticians were largely overlapping groups of thinkers (e.g. the Pythagoreans) exposed to the same general polemical background of Athenian democracy (though, of course, not all of them were Athenians). Tradition has it that the sentence, 'Let no one ignorant of geometry enter' was engraved on the door of Plato's Academy, and indeed Plato offers extensive discussions of mathematics in many of his dialogues – including in the *Republic*, purportedly a dialogue on moral and political philosophy. For Plato, future rulers of the city must be extensively trained in mathematics, as mathematics is also 'good for the soul' (Burnyeat, 2000).[7]

A specific passage from Netz (parts of which are quoted elsewhere in this book) perfectly summarizes what is so distinctive about this mathematical tradition, and how it is connected to the Greek social and political context:

Greek mathematics reflects the importance of persuasion. It reflects the role of orality, in the use of formulae,[8] in the structure of proofs, and in its reference to an immediately present visual object. But this orality is regimented into a written form, where

---

[6] In Chapter 6, when discussing the Chinese logical tradition, Lloyd's thesis will be further discussed.

[7] A topic I would have liked to discuss more extensively here is the extent to which Plato's analyses of mathematics echo the main claims in this chapter concerning the genealogical development of deduction in Ancient Greece. For reasons of space (and time), this important topic has not received the treatment it deserves here.

[8] Formulae are strings of words (short phrases) that are used frequently and consistently for a certain concept, roughly what we might describe as 'technical terms.'

vocabulary is limited, presentations follow a relatively rigid pattern, and the immediate object is transformed into the written diagram – doubly written, for it is now inscribed with letters, so that even the visual object of mathematics becomes incomprehensible for one's less privileged compatriots. It is at once oral and written, a feature we have stressed many times so far in the book. We can now begin to see that this intersection represents an even more basic one – in simple terms, the intersection of democracy and aristocracy. (Netz, 1999, pp. 297–298)

What a mathematical proof in its early, still purely oral stages might have looked like is captured in a famous passage from Plato's *Meno* (82b–85d), where Socrates shows a young slave how to double the area of the square:[9]

SOCRATES: Tell me, boy, do you recognize that a square area is like this?
SLAVE: Yes.
SOCRATES : So a square area is one with all these lines equal, all four of them?
SLAVE: Certainly.
SOCRATES: And doesn't it also have these equal lines across the middle?
SLAVE: Yes.
SOCRATES: Now an area of this shape might come in different sizes?
SLAVE: Certainly.

The argument begins with a reference to an "immediately present visual object" (see Netz's quote above), presumably drawn in the ground: "a square area is like *this*," "*these* equal lines," etc. Socrates then goes on to show that the boy's initial intuitive answer to the problem of doubling the area of the square, namely to double the length of the lines that form the square, does not work (as the area is then quadrupled).[10] Instead, the area of a square is doubled by a square whose extremities correspond to the *diagonal* of the original square. This is shown by means of a clever diagram, which is an extremely effective device for persuasion. The boy (and the presumed audience) inevitably becomes convinced that this is the correct procedure to double the area of the square, as he is led to the answer by Socrates' astute questioning and the cognitive boost afforded by the diagram (which is constructed as the proof progresses, as is typical for diagrams in Euclidean proofs). The diagram allows the boy literally to *see* the correct answer.[11] Notice, however, that here the diagram is not yet lettered; even though it is customary in modern editions (e.g. Plato, 2010, from which the text above is

[9] In the *Meno*, the argument is intended to illustrate Plato's theory of recollection, according to which a soul before birth possesses full knowledge of the perfect forms, which is then lost through embodiment. Humans must thus 'recollect' the knowledge they once possessed.

[10] This step in the argument can be construed as an *elenchus*, a refutation whereby someone's initial beliefs are shown to lead to inconvenient consequences. See below for a detailed discussion of *elenchus*.

[11] The cognitive import of diagrams has been much discussed in the recent literature in the philosophy of mathematical practice. As noted in Carter, 2019 (which also contains a section on diagrams in Euclidean proofs), "moving about in the diagram, following the instructions made in the text, one comes to *see* that the proposition holds."

quoted) to add letters to the diagrams that accompany the text to refer to specific points (the diagrams themselves are also later additions),[12] the procedure is not part of the original text.

Now, while this proof cannot be said to be an instantiation of a Prover–Skeptic dialogue (given that the boy does not act as a skeptic), it does have a number of elements in common with the Prover–Skeptic model. Socrates, as the Prover, states the basics of the problem at the beginning and then proceeds to propose statements that his interlocutor may accept or reject, occasionally asking questions that require a more substantive answer from his interlocutor. Socrates allows the boy to explore an apparently intuitive answer, but subsequently shows that it is not correct. After a brief period of puzzlement for the boy, they backtrack and eventually reach the correct solution.

A comparison with a later proof, for example, the famous proof of the Pythagorean Theorem in Euclid's *Elements* (proposition 47 of Book I), is instructive to illustrate the transformations that had occurred in the meantime (the *Meno* is thought to have been written around 385 BCE, and the *Elements* is dated to circa 300 BCE).[13] The theorem was known before Euclid's proof, in fact also in Egyptian mathematics, and so before Pythagoras himself (see Thomas Heath's extensive commentary on the proof, 1908, Vol. 1, pp. 350–368). What is special about the proof in the *Elements* is that it follows rigorously and systematically from the postulates and axioms previously stated in the book.

Like the proof of how to double the area of the square in the *Meno*, Euclides' proof of the Pythagorean Theorem relies crucially on the construction of a diagram to obtain its persuasive effect.[14] Modern editions of the text (e.g. Heath) contain the final diagram constructed through the proof, but mere inspection of the final diagram is not likely to produce much persuasive effect. Instead, the diagram must be *constructed* following the steps described in the proof in order for explanatory persuasion to come about. In this proof, Euclid as the Prover is not only putting forward propositions for Skeptic to grant or reject: he is issuing *imperatives* for the reader to execute a number of procedures (see Chapter 3 on imperatives in Prover–Skeptic dialogues). We may thus say that the proof represents a 'dialogue' between the author of the text and its readers, who are instructed to carry out certain procedures.

---

[12] The diagrams in Euclid's *Elements* may also be later additions dating back to medieval manuscripts, rather than elements present in the original texts (Saito & Sidoli, 2012).

[13] Admittedly, it is not a given that a mathematical demonstration presented in a non-mathematical (philosophical) textual context can be taken to represent the status quo of mathematics then.

[14] There is an important distinction in the *Elements* between *theorems* and *problems*, and it is tempting to think that deductions pertain to theorems while constructions pertain to problems. However, constructions can also be used for theorems (Sidoli, 2018). Either way, for the present purposes, I am taking 'deduction' in a broad sense, thus covering different forms of arguments in the *Elements* (including constructions and answers to problems).

However, we also observe some of the crucial changes described by Netz. Here the elements of the diagram are given 'names' by means of letters, which by then had become established practice. Moreover, the use of third-person (passive) imperatives in the proof, another common feature in the *Elements*, and in fact more generally in Ancient Greek proofs,[15] suggests an 'impersonal' interlocutor rather than a specific interlocutor – for example, the boy in the passage from the *Meno*, where second-person imperatives are more naturally used. (Third-person imperatives are usually translated in English with expressions such as, 'let there be a triangle ABC . . .')

This concludes my brief discussion of Ancient Greek mathematics. For reasons of space, it must remain superficial, thus failing to do justice to the sophisticated scholarship produced on the topic by authors such as Heath, Wilbur Knorr, and Netz himself, whose work provides the basis for the present analysis. Nevertheless, these brief considerations should suffice to illustrate the general claim that, also in mathematics, deduction is born from a largely dialogical framework but then fairly quickly undergoes significant transformations.

5.5   Ancient Greek Dialectic

In this section, I discuss the practice of ancient dialectic, which provides the background (or so I argue) for the emergence of the first fully-fledged theory of deductive reasoning in Aristotle's syllogistic (to be discussed in Chapter 6).

5.5.1   General Background

In Section 5.2, I briefly mentioned the rhetoricians known as the sophists, who taught much-needed rhetorical skills to the citizens of Athens. Socrates, at least as portrayed in Plato's dialogues,[16] was particularly critical of the sophists for aiming only at persuasion, thus disregarding truth. Philosophers such as Socrates, Plato, and Aristotle rejected the sophists' (presumed) disregard for truth and their focus on superficial persuasion, and sought to establish a different model of intellectual inquiry (Irani, 2017).

Indeed, as vividly (though somewhat unfairly)[17] depicted in Plato's dialogue *Gorgias*, the *logos* of rhetoricians/sophists essentially consists in telling audiences what they want to hear rather than the hard truth (naturally, something

---

[15]   See Knorr, 1989 for the pervasiveness of these conventions, and an exception in a proof by Philo of Byzantium.

[16]   To many of his contemporaries, Socrates in fact belonged to the same 'ilk' as the sophists (Nehamas, 1990).

[17]   Throughout this section, my portrayal of the sophists will be restricted to the Socrates/Plato critical characterization of them. But most recent interpretations of the sophists as an intellectual movement shed a more positive light on them (Notomi, 2014).

particularly relevant in the context of garnering votes at the assembly). While, in theory, rhetoric has the potential to be used for the betterment of individual and society, Socrates maintains that, in practice, it is no more than a form of *flattery*, to be compared to pastry-baking and cosmetics, which may be pleasant at first but is ultimately detrimental (Moss, 2007).[18] The philosopher, by contrast, aims at the truth, even if exposure to the truth can be an unpleasant experience; philosophy is a 'bitter draft' (*Gorgias* 522a).

But the fact that Socrates and his followers aimed at truth does not mean they could ignore persuasion completely; indeed, they still lived in a democratic city where oral skills of persuasion remained of paramount importance. Arguably, they simply could not afford the luxury of disregarding debating skills and persuasion completely, as attested by Aristotle's very concrete instructions on how to be a good debater in the *Topics* and *Sophistical Refutations*. And thus, rather than aiming at truth *instead of* persuasion, we may say that they aimed at truth *with* persuasion (Irani, 2017). Indeed, even in the *Apology*, where he begins by contrasting persuasive speech and truth-telling, Socrates then goes on to try to convince the jury of his innocence (something he states explicitly). What they reject is persuasion that is mere flattery, causing a fleeting pleasurable experience but doing nothing to promote a virtuous life or the pursuit of intellectual inquiry.

A feature of this 'Socratic' conception of *logos* that differs from that of rhetoricians, and one of crucial significance for the present investigation, is that, instead of the long speeches of rhetoricians (presumably modeled on the debating procedures in the assembly and in court), the focus is on *dialogical interactions* where speakers take turns in quick succession. (Socrates explicitly eschews the long speeches of Gorgias in favor of a short style of speech; *Gorgias* 449b–c.) These dialogues came to be known as the practice of *dialectic*, which consists in conversations following a specific, fairly systematic structure: verbal bouts between two interlocutors, a questioner and an answerer, in front of an audience, possibly with a referee or judge.

The art of dialectic seems to predate Socrates and Plato, understood in its literal sense of *dialektikē*, 'the art of conversing': a debating practice that takes places in a concrete, multi-agent setting.[19] Some texts in fact attribute skills of question-and-answer bouts to the sophists themselves (Nehamas, 1990), and

---

[18] In the *Gorgias*, and in more detail in the *Republic*, Plato famously argued that the fact that politicians will always say what voters want to hear in order to garner support means that democracy itself is ultimately doomed as a political system.

[19] Scholars disagree on how best to understand the concept of dialectic, even in the restricted context of Ancient Greek thought (Duncombe & Dutilh Novaes, 2016). One popular view is that dialectic corresponds to the discovery of first principles. It is important to bear in mind that Socratic dialectic, as depicted in Plato's early dialogues, is different from the notion of dialectic that emerges from Plato's later dialogues. For our present purposes, however, it is obviously the dialogical sense that is relevant, and so predominantly *Socratic* dialectic.

the philosophers of the Eleatic school (Parmenides, Zeno) may also have engaged in such dialogues. Benoît Castelnérac and Mathieu Marion (2009, 2013) (following Wilpert, 1956/57) argue that the philosophers of the Eleatic school already relied on the practice of contradicting, for which the name 'antilogic' was used. Dialectic in this sense would be a version of 'antilogic':[20]

In Plato and Aristotle (and others before them), *antilogikē* refers to the practice of contradicting, and thus equally applies to long rhetorical speeches with opposite conclusions or the practice of arguing through short questions and answers to lead an opponent into contradicting himself. (Castelnérac & Marion, 2013, p. 2)

The practice of contradicting is thus the genus to which long and short speeches may belong, as long as they expose contradictions. That contradicting was a widespread discursive practice is, of course, not surprising, given the polemical social and political background. In a polemical context (be it political or intellectual), it is not sufficient to argue in favor of one's preferred position; it is also essential to be able to show the incongruity of the position of one's opponent, and to this end exposing its internal inconsistencies or its absurd implications is a particularly suitable method. A term used for the testing of an interlocutor's position is *elenchus*, which is usually translated as 'refutation' and will be discussed in detail in the next section.

What does a dialectical encounter look like, concretely? There are a number of detailed reconstructions of the basic features of this practice in the literature (Castelnérac & Marion, 2009, 2013; Fink, 2012). Aristotle's *Topics* and its 'ninth chapter,' the *Sophistical Refutations*, may be read as the (presumably) first regimentation and systematization of practices hitherto dictated by tacit rather than explicit rules. Aristotle's text thus provides support for a general description of these practices in the following terms:

First of all there are the agents: the questioner and the answerer. There may also have been an audience (*Sophistical Refutations* 16 175a20–30). The questioner has two main jobs: first, to extract a thesis, the 'starting point' for the debate from the answerer; second, to try to force the answerer to admit the contradictory of that starting point, by getting the answerer to agree to certain premises. Alternatively, the questioner can try to reduce the thesis to absurdity. In either case, the questioner aims to refute the answerer. Crucially, the starting point should be something that can be affirmed or denied (*Topics* 8.2. 158a14–22). For example, 'what is knowledge?' would not be allowed as a starting point, as the answerer cannot reply 'yes' or 'no.' The answerer, on the other hand, has only one task, which is to remain un-refuted within a fixed time (*Topics* 8.10. 161a1–15). If the answerer is refuted, then the answer should make clear that it is not their fault, but is due solely to the starting point (*Topics* 8.4. 159a18–22). (Duncombe & Dutilh Novaes, 2016, p. 3)

---

[20] However, on the conception of dialectic that emerges from Plato's later dialogues, which is closely connected with the theory of Forms, dialectic is strictly distinct from frivolous 'antilogic' (Nehamas, 1990).

Notice here the (apparently) adversarial character of these dialogues: questioner wants to refute answerer (or answerer's position), whereas answerer tries to maintain the consistency of her discursive commitments (Castelnérac & Marion, 2009), thus avoiding refutation. However, as we will see shortly, there is a complex interplay between adversariality and cooperation in dialectical encounters that deserves further scrutiny.

Crucially, the dialogical form may be more conducive to truthful speech than long speeches, because questioner and answerer can keep each other in check, as it were. A passage from *Republic* VII illustrates this point:

> The man who cannot by reason distinguish the Form of the Good from all others, who does not, *as in a battle, survive all refutations*, eager to argue according to reality and not according to opinion, and who does not come through all the tests without faltering in reasoned discourse – such a man you will say does not know the Good itself, nor any kind of good.[21] (534b–c, trans. Grube, emphasis added)

Moreover, for pedagogical purposes, short speeches are more conducive to enhancing the understanding of the pupil, who is required to engage actively with each step along the way (as in the passage from the *Meno* quoted above; see also Socrates' portrayal of himself as a midwife in the *Theaetetus*). Dialectical encounters thus allow for a careful scrutiny of views, whereas the long speeches of rhetoricians may mislead the audience (who are not allowed to ask pointed questions). (One is reminded here of John Stuart Mill's comment on the value of arguing with dissenters in *On Liberty*: "Both teachers and learners go to sleep at their post, as soon as there is no enemy in the field.") Indeed, it is the presupposition of a certain level of *adversariality* between questioner and arguer, or at least a highly critical stance, that ensures the truth-conduciveness of dialectic.

5.5.2   Elenchus

A key component of dialectic is thus the concept of *refutation*, or *elenchus* in Greek: questioner aims at refutation, answerer tries to avoid being refuted. But what exactly is an *elenchus*? Readers of Plato will undoubtedly recall the numerous instances where Socrates, by means of questions, elicits a number of discursive commitments from his interlocutors, only to go on to show that, taken together, these commitments are incoherent.[22]

---

[21] I owe reference to this passage to Luca Castagnoli. The battle metaphor for a dialectical encounter is also present in the *Philebus*.

[22] However, we should not take Plato's account as telling the whole story about what *elenchi* were for his immediate predecessors and his contemporaries (Lesher, 2002). More likely, the term was used to cover related but nevertheless diverse argumentative strategies (Castelnérac & Marion, 2009).

An *elenchus* is arguably best understood as a *test* of the overall coherence of a person's beliefs: "a test that shames those who fail it, and which cleanses their soul through that shaming" (Castelnérac & Marion, 2009, p. 51). The etymology of *elenchus* is related to shaming (Lesher, 2002), and, at least in some cases, it seems that Socrates is out to shame the interlocutor by exposing the incoherence of their set of beliefs. However, as noted by Socrates himself in the *Gorgias* (470c7–10), refuting is also what friends do to each other, a process whereby someone rids a friend of mistaken beliefs. (Similarly, an *elenchus* can also have pedagogical purposes, in interactions between masters and pupils.) Indeed, for the Greeks, shame did not have the same negative connotation that it presently has; it is best understood in the sense of virtues such as *honesty* and *humility*. Thus understood, an *elenchus* is essentially 'ad hominem' in that it is directed at the person rather than the thesis she maintains, but need not be construed as a personal attack.

This conception of *elenchus* is, however, not unanimously endorsed, and in fact there has been much discussion in the secondary literature on what exactly an *elenchus* is.[23] Vlastos (1982) proposed a particularly influential account, where two kinds of *elenchi* are distinguished: indirect *elenchus* and standard *elenchus*:

> Here [in the indirect *elenchus*] Socrates is uncommitted to the truth of the premise-set from which he deduces the negation of the refutand. This mode of argument is a potent instrument for exposing inconsistency within the interlocutor's beliefs. But it cannot be expected to establish the truth or falsehood of any particular thesis. For this Socrates must turn to standard *elenchus*. (Vlastos, 1982, p. 711)

He then goes on to describe what he dubs the standard *elenchus*:
(1) The interlocutor, "saying what he believes," asserts *p*, which Socrates considers false, and targets for refutation.
(2) Socrates obtains agreement to further premises, say *q* and *r*, which are logically independent of *p*. The agreement is ad hoc: Socrates does not argue for *q* or for *r*.
(3) Socrates argues, and the interlocutor agrees, that *q* and *r* entail *not-p*.
(4) Thereupon Socrates claims that *p* has been proved false, *not-p* true. (Vlastos, 1982, p. 712)

Vlastos' account of the 'standard *elenchus*' has been criticized by a number of scholars (e.g. Benson, 1995), who point out that the Socratic *elenchus* can only have a negative function, that is, merely to show that *p* is inconsistent with the interlocutor's other commitments but not that *p* is false. It is step (4) in Vlastos' reconstruction that is particularly contentious, as up to step (3) what has been achieved is merely to show the incoherence of the interlocutor's simultaneous commitment to *p*, *q*, and *r*.

---

[23] A useful recent review is Wolfsdorf, 2013.

But Vlastos' account highlights the similarities between an *elenchus* and a reductio ad absurdum argument; essentially, a reductio (where a reasoner states the initial hypothesis, goes on to show that it leads to absurdity, and then concludes the contradictory of the initial hypothesis) is an *elenchus* with one additional component, namely the final step where the falsity of the initial hypothesis is claimed. And so, dialectical refutations might be considered as *genealogical ancestors* of reductio arguments (Dutilh Novaes, 2016b).[24] It is not entirely unreasonable to conjecture that the practice of dialectical refutations may have had some influence on the development of the technique of reductio arguments, which is widespread in Greek mathematics and in Aristotle's theory of syllogistic.[25]

To illustrate this point, consider Zeno's paradoxes (recall that, according to Castelnérac and Marion, dialectic was possibly already practiced by the Eleatic philosophers). Indeed, they can be interpreted either as straightforward reductios or as *elenchi*. On the first interpretation, the result achieved is the establishment of the truth of Parmenides' theses to the effect that there is no plurality, no change, no movement, etc., once Zeno shows that assuming that there are such things leads to incoherence. On the second interpretation (and this is the position that Plato attributes to Zeno in *Parmenides* 128a–e), what is achieved is merely to show that the positions of the opponents of Parmenides lead to absurdity, and thus that they are not obviously correct, despite the apparent strangeness of Parmenides' own views. On this interpretation, an *elenchus* would function above all as a 'dialectical silencer' (Castagnoli, 2010) whereby the incoherence of the position of an interlocutor is made manifest.

For our purposes, what is essential in the interpretation of *elenchi* as aiming at a *person* – the discursive commitments of an interlocutor in a given dialectical encounter – rather than at a thesis or proposition is that it illustrates a stage in the genealogy of deduction where the dialogues in question are still very much 'personalized': concrete dialogical situations involving specific participants.[26] A successful *elenchus* shows that the interlocutor is confused in her beliefs taken together, and so would do well to revise them, without determining exactly what needs to be revised. (An *elenchus* can also simply

---

[24] I am here presupposing that *elenchi* are chronologically older than reductio arguments, which may not be the case (as precise dates for such developments in this period is a delicate matter, given scarce availability of earlier sources). However, nothing much hinges on a specific chronological order for my purposes: if *elenchi* and *reductio* arguments appeared roughly at the same period, the dialogical link still stands.

[25] Naturally, much more work would be required in order to substantiate the claim that dialectical refutations are genealogical ancestors of reductio arguments, in particular, extensive textual analysis. At this point, I offer it merely as a plausible hypothesis for further investigation.

[26] Another interesting aspect of Plato's views on dialectic that intersects with my dialogical account of deduction is the idea of internal discourse (Duncombe, 2016), which echoes the concept of an internalized interlocutor (see Chapters 4 and 9). Unfortunately, for reasons of space, I cannot offer a full discussion of this point here.

lead to *aporia*, i.e. showing that every viable option leads to undesirable consequences.) Moreover, this interpretation highlights the limits of dialectic as a method for truth-seeking; it cannot positively establish the truth or falsity of theses, only the coherence or incoherence of discursive commitments (sets of propositions) taken as a whole (though some theses may be more certain than others, i.e. those that are viewed as *endoxa*, widely held beliefs).

However, thus understood, dialectic does presuppose a tacit notion of relations of logical implication among propositions – for example, when an interlocutor affirms p and grants q and r, as in Vlastos' schema above, and it is shown that q and r together imply *not-p*. It is this relation of logical implication, for which Plato occasionally uses the term 'to syllogize' (e.g. *Gorgias* 479c),[27] that Aristotle will seek to systematize both in the *Topics* and in the *Prior Analytics* (see Chapter 6).

5.5.3   Adversariality and Cooperation in Dialectic

Thus seen, dialectic may appear as an essentially or even exclusively adversarial enterprise: questioner seeks to expose the incoherence of answerer's position, thus shaming answerer, whereas answerer does her best to defend herself from such 'attacks.' However, on closer inspection, dialectic also depends on a fair amount of *cooperation and goodwill* among interlocutors. Moreover, being exposed to shame through refutation can also serve as a possibly painful but beneficial 'treatment' to rid one of false beliefs.

In fact, being overly adversarial is precisely one of the reproaches addressed once again against the sophists, who according to Socrates/Plato are only interested in overpowering their interlocutors and 'scoring points' in purely eristic encounters (Nehamas, 1990). By contrast, the dialectical/philosophical goal of argumentation is to benefit oneself and others by revealing deeper truths about how to lead a virtuous life. Admittedly, Socrates is sometimes singularly nasty to his opponents, but he typically tailors his argumentation to the specific social position, interests, and dispositions of his interlocutors (Moulton, 1983). Arguably, he is nasty only when this is what is required to deal with recalcitrant interlocutors. Irani brings out the contrast between rhetoricians and philosophers in terms of

... the different interpersonal attitudes that Plato believes distinguish the rhetorical ethos from the philosophical ethos: whereas the former seeks to dominate or otherwise win over an audience, the latter seeks to benefit others. A philosophical attitude

---

[27] De Strycker, 1932 presents an extensive list of uses of *syllogismos* and related terms in Plato's dialogues. The term is used in different senses, and only a few of them can be read in the sense of inference/implication. One interesting sense refers to calculations, to 'add things up,' as also noted in Striker, 2009.

towards argument thus fundamentally requires a form of care according to Plato. (Irani, 2017, p. 6)

In this context, *friendship* emerges as a key factor for a successful dialectical encounter (and in fact as a central component of the philosophical attitude as a whole; Nichols, 2009). Indeed, Socrates explicitly says that refuting is what friends do to each other: "Then I'll be very grateful . . . to you if you refute me and rid me of nonsense; now don't be slow to benefit a friend, and refute me" (*Gorgias* 470c7–10). Moreover, a background of friendship is required for a dialectical encounter to be a legitimate truth-seeking enterprise, as described in the following passages where Socrates is addressing Callicles, his most formidable 'opponent' in the *Gorgias*:

> For I believe that someone who is to test adequately the soul which lives rightly and the soul which does not should have three things, all of which you have: knowledge, goodwill, and free speaking. (*Gorgias* 487a)
>
> Clearly, then, this is how it is now with these questions: if you agree with me about anything in the discussion, then this will have been adequately tested by me and you, and it will no longer need to be brought to another touchstone. For you would never have conceded it either from lack of wisdom, or from excess of shame,[28] nor would you concede it to deceive me; for you are a friend to me, as you say yourself.[29] In reality, then, agreement between you and me will finally possess the goal of truth. (*Gorgias* 487e)

(Here again we encounter what looks like an attribution of truth-conduciveness to dialectical encounters, as in the passage from the *Republic* quoted above.)

But just as friends sometimes need to share painful truths, the 'friendly' treatment of submitting someone to a refutation may be an unpleasant experience. Indeed, on this account of *elenchus*, shame is a fundamental component of the process (Tarnopolsky, 2010). It is the irritation and shame of being exposed as incoherent that clears the way for a sincere reconsideration of one's prior views (recall the passage from the *Meno* where Socrates shows to the boy that his initial idea on how to double the area of a square is incorrect). Having one's views challenged may lead to a *cleansing of the soul*, as described in a famous passage of the Sophist (230b–e). Ideally, the person refuted becomes angry at him/herself rather than at the refuter, and "it is in this way that they are liberated from those great, obstinate beliefs about themselves" (*Sophist*, 230c1–2).[30]

Indeed, Socrates presents himself as a 'doctor of the soul,' analogous to the physician who tends to the health of the body. The rhetorician is like a pastry

---

[28] The point here is that it takes courage to speak truthfully, i.e. to say what one really thinks.

[29] Of course, there is a fair amount of irony in this comment, as Callicles had so far presented himself as a cynical immoralist, with not much of a friendly disposition towards Socrates.

[30] I owe the reference to this passage to Tushar Irani.

chef, who offers delicious but unhealthy treats, whereas the philosopher is like a true doctor, who restores the health of a sick person even if the treatment itself is rather disagreeable. Philosophy is a beneficial craft, whereas rhetoric (as pastry-baking) is nothing but a flattering knack. (And yet, between the doctor and the pastry chef, the ignorant will oftentimes choose the pastry chef; Moss, 2007.) The medical metaphor thus highlights the idea that the goal of refuting someone is primarily not competitive, but rather to benefit the interlocutor.

A similar interplay between adversariality and cooperation underpins Aristotle's description of dialectic in the *Topics*. In chapter 4 of Book VIII, Aristotle distinguishes three modes of engaging in argumentation: eristic, which is purely competitive; didactic, for teachers and learners; and dialectic, for inquiry. He then claims that the details of the third mode have never been properly described, which he then sets out to do:

> But when it comes to dialectical meetings among people who engage in arguments not for the sake of competition, but for testing and inquiry (*peiras kai skepseos*), it has never been spelt out what the answerer must aim at, or what sorts of things he must grant and what not in order to <count as> defending his thesis well or not. (*Topics* 159a33–37)

The key notions here are 'testing and inquiry.' Testing echoes the notion of *elenchus* as testing described above; inquiry, in turn, seems to be "a means for exploring the consequences of different opinions as a part of philosophical inquiry" (Smith, 1997, p. 129). Inquiry, in particular, is a cooperative endeavor at a higher level, as there is a 'common work' to be accomplished. However, when one of the interlocutors is not sufficiently cooperative, then the dialogue becomes purely adversarial and is thus no longer dialectical:

> For it is not in the power of one participant alone to see that their common work is well accomplished. There are times, then, when it is necessary to attack the speaker, not the thesis – when the answerer is particularly abusive and ready to pounce on the questioner with the contrary of whatever he asks for. By being cantankerous, then, these people make discussions competitive and not dialectical. (*Topics* 161a20–25)
>
> And since it is a poor participant who impedes the common work, so it is clearly also in an argument. For there is also a common project in these (except for competitive ones: in these, it is not possible for both to achieve the same goal, for it is impossible for more than one to win.) (*Topics* 161a37–161b1)

And so, just as for the Lakatosian dialectic of proofs and refutation (Chapter 3), dialectic thus understood is characterized by a complex relationship between adversariality and cooperation. While at a lower level the practice appears purely competitive (questioner seeks to refute answerer; answerer seeks to avoid being refuted), at a higher level participants are in fact cooperating toward a common goal. (Recall option (4) of the different combinations of adversariality and cooperation discussed in Section 3.4 of Chapter 3.)

5.6   Conclusion

In this chapter, I have presented an account of the historical background for the emergence of the first worked-out theory of deduction with Aristotle's theory of syllogistic, to be presented in Chapter 6. The two main sources of influence for Aristotle were deductive argumentation in mathematics and practices of dialectic, both discussed in this chapter. In other words, while deduction in practice existed prior to Aristotle's logical works, it is in *Prior Analytics* that deduction as such is theorized explicitly for the first time, as we will see in the next chapter.

6   Aristotle's Syllogistic and Other Ancient Logical Traditions

6.1   Introduction

In this chapter, I discuss the first fully-fledged theory of deduction, namely Aristotle's syllogistic, focusing in particular on *Prior Analytics* (the theory of demonstration of *Posterior Analytics* will occasionally be referred to). Aristotle often claims in his writings to be the first to accomplish a number of important feats, drawing on his predecessors but faulting them for failing to get to the full picture. With respect to deduction, though, this is not a mere rhetorical device: he really seems to have been the first to systematize the concept of deduction as such, in particular the crucial clause 'resulting by necessity,' which is what differentiates deduction from other forms of reasoning and argumentation such as induction and analogy.

However, Aristotle's logic, and Greek logic more generally, was not the only ancient logical tradition where sustained attention was devoted to argumentation and inferential relations. In particular, sophisticated investigations on this topic can also be found in Chinese and especially Indian writings. Given the emphasis on the role of social and political conditions for the emergence of logical theories in the present investigation, it makes sense to consider social and political conditions that are significantly different from those found in Greece (and Athens in particular), and the logical theories emerging in these other contexts. We will see that, as predicted by the model adopted here (which is inspired by the work of G.E.R. Lloyd and Reviel Netz), in these different circumstances, the logical theories emerging are substantially different, in particular in that they do not single out the class of arguments having the property of necessary truth-preservation as particularly significant (though later Indian logicians seem to do so). In other words, specific theories of deduction are not to be found in these other ancient traditions. However, this does not mean that they are more 'primitive' or elementary; it simply means that classical Indian and Chinese thinkers had other interests and goals, for which necessary truth-preservation was not especially relevant.

We start with Aristotle's syllogistic, focusing on its roots in dialectic, the influential definition of syllogism at the beginning of *Prior Analytics*, the celebrated theory of the figures developed in the early chapters of this book, and arguments 'leading to the impossible.' Next, we turn to logic in India and then to logic in China.

6.2   Aristotle's Syllogistic

As we've seen, the discursive practices of Aristotle's predecessors, dialectic in particular, presupposed a tacit, non-theorized notion of implication as a relation holding between statements. Aristotle was the first to formulate a precise theory of implication: the theory of syllogistic as presented in *Prior Analytics*. This theory is rightly described as the first regimentation of deductive reasoning in the history of logic, and thus as the first logical theory as such.

6.2.1   From Dialectic to Syllogistic

The relations between dialectic and Aristotle's logic, in particular syllogistic, have been fiercely debated in the literature (Duncombe & Dutilh Novaes, 2016). One frequently discussed question is genetic/historical: does syllogistic *originate* from dialectical practices? It is generally thought that Aristotle's so-called dialectical texts (*Topics* and *Sophistical Refutations*) were composed before the two *Analytics*, but this is not sufficient to establish a stronger genetic, causal relation between his reflections on dialectic and the emergence of syllogistic. Some scholars (e.g. Smith, 1994) maintain that syllogistic's origins are not to be found in dialectical practices but rather in Aristotle's concern with the concept of *scientific demonstration*, which is the object of the *Posterior Analytics*. Because a demonstration is a kind of deduction, he first needs to provide a theory of deduction in the *Prior Analytics* in order to ground the theory of demonstration in the *Posterior Analytics*.

Others contend that syllogistic is indeed best understood as emerging from a dialectical matrix; it presupposes a dialectical framework and responds to needs that arise in the context of these dialogical practices (Kapp, 1975; Hintikka, 1995). Arguments in favor of the view that there is a strong relation between dialectic and Aristotle's logic may be philological; for example, Benoît Castelnérac (2015) identifies significant terminological similarities between Plato's *Gorgias* and Aristotle's *Analytics*. Such arguments may also be conceptual if they show that, in order to understand certain otherwise puzzling features of syllogistic, we must take into account the dialectical background. For example, Mathieu Marion and Helge Rückert (2016) argue that the famous principle of *dictum de omni* stated in the *Prior Analytics* is closely related to the rule for the universal quantifier as stated in the *Topics*.

Indeed, as noted by Benedict Einarson (the very scholar who first identified the terminological similarities between the *Analytics* and mathematics), "the point of view of the dialectician is always taken into account in the *Prior Analytics*" (Einarson, 1936, p. 37).

Notice though that, in a sense, this is a false dichotomy: it is perfectly plausible that different interests of Aristotle's will have influenced the development of syllogistic simultaneously. (Castelnérac, 2015 makes a similar point.) Indeed, at the very beginning of the *Prior Analytics*, Aristotle distinguishes between two kinds of deductions (*syllogismoi*),[1] dialectical and demonstrative deductions, and this suggests that both sets of considerations, dialectical *and* scientific, are relevant for the theory of syllogistic. Moreover, dialectic and mathematics were not completely distinct enterprises: as noted in Chapter 5, in Plato's dialogues, comparisons between mathematical and dialectical contexts and procedures/reasoning abound. In the *Theaetetus*, for example, Socrates' interlocutor is Theaetetus, a promising young mathematician and philosopher, chosen as an interlocutor to illustrate general features of the Socratic method. In passage 147d–148b, an explicit analogy is presented between the Socratic method and mathematical reasoning/argumentation (in this case, referring to what we now call the roots of non-square numbers).[2]

Now that the dialectic vs. mathematics dichotomy has been shown not to hold, let us first discuss how syllogistic may have been motivated by dialectical concerns. Recall that, in an *elenchus*, questioner first secures answerer's commitment to a thesis *p*. She then asks answerer to grant some additional propositions *q* and *r*, so as to show that *q* and *r* imply *not-p*, and thus that answerer's discursive commitments as a whole are incoherent. But what is the exact nature of the relation of implication between premises *q* and *r* and conclusion *not-p*? Is it one of *deductive* implication, where the premises necessitate the conclusion?

Plato's dialogues and other textual evidence suggest that, in dialectical encounters, various kinds of arguments – analogical, inductive, enthymematic, etc. – were presumably used to establish that, from *q* and *r*, *not-p* follows, in different senses of 'following' (De Strycker, 1932). In other words, it seems that an *elenchus* does not require, in the strict sense, a relation of implication that is necessarily truth-preserving; an *elenchus* may expose a tension in answerer's set of beliefs, even if *q* and *r* are compatible with *p* but make *not-p* much more plausible: reasonable doubt (rather than necessity) is already

---

[1] It is not obvious how to translate the Greek term συλλογισμός as used by Aristotle. Robin Smith translates it as 'deduction,' following a tradition initiated by Corcoran (Smith, 1994), while Gisela Striker (Striker, 2009) maintains the neologism 'syllogism.' 'Deduction' may be too broad, as Aristotle's definition of a syllogism excludes some arguments that we would be prepared to describe as deductions (e.g. single-premise arguments). But 'syllogism' is too narrow in that it is strongly associated with the restricted class of arguments for which Aristotle develops a formal theory in the *Prior Analytics*, restricted to categorical sentences of the A, E, I, and O forms.

[2] I owe the reference to this passage to Tushar Irani.

sufficient. In this case, the set of beliefs $\{q, r, not\text{-}p\}$ would be more plausible than the set $\{q, r, p\}$, even if the latter is still not entirely impossible.

However, if the relation of implication between premises q and r and conclusion $not\text{-}p$ is one of *necessity*, then an *elenchus* will be a much more powerful tool to show the incoherence of a set of discursive commitments than if the relation of implication in question is weaker. In this case, $\{q, r, not\text{-}p\}$ is the *only* coherent option available, so answerer is more strongly compelled to revise her beliefs, as $\{q, r, p\}$ will have been shown to be entirely impossible. This means that, while perhaps not mandatory for an *elenchus* as originally conceived, in a dialectical context a deductive relation of implication, where the premises *necessarily* imply the conclusion, is much to be preferred over other, weaker types of implication. At this stage, necessary truth-preservation is *strategically advantageous* for questioner, who seeks to expose the incoherence of answerer's discursive commitments, even if an *elenchus* may also go through with weaker types of implication. This alone would provide significant motivation for someone like Aristotle to develop a detailed theory of deductive implication, given the clear advantages it would confer on anyone participating in a dialectical encounter over weaker types of inference.

But Aristotle goes a step beyond, and declares at the beginning of the *Sophistical Refutations* that a deduction is a *constitutive* feature of an *elenchus*: "A refutation is a deduction (*syllogismos*) together with the contradictory of the conclusion" (165a2–3). In other words, for Aristotle, the argument from q and r leading to $not\text{-}p$ in an *elenchus* must be a necessarily truth-preserving argument, as indeed required by the definition of *syllogismos* offered in the *Sophistical Refutations*:[3]

A deduction is from certain things which have been assumed, in such a way as to *necessarily* lead to the assertion of something else than what has been assumed, through what has been assumed. (164b27–165a2, emphasis added; translation from Malink, 2014)

We are thus quite far from Plato's more liberal uses of arguments in dialectic.[4] Indeed, Aristotle seems to exclude arguments that are not necessarily truth-preserving from the realm of dialectic by stipulating that a refutation must always be constituted by a deductive implication (though in practice, in the *Topics*, he discusses other kinds of arguments too). Equally important is the observation that many features of the very definition of *syllogismos* appear to

---

[3] Aristotle formulates very similar (though not identical) definitions of *syllogismos* in the *Topics*, *Sophistical Refutations*, *Rhetoric*, and *Prior Analytics*.

[4] See Shorey, 1924 and Solmsen, 1951 for opposing views on the extent to which the gist of Aristotelian syllogistic is already present in Plato's dialogues. One recurrent suggestion in the literature is that Plato's method of division may have been a source of inspiration for the development of syllogistic (De Strycker, 1932).

be motivated by the need to avoid (and to spot) fallacious arguments (the topic of the *Sophistical Refutations*), as argued in Malink, 2014.

And yet, it is undeniable that there are fundamental differences between Aristotle's analyses of *syllogismoi* in his dialectical texts, *Topics* and *Sophistical Refutations*, and the theory presented in the *Prior Analytics*. Crucially, in the dialectical texts there is no mention of the theory of the figures that is presented in the first chapters of the *Prior Analytics* (to be discussed shortly) and is rightly viewed as a colossal breakthrough in the history of logic. There are, moreover, other significant differences that clearly indicate an important transformation in the genealogical development of the concept of deduction from Aristotle's dialectical texts to the theory of syllogistic in *Prior Analytics*. As mentioned at the beginning of Chapter 5, the two main transformations concern a 'de-personalization' of discourse in the move from dialectical to logical contexts (hints of which are already present in Plato's dialogues), and the recourse to the written medium. I now focus on the former, and discuss the latter in Section 6.2.3.

Marko Malink (2015) poses the question of what is distinctive about the *Prior Analytics* in terms of what makes the theory presented in this text formal (in a modern sense of 'formal'). While the question of formality as such is not our main concern here, the features identified by Malink as differentiating deduction in the *Topics* from deduction in *Prior Analytics* indicate a process of de-personalization. While in the *Topics* Aristotle is concerned with more or less concrete dialogical situations involving specific participants, in the early chapters of *Prior Analytics* he focuses on deductive arguments in abstraction from these specific situations. For one thing, while in dialectical contexts the relevant speech acts are questions and answers to elicit discursive commitment from the answerer,[5] in the *Prior Analytics* the basic units considered are categorical sentences, which are considered in abstraction from specific dialogical interactions. This is precisely the point where the relevant dialogues come to involve a Prover and a (tacit, silent) Skeptic rather than questioner and answerer. Malink identifies a number of other significant differences:

First, the *Prior Analytics* abstracts from speaker meaning and only takes into account the literal meaning of the sentences involved in a deduction. Nothing of relevance is left to tacit understanding between speaker and hearer … Secondly, Aristotle is concerned to make explicit all premises that are necessary to deduce the conclusion in a given argument. Thirdly, Aristotle provides a criterion for determining when all the necessary premises have been made explicit … Fourthly, deductions are formulated in a language that is supposed to be free from homonymy and ambiguity. (Malink, 2015, pp. 300–301)

---

[5] As noted in De Strycker, 1932, in Plato's dialogues there are virtually no occurrences of arguments that run continuously from premises to conclusion without interventions from the secondary interlocutor-answerer, if only to answer with a simple 'yes.'

Malink views the requirement that all premises needed for the argument to go through be made explicit as particularly significant. Indeed, what distinguishes deductive argumentation from other forms of argumentation is that all the relevant information must be 'on the table'; no hidden assumptions are tolerated (as discussed in Chapter 1). In a dialectical context, participants typically share a fair amount of tacit assumptions, *endoxa*, which need not be made explicit. But when one abstracts from a specific context/interlocutor and addresses a *universal audience*,[6] then all premises must be made explicit. More than the mathematical theory of figures, what makes the *Prior Analytics* the first treatise on deductive logic proper is the concern with making fully explicit all the premises that are necessary to derive the conclusion in a given deduction. This, I argue, results from moving away from embodied, situational elements of concrete dialogical situations towards a more abstract, 'de-personalized' approach to argumentation (which is evident also in the focus on literal meaning rather than on speaker's meaning identified by Malink), in particular with increased focus on demonstration instead of *elenchus*.

But while we may speak of a real transformation from dialectic to syllogistic in the conception of *syllogismos*, dialectical/dialogical features remain pervasive in *Prior Analytics*. The theory of the figures in the first chapters of Book I (including modal syllogistic) is the most celebrated contribution of *Prior Analytics*, but taken as a whole, many more pages are dedicated to dialectical aspects (especially in the unjustly neglected Book II) than to the formal/ mathematical approach. One recurring concern, particularly conspicuous in chapter 27 of Book I, is with a method to find the premises needed in order to establish a given conclusion. This method is especially useful in dialectical contexts, where one starts with a certain thesis as accepted by answerer and must look for premises that will imply the contradictory of the thesis accepted. Moreover, there is much attention in *Prior Analytics* to methods that allow for the regimentation of arguments in ordinary language so as to make them fit the machinery of the mathematical theory of syllogistic (Dutilh Novaes, 2015c), precisely because the goal is to show that this mathematical theory is also applicable in a wide range of concrete situations of argumentation.

6.2.2   The Definition of Syllogismos

To further argue that dialectical traces are still very much present in the conception of *syllogismos* of *Prior Analytics*, I now discuss in detail Aristotle's definition of *syllogismos* from *Prior Analytics* 24b18–22. Tellingly, he offers very similar definitions of *syllogismos* in the *Topics*, *Sophistical Refutations*, and the

---

[6] This is a concept developed by Chaim Perelman within the 'new rhetoric' approach (Perelman & Olbrechts-Tyteca, 1969).

Rhetoric, which suggests a general, unified conception of deduction present in these different domains of application. In Striker, 2009 (emphasis added), the definition is translated as:

A *syllogismos* is an argument (*logos*) in which, (i) certain *things* being posited (*tethentōn*), (ii) something *other* than what was laid down (*keimenōn*) (iii) results by *necessity* (*ex anagkēs sumbainei*) (iv) because these things are so. By 'because these things are so' I mean that it results through these, and by 'resulting through these' I mean that no term is required from outside for the necessity to come about.

A *syllogismos* thus has four main features:
  (i) There are at least two premises which are posited.
 (ii) The conclusion is different from the premises.
(iii) The conclusion follows necessarily from the premises.
(iv) The premises imply the conclusion by themselves; they are jointly necessary and sufficient for the conclusion to be produced.[7]

Each of these clauses can receive natural dialogical interpretations, pertaining both to dialectic and to demonstrations.[8] As Aristotle presents it in the first chapter of *Prior Analytics*, the distinction between dialectical and demonstrative syllogisms seems to pertain exclusively to the status of the premises: if known to be true and more primary than the conclusion, then the syllogism will be demonstrative; if merely 'reputable' (*endoxa*), then the syllogism is dialectical. But with respect to the *pragmatics* of the two situations, there are other relevant differences. In particular, demonstrative syllogisms used in the context of teaching will presuppose an asymmetric relationship between the interlocutors (teacher and pupil), whereas in a dialectical context, although questioner and answerer have different roles to play, their statuses are usually comparable – they are peers. Indeed, the overall goals of a demonstration are quite different from the goals of a dialectical disputation, even if both can rely on syllogistic as a background theory of argumentation.

(i) **Multiple premises.** This requirement excludes single-premise arguments as deductively valid. In the mathematical theory of the figures subsequently developed in *Prior Analytics*, the arguments considered are almost exclusively those that we now refer to as syllogistic arguments, namely those composed of two premises and one conclusion, all of which are categorical sentences of the

[7] This gloss should not be understood in the sense that a *unique* set of premises is what allows for the derivation of a given conclusion; often, alternative sets of premises are equally able to produce a given conclusion. Rather, it should be understood as stating that the set of premises is *sufficient* for the necessary truth of the conclusion (no 'hidden premises'), and that the removal of any of the premises from the set would make the conclusion no longer deductively derivable. (I owe this point to Paul Thom.)

[8] See Barnes, 1969 for an interpretation of Aristotle's theory of demonstration (as presented in *Posterior Analytics*) according to which the primary use of this theory was didactic, thus referring to a teacher–pupil form of dialogical interaction.

A, E, I, or O forms. But this definition excludes, for example, the conversion rules (from 'Some A is B' infer 'Some B is A' and vice versa; from 'No A is B' infer 'No B is A' and vice versa). Moreover, consider the following description of the general enterprise:

Aristotle intended his syllogistic to serve as a general theory of valid deductive argument, rather than a formal system designed for a limited class of simple propositions. (Striker, 2009, p. 79)

If we accept this interpretation of syllogistic (which I've also defended in Dutilh Novaes, 2015c), then the specific features of the theory later developed in *Prior Analytics* should not be taken to explain the general definition at the beginning; this would amount to putting the cart before the horse, as it were. Indeed, it is the mathematical theory that is meant to offer a regimented account of the conceptual starting point, which is the general notion of a valid deductive argument. So the fact that the arguments considered later in the text always have exactly two premises cannot be summoned to explain the multiple-premise requirement.

What could then explain this requirement? As noted in Striker, 2009 (p. 79) and De Strycker, 1932, the verb 'to syllogize' also means 'to add up,' 'to compute/calculate,' and so it suggests the idea of 'putting things together,' of a fusion of multiple elements. Especially from a dialectical perspective, the multiple premises requirement makes good sense. In a dialectical situation, questioner elicits a number of discourse commitments from answerer, and then goes on to show that they are collectively incoherent in an *elenchus*. Typically, a refutation will not come about with only one discursive commitment: it is usually the *interaction* of multiple commitments that gives rise to interesting (and sometimes embarrassing) conclusions.

Notice also the use of the terms 'posited' and 'laid down,' which are frequently used in connection with dialectic. They introduce the dimension of a speech act, of an agent actually putting forward premises to an interlocutor or audience, again suggesting multi-agent situations (though here in the third-person passive imperative, incidentally the same grammatical construction found in Euclid's demonstration mentioned in Chapter 5). Later authors such as Boethius will make the multi-agent dimension even more explicit, adding that the premises are not only laid down by the producer but also granted by the receiver. (I discuss Boethius' definition briefly in Chapter 7.)

(ii) **Irreflexivity.** Aristotle's requirement that the conclusion be different from the premises seems puzzling at first sight, since it entails that the consequence relation underlying syllogistic is irreflexive. This is in tension with the currently widely accepted idea that reflexivity is a core feature of deductive validity, i.e. A implies A for all A. (See Chapter 4 for a discussion of reflexivity as a property of the consequence relation.)

However, here again, taking into account the various contexts of application of syllogistic arguments, irreflexivity makes good sense for each of them (as argued in Duncombe, 2014). Indeed, in a demonstrative context, the function of a syllogism is to lead from the known to the unknown, and so obviously premises and conclusion should be different. (In more technical terms, the relation between premises and conclusion in a demonstration is a relation of *grounding*, which is irreflexive and asymmetric.) In a dialectical context, it makes no sense to ask an interlocutor to grant as a premise precisely that which one seeks to establish as a conclusion; this would amount to an instance of *petitio principii*. Thus, the irreflexivity of the syllogistic consequence relation is exactly what one would expect, given the applications Aristotle has in mind when developing the theory.

(iii) **Necessary truth-preservation.** Aristotle distinguishes deductive arguments from those whose premises make the conclusion likely but not certain, such as induction (*Prior Analytics* 23) or arguments from example (*Prior Analytics* 69a). When defining *syllogismos*, he stresses in particular the property of necessary truth-preservation as what distinguishes a *syllogismos* from these other kinds. (Naturally, necessary truth-preservation is a necessary but not sufficient condition for deductive validity, in light of the three other clauses.)

While it is an excessive demand for most (practical) purposes, the 'results by necessity' clause makes sense in what are presumably the main contexts of application of deductive arguments, demonstrative and dialectical contexts. As argued above, in a dialectical context, an argument having this property will 'force' an interlocutor to grant the conclusion, if she has granted the premises (the conclusion *must* be true if the premises are), and so it is a strategically advantageous property for questioner. (As discussed in Chapter 3, in game-theoretical terms, the property of necessary truth-preservation ensures that the argument will be a *winning strategy* for the person proposing it.) In a demonstrative context, Aristotle's whole theory of demonstration is premised on the idea of deriving rock-solid conclusions from self-evident axioms (Barnes, 1969), and thus again necessary truth-preservation becomes advantageous to ensure certainty. So, for different reasons, necessity makes sense both for dialectical and for demonstrative applications of arguments.

(iv) **Sufficiency and necessity of the premises.** This is the most obscurely formulated of the four clauses in the definition. In the *Topics*, his gloss of this clause is more transparent than in *Prior Analytics*, as described by Striker:

The definition as given in the *Topics* is clearer in this respect: it has the clause 'through the **things** laid down' instead of 'because these things are so.' In this passage, Aristotle adds the remark that this clause should also be understood to mean that all premises needed to derive the conclusion have been explicitly stated. (Striker, 2009, p. 81)

This clause has been variously interpreted by commentators; some of them read it as a strictly logical requirement, others as a metaphysical requirement. Some commentators, in particular in the Arabic tradition, have interpreted this clause as a requirement for an essential, metaphysical connection between premises and conclusion (Thom, 2016). But the clause can also be interpreted logically as stating that no premise should be *redundant* for the conclusion to come about; all of them are de facto needed for the conclusion to result of necessity. This is indeed one of the two main formulations of the requirement of relevance in modern relevant logics, known as 'derivational utility' (Read, 1988, section 6.4), and in this sense Aristotelian syllogistic is very naturally interpreted as a relevant system (Steinkrüger, 2015).

Moreover, as Aristotle's gloss suggests, this clause can also be read as a requirement that *everything* that is needed for the conclusion to result of necessity be explicitly stated; there are no hidden premises required ("no term is required from outside"). As discussed in Section 6.2.1 and argued in Malink, 2015, the demand that all premises be made explicit is arguably what truly distinguishes the approach in *Prior Analytics* from the *Topics*. And so, this clause as a whole may be read as the requirement that the premises laid down are *exactly* those needed for the conclusion to come about; no more, no less.

In demonstrative contexts, this clause is very reasonable: for Aristotle, a demonstration is an explication unearthing the *causes* of a given phenomenon, and so both redundancy and 'missing premises' go against this desideratum. In dialectical contexts, however, both these requirements are less straightforward: the participants may have a fair amount of *endoxa* in common, which could plausibly be taken for granted without having to be explicitly put forward; and redundancy may be advantageous in purely adversarial contexts, as asking for various redundant premises may serve the strategic purpose of confusing one's opponent. But as we've seen in Chapter 5, in the *Topics* Aristotle wants to move away from purely adversarial dialectical disputes towards a more cooperative model – dialectic as inquiry, where two parties together consider what would follow from given assumptions. In such contexts, redundancy would be out of place, and relevance comes out as a notion related to cooperativeness (as argued in Dutilh Novaes & French, 2018).

But what does this all mean? I do not take this dialogical interpretation of the definition of *syllogismos* to constitute decisive evidence for the claim that the theory of syllogistic as presented in *Prior Analytics* is ultimately a theory of dialectic, or that it emerges exclusively from dialectical considerations. In fact, I've also referred to demonstrative contexts several times. Following the principles of conceptual genealogy, I take it that the notion of deduction (*syllogismos*) in *Prior Analytics* is already a hybrid notion, containing dialectical/dialogical components which are now mixed with other strands of Aristotle's thought – in particular his theory of demonstration, the inspiration from mathematics, and a concern with speaking to 'universal audiences' beyond specific dialectical situations.

6.2.3   The Theory of the Figures

From the point of view of contemporary logic, the most impressive achievement of *Prior Analytics* is the mathematical theory of the figures, presented in the early chapters of Book I. It consists of a systematic study of a rather small class of arguments, namely those composed of two premises and one conclusion, all of which display one of four possible structures, the so-called categorical sentences:

>   **A**: All A is B.
>   **E**: No A is B.
>   **I**: Some A is B.
>   **O**: Some A is not B.

(Aristotle himself actually mostly uses different formulations, such as 'B belongs to all A,' but for convenience of presentation I stick to the more familiar subject–copula–predicate structure.) Aristotle systematically investigates which combinations of premises in this class produce necessary conclusions. He defines two properties of such arguments: figure and mood. Figure pertains to the mutual disposition of the three terms that must occur in a syllogistic argument: the major term is the predicate of the conclusion, the minor term is the subject of the conclusion, and the middle term is the one which occurs in both premises but not in the conclusion. The three figures are as follows (M for middle term, S for subject of the conclusion, and P for predicate of the conclusion):[9]

First	Second	Third
M/P	P/M	M/P
S/M	S/M	M/S
S/P	S/P	S/P

Mood pertains to the quantity (universal or particular) and the quality (affirmative or negative) of the sentences. There are invalid as well as valid moods; the valid ones acquired special names intended as mnemonic devices in the Middle Ages. Of the 256 possible combinations of premises and conclusion, twenty-four are said by Aristotle to constitute valid deductions.

Aristotle posits that some moods in the first figure are perfect/complete in that their validity is immediately apparent to us (later known as Barbara, Celarent,

---

[9] Combinatorially, there is a fourth figure possible, but it is usually viewed as equivalent to the first figure.

Darii, and Ferio); importantly, perfection/completion is an *epistemic* property of a syllogism, pertaining to its self-evidence (Corcoran, 2003). He then goes on to show for the other twenty valid moods that they can be deduced from the perfect syllogisms and a few other rules of inference, in particular conversion (from 'No A is B' infer 'No B is A'; from 'Some A is B' infer 'Some B is A') and subalternation (From 'All A is B' infer 'Some A is B') (Andrade-Lotero & Dutilh Novaes, 2012). For combinations of premises that do not deliver a necessary conclusion, he shows them to be compatible both with a putative conclusion *p* and its contradictory. Eventually, he has a complete characterization of validity for this limited class of arguments in that, for each pair of premises, it can be determined whether it produces necessary conclusions.

A crucial feature of the theory is its use of schematic letters. Netz (1999) explicitly relates the use of schematic letters by Aristotle in the two *Analytics* to the practice of using letters to denote points in geometrical diagrams. He hypothesizes that Aristotle may have been inspired by this (by then) well-established mathematical practice for the introduction of schematic letters in his logical work. In effect, the generality afforded by the use of letters in diagrams may have been Aristotle's inspiration to use letters to designate arbitrary terms.[10] This feature also allows for meta-properties of the system to be investigated, as in the first chapters of *Prior Analytics*.

Smith (1978) concurs with Netz on the geometrical origin for the use of schematic letters in the *Prior Analytics*, and goes a step further: inspired by the terminological similarities between the language of Aristotle's logical writings and that of Ancient Greek mathematics identified in Einarson, 1936, he claims that the theory of the figures simply *is* a mathematical theory, modeled after proportion theory and harmony (both established branches of mathematics at the time). Smith documents a number of striking similarities between arguments presented in the *Prior Analytics* and mathematical texts in the 'Euclidean' tradition, thus convincingly establishing that Aristotle's syllogistic was heavily inspired by the mathematics of his time.

However, Smith's conclusion that syllogistic is thus *not* a logical theory (because it is a *mathematical* theory) is less convincing. He claims that "syllogistic probably did not develop from Aristotle's reflections on argument so much as from his early attempts to carry out a Platonic program for mathematizing epistemology" (Smith, 1978, p. 209). Smith is of course aware that the bulk of *Prior Analytics*, especially all of Book II, is explicitly concerned with arguments, but he thinks that these are later additions to the theory. It seems, though, that here

---

[10] Notice that the concept of schematic letter (placeholder) must be distinguished from the concept of a (functional) *variable*, which emerged much later within mathematics: a mathematical variable stands for an unknown but determinate value, whereas a schematic letter is a device of generality, indicating a range of possible instantiations. Moreover, in the modern usage of these concepts, schematic letters range over terms while variables range over objects of the domain.

again we are dealing with a false dichotomy: the theory can very well be both a mathematical *and* a logical theory, in different senses. On my interpretation, the theory is a response to the need for a precise theory of implication both in dialectic and in scientific demonstration, and so in this sense *logical*. But it is simultaneously a *mathematical* theory in that the formal apparatus that Aristotle develops is inspired by mathematics. The structure of the theory is mathematical; the content is not.

Be that as it may, it is clear that the use of schematic letters and reference to visual categories such as the relative disposition of terms in an argument (to differentiate the three figures) indicates significant influence of the written medium.[11] It is in this sense that, just like mathematics, Aristotle's syllogistic is "at once oral and written" (Netz, 1999, p. 298).

6.2.4   Arguments 'Leading to the Impossible' in Prior Analytics

A distinctive feature of *Prior Analytics* is the extensive use of what we now call reductio ad absurdum arguments; this feature, too, indicates a strong connection both with mathematics, where reductio proofs were already widely used in Aristotle's time, and with dialectic, given that an *elenchus* is essentially a reductio argument minus the final step of retracting one of the initial assumptions and thus coming to a positive conclusion (as argued above). More generally, as argued in Castelnérac, 2015, the concept of impossibility (*adunaton*) plays an important role in *Prior Analytics* also beyond arguments 'leading to the impossible' (*apagōgē dia tou adunatou*), as Aristotle calls reductio arguments. But, for our purposes, it is these arguments that are particularly relevant. Aristotle contrasts ostensive arguments (starting with categorically stated premises) with arguments from an assumption/hypothesis (*Prior Analytics* A23). Arguments leading to the impossible are for him a kind of argument from an assumption/hypothesis. Tellingly, Aristotle offers a *mathematical* example of an argument leading to the impossible, namely the proof of the incommensurability of the diagonal (41a26–28), which again confirms the influence of mathematics.

These arguments in *Prior Analytics* are important not only because they highlight once again the connections of syllogistic both with dialectic and with mathematics. As we will see in Chapter 7, these arguments are at the very origin of the term 'deduction,' as Medieval Latin authors will use the expression *ad impossibile deductio/deducere* to translate εἰς τὸ ἀδύνατον ἀπαγωγή/ἀπάγειν, that is, to refer precisely to these arguments leading to the impossible.

As noted in Section 6.2.3, one of the main goals of *Prior Analytics* is to show that valid syllogisms in the second and third figures and the non-perfect ones in

---

[11] In Dutilh Novaes, 2012a, I offered a detailed analysis of the importance of the written medium for logical and mathematical reasoning in general.

the first figure can be shown to be valid by means of a process of 'perfection' (or 'completion'), which consists in applying certain rules of transformation (the perfect syllogisms themselves, plus conversion and subalternation) to pairs of premises so as to obtain a conclusion. So for example, the pair 'No P is M, Every S is M' (second figure) can be shown to produce the conclusion 'No S is P' by an application of conversion to the first premise, which results in 'No M is P,' and then we have Celarent, which is one of the first-figure perfect syllogisms.

Conversion consists in switching positions for subject and predicate in a sentence. Naturally, since it is a matter of changing the relative disposition of the terms in the premises so as to obtain the disposition that characterizes the first-figure syllogisms, conversion is the key device. But only the **E** and the **I** propositions convert simpliciter: from 'No A is B' we can infer 'No B is A' (and vice versa), and the same for 'Some A is B.' The **A** and **O** sentences do not convert (the **A** sentences are said to convert accidentally: 'Every A is B' converts to 'Some B is A'). So, when we have a pair of **A** and/or **O** premises, the rules of conversion alone do not provide the resources to 'perfect' the pair in question, even though some such combinations do produce conclusions necessarily, such as Baroco (second figure: 'Every P is M, some S is not M, thus some S is not P') and Bocardo (third figure: 'Some M is not P, every M is S, thus some S is not P'). This is where arguments leading to the impossible come in.

To perfect such syllogisms, what Aristotle calls the ostensive (direct) approach (in the Striker translation; 'probative' in the Smith translation) will not do. Instead, to perfect the syllogisms that cannot be perfected ostensively, i.e. those containing premises and conclusions that cannot be converted, Aristotle resorts to arguments leading to the impossible. His usual procedure is the following: to show that premises A and B produce conclusion C, take A and the contradictory of the conclusion, not-C, and show that one can deduce not-B from A and not-C. But not-B and B lead to absurdity (to the impossible). The general idea can be represented as follows:

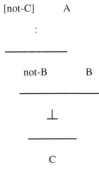

One can thus deduce C from A and B, but with the auxiliary hypothesis/ assumption of the contradictory of C. The subproof from [not-C] and A to not-B is constituted of direct applications of the usual rules of inference of the system (conversion and/or one of the perfect syllogisms). The fact that [not-C] is treated as a hypothesis is at this point an extra-logical, quasi-pragmatic property of the proof (it is in fact tacitly accepted as a 'false assumption'; 29a35), hence the use of the [ ] notation to signal its hypothetical status. (Aristotle uses the phrase 'reached through an agreement' [41a40] to refer to the status of the hypothesis in such arguments, which clearly has a dialectical flavor.) The structural similarities with an *elenchus* should be evident enough by now: questioner first secures answerer's assent to A, B, and not-C, and shows that these three commitments taken together lead to something absurd (because A and not-C imply not-B). Answerer then needs to backtrack and retract at least one of the previous commitments; assuming the law of non-contradiction (which Aristotle famously recognizes as valid), retracting non-C (which had only been assumed while tacitly recognized as false) leads to conclusion C.[12]

Here is a concrete example: Baroco ('Every P is M, some S is not M, thus some S is not P') is perfected by taking the first premise 'Every P is M' and the contradictory of the conclusion, which is 'Every S is P,' as the starting point. From these two, through a regular application of Barbara, one obtains 'Every S is M.' However, this is the contradictory of the second premise, 'Some S is not M,' so from these two premises we obtain the impossible. We can then reject the initial assumption of 'Every S is P,' thus obtaining its contradictory 'Some S is not P' as a conclusion, on the assumption of the two original premises.

6.2.5   Conclusion

In this section, we turned to the first fully-fledged logical theory in history, Aristotle's syllogistic, and analyzed some of its components from a dialogical perspective. I've argued that syllogistic has strong dialogical components, in particular given its roots in dialectic. But a number of other elements and strands converge for the development of syllogistic, especially concerns pertaining to scientific demonstration and inspiration from mathematics.

In a number of later intellectual traditions (late antiquity, Christian medieval, Arabic medieval, Byzantine), syllogistic remained for millennia the quintessential model for logic and argumentation (although some alternative systems

---

[12] "Here, Aristotle is reducing an internalized opponent to silence. This shadow-boxing (fictitious or historical) is evidence that demonstrating through impossibility retains characteristics of a dialectical exchange" (Castelnérac, 2015, p. 311).

such as Stoic logic also emerged, they never became as influential). It is thus to a great extent thanks to the influence of syllogistic (alongside Euclidean mathematics) that the concept of a deductive argument remained so central in these different intellectual traditions.

6.3   Asian Logical Traditions

As mentioned in Section 6.1, there are (at least) two other formidable ancient logical traditions, which (as far as we know, at least) arose independently from the Greek tradition and from each other: logic in India and logic in China. (At a later stage, logic in China is heavily influenced by Buddhism imported from India.) Given the general historiographical hypothesis of this book, namely that broader social, cultural, and political conditions greatly influence the development of scientific knowledge, a comparative analysis between logical traditions that emerged in very different contexts should find that the logical theories developed in each of them differ substantively. In particular, we will see that fully-fledged deduction does not emerge in China or India (though at later stages in India something like deduction seems to have been theorized), even if in both places (especially in India) debating practices were of paramount importance.

This is not to say that having given rise to the concept of deduction makes Ancient Greek logic automatically superior. In fact, regarding complexity and sophistication, it is fair to say that classical Indian logic, in particular, is on a par with Ancient Greek logic. (Classical Chinese authors were admittedly less interested in theorizing and systematizing relations of entailment.) And yet, it is crucial to attend to the important dissimilarities between these traditions, and to the broader social, cultural, and political backgrounds that gave rise to these different traditions.

6.3.1   Logic in India

The classical Indian tradition shares with the Ancient Greek tradition the central position occupied by debating practices.[13] In fact, it might seem that Indian thinkers relished engaging in lively debates even more than their Greek peers,[14] as attested by the sophisticated theories of argumentation that they have produced (both for instruction and practice, and as theoretical investigations) (Matilal, 1998, chapters 2 and 3; Solomon, 1976).

---

[13] Thanks to Elisa Freschi for advice on this section. Tellingly, the distinguished economist and philosopher Amartya Sen entitled one of his books *The Argumentative Indian* (Sen, 2005).

[14] In fact, it is more accurate to refer to South Asian thinkers, as many of them lived in today's Pakistan and Afghanistan. For convenience, I will continue to use 'India' in what follows, despite this caveat.

While the emergence of sustained debating practices in Ancient Greece was primarily defined by a political, democratic background (as argued in Chapter 5), in India debating practices emerged as a response to different circumstances, in particular to address metaphysical, epistemological, and religious issues. As is well known, Indian philosophy is extremely diverse, branching into a plethora of schools. These essentially fall within two groups: Brahmanical schools, which accepted the validity of the Vedic sacred texts (such as Nyaya and Yoga), and schools that rejected the authority of the Vedas (such as Buddhism and Jain). These different schools all disagreed with each other, generating ample opportunity for lively discussions. Historical records suggest that kings and rulers encouraged and patronized such debates between sages, thus providing an institutional, social embedding quite different from the background for intellectual endeavors in Ancient Greece. On the whole, as noted in Matilal, 1998 (p. 31), while the Greeks were primarily interested in moral and political issues, Indian thinkers mainly focused on ontological, epistemological, and religious questions such as the distinction of the soul from the body, the purpose of life, the different sources of knowledge, and the existence of the afterlife.

The popularity of debate dates back to the early stages in the history of Indian thought (i.e. the Upanishads period), but theories of debating only appeared around the time of the Buddha and other religious reformers (sixth century BC). By the third and second centuries BC, monks and Brahmans were required to have training in the art of debating.[15] Debating manuals were written within the different sectarian schools (Matilal, 1998, p. 32), containing accounts of highly regimented debating practices displaying the same level of sophistication (if not beyond) as Greek dialectic and medieval scholastic disputations (see Chapter 7). The Indian authors distinguished between friendly, honest debates, where presumably the common goal was the search for truth, and competitive ones, where the goal was mere victory.[16] Relatedly, these manuals contained instructions on how to perform at honest debates as well as discussions of clever argumentative tricks that may be used by disputatious opponents in competitive debates, so as to help the novice to identify and rebut these tricks. In other words, Indian philosophers also developed sophisticated theories of fallacies (Phillips, 2017) that served purposes very similar to Aristotle's *Sophistical Refutations*.[17]

---

[15] Astonishingly, versions of these practices still survive to this day and age. For example, Liberman, 2007 presents a detailed ethnographic study of philosophical public debates among Tibetan Buddhist scholar-monks.

[16] In the influential *Nyaya-sutra* manual, attributed to Akṣapāda Gautama and widely available by AD 150 (exact dates of composition are uncertain), the former were called *vada*, while the latter were called *jalpa*.

[17] "In short, the *Nyaya-sutra* could almost have been a work of Greek philosophy" (Ganeri, 2001, p. 5).

This comparison with the Ancient Greek dialectical tradition is, however, not intended to suggest that Indian logic/argumentation theory is interesting to us only insofar as it resembles its Greek counterpart. While there are a number of striking similarities, what is arguably even more interesting in these Indian theories is precisely the ways in which they differ from Greek logic and dialectic. There is a historiographical tradition dating back to the nineteenth century of using Ancient Greek logic, syllogistic in particular, as a metric to assess the sophistication and correctness of Indian logical theories (and of other non-European theories for that matter). Naturally, the nineteenth-century colonial background, when Europe was taken to be the pinnacle of rationality and civilization, provides the ideological underpinning for this questionable approach (Ganeri, 2001). Unsurprisingly, this extraneous metric delivers a negative verdict; if Indian theories such as the one found in *Nyaya-sutra* are viewed as theories of syllogistic (of sorts), the unavoidable conclusion will be that they are rather subpar theories. However, if they are in fact theories *of something else* altogether (not about the relation between premises and conclusion in a deduction, but perhaps theories describing correct ways of conducting a debate), then it is not clear what the value of the comparison might be. Instead, a number of scholars have attempted to offer reconstructions of Indian logical theories in their own terms, rejecting both Aristotelian syllogistic and modern predicate logic as their starting points (Matilal, 1998, chapter 1; Ganeri, 2003).

What is most significant for our purposes is that, just as in the Greek tradition, logical theories in India emerged first and foremost as theories of debating and argumentation. We thus have an independent instance of logic – understood as a general theory of inference and reasoning – emerging from dialogical practices and needs.[18] True enough, Indian logical theories also tend to have a strong epistemological focus, with a concern for the nature of evidence and discussions on the means of knowledge, *pramanas*. The *Nyaya-sutra*, for example, can be read as offering a formulation of acceptable and sound methods for philosophical discourse and inquiry. Inference (*anumana*) was viewed by the Nyaya philosophers (as well as by other schools of thought) as one of the *pramanas*, one of the means of knowledge. But Indian thinkers saw no contradiction between dialectical and epistemological approaches to logic; as is clear in particular in the works of the influential fifth-to-sixth-century AD Buddhist thinker Dignāga, inference, the cognitive process taking one from the known to the unknown, and argument, a device of persuasion, "are but two sides of a single coin" (Gillon, 2016, section 4).

---

[18] While there has been much speculation on whether Indian logic may have been influenced by Greek logic or vice versa, so far there is no real evidence for actual points of contact and systematic cross-pollination between the two traditions.

There are, however, some important disanalogies between Indian logical theories and both the Greek tradition discussed in Chapter 5 and contemporary conceptions of logic and deduction (Matilal, 1998, section 1.3). First, while in Ancient Greece logic and philosophy were intimately related to mathematics, in the Indian context the main influence was that of *linguistics*. Language was a central topic of inquiry for Indian thinkers from early on, as attested by the first linguist in history (that we are aware of at least), the great Panini (variously dated to the sixth, fifth, or fourth century BC). Second, it seems that early Indian thinkers did not distinguish sharply between (what we now call) deductive and inductive reasoning. (Recall that Aristotle explicitly distinguishes between *syllogismos*, deduction, and *epagoge*, induction). Inferential knowledge was viewed as the product of repeated observations of individual cases, and most thinkers in the earlier period seemed to view these inferences as sufficiently reliable (with the exception of some skeptical thinkers who emphasized precisely the fact that these inferences were in fact not necessarily truth-preserving; Matilal, 1998, p. 16).

In fact, given the presupposition that background knowledge is always involved in reasoning and inference – especially in the context of debates, as again stressed by *Nyaya-sutra* (Ganeri, 2003, pp. 42–43) – classical Indian logical theories seem to resemble recent non-monotonic logical systems such as default logics (Oetke, 1996) rather than deductive, monotonic logical systems such as syllogistic or modern predicate logic.[19] It was only later, with Dignāga, that the criterion of invariant concomitance between premises and conclusion was explicitly formulated as a necessary condition for the goodness of an inference.

We may speculate on why strictly deductive reasoning and the idea of necessarily truth-preserving inferences were not as salient for earlier Indian thinkers as they were in the Greek tradition. Did the antagonism and polemical context in Athenian democracy intensify the need for incontrovertibility (as argued in Lloyd, 2013), a feature missing in the Indian context? Be that as it may, what the case of Indian logic shows is that a formidable debating tradition may emerge in a non-democratic social context, in fact under the patronage of powerful rulers, and then give rise to sophisticated logical theories.[20] Moreover, later authors such as Dignāga did go on to formulate what appear to be deductive canons for reasoning, even in the absence of these specific

---

[19] However, Taber, 2004 contests this interpretation, and instead claims that classical Indian logicians from early on already implicitly presupposed deductive ideals, which were later refined and systematized by Dignāga and Dharmakīrti.

[20] Classical Indian logical theories continue to attract the interest of logicians and philosophers of logic, who see in these theories potential lessons for the contemporary logician – see for example Priest, 2018 on the Buddhist principle *catuṣkoṭi*, according to which every claim is true, false, both, or neither. See also a reconstruction of the Jain theory of viewpoints from the perspective of modern dialogical logic in Clerbout, Gorisse, & Rahman, 2011.

sociopolitical polemical conditions. In other words, while in the Greek case the connection between a polemical social context and the emergence of deduction is plausible, Indian logic shows that the former may not be a necessary condition for the emergence of the latter. (It does not seem to be sufficient, either.)

6.3.2 Logic in China

Another great ancient intellectual tradition emerged in China.[21] For our purposes, the Chinese tradition is particularly significant because it has been systematically compared to the Greek tradition by G.E.R. Lloyd (1990, 1996, 2013). In order to emphasize the importance of the polemical background in Ancient Greece (in particular in democratic cities) for the specific ways in which scientific knowledge developed there, Lloyd argues that it is no happenstance that in China, against a very different sociocultural, political background, scientific knowledge developed in different ways. In particular, he stresses that the need for incontrovertible arguments was not felt to the same extent in China as it was in Greece. According to Lloyd, most intellectuals in ancient China saw themselves primarily as political advisers to rulers, and often went from kingdom to kingdom to advise different rulers. (Importantly, the relevant period is the period prior to the unification of China, which took place with the Qin's wars of unification, 230–221 BC – thus a period of warfare and diffused political power among several local rulers.) Lloyd argues that, in these circumstances, these itinerant advisers did not seek to formulate, let alone theorize about, indefeasible arguments:

> But those political and legal contexts of the mass persuasion of fellow-citizens [in Greece] simply had no counterpart in the experience of Chinese advisers. Accordingly such contexts could not act as a negative model to stimulate the analysis of an argument schema that would purportedly be immune to doubt. Incontrovertibility simply does not figure as a goal for interpersonal exchange in China, whether in politics, in the law, or in more purely intellectual contexts, such as mathematics. Considerations of motivation were certainly important, as was morality, and as was what was in the interests not just of the ruler but of the state, the welfare, as they said, of 'all under heaven' ... Working out what should be done, and persuading rulers to do it, was the focus of attention. The goal of certainty, of incontrovertibility, secured by a combination of indemonstrable self-evident primary premises and valid deductive argument, would have seemed chimerical if it had been suggested to any classical Chinese thinker. (Lloyd, 2013, p. 451)

Lloyd's interpretive hypothesis is appealing, but it seems to downplay the importance of disputations, including competitive disputations, in ancient

---

[21] Thanks to Chris Fraser for advice on this section.

China. While perhaps not as much as their Greek and Indian peers, Chinese intellectuals also engaged in (public) debates and disputations, a practice described in classical Chinese texts as *biàn* or *biàn shuō*. In particular, the thinkers associated with the so-called 'School of Names' were especially keen on disputations, including idle contests of wits (at least according to their critics). Indeed, some of these thinkers have been described as the 'Chinese sophists,' given the (at least superficial) similarities with the Greek sophists (Fraser, 2015). Moreover, Chinese thinkers also dealt with contexts of 'mass persuasion,' that is, persuasion of large groups of people (even if they were not fellow citizens like in Greece), such as groups of followers of different masters. So, in this sense, Chinese thinkers did have exposure to the kind of competitive disputation that, on Lloyd's account of the evolution of Greek thought, was a crucial component for the emergence of deductive argumentation by offering a negative model. The demand for powerful, irrefutable argumentative techniques was certainly felt.[22]

Biàn is in fact a more general concept, its core meaning pertaining to drawing distinctions, "as a verb referring to the act of distinguishing or discriminating things from each other and as a noun referring to distinctions" (Fraser, 2013, p. 4). But for these classical Chinese thinkers, a debate or argument is in fact an activity primarily aimed at drawing distinctions, hence the secondary meaning the term acquired as referring to disputation and argument. Essentially, the question in a disputation is usually whether a given name is suitably applied to a given object (or event) or not, as revealed by a passage from the Mohist Dialectics (A74, cited in Fraser, 2018, note 25):

CANON : *Biàn* is contending over converses. Winning in *biàn* is fitting the thing.
EXPLANATION : One calls it 'ox,' the other calls it 'non-ox.' This is contending over
    converses. These do not jointly fit the object. If they do not jointly fit, it must be that
    one does not fit.

While this may seem like an idle discussion, Chinese thinkers took 'correcting names' to be of paramount importance. If speakers do not use names and terms uniformly, chaos and anarchy will ensue. In particular, they will not be able to follow commands as intended by their superiors, as these thinkers emphasized action-guiding over descriptive functions of language (Fraser, 2015, supplement 'Disputation in context').

---

[22] An important difference with respect to the Greek tradition is that early Chinese mathematics did not rely on practices of deductive proofs. This tradition focused on algorithms, not proofs, and much attention is devoted to distinguishing different kinds of similar problems, to which 'the same' algorithmic methods are applicable. By contrast, as shown earlier in this chapter, Aristotle was profoundly influenced by the mathematics of his time for the development of syllogistic. (I owe this point to Chris Fraser.)

While intellectuals of all main traditions in the classical period discussed (and presumably engaged in) *biàn*, there are three main (interrelated) accounts of argumentation in classical Chinese thought: that of the early Mohists in their rebuttal of fatalism, that of the later Mohist dialectic, and that of Xúnzǐ (a prominent thinker in the Confucian tradition). And yet, while they contain sophisticated analyses of proper and improper uses of language in disputations, they remain fundamentally different from the theories of argumentation found in Aristotle's texts, in particular in that there is no explicit articulation of deductive principles – even if implicitly they seem to endorse certain principles, such as the principle of non-contradiction when stating that something cannot both be called 'ox' and 'non-ox' (see passage quoted above). Instead, the key concept in the Chinese context is that of *analogical argumentation and inference*: "inference is thus understood as the act of distinguishing something as a certain kind of thing on the basis of having distinguished it as similar to a relevant 'model' or 'standard'" (Fraser, 2013, p. 4).

Naturally, analogy is also a key component of Ancient Greek modes of argumentation, as illustrated by e.g. Plato's dialogues (e.g. the analogy between rhetoric and pastry-baking, as opposed to philosophy and medicine in the *Gorgias*). So it would be utterly inaccurate to claim that Chinese argumentation is purely analogical while Greek argumentation is purely deductive. Instead, analogical reasoning is widely present in both traditions, but in the Greek tradition it coexists with other modes of reasoning, including deductive reasoning. In this respect, we may say that, while for the Greeks a specific class of arguments displaying the property of necessary truth-preservation became salient, this property did not stand out for the Chinese thinkers, who were primarily concerned with language–world relations rather than with relations between sentences (as part of a more general pragmatic intellectual orientation).[23] Whether this difference can be explained *solely* in terms of the different background political and social conditions – one more polemical than the other – is of course an issue that is difficult, perhaps impossible, to adjudicate conclusively. Still, here again we have an argumentative tradition that primarily suits the needs of its practitioners in their own sociocultural circumstances.

6.4   Conclusion

In this chapter, I have examined Aristotle's theory of deduction as presented in his logical texts (mostly in *Prior Analytics*). I have also briefly presented some of the main features of logical traditions in India and China, where sustained

---

[23] Fraser, 2013, footnote 1 takes issue with the tendency in some previous studies to overemphasize possible similarities between Ancient Greek and ancient Chinese logical theories.

attention was also devoted to inferential relations in the context of dialogical, debating practices but with different results. These discrepancies highlight the elements of *contingency* involved in the emergence and development of logical theories at different times and places, thus suggesting a weak form of social constructivism. (I return to social constructivism in the Conclusions chapter.)

7   Logic and Deduction in the Middle Ages and the Modern Period

7.1   Introduction

In the previous chapters, I presented an account of the birth of deduction in Ancient Greek mathematics and philosophy, according to which dialogical practices provided the background for the emergence of deductive reasoning and argumentation. But already early on, deduction also acquired non-dialogical traits, in particular (but not exclusively) as the written medium became increasingly important, and with a move towards 'de-personalized' discourse aimed at general audiences rather than specific interlocutors.

In this chapter, a genealogical narrative of deduction for later periods is presented, following in particular developments in the Latin medieval tradition.[1] We begin with an analysis of the etymology and history of the term 'deduction' in connection with logic in the Latin medieval tradition; as we will see, its origin is to be traced back to the Latin translation of the *Prior Analytics*. We then turn to an examination of the changing definitions of a *syllogismos* in response to Aristotle's definition (discussed in Chapter 6). In Section 7.2.3, the general dialogical background of scholasticism, i.e. the practice of *disputations*, is discussed, as well as a turn towards more mentalistic conceptions of logic in the fourteenth century. In Section 7.2.4, the Arabic tradition in logic is briefly presented; I argue that, while the starting point was the same as for Latin medieval logic – Greek philosophy, and Aristotelian logic in particular – Arabic logic developed in different, less markedly dialogical directions. Section 7.3 brings us back to Christian Europe; it describes the steps through which the dialogical origins of logic were all but forgotten in the early modern period (Section 7.3.1) and in the nineteenth century, with the birth of mathematical logic (Section 7.3.2).

---

[1] For reasons of space and time, the rich period between Aristotle and Boethius, which includes very important developments, such as Stoic logic, will regrettably not be treated here at all. The concept of dialectic continued to occupy a central position in the Hellenistic and Late Antiquity periods, but it acquired a number of different meanings and guises (Barnes, 2007).

Philosophically, this chapter accomplishes two important tasks: it explains why and how the dialogical origins of logic and deduction were slowly but surely forgotten in Europe, and highlights some of the contingent aspects of the development of logic in European traditions by means of comparisons with a sister tradition, Arabic logic.

7.2   Medieval Aristotelian Logical Traditions

7.2.1   The History of the Term 'Deduction'

I've been using the English term 'deduction' to refer to the developments in Ancient Greece described in the previous chapters, both in mathematics and in logic/philosophy;[2] this is not unusual, and indeed both Reviel Netz (1999) and Robin Smith (1997) use the term for mathematical proofs and for Aristotle's *syllogismos*. However, the term itself is obviously of Latin origin, and thus a later development: its etymological root is the verb *ducere*, which means 'to lead,' conjoined with the prefix *de-*, which means 'from.' *Deducere* thus means 'to lead from,' indicating a given starting point from which the 'leading' occurs. Implicitly, there is also an endpoint in the process, which can be explicitly indicated by the preposition *ad*, 'towards,' plus whatever the end-point is. So, etymologically, a deduction denotes a process leading from a starting point towards an endpoint, which may naturally be interpreted as the process leading from premises to conclusion. However, the actual maturation of the term *deductio* as technical term in the logical sense is a more convoluted story than a superficial inspection of its etymology may suggest.

The term *deductio* (and cognates, including the verb *deducere*) appears to have made its debut in logical contexts in Boethius' translations of Aristotle's *Prior Analytics* and *Sophistical Refutations*, and specifically to refer to arguments leading to the impossible: εἰς τὸ ἀδύνατον ἀπαγωγή/ἀπάγειν is translated as *ad impossibile deductio/deducere* or similar constructions. Interestingly, the two versions of Boethius' translation of *Prior Analytics* included in the *Aristoteles Latinus* volume (Minio-Paluello, 1962) disagree on their translations of the title of chapter 25 of Book II: one features *De deductione*, while the other has *De reductione*, indicating some fluidity in uses of these two terms, *deductio* and *reductio*, more or less interchangeably. (Etymologically, they are obviously closely related, as the prefix *re-* denotes 'again' or 'back.')

Importantly, at this stage (i.e. in Boethius' translations) a process of deduction leads a given (grammatical) object from a starting point to an endpoint. In

---

[2] This section has been written in collaboration with Mark Thakkar, who conducted the systematic textual research. The emphasis was on logical texts, which is methodologically justifiable given our focus here, but ideally a more systematic search would include non-logical philosophical texts, as they may contain interesting uses of the term as well.

a dialectical context, the object that is led is either an interlocutor or a thesis maintained by an interlocutor: an *elenchus* leads *an interlocutor* (or his thesis) *from* the assumptions made *to* some embarrassing result/endpoint, such as an impossibility. It is thus a process relating three relata: a starting point, the object being led, and an endpoint. At this stage, the endpoint is invariably an undesirable result, in particular an impossibility, thus indicating a restricted sense for deduction only as pertaining to (what we now call) reductio ad absurdum arguments.

As is well known (Dod, 1982, p. 46), Boethius' translations of *Prior Analytics* and *Sophistical Refutations* were not read by Latin authors until the twelfth century, when (roughly from 1120 onwards) there was a rediscovery of the original Aristotelian corpus.[3] (Until then, the logic curriculum consisted in Boethius' translations of the *Categories* and *De interpretatione*, Porphyry's *Isagoge*, and Boethius' own texts on syllogistic.) For our purposes, this means that the history of the terms *deductio* and *deducere* only really starts with the rediscovery of *Prior Analytics* and *Sophistical Refutations* among Latin medieval authors in the twelfth century. Interestingly, the earliest known Latin commentary on *Prior Analytics*, *Anonymus Aurelianensis III* (Thomsen Thörnqvist, 2014), does not contain any occurrence of *deductio* and cognates, thus deviating from the terminology introduced in Boethius' translation (indeed, the commentary is thought to be based on the original text in Greek rather than a Latin translation).

While it occurs sporadically in Latin logical texts in the twelfth and thirteenth centuries, in particular in commentaries on Aristotle, *deductio* was certainly not a technical logical term in this period. Tellingly, two of the major logical textbooks of this period, Peter of Spain's and William of Sherwood's, contain no occurrences of the term at all. Occurrences in logical texts (e.g. Abelard's *Dialectica* has nine occurrences, but five of them are in non-logical senses) vary in meaning, sometimes in the general sense of 'to escort' or 'lead to.' Virtually all of the earlier uses of *dedu-* in a logical sense refer to arguments leading to the impossible (e.g. Albert the Great's commentary on *Prior Analytics* contains 100 occurrences, the wide majority of them for this kind of argument), or else to explicit dialectical contexts (such as in Roger Bacon's *Summulae dialectices*, where the term is used four times in connection with sophistical refutations).

For the modern meaning of deduction to emerge (where a conclusion is deduced from premises), two key transformations had to take place: (1) **generalization**, so that the endpoint of a deduction can be any kind of outcome, not necessarily an undesirable or inconvenient one, and (2) **reorientation**, so that the (grammatical) object of a deduction is the conclusion, not an opponent or an

---

[3] One of the great mysteries in the history of logic is how and where Boethius' translations, which had been composed some six centuries earlier, were rediscovered in the twelfth century.

opposing thesis.[4] For (2) in particular, a significant grammatical transformation had to occur, namely the disappearance of the preposition *ad* ('to') to indicate the endpoint of a deduction; indeed, we now say that a reasoner deduces *a conclusion* (a direct object), not that a reasoner deduces (escorts) an interlocutor or thesis *towards/to* a conclusion. And while there were occasional earlier occurrences that suggested a generalized, reoriented meaning of deduction,[5] for the most part the term *deductio* was used exclusively in connection with arguments leading to the impossible well into the fourteenth century. The great logicians of the first half of the fourteenth century, such as Ockham, Burley, and Buridan, do not use *deductio* in a technical sense at all; instead, much of what we now understand under the concept of deduction was treated by them under the notion of *consequentia* (Dutilh Novaes, 2016a).

As far as we could establish, the first author who systematically uses *deductio* in the generalized, reoriented sense is John Wyclif, whose *Tres tractatus de probationibus propositionum* (composed c. 1370) contains many occurrences of the term. Importantly, of the thirty-six occurrences of *dedu-*words in this text, only seven are for the vestigial *reductio* usage; the remaining twenty-nine are all in a recognizably more modern sense, such as references to conclusions that have been deduced or are deducible. In Paul of Venice's *Logica magna* (composed in 1396–99), there are also a number of occurrences of *dedu-* words, some in the older *reductio* usage and others in newer senses. But in all of the books of the *Logica magna* that have received modern editions (seven volumes), there are only nineteen such occurrences, which again suggests that it had not yet in any way become a technical, established term. (By contrast, in Descartes' *Regulae*, a rather short text of only twenty pages in the English translation (Descartes, 1988), there are over sixty occurrences.)

The early history of the term 'deduction' in the Latin medieval tradition thus follows quite closely the genealogical development of the notion of deduction as sketched in the previous chapters. Initially, the term is used almost exclusively in connection with the *elenchus* and its genealogical descendant, namely arguments leading to the impossible. At this point, the term has a clear dialogical flavor, in that it involves an interlocutor or his thesis and the process of escorting him from assumptions towards something undesirable/inconvenient. At a later stage, however, it begins to be used in a 'de-personalized' sense, where what is deduced is a *conclusion* from given premises (the interlocutor has disappeared), as seen in Wyclif's text. This newer meaning is then fully consolidated by the time of Descartes (see Section 7.3.1), which in turn provides the background for the further development of modern meanings for the term 'deduction.'

---

[4] The terms 'generalization' and 'reorientation' were proposed by Mark Thakkar.
[5] For example, in Aquinas' commentary on *Posterior Analytics* (1271–72).

7.2.2   Changing Notions of Syllogismos

The changing definitions of the term *syllogismos* also provide a useful trail to track a number of interesting developments.[6] Every medieval logic compendium, and every medieval commentary on *Prior Analytics*, addresses the question of what a syllogism is, so there is plenty of textual material to draw from. We observe (again) a general turn away from explicitly dialogical practices towards de-personalized discourse, and towards a conceptualization of syllogisms in terms of the mathematical theory of figures discussed in Chapter 6.

For convenience, I quote Aristotle's definition again:

A *syllogismos* is an argument (*logos*) in which, (i) certain *things* being posited (*tethentōn*), (ii) something *other* than what was laid down (*keimenōn*) (iii) results by *necessity* (*eks anagkēs sumbainei*) (iv) because these things are so. By 'because these things are so' I mean that it results through these, and by 'resulting through these' I mean that no term is required from outside for the necessity to come about.

This definition was extensively commented upon by medieval authors, both in the Latin tradition and in the Arabic tradition (Thom, 2016), but here we focus on the Latin tradition. As mentioned in Section 7.2.1, the main bridge between Ancient Greek logic and medieval Latin logic is provided by Boethius, who translated *Prior Analytics* and wrote influential textbooks on syllogistic. In one of those, *De syllogismo categorico*, he explains what makes an *oratio* (his translation of *logos*) a *syllogismus*. The formulation of the definition that he uses deviates in one important aspect from Aristotle's definition:

A syllogism is a locution in which, certain things being posited *and granted*, something other than what are posited *and granted* occurs necessarily through the things that are *granted*. (Boethius, *De syllogismo categorico* 821A; emphasis added)

The key deviation is the addition of 'granted' (notice also that 'granted' is repeated no fewer than three times). Boethius seems to restrict the notion of a syllogism to dialectical, disputational contexts, as granting is typically something that happens in these contexts, whereas Aristotle's goal was presumably to cover both dialectical and demonstrative syllogisms. Another point worth noting in his subsequent discussion of the different clauses is his description of syllogisms where the conclusion is among one of the premises as 'ridiculous,' as it would be absurd to view as granted precisely what is not yet established (the conclusion). This raises the question of whether such arguments are syllogistically valid after all, even if of the ridiculous kind, or simply not valid at all, given that they infringe clause (ii) in Aristotle's definition.

---

[6] This section draws substantially from Dutilh Novaes, 2017a, where these developments are presented in more detail.

Fast-forwarding to the thirteenth century, Robert Kilwardby's treatment of the syllogism in his commentary on *Prior Analytics* represents another important step in these developments. In particular, he takes 'posited' and 'laid down' to refer not to the performative nature of a syllogistic argument (involving the speech act of stating premises), but rather to the requirement that a syllogistic argument must be in a figure and a mood. 'Laid down' (*keimenōn*) is understood in the sense of a specific *arrangement* of terms and propositions (Thom, 2016, p. 301). Thus, he reads the Aristotelian definition as encoding properties of syllogistic which are fully specified only later in *Prior Analytics*, such as the notions of figure and mood, and which pertain only to the restricted class of arguments having two premises of the A, E, I, O forms (see Chapter 6). And so, rather than taking the initial definition to be broad and general, Kilwardby interprets the initial definition as already aiming at the restricted class of arguments that we now refer to as syllogistic arguments.

In the fourteenth century, two influential authors, William of Ockham and John Buridan, represent different approaches to the definition of *syllogismos*: Ockham's definition is very different from Aristotle's, while Buridan's definition stays closer to the original. Ockham's definition runs as follows:

A syllogism is a discourse in which, from two premises arranged in figure and mood, a conclusion follows of necessity. For this definition, it does not matter whether the premises are true or false. (Ockham, 1974, *Summa Logicae* III.1, chapter 1)

Ockham is here deviating considerably from Aristotle's original definition, in particular by excluding what are arguably its characteristic dialectical/dialogical components. The only clause that appears unaltered is (iii), pertaining to the necessity with which the conclusion follows from the premises. Regarding clause (i), rather than stating that *at least* two premises are needed (as Aristotle), Ockham says that *exactly* two premises are needed, which is indeed a specific feature of the formal theory of the figures. Notice also that 'arranged in figure and mood' comes to replace 'laid down,' thus making explicit something that Kilwardby took to be implicit. Moreover, Ockham skips clause (ii) altogether, as no reference is made to the requirement that the conclusion be other than the premises. Regarding (iv), nothing is said about redundant or hidden premises. The only part of the definition that is somehow reminiscent of (iv) is his observation that the truth-value of the premises is irrelevant for the validity of the syllogism in general.

Indeed, Ockham relegates the concerns expressed in (ii) and (iv) of Aristotle's formulation to the pragmatic aspects of *using* syllogisms in a debating context, as revealed by his treatment of fallacies in *Summa Logicae* III.4, chapter 15. What is wrong with arguments that have the conclusion (or some suitably equivalent proposition) among the premises is that they are unconvincing, as in such cases respondent is asked to grant precisely that which opponent wants to convince him of. But arguments like this can still be valid syllogistic arguments, as Ockham does not consider the conclusion being different from the premises as a constitutive feature.

By contrast, Buridan's definition of the syllogism in the *Summulae de dialectica* is much closer to the original Aristotelian definition, both in word and in spirit (Dutilh Novaes, 2017a). Moreover, he rejected the Kilwardby–Ockham interpretation of 'laid down' as pertaining to the arrangement of premises and conclusion in a figure and a mood (which he describes as the 'common view'). He favored instead an interpretation of Aristotle's definition as aiming at a general notion of deductive validity, which is then expressed in terms of a formal system that allows for the systematic study of valid and invalid arguments (Thom, 2016).

In sum, the development of definitions of a syllogism in the Latin medieval tradition illustrates a move away from dialectical/dialogical concerns, which are present in Boethius and later authors following him (e.g. Abelard in the twelfth century), but by the thirteenth century seem to have largely vanished, at least specifically regarding the definition of a syllogism.[7] In turn, the formal theory of the figures (Chapter 6) comes to be seen as an integral component of the very definition, as illustrated by Ockham (but rejected by Buridan). Prima facie, this is a somewhat puzzling development, given the centrality of oral disputations in the scholastic tradition (to be discussed in the next section). But here is another reminder that, rather than a neat linear narrative, the genealogy of deduction (as of most philosophically interesting concepts) corresponds to a complex story where multiple lines of influence intertwine, resulting in multilayered stages of development.

7.2.3   Scholastic Disputations and Mental Languages

While very influential, Aristotelian logic in general and *Prior Analytics* in particular were not the only topics that interested Latin medieval logicians. They were in fact interested in a wide range of topics, both inspired by Aristotle's logical works as well as some genuinely novel contributions (Dutilh Novaes & Read, 2016). However, a common denominator of intellectual practices in the Latin medieval tradition is the focus on *debating*, in particular as crystalized in what is known as 'scholastic disputation.' Scholastic disputation is a formalized, rigorous procedure for debate, based on fairly strict rules, which became one of the main approaches for intellectual inquiry in medieval Europe (Novikoff, 2013). It was inspired by Ancient Greek argumentation methods, and was then further developed in the monasteries of

---

[7] As shown in Thom, 2016a, Kilwardby discusses disputations extensively in his commentary on *Prior Analytics*, so the dialogical element is still present after all (see Section 7.2.3).

the early Middle Ages. It reached its pinnacle from the twelfth century onwards, especially with the birth and expansion of universities, where it became one of the main teaching methods (alongside textual commentary). The influence of disputations went well beyond universities, expanding into multiple spheres of cultural life.

What do such disputations look like? Here is an informative schematic description:

> [A disputation] is a regular form of teaching, apprenticeship and research, presided over by a master, characterized by a dialectical method which consists of bringing forward and examining arguments based on reason and authority which oppose one another on a given theoretical or practical problem and which are furnished by participants, and where the master must come to a doctrinal solution by an act of determination which confirms him in his function as master. (Bazán et al., 1985, p. 40, quoted in Sweeney, 2008)

In other words, a disputation starts with a statement, and then goes on to examine arguments in favor of and against the statement – a procedure that is clearly reminiscent of the game of questions and answers described by Aristotle in the *Topics*. A disputation is essentially a dialogical practice in that it features two (possibly fictive) parties disagreeing on a given statement and producing arguments to defend their respective positions, even if both roles can be played by one and the same person. The goal may simply be that of convincing an interlocutor and/or the audience, but the implication is typically that something deeper is achieved, namely coming closer to the truth by examining it from many different angles – in fact, not unlike Socratic dialectic, as discussed in Chapter 5.

Medieval intellectuals engaged in 'live' disputations – both privately, between a master and a pupil, and at grand public events attended by the university community at large – but the general structure is also used extensively in some of the most prominent writings by these authors (some of them are in fact written-up versions of disputations that had actually taken place, known as *reportatio*). For example, Aquinas' *Summa Theologica* – possibly the most influential work from the scholastic tradition – follows the structure of a disputation, with arguments for and against specific claims being examined. Indeed, disputation became one of the chief methods for intellectual inquiry in general, and medieval treatises on philosophical topics typically contain a fair amount of disputational vocabulary. The widespread presence of disputations and related genres has been described as 'the institutionalization of conflict' in scholasticism (Sweeney, 2008).

Importantly, logical textbooks were expected to provide the required training to excel in the art of disputation, with chapters on fallacies, consequence, the logical structure and meaning of propositions, *obligationes* (a special kind of disputation), etc., all of which are directly relevant for the art of disputation. In fact, to a great extent Latin medieval authors did not differentiate between *logica* and *dialectica*, as attested by the fact that a number of influential logical textbooks – Abelard's *De dialectica*, Buridan's *Summulae de dialectica* – bore the term *dialectica* in their titles. Thus, the cultural significance of scholastic disputations and the fact that the required training to be a competent disputant fell within the scope of logic/dialectic entailed a strong association between logic and dialogical practices in this period. To be sure, the topics covered by logical textbooks went beyond matters pertaining exclusively to disputations, but even in the sixteenth century the Spanish scholastic author Domingo de Soto could claim that "dialectic is the art or science of disputing" (Ashworth, 2011).

Simultaneously, however, a number of authors came to associate logical concepts to entities belonging to the mental realm. The influential Persian philosopher Avicenna (eleventh century – see Section 7.2.4) had claimed that logic is about 'second intentions,' roughly what we now call second-order concepts, or concepts of concepts, and this view came to exert significant influence on Latin medieval authors (Hasse, 2014, section 3). Moreover, in the first half of the fourteenth century, William of Ockham developed a sophisticated theory of mental language, which came to play a fundamental role in his logical theories (Panaccio, 2004, chapter 8). His motivations were predominantly metaphysical; as a nominalist, he denied the reified existence of universals, and instead claimed that terms for universals such as 'species' in fact signified mental terms rather than extra-mental entities (Dutilh Novaes, 2013a). Partly as a result of Ockham's influence, there was increased emphasis on the role of the agent and her (mental) acts as providing the foundations for semantic and logical phenomena. One of the manifestations of this tendency are accounts of syncategorematic terms – which include, among others, what we now describe as 'logical constants' – in terms of mental acts and operations of the mind (Klima, 2006; Spruyt & Dutilh Novaes, 2015). For Buridan, for example,

the copulas 'is' and 'is not' signify different ways of combining mental terms in order to form mental propositions, and these different ways [of combining] are in their turn complexive concepts ... And so also the words 'and,' 'or,' 'if,' 'therefore,' and the like designate complexive concepts that combine several propositions or terms at once in the intellect, but nothing further outside the intellect. (Buridan, 2001, p. 234)

Moreover, according to one influential conception of consequence in the Latin medieval tradition, in a valid consequence, the conclusion (consequent) is *contained/understood* in the premises (antecedent). In the fourteenth century, in particular among British authors, this notion of consequence came to be interpreted in terms of mental acts of the understanding, so again in mentalistic terms (Dutilh Novaes, 2016a, section 3.4). These developments all paved the way for a shift away from dialogical/dialectical conceptions of logic and towards conceptions where the mental realm and operations of the mind are emphasized, which became the predominant view in the early modern period (Normore, 1993). So here, again, we have a confluence of different strands of thought, sometimes pulling in opposite directions, reminding us that genealogical narratives must avoid simplified accounts, where different modes of thought neatly correspond to specific periods and follow each other in succession. In the medieval Latin period, dialogical conceptions of logic were pervasive, but they shared the stage and intermingled with decidedly non-dialogical conceptions as well.

7.2.4   Arabic Logic

Roughly in the same period, another formidable intellectual tradition was emerging, which had the same starting point as the Latin tradition (Ancient Greek philosophy) but then went on to develop in different ways.[8] In this tradition, too, logic came to occupy an important position. Arabic logic began with translations of Ancient Greek logical texts into Arabic,[9] but then gave rise to a number of original, novel and sophisticated ideas and theories (see Street, 2013, Hasnawi & Hodges, 2016, and El-Rouayheb, 2016 for reviews). The Arabic term for logic in this tradition is *mantiq*, meaning 'speech' or 'utterance.'

The advent of the Abbasid Caliphate (750–1258) marked the beginning of systematic efforts to translate a wide range of Ancient Greek philosophical texts, in particular texts by Aristotle and his commentators, under the protection and sponsorship of these rulers. (Indeed, a patronage system of support from rulers and other powerful people is what sustained intellectual activity in this tradition, at least initially.) The translation movement culminated around 830 in the circle of al-Kindī in Baghdad, who is the first outstanding figure in Arabic philosophy. These translations inaugurated the intellectual tradition of *falsafa* (an alliteration for the Greek word *philosophia*), which, at least initially, was viewed as a competitor for the 'indigenous' traditions of *kalam* (rational theology) and *fiqh* (Islamic jurisprudence). The latter also offered accounts of reasoning and argumentation (in their specific domains), but until the eleventh century there was little cross-pollination between them and the foreign innovations of Greek-inspired logic and philosophy.

Within *falsafa*, the logic studied was initially simply that of the classical Aristotelian *Organon*.[10] By the mid-ninth century, most of Aristotle's logical

---

[8] Thanks to Khaled El-Rouayheb for advice on this section.

[9] Indeed, it is above all a tradition defined by a unifying language, Arabic, though there are texts belonging to the tradition originally written in other languages as well (e.g. Farsi, for some of Avicenna's texts).

[10] Aristotle's *Organon* is composed of the *Categories, On Interpretation, Prior Analytics, Posterior Analytics, Topics, and Sophistical Refutations*; the selection of texts and order is the result of intense editorial activity in the first century BC, so not Aristotle's own choice. In some traditions, the *Organon* also includes Aristotle's *Rhetoric* and even his *Poetics*. Another

texts had been translated. By the early tenth century, a group of self-declared Peripatetics in Baghdad presented themselves as the defenders of Aristotelian orthodoxy, in particular with respect to logic. The most famous member of this group was Alfarabi, who composed a series of commentaries on the books of the *Organon*. At this stage, unsurprisingly, Arabic logicians were predominantly interested in the key topics of Aristotle's logical canon such as syllogistic, dialectic, and demonstration.

All this was to change thanks to the larger-than-life figure of Avicenna (ca. 970–1037), who was born in the city of Bukhara (currently in Uzbekistan), then the capital of the Samanids, a Persian dynasty. (He wrote both in Farsi and Arabic.) Avicenna was an extremely prolific writer, a polymath proficient in virtually all philosophical/scientific topics of his time, including medicine, which was one of his main interests. He had comprehensive knowledge of the Hellenistic tradition of late antiquity, but was above all an independent, original thinker. In particular, with respect to logic, while thoroughly familiar with Aristotle's logic, he set out to correct what he considered to be shortcomings of these theories. Avicenna was without a doubt one of the greatest logicians of all times, and even now his logical theories have much to teach contemporary logicians.[11]

For our purposes, what is particularly relevant is that Avicenna diverged significantly from the Aristotelian canon in his conception of the subject matter of logic. The Ancient commentators of Aristotle had discussed this issue at length, arriving at different verdicts (Sorabji, 2004), but none of them was particularly mentalistic in their approaches to logic. Avicenna famously identified *concepts* as the subject matter of logic, in particular what scholars of Arabic philosophy have translated into English as 'secondary intelligibles' (Street, 2013), or second-order concepts (in the Latin tradition known as 'terms of second intention'). Arabic logicians before Avicenna recognized the distinction between conception and assent (in Street, 2013's terminology), or conception and assertion (in Strobino, 2018's terminology). Conception pertains to terms and definitions, while assent/assertion pertains to sentences or propositions, and is elicited by an argument (proof) in support of a given conclusion. For Avicenna, insofar as it deals with the theory of conception and assent, logic will deal with second-order notions such as 'genus,' 'species,' etc.:[12]

canonical text in many traditions is Porphyry's *Isagoge*, which is supposed to be an introduction to the whole *Organon*.
[11] Wilfrid Hodges (2017, 2018) has recently offered painstaking reconstructions of Avicenna's logical theories from the point of view of contemporary logic, thus revealing the sophistication and complexity of these theories.
[12] "Avicenna had presented the subject matter of logic as being 'second intentions,' i.e. accidents that only accrue to quiddities insofar as these quiddities are in the mind, such as a quiddity being a 'genus' or a 'species' or a 'subject' or a 'predicate'" (El-Rouayheb, 2016, p. 69).

The subject matter of logic, as you know, is given by the secondary intelligible meanings, based on the first intelligible meanings, with regard to how it is possible to pass by means of them from the known to the unknown, not in so far as they are intelligible and possess intellectual existence ... (Avicenna, *Metaphysics*, quoted in Street, 2013)

Notice that this is a decidedly *epistemological* conception of logic, as its stated purpose is to lead from what is known to what is unknown (somewhat reminiscent of Indian approaches to logic, which Avicenna may have had some knowledge of).[13] It is thus fundamentally different from Aristotle's own conception, as even in his theory of demonstration in the *Posterior Analytics* the goal is to go from what is known with more certainty to what is known with less certainty (it is a theory of exposition rather than discovery). An epistemological account of logic in these terms is arguably also not to be found in the Latin medieval tradition. Curiously, Avicenna's approach to logic is surprisingly similar to the *anti*-scholastic conception of logic to be formulated by Descartes centuries later (see Section 7.3.1). Thus, Avicenna's approach seems overall less dialogical and more epistemic and mentalistic than what one encounters among Ancient Greek thinkers or Latin medieval thinkers.[14]

While very influential, Avicenna's approach to logic was not unanimously embraced by later authors, as some of them considered his focus on secondary intelligibles as too narrow, and identified the subject matter of logic as 'known concepts and assents' (El-Rouayheb, 2016; Street, 2013). By and large, though, Avicenna's theories replaced Aristotle's theories as the canon determining how logic should be approached at all in the Arabic tradition. In particular, the texts that later authors engaged with were predominantly those of Avicenna (even if to criticize or disagree with him). True enough, one strand within Arabic philosophy followed Alfarabi and remained resolutely Aristotelian; Averroes is the main, and in fact the last, notable representative of this tradition. But Averroes had little influence on developments in Arabic philosophy (while being hugely influential for the Latin tradition), in part due to his geographic isolation (he was born and lived in Spain, far from the main centers of Islamic intellectual activity). Thus, after an initial Aristotelian phase, Arabic logic became essentially Avicennian, even if later authors continued to produce innovations – these later authors can be divided between 'Avicennians' and 'revisionist Avicennians' (but Avicennians nevertheless; El-Rouayheb, 2016).

---

[13] Avicenna was born and educated in Bukhara and then Balkh, two Silk Road cities which were both centers of religious learning and attracted scholars from across the Islamic world.

[14] Admittedly, it is possible that the epistemological and mentalistic focus of Avicenna, and possibly of other Arabic authors before him, can be traced back to Late Antiquity authors such as Galen or the Stoics. For my purposes, nothing much hinges on whether this conception of logic is original to Arabic authors or borrowed from Late Antiquity authors. I stand by the claim that it is *not* Aristotle's conception of logic.

Avicenna's influence extended as far as the Latin tradition, especially with respect to the concept of second intentions (as mentioned above), even if Latin medieval logic remained by and large Aristotelian.

In later periods, the 'foreign' logic of the *falsafa* tradition was finally (partially) incorporated into the original traditions in jurisprudence, law, and theology, in particular with the rise of the madrasa system starting in the late eleventh century. (Madrasas were official institutions of learning, functionally similar to European universities.) In the madrasas, the Arabic scholastic method became consolidated and widely disseminated, a method where logic occupied pride of place (Street, 2013). In this context, logic came to be divorced from *falsafa* tradition and became more of an instrumental discipline deemed useful for jurists and theologians, alongside grammar and rhetoric (El-Rouayheb, 2016).

Thus, despite the common starting point, namely Greek and Hellenistic philosophy, Arabic medieval logic took its own developmental path when compared to Latin medieval logic, in particular (but not exclusively) regarding the influential Avicennian epistemic and mentalistic conception of logic. Overall, the significance of dialogical practices for logical theorizing is felt less in the Arabic tradition than in its sister tradition, even though argumentative practices were, of course, not unimportant for Arabic thinkers. Indeed, in the madrasa tradition, theories of disputation tended to be studied as an independent discipline, called 'the science of disputation' (*'ilm al-munazara*) or 'the rules of discussion' (*adab al-bahth*) (Miller, 1984), whereas logic (*mantiq*) remained focused on epistemological concerns.

7.3   Forgetting the Dialogical Origins of Logic

In this section, I offer a brief account of how the dialogical origins of logic, of which Latin medieval authors were still keenly aware, came to be overlooked or outright rejected in the following centuries.[15] This led to profound transformations in how logic came to be conceived of.

7.3.1   *Renaissance and Early Modern Period, up to Kant*

Let us now turn to Christian Europe again. After the golden age of the scholastic period, starting in the fifteenth century logic as a discipline underwent a slow but steady decline. Much of the scholastic sophistication got lost, and the logic taught at universities during the early modern period was for the most part watered-down versions of medieval scholastic logic. To be sure, the decline did not happen at once, and in some regions (e.g. Spain) innovative

---

[15] This section draws substantially on Dutilh Novaes, 2017b.

work in the scholastic tradition continued to emerge well into the sixteenth century (Ashworth, 2016). However, generally speaking, scholastic logic became less and less prominent after the end of the Middle Ages, except for educational purposes at universities. What explains this decline? Tellingly, the decline of scholastic logic coincides with the gradual divorce between logic and its dialogical origins.

As is generally the case, this is probably a multi-causal development. One well-known cause for the demise of scholastic logic was the damning criticism by Renaissance authors such as Lorenzo Valla (Nauta, 2009). These authors deplored the lack of applicability of scholastic logic; Valla, for example, saw syllogisms as an artificial type of reasoning, useless for orators on account of being too far removed from natural ways of speaking and arguing. They harshly criticized the cumbersome, artificial, and overly technical Latin of scholastic authors, and defended a return to the classical Latin of Cicero and Vergil. For the most part, Renaissance authors did not belong to the university system, where scholasticism was still the norm in the fifteenth century; instead, they tended to be civil servants, and were thus involved in politics, administration, and civic life in general. As such, they were much more interested in rhetoric and persuasion than in logic and demonstration.

Moreover, it is not happenstance that the downfall of the scholastic disputational culture roughly coincides with the introduction of new printing techniques in Europe, around 1440. Before that, written material such as books were a rare commodity, and education was conducted almost exclusively by means of oral contact between masters and pupils: expository lectures in which textbooks were read out loud, disputations of various kinds, and so forth. While a change of culture did not happen immediately, by the time of Descartes (roughly two centuries later), the idea that a person could educate themselves on their own by means of books was already well established.

The abandonment of predominantly dialectical, disputational modes of intellectual inquiry also explains why logic gradually lost its prominence in the modern period. A passage by Descartes represents this shift quite clearly. Speaking of how the education of a young pupil should proceed, he writes:

After that, he should study logic. I do not mean the logic of the Schools, for this is strictly speaking nothing but a dialectic which teaches ways of expounding to others what one already knows or even of holding forth without judgment about things one does not know. Such logic corrupts good sense rather than increasing it. I mean instead the kind of logic which teaches us to direct our reason with a view to discovering the truths of which we are ignorant. (Descartes, 1985, p. 186)

Descartes correctly observes that the logic of the Schools, and more generally Aristotelian logic, is not really a logic of discovery. Instead (as also argued in Chapter 6), its chief purpose is that of justification and exposition, which makes sense in particular against the background of dialogical practices, where different interlocutors explain and debate with others what they themselves already know. Indeed, for much of the history of logic up to Descartes' time, one of the chief applications of logical theories had been to teach students to perform well in debates and disputations, and to theorize more generally on the logical properties of what follows from what insofar as this is an essential component of such argumentative practices. But as a result of the rejection of scholasticism, the very term 'logic' came to be used for something other than what the scholastics had meant, as the passage above indicates. Instead, early modern authors emphasize the role of novelty and individual discovery, as exemplified by the influential *Port-Royal Logic* (1662) – essentially the logical version of Cartesianism, based on Descartes' conception of mental operations and the primacy of thought over language (Buroker, 2014). Tellingly, the original title of what became known as the *Port-Royal Logic* was *La logique ou l'art de penser*: logic as the art of *thinking*, not as the art of disputing (as the sixteenth-century scholastic author Domingo de Soto had claimed).

For Descartes, this 'logic of discovery' is based on two basic actions of the intellect through which one can arrive at knowledge that is immune to mistakes: intuition and deduction. On deduction, he says:

> There may be some doubt about our reason for suggesting another mode of knowing in addition to intuition, viz. deduction, by which we mean the inference of something as following necessarily from some other propositions which are known with certainty. But this distinction had to be made, since very many facts which are not self-evident are known with certainty provided that they are inferred from true and known principles through a continuous and uninterrupted movement of thought in which each individual proposition is clearly intuited. (Descartes, 1988, p. 3)

Notice, however, that what Descartes means by 'deduction' is not exactly the same as twenty-first-century logical conceptions of this notion (as described in Chapter 1), in particular with respect to the clause of necessary truth-preservation, despite his own use of the term 'following necessarily' (Normore, 1993). (Notice also the requirement that the premises must be known with certainty, which is not a constitutive component of current conceptions of deduction, *pace* Frege.) Instead, the key notion here is that of a 'continuous and uninterrupted movement of thought' which is expected to ensure transmission of certainty. It is in this sense that I can infer with absolute certainty from the fact that I think that I exist (*cogito, ergo sum*). With Descartes, we have what is perhaps the first systematic, technical use of the term 'deduction' as applied to a form of inference where certainty (necessity) is transmitted from premises to conclusion.

And thus, during the early modern period, picking up on a thread that dates back at least to Avicenna and had a certain amount of influence among Latin medieval authors (as discussed in Section 7.2.3), in the early modern period conceptualizations of the nature of logic in terms of faculties of the mind came to prevail (Hatfield, 1997). This tendency then culminates in Kant, for whom logic pertains above all to the structure of thought as such and the operations of the mind, as in his interpretation of Aristotelian categories. For Kant, quintessential logical concepts such as drawing an inference from premises to conclusion are explicitly associated with internal operations of the mind rather than with moves in an argumentative situation:

> As general logic, it abstracts from all content of knowledge of understanding and from all differences in its objects, and deals with nothing but the mere form of thought. (*Critique of Pure Reason* A54/B78, Kant, 1998)

Kant thus systematized and consolidated the close connection between logic and thinking/reasoning, which was to remain pervasive and influential throughout the nineteenth and twentieth centuries (MacFarlane, 2000). He selectively absorbed the notions of 'judgment,' 'form,' and 'categories' as found in the logical textbooks of the time, and put them to use so as to describe the very conditions of possibility for our thinking and perceiving. The concept of judgment, for example, traditionally used to refer to linguistic claims made by speakers in the public sphere, is transformed into the mental act involved in the apperception of objects. Thus, with Kant, logic concerns exclusively the inner mental activities of the (lonesome) thinking subject.

7.3.2   The Birth of Mathematical Logic

While Kant's views on logic remained influential throughout the nineteenth century and beyond, it is also in the nineteenth century that logic took yet another turn, different both from the scholastic disputational conception and the early modern mentalistic conception, namely a turn towards *mathematics*. (But then again, recall the close connections between logic/philosophy and mathematics among the Ancient Greeks.) The founding figure here is George Boole, a highly innovative mathematician who in 1847 wrote an essay called *The Mathematical Analysis of Logic*, thus inaugurating a new research program. This approach had antecedents in the seventeenth century (Mugnai, 2010), especially but not exclusively with Leibniz. However, Boole appears to have been largely unaware of these earlier developments, as he was an autodidact with no formal education on either the history of logic or mathematics.

Similar to what Leibniz had achieved with his numerical interpretation of syllogistic (Andrade-Lotero & Dutilh Novaes, 2012) but going far beyond (and helped by the significant advances that had occurred in mathematics since the seventeenth century), Boole developed a method to 'calculate' whether an argument was valid or not, in stark contrast with the catalogue-based approach of traditional logic. Boole's work inaugurated what is known as the 'algebra of logic' tradition (Burris & Legris, 2015), and pushed forward the idea of using mathematical symbolism in connection with logic. Boole was not working in a vacuum, as indeed he was responding to a growing interest in logic among mathematicians (Peckhaus, 2009). In many senses, he remains a 'Kantian' (as attested by the title of his 1854 masterpiece, *The Laws of Thought*), but his work undoubtedly represents a turning point in the history of logic: it kicks off the mathematical period singled out by Joseph Bocheński (1961) as one of the most prolific periods in the history of logic.

The other towering figure in nineteenth-century logic is, naturally, Gottlob Frege. While Boole used mathematics to analyze logic (syllogisms), Frege's project was the converse: to use logic to analyze mathematics, more specifically to provide purely logical foundations for mathematics (in what is known as the 'logicist program'). In other words, Frege intended to derive all truths of arithmetic from purely logical principles (axioms), using logical rules. To this end, however, Frege had to 'mathematize' logic so as to make it suitable for the logicist program, in particular by taking the mathematical notion of a *function* as the main conceptual building block of his system. Moreover, explicitly inspired by the seventeenth-century tradition of artificial languages, Leibniz's work in particular, Frege devised an entirely new notation for his system, which he called 'concept-script' (*Begriffsschrift*). In the preface to the *Begriffsschrift*, he offers an illuminating description of his motivations for introducing this new language:

My initial step was to attempt to reduce the concept of ordering in a sequence to that of logical consequence, so as to proceed from there to the concept of number. To prevent anything intuitive from penetrating here unnoticed, I had to bend every effort to keep the chain of inferences free of gaps. In attempting to comply with this requirement in the strictest possible way I found the inadequacy of language to be an obstacle; no matter how unwieldy the expressions I was ready to accept, I was less and less able, as the relations became more and more complex, to attain the precision that my purpose required. This deficiency led me to the idea of the present concept-script. Its first purpose, therefore, is to provide us with the most reliable test of the validity of a chain of inferences and to point out every presupposition that tries to sneak in unnoticed, so that its origin can be investigated. (Frege, 1967, pp. 5–6)

The idea that ordinary language is expressively inadequate to account for mathematical (or even logical) reasoning became a recurring theme in the ensuing tradition of mathematical logic, so much so that the term 'symbolic logic' became synonymous with this tradition: to 'do logic' simply means working with special symbols, not with ordinary words (Dutilh Novaes, 2012a). In this respect, recall that the humanist authors had criticized the Latin of scholastic logicians precisely as 'too artificial'; even the Greek language that Aristotle relies on for syllogistic is rather regimented and far removed from ordinary ways of speaking at the time. In a sense, perhaps a certain degree of 'artificiality' is at the core of logic throughout its history, as it operates at levels of abstraction that are at odds with ordinary language usage. And thus, there is perhaps an inherent tension within logic, insofar as it emerges from dialogical practices conducted in ordinary languages but must then contend with the irregularities and inadequacies of these languages for the purposes of systematizing relations of entailment.

As is well known, Frege's impressive cathedral unfortunately lay on shaky grounds, as revealed by Russell's paradox: Frege's system allows for the existence of a collection that both does and does not belong to itself. It was with the goal of rescuing and further developing the logicist program that Russell and Whitehead went on to develop the monumental system presented in their *Principia Mathematica* (Russell & Whitehead, 1910–13). The rest is history: essentially, all major developments in logic in the twentieth century are premised, directly or indirectly, on *Principia Mathematica*.

However, traces of logic's dialogical origins still persist in recent developments, as argued throughout this book. Thus, taking the dialogical/dialectical perspective into account remains essential to obtain a thorough understanding of the nature of logic even in its recent, mathematical instantiations (also because mathematics itself is characterized by dialogical features, as argued in Chapter 11).

7.4   Conclusion

This chapter offered a condensed (and thus inevitably incomplete) account of transformations in conceptions of logic and deduction in the European tradition (with a brief foray into Arabic logic) from Boethius to the early twentieth century. The starting point is dialectical conceptions of logic inherited from Ancient Greece, which continue to thrive in the Latin Middle Ages. However, also during the Latin medieval period, mentalistic conceptions of logic began to emerge, in part owing to the influence of Avicenna. Mentalistic approaches then gained the upper hand in the early modern period, and in many senses are still with us (e.g. in discussions on the normativity of logic for thought, see Chapter 4). In the nineteenth century, yet another approach to logic and deduction joined the party, namely mathematical logic, which remains influential to this day. Yet, as predicted by the genealogical model, each of these instantiations leaves traces that are carried over to newer instantiations, despite transformations.

Part III

Deduction and Cognition

8   How We Reason, Individually and in Groups

8.1   Introduction

The next three chapters discuss empirical evidence that bears on the hypothesis that deductive reasoning is best understood in dialogical terms. The evidence to be examined comes from different fields, especially psychology of reasoning, cognitive science, and mathematics education. In this chapter, I look into the empirical evidence on how humans reason, individually as well as in groups, specifically with respect to deductive problems. In Chapter 9, I address the ontogenetic question of how deductive reasoning skills emerge in a particular human agent, stressing the importance of dialogical scaffolding for the relevant learning processes. In Chapter 10, I address the phylogenetic question of the presumed evolutionary basis for deductive skills: Are they a product of genetic evolution or of cultural evolution?

Before moving on, let us start by considering in more detail a useful distinction between the different timescales in which (cultural) processes may change human minds: phylogenetic timescales, historical timescales, and ontogenetic timescales (Tomasello, 1999; Menary & Gillett, 2017). The development of deductive reasoning on the historical timescale has been treated extensively in Chapters 5, 6, and 7; we've seen that it is a thoroughly cultural phenomenon, largely confined to niches of specialists. Most of Chapters 8 and 9 focus on the ontogenetic timescale, and on how the emergence of deductive reasoning skills depends on specific kinds of social/cultural experiences that an individual undergoes. As for the phylogenetic timescale, it will be treated in Chapter 10, where I offer some tentative, cautious hypotheses on what might be the phylogenetic basis for deductive reasoning to emerge. Indeed, an encompassing account of a particular aspect of human cognition and the extent to which it is shaped by cultural processes must arguably tackle all three timescales. The dialogical hypothesis allows precisely for such a unified account of deduction.

In this chapter, I start by reviewing some of the evidence, amassed by decades of research in the psychology of reasoning, suggesting that humans are 'bad' at deductive reasoning. These are well-known results that have been extensively discussed by psychologists and philosophers (and are reviewed in detail in Dutilh Novaes, 2012a, chapter 4). Many of the reasoning 'biases' identified in this literature can be explained by one basic cognitive tendency in humans, which cognitive scientist Keith Stanovich describes as a 'fundamental computational bias': "the tendency to automatically bring prior knowledge to bear when solving problems" (Stanovich, 2003, p. 292). This tendency impacts in particular a reasoner's ability to reason following necessary truth-preservation, and her ability to bracket belief when reasoning deductively. In Section 8.3, I review evidence indicating that performance in deductive reasoning tasks improves in groups, in particular if reasoners are allowed to deliberate and engage in dialogue with each other. The question then becomes: What are the features of group situations that give rise to these significant differences in performance? This question will be addressed in detail in Chapter 9.

8.2   Our 'Poor' Deductive Reasoning Skills

Deductive reasoning skills in humans have been systematically investigated experimentally since the 1960s (with a few notable earlier investigations such as Wilkins, 1928). The starting point for this tradition (in particular in the pioneering work of Peter Wason) was the (Kantian/Piagetian) assumption that the canons of deductive reasoning (as captured in e.g. syllogistic logic) provided the foundation for rationality, and the assumption that humans are indeed rational. These two assumptions together led to the prediction that humans would for the most part be skilled deductive reasoners. But already in the early days of this research tradition, this prediction was contradicted by the experimental results obtained: by and large, human reasoners seemed to fail miserably in deductive reasoning tasks (at least in experimental settings). (For reviews, see Evans, 2002; Dutilh Novaes, 2012a, chapter 4.)

Still, for decades researchers continued to operate within the (so-called) *deduction paradigm*, which was premised on dissociation between deductive reasoning, understood as rule-based reasoning with logical forms, and the content and context in which reasoning occurs (Elqayam, 2018). In experiments, participants are expected (and sometimes explicitly told) to disregard their own doxastic attitudes with respect to the sentences in the arguments presented to them, in order to focus solely on the logical connections between premises and conclusion when deciding whether the argument is valid or not.[1] And yet, as numerous experimental results have shown, content in general and background beliefs in particular have a strong effect on reasoning performance, and this

---

[1] "Thus, in the deduction paradigm, participants are typically instructed to assume that the premises are true, a manipulation intended to neutralise the effects of belief" (Elqayam, 2018, p. 134).

includes both facilitating effects (e.g. some contentful versions of the Wason selection task lead to results much closer to the deductive normative responses) as well as hindering effects (e.g. the widely discussed belief bias effects).

8.2.1 Belief Projection

The discrepancy between experimental results and the deductive normative responses to the different reasoning tasks revealed that, as a matter of fact, humans do not typically reason according to the Piagetian 'formal operations' model (Dutilh Novaes, 2012a, chapter 4). Instead, humans systematically bring background beliefs to bear when reasoning, thus operating on the basis of content rather than logical structure/form. This general tendency towards projecting one's beliefs into a problem has been described as a 'fundamental computational bias' by Stanovich.[2] Commenting on a specific reasoning problem (part of a study reported in Sá et al., 1999), where reasoners perform much closer to the deductive normative response with an argument containing made-up words ('hudon,' 'wampet') than with an argument containing familiar words ('rose,' 'water') and a believable conclusion, Stanovich concludes:

The rose problem illustrates one of the fundamental computational biases of human cognition – the tendency to automatically bring prior knowledge to bear when solving problems.[3] That prior knowledge is implicated in performance on this problem even when the person is explicitly told to ignore the real-world believability of the conclusion, illustrates that this tendency toward contextualizing problems with prior knowledge is so ubiquitous that it cannot easily be turned off – hence its characterization here as a fundamental computational bias (one that pervades virtually all thinking whether we like it or not). Of course, the tendency to use prior knowledge to supplement problem solving is more often a help than a hindrance. Nevertheless, it will be argued below that there are certain improbable but important situations in modern life in which the fundamental computational biases must be overridden, and that failure to do so can have negative real-life consequences.[4] (Stanovich, 2003, pp. 292–293)

One of the most extensively studied phenomena in the psychology of reasoning literature since the 1980s, which is a specific manifestation of the tendency to bring prior beliefs to bear when solving problems, is known as *belief bias*. Belief bias is the tendency to let the (un)believability of the

---

[2] Stanovich, 2003 discusses four main computational biases in humans: (1) automatic contextualization (the use of prior knowledge and context); (2) the tendency to "socialize" abstract problems; (3) seeing intentional design in random events; (4) narrative modes of thought. For our purposes, 1 and 2 are especially relevant.

[3] Stanovich then clarifies that 'belief' may be a more appropriate term than 'knowledge,' especially given that the philosophical meaning of 'knowledge' involves factivity. He introduces the term 'belief projection' for this phenomenon.

[4] Stanovich goes on to discuss some of these situations: medical diagnosis and medical decision-making; legal proceedings; large-scale public spending; financial judgment.

conclusion influence judgments of the (in)validity of arguments. It has been described as "perhaps the best known and most widely accepted notion of inferential error to come out of the literature on human reasoning" (Evans, 1989, p. 41), though more recently its status as a straightforward 'inferential error' has been reconsidered (now that the strict deductivist paradigm in psychology of reasoning is by and large viewed as outdated; Elqayam, 2018). Error or not, belief bias is closely related to a number of other empirically observed cognitive phenomena which all point in the same direction: human reasoners typically seek to maintain the beliefs they already hold and, conversely, to reject contradictory incoming information (a tendency also known as *confirmation bias*; Nickerson, 1998), thus typically letting background belief play an important role in reasoning processes.

Elsewhere, I have extensively discussed the classical belief bias results (Dutilh Novaes, 2012a, chapter 4; Dutilh Novaes & Veluwenkamp, 2017), so there is no need for another detailed discussion of these results in the present context. (Recent reviews of the literature are Ball & Thompson, 2018 and Evans, 2016.) But for readers unfamiliar with this literature, here follows a brief primer.

Belief bias is typically studied using fully formulated categorical syllogisms;[5] participants are then asked to evaluate whether the conclusion follows from the given premises. The different syllogisms used are such that the validity and believability of conclusions are manipulated, thus defining four classes of arguments: (1) deductively valid arguments with a believable conclusion; (2) deductively valid arguments with an unbelievable conclusion; (3) deductively invalid arguments with a believable conclusion; and (4) deductively invalid arguments with an unbelievable conclusion.[6] The systematic combination of argument validity and conclusion believability produces problems in which validity and believability are either in opposition (known as conflict items, classes 2 and 3) or problems in which validity and believability are congruent (known as no-conflict items, classes 1 and 4); indeed, what is under investigation is the presumed conflict between 'logic and belief' (as stated in the title of the seminal study Evans et al., 1983).

A very robust pattern of results in these experiments is that, typically, 'belief trumps logic' for conflict items: participants generally endorse invalid arguments with believable conclusions, and (though to a lesser extent)[7] often deem

---

[5] One exception is Oakhill & Johnson-Laird, 1985, which is a conclusion-generation study. However, there are no significant discrepancies between results for conclusion-evaluation and those for conclusion-generation.
[6] Some studies use a fifth class of arguments, namely arguments with 'neutral' conclusions with respect to believability, for example arguments with made-up words such as 'jamtops' and 'opprobine' (Sá et al., 1999). These are referred to as 'neutral items.'
[7] This difference is interesting in itself: note that in the data from Evans et al., 1983, in 71 percent of the cases participants mistakenly endorsed an invalid argument with a believable conclusion, whereas in 44 percent of the cases participants mistakenly rejected a valid argument with an

valid arguments with unbelievable conclusions as invalid (thus in both cases making a mistake according to the deductive canons). In Evans et al., 1983, the results were as follows: 71 percent of 'wrong' answers for invalid arguments with believable conclusions, and 44 percent of 'wrong' answers for valid arguments with unbelievable conclusions:

	% of validity endorsements	
	Believable conclusions	Unbelievable conclusions
Valid	89	56
Invalid	71	10

Researchers agree unanimously on the pervasiveness of the belief bias phenomenon but disagree on the underlying mechanisms (Ball & Thompson, 2018). For example, in the 1980s and 1990s, one influential account relied on the mental model theory of reasoning (Oakhill & Johnson-Laird, 1985). According to this account, reasoners first establish an integrated representation of the premises (an initial mental model). A conclusion that is supported by this initial model will simply be accepted if it is believable, but if a conclusion is unbelievable, it will be examined more rigorously against alternative, potentially falsifying models of the premises. Subsequently, experimental data emerged suggesting that most people do not spontaneously seek counterexamples when asked to evaluate an argument, but rather base their assessment on the first model that comes to mind. This observation led to the formulation of the selecting processing model (Evans et al., 2001): when evaluating syllogistic arguments, reasoning typically proceeds by

an effort to construct just a single model of the premises. This construction process is, however, biased by the believability of presented conclusions, so that for a believable conclusion an attempt is made to construct a single model that supports the conclusion, whereas for an unbelievable conclusion an attempt is made to construct a single model that refutes the conclusion … When conclusions are valid [i.e. follow deductively from the premises], despite unbelievable content motivating a search for a counterexample model, such a model cannot be found, thus limiting the influence of belief bias. When conclusions are invalid, however, models exist that both support and refute such conclusions, thus leading to high levels of erroneous acceptance of invalid–believable items and high levels of correct rejection of invalid–unbelievable items. (Ball & Thompson, 2018, p. 20)

This description prompts a number of important observations for our purposes. Indeed, to verify the validity of a deductive argument, a reasoner must

---

unbelievable conclusion. Indeed, it has been proposed that "unbelievable conclusions may serve to debias reasoning" (Ball & Thompson, 2018, p. 20), but 44 percent of non-normative responses is still quite significant, showing that the presumed debiasing effect is limited.

consider *all* models of the premises, and see whether the conclusion holds in *all of them* (as observed in earlier chapters). Now, if people's spontaneous tendency is to construct a single model of the premises (with additional background information), then clearly they are not doing what is expected of them in deductive reasoning. Similarly, how readily reasoners engage in the task of looking for counterexamples when trying to establish the invalidity of a deductive argument is also a crucial question. While the initial mental models account posited that reasoners would proceed to look for counterexamples in the case of arguments with unbelievable conclusions, later theories questioned this claim, as it transpired that only a subset of reasoners tended to seek counter-examples (Torrens et al., 1999).

In other words, on this account, what reasoners are in fact doing when asked to evaluate the (in)validity of deductive arguments – constructing single, most plausible models of the premises and evaluating the conclusion on this first model that comes to mind (Evans et al., 1999; Newstead et al., 1999) – is not at all what they should be doing as far as the deductive canons are concerned. They are not considering *all* of the models of the premises (for validity), and they are not specifically looking for counterexamples to invalidate arguments (for invalidity).[8] Instead, they produce a single model of the premises with additional background belief, and then check whether the conclusion looks plausible (rather than following necessarily from premises) in this single model.[9]

In recent years, research on belief bias has moved towards more sophisticated experimental setups, for instance by tracking more than just participants' responses (e.g. by also tracking response time and eye movement), and/or by introducing interesting task manipulations such as speeded responses and additional cognitive demands during the experiments (so as to probe the contribution of working memory). These methodological innovations have delivered results that are often inconsistent with the earlier accounts of belief bias, thus forcing researchers to go back to the drawing board (Ball & Thompson, 2018). For example, it has been shown that people may take longer to reason when responding to *believable* conclusions (Thompson et al., 2003), whereas the original mental model theory predicts that they would take longer

---

[8] Researchers in this tradition sometimes still formulate the distinction in terms of an opposition between abstract, rule-based reasoning (construed on a simplistic understanding of the notion of logical form) and belief-based reasoning. However, given the conceptualization of deduction developed here, where the notion of logical form has no central role to play (as explained in Chapter 1), this is a misguided way of drawing the distinction. Instead, what seems to be at stake is the difference between reasoning where the reasoner's background implicit beliefs are activated by default, and reasoning where only the explicitly stated premises are taken into account and background belief is bracketed.

[9] Notice that this description is perfectly aligned with the notion of *preferential models*, introduced in the computer science literature on non-monotonic reasoning, and discussed in connection with belief bias in Dutilh Novaes & Veluwenkamp, 2017.

with unbelievable conclusions, and the selective processing model predicts that there would be no difference in response time between believable and unbelievable conclusions (given that, in both cases, reasoners would be operating with the first model coming to mind). (However, there is also evidence that rapid responding increases belief bias; Evans & Curtis-Holmes, 2005.)

8.2.2   Dual-Process Theories and Individual Differences

While the existence of belief effects as such remains unchallenged, the exact mechanisms underlying these reasoning processes are still disputed. In particular, two themes have received significant attention from researchers in the last decades: dual-process accounts of belief bias, and focus on individual differences in reasoning.

Originally, dual-process theories postulated a strict dichotomy between two different kinds of mental processes:

> Dual-process theories hold that there are two distinct processing modes available for many cognitive tasks: one (Type 1) that is fast, automatic and non-conscious, and another (Type 2) that is slow, controlled and conscious. Typically, cognitive biases are attributed to type 1 processes, which are held to be heuristic or associative, and logical responses to type 2 processes, which are characterised as rule-based or analytical. (Frankish, 2010, p. 914)

Indeed, from the original dual-process perspective, belief bias effects are readily explained in terms of predominant Type 1 belief-based processes, which are occasionally overridden by Type 2 processes. However, recent experimental results have significantly complicated this simple picture.[10] For example, it has been observed that sometimes the 'logical' (presumably Type 2) response is faster than the belief-based (presumably Type 1) response (Trippas et al., 2017), which goes against one of the basic tenets of dual-process theories. Moreover, the simplistic association between Type 1 processes and biased responses, on the one hand, and Type 2 processes and normative responses, on the other hand, has also been shown not to hold. These results have compelled researchers to embrace a more nuanced position on dual-process accounts of belief bias:

> although Type 1 and Type 2 processes are qualitatively different in terms of what triggers them and how much they draw on WM [working memory] capacity, they do not necessarily differ in terms of the answer that they can produce (cf. Evans & Stanovich, 2013a). That is, we need to assume – as indeed the recent evidence appears to show convincingly – that answers based on belief or on logic can arise from either Type 1 or Type 2 processes. (Ball & Thompson, 2018, p. 29)

---

[10] For my own criticism of the dual-process framework in general, see Dutilh Novaes, 2012a, section 7.2.2.

In other words: the belief bias effect simply does not cut neatly across the Type 1/Type 2 distinction. However, even if the emerging picture is much less straightforward than originally thought, it is still the case that taking into account background knowledge and belief when reasoning is the most typical, spontaneous response. Stanovich's 'fundamental computational bias' still stands, even if 'bias' here should not be understood as a cognitive error; the more neutral term 'belief projection,' also used by Stanovich, seems more apt. (Indeed, according to a competing normative system, Bayesian probability calculus, taking background belief as one's starting point when reasoning is precisely what one ought to do – more on this shortly.) At the same time, it has become clear that, under certain conditions, and with specific triggers in place, at least some reasoners are able to override the pull of background beliefs. And insofar as deductive reasoning requires exactly the suppression of background, implicit beliefs, findings on when and how this occurs are directly relevant for the present investigation. Indeed, experimental results seem to suggest an important component of *individual differences* with respect to belief effects on reasoning.

While reasoning experiments originally tended to look at overall percentages of different responses, with no attention paid to the cognitive profiles of participants giving different responses, most of the key experiments in this literature display significant variation in response patterns. Even in the classical formulation of the Wason selection task, while very few people (typically between 5 and 10 percent) give the normative response according to classical logic, the remaining participants still show quite some disagreement (two frequent non-normative responses being: turn only the card that matches the antecedent, or the card that matches the antecedent and the card that matches the consequent of the conditional rule being tested). In the classical belief bias study cited above (Evans et al., 1983), in 71 percent of the instances participants deemed invalid arguments with a believable conclusion to be valid; a large number indeed, but with a significant minority of 29 percent giving the normative response (assuming that there were only two options). In the case of valid syllogisms with unbelievable conclusions, the responses were almost evenly split: 56 percent of normative responses vs. 44 percent of non-normative responses. Indeed, for every single reasoning task studied in the literature, even the notoriously difficult original formulation of the Wason selection task with abstract materials, some people *do* provide the deductive normative response.

Against this background of variability, Stanovich and colleagues have undertaken a sustained research program on individual differences in reasoning in the past decades (Stanovich, 1999, 2012), including studies specifically on belief bias effects (Sá et al., 1999). These studies have investigated the significant variability that is already implicitly present in standard reasoning studies, focusing in particular on the features of a person's cognitive profile that would predict different reasoning outcomes.

At first sight, it might be thought that performance in reasoning tasks would simply strongly correlate with standard measures of intelligence and cognitive ability, e.g. IQ tests, but in fact there are a number of other factors involved (as research on the Cognitive Reflection Test developed by Shane Frederick [2005] has shown; Stanovich & West, 2008). Specifically with respect to belief bias, it has been argued that the capacity to override belief-based responses does correlate with typical measures of cognitive ability (working memory capacity being one reliable indicator), but other epistemic features also seem to play a role, such as open-minded thinking (indicating openness to belief change and cognitive flexibility) and skills in cognitive decontextualization (Sá et al., 1999).

A more recent study of individual differences in belief bias was motivated by the observation that "*no-one* should be able to respond logically to invalid/believable problems via either the heuristic or the analytic routes within the current version of the selective processing model" (Stupple et al., 2011, p. 933), whereas typically a significant minority (29 percent in the seminal Evans et al., 1983 study; 22 percent in the 'rose problem,' Stanovich, 2003) *do* identify a deductively invalid syllogism with a believable conclusion as invalid. What are these reasoners doing differently from others? Edward Stupple and colleagues focused on inspection time measures for three different groups of participants, divided according to the deductive accuracy of their responses:

(1) a low-logic group (overall accuracy below 56 percent) showing high levels of belief bias and very fast response times;

(2) a medium-logic group (overall accuracy 57–74 percent) showing moderate belief bias and slower response times;

(3) a high-logic group (overall accuracy above 75 percent) showing low belief bias, where such responses were also associated with increased processing times, especially for invalid–believable conclusions.

The authors interpreted these results as lending support to a slightly revised version of the selective processing model, and thus to the general dual-process framework underpinning this theory. Indeed, it seems natural to view the fact that participants who give the deductively correct response tend to take more time to respond as an indication of (effortful, time-consuming) Type 2 processing overriding (fast and frugal) Type 1 processing. But even if this interpretation can be questioned (in view of the more recent reformulations of the Type 1/Type 2 dichotomy with respect to biases, as discussed above), the chronometric data give us some indication of the strategies adopted by different reasoners in these tasks.

One plausible account of the reasoning strategies adopted by the reasoners who, in the experiments at least (but perhaps also in more ecologically valid environments), are able to override the spontaneous tendency to bring in background belief, is that these strategies are not 'natural,' genetically encoded dispositions in these individuals but rather culturally induced modes of thinking. Stanovich sums up this hypothesis in the following terms:

> In short, in situations where the present human environment is similar to the EEA [environment of evolutionary adaptedness], the human brain is characterized by fundamental computational biases that bring massive amounts of stored contextual information to bear on the problem. However, when technological societies throw up new problems that confound these evolutionarily adapted mechanisms, humans must use cognitive mechanisms that are in part cultural inventions to override the fundamental computational biases that, in these situations, will prime the wrong response. These culturally induced processing modes more closely resemble the abstract, rule-based, serial processes in many more traditional models of problem solving. (Stanovich, 2003, pp. 293–294)

Individual differences in reasoning outcomes would then be at least partially explained in terms of the different degrees to which reasoners are exposed to and adopt these culturally induced modes of thinking (which, of course, never completely replace other, more spontaneous modes of thinking; Dutilh Novaes, 2013b). This in turn would be a function both of the right kind of cultural exposure and of the reasoner's individual cognitive inclinations, which entails that even among cognitive agents who have had the same kind of formal education, relevant differences in reasoning performance may still occur. (The notion of culturally induced modes of thinking will feature prominently in Chapters 9 and 10.)

8.2.3   Belief Projection and Deductive Reasoning

To sum up, I have argued that the main source for the difficulties with deductive reasoning that most human reasoners seem to experience is what Stanovich has described as the tendency to systematically bring background information and belief to bear when reasoning (i.e. belief projection). This tendency is perfectly natural and adaptive for most intents and purposes, but it clashes with the requirement to block interference of background beliefs when reasoning deductively. The phenomenon has been extensively studied in the belief bias literature, including a number of proposals for the putative mechanisms involved. What also emerges from these studies, though, is the fact that a significant minority does seem to be able to override the pull of prior beliefs and deliver deductive normative responses, even when a different response is more salient as a result of belief projection. This means that deductive reasoning is something that (some) human reasoners are able to perform, given the right kind of triggers. In Chapter 9, we look into what these triggers might be.

In terms of the three key features of deductive reasoning that provide the basis for the present analysis (Chapter 1), it is particularly with respect to necessary truth-preservation and belief-bracketing that the tendency towards belief projection is at odds with the precepts of deductive reasoning. While much of the psychology literature still associates logical forms and schemata to deduction as a rule-based mode of reasoning, what is in fact truly distinctive of deductive reasoning (or so I claim) is that, for an argument to be deductively valid, the conclusion must hold in *all* situations where the premises hold (necessary truth-preservation). This requires the reasoner to consider also very far-fetched, implausible models of the premises, whereas a more spontaneous cognitive tendency is to consider only a subset of the premises' models, namely the more plausible ones – which have been described as the *preferred models* of the reasoner in the literature on non-monotonic reasoning (Dutilh Novaes & Veluwenkamp, 2017). Arguably, the limited range of models considered is at the root of the non-monotonicity of most ordinary reasoning, and what determines the models to be considered are the background beliefs of the agent. By contrast, deductive reasoning requires that *all* models of the premises be considered, a cognitively costly task that, for most intents and purposes, is not pragmatically warranted. Thus, to ensure that a reasoner moves towards deductive reasoning (in the appropriate situations), what is required are triggers that would force her to consider *all* the models of the premises instead of only her belief-induced preferred models.

Another feature of deductive reasoning that is at odds with the more spontaneous, belief-driven reasoning modes described above is the requirement that premises be taken at face value, i.e. taken as if they were true regardless of the reasoner's own doxastic position towards them – in my terminology, belief-bracketing. Some belief bias experiments specifically include instructions to this effect in the task materials. Sá et al., 1999, for example, had the following:

In the following problems, you will be given two premises *which you must assume are true*. A conclusion from the premises then follows. You must decide whether the conclusion *follows logically* from the premises or not.[11] You must *suppose that the premises are all true* and limit yourself only to the information contained in the premises. This is very important. Decide if the conclusion follows logically from the premises, assuming the premises are true, and circle your response. (Sá et al., 1999, p. 500, emphasis in the original)

But even when given explicit instructions to do so, reasoners tend to experience difficulty with reasoning on the basis of premises that they themselves do not believe – a phenomenon also identified and discussed in the critical thinking literature, where the ability to "reason from starting points with which they disagree without letting the disagreement interfere with reasoning" (Norris &

---

[11] It is not clear, however, that participants would be in a position to give the intended interpretation to 'follows logically.' The results in Evans et al., 1994 confirm that a modicum of instruction on the very notion of 'following logically' already has the effect of bringing participants' responses closer to the deductively normative responses. But even then, belief bias effects are not completely eliminated.

Ennis, 1989, p. 12) is viewed as an essential but demanding component. Indeed, in Chapter 9, I discuss findings showing that participants with low levels of schooling tend to avoid drawing conclusions from premises that they have no knowledge of, suggesting that this ability must be taught and cultivated.

However, even highly schooled WEIRD reasoners (from societies that are Western, educated, industrialized, rich, and democratic; Henrich et al., 2010), the typical undergraduates in reasoning experiments, may fail to fully integrate the premises of a given argument if they clash with their background beliefs. This may explain why a significant portion of participants fails to identify as valid a valid syllogism with an unbelievable conclusion. Arguably, they do not in fact perform the required (temporary, artificial, hypothetical) update in their belief sets with the given premises in order to ascertain the validity of the argument (Dutilh Novaes & Veluwenkamp, 2017), despite being told to do so. Indeed, premise integration is a complex but often overlooked component of (deductive) reasoning, and belief effects can interact with premise integration processes (Andrews, 2010). So, given our tendency to bring in background beliefs when reasoning, it is no wonder that, for most human reasoners, deductive reasoning remains challenging.[12]

Before moving on to the next section, a few observations on a competing normative account of reasoning are in order, namely Bayesian rationality. The Bayesian challenge, first articulated by Oaksford and Chater in the 1990s (Oaksford & Chater, 1994, 1991), was the first significant blow to the deductive paradigm that had reigned uncontested for decades in the psychology of reasoning. Outliers at first, the Bayesians have now become central figures in the new paradigm of research on reasoning (Elqayam, 2018), even if it would be an overstatement to say that all researchers in the field have become card-carrying Bayesians.

For our purposes, it is crucial to notice that, while in the deduction paradigm the effects of belief on reasoning were initially described as 'biases' (a 'bug'), in the Bayesian framework, prior beliefs are precisely what reasoners must take as their starting point when reasoning (a 'feature').[13] In other words, while virtually all researchers now choose not to view belief effects as straightforward

---

[12] Some researchers maintain that human reasoners display a considerable amount of 'logical intuition' (De Neys, 2014), corresponding to what could be described as 'Type 1 logic,' a claim that I contest. See Ball & Thompson, 2018 for a discussion of the limitations of the research purportedly demonstrating the existence of Type 1 logic. See also Chapter 10 on inference in non-human animals, where it is argued that even if an agent may seem to be displaying 'logical behavior,' equally compelling non-logical explanations can typically be given for the behavior.

[13] "[O]n this view, people should make decisions by using all of their relevant knowledge and beliefs. From this Bayesian perspective it can be argued that reasoners will be rightly reluctant to set aside their beliefs, which are based on many years of learning and experience, so as instead to privilege an experimenter's artificially presented arguments (cf. Evans & Over, 1996)" (Ball & Thompson, 2018, p. 32).

cognitive errors, for the Bayesians, background beliefs (or credences, in more technical parlance) are the very things that reasoning operates with, as captured by the key theoretical notion of *prior probabilities*. From a Bayesian perspective, researchers on reasoning should not have been in the least surprised to discover the strong effects of belief on reasoning; this is exactly how it is and should be (Hahn & Oaksford, 2008).[14]

8.3   The Strength of Group Deductive Reasoning

While performance in deductive tasks undertaken individually tends to be poor (both in the lab and in the 'wild'), there are some robust results suggesting that deductive performance improves significantly when reasoners are allowed to tackle deductive tasks in groups (even if groups tend to need more time than individuals to reach conclusions). In fact, there is abundant evidence for the effectiveness of group problem-solving on a wide range tasks, not only deductive ones (Laughlin, 2011; Mercier, 2018). This may come as a surprise to those familiar with the phenomena of group polarization (Sunstein, 2002) and groupthink (Solomon, 2006). Indeed, in view of these phenomena, it seems that, in many circumstances, group problem-solving in fact leads to suboptimal solutions. However, an important distinction to keep in mind is the one between *intellective* and *judgmental* problems (though these are more helpfully conceived of as two extreme points on a continuum rather than as a sharp distinction):

Laughlin (1980) proposed a group task continuum anchored by intellective and judgmental tasks. Intellective tasks have a demonstrably correct solution within a mathematical, logical, scientific, or verbal conceptual system ... In contrast, judgmental tasks are evaluative, behavioral, or aesthetic judgments for which no generally accepted demonstrably correct answer exists. (Laughlin, 2011, p. 5)

Generally speaking, group problem-solving achieves better results in intellective than in judgmental tasks, and deductive tasks are paradigmatic examples of intellective tasks (at least within a well-defined conceptual system).[15] Indeed, there are a few experiments with deductive tasks in the literature that offer striking displays of the strength of group problem-solving; I now discuss two of them in detail.

---

[14] However, the Bayesian approach has also been criticized for adopting a monolithic, overly normative conception of rationality: "But why do we need a normative system at all? Arguably, all the new paradigm is doing is repeat the mistakes made by the traditional paradigm – the same old game, only with the normative system replaced" (Elqayam, 2018, p. 145).

[15] In view of considerations on logical pluralism (discussed in Chapter 4), it may well seem that deductive tasks will also have a strong judgmental component, at least insofar as ascertaining whether an argument is deductively valid or not presupposes a substantive choice of what counts as 'deductively valid' (i.e., if there are competing accounts of deductive validity). However, for the relatively simple deductive tasks discussed in this literature, issues related to logical pluralism do not arise.

Perhaps the best known of these studies is that of David Moshman and Molly Geil (1998), which focuses on how groups solve the classical, abstract version of the Wason selection task (with letters and numbers). The study was motivated by Moshman's years of experience in classroom settings, where he let students engage in the Wason selection task in groups and observed that the correct answer from the point of view of the deductive canons (turn the *p* and the *not-q* cards to test the 'If *p* then *q*' conditional) was obtained much more often than in experiments with individuals (where typically between 5 and 10 percent of participants give the correct deductive response). The materials for the experiment were as follows (a classical formulation of the Wason selection task, quoted here in full in the unlikely event that some readers may not yet be familiar with the task):

[Students] were presented with four cards pictured on a sheet of paper. Each card had either a letter or a number on it. The letter E was shown on the first card, K on the second card, 4 on the third card, and 7 on the fourth card. It was indicated that each card pictured had a letter on one side and a number on the other. Below the letters was the following hypothesis: "If a card has a vowel on one side then it has an even number on the other side." Students were asked to test the hypothesis by selecting the card(s) they would need to turn over to determine conclusively whether the hypothesis was true or false for the set of four cards shown. (Moshman & Geil, 1998, p. 233)

The 143 students who participated in the study were divided into three experimental conditions: an individual control condition (thirty-two participants); an interactive condition (fifty-four participants, who were immediately divided into groups of five or six members); and an individual/interactive condition (fifty-seven participants, who first approached the task individually such that their individual responses were registered, and then divided into groups of five or six which went on to solve the task in interactive ways, as in the second condition). Importantly, the two group conditions specifically required participants to discuss different proposals with one another, that is, to 'work together' until they reached a unanimous view. The individual/interactive condition is particularly ingenious, because it allowed the experimenters to track the specific effects of deliberation, when compared to their initial responses.

The results were striking: "In the individual condition, 9.4% selected the correct *p and not-q* combination. In the interactive condition, 70% of the groups selected the correct *p and not-q* combination; in the individual/interactive condition, 80% of the groups selected this combination." (Moshman & Geil, 1998, p. 235) (The hypothesis being tested is represented by the schematic 'If *p* then *q*' conditional.) In other words, in the individual condition the results were aligned with the 'usual' performance of participants in the classical Wason selection task, but the two interactive conditions saw a dramatic increase in correct responses.

What is perhaps even more significant is the fact that, in the individual/ interactive condition, even groups where all participants had failed to obtain the correct response at the individual stage then went on to find it at the interactive stage:

Seven of the ten groups had at least one member who initially selected the correct *p and not-q* combination. In no case was this the modal response. Nonetheless, five of these groups selected the correct pattern after collaboration; only two did not. In the remaining three groups, none of the members initially selected the correct response. Nevertheless, each of these groups ultimately agreed on the correct *p and not-q* combination. Thus, having a member who initially selected the correct cards was neither a necessary nor sufficient condition for group success. (Moshman & Geil, 1998, p. 237)

These results are significant because they conflict with the (otherwise plausible) hypothesis that what ensures the improved performance of groups is simply that the (few) participants who had individually arrived at the correct answer were then able to convince the other participants of its correctness – what is known as the 'truth wins' model: the observed group superiority is attributed to the abilities of the members of the group rather than to their interaction (Laughlin, 2011). By contrast, in the Moshman & Geil, 1998 study, three groups where none of the members initially selected the correct solution went on to agree on the correct solution by 'working together' through deliberation and the exchange of reasons. (The article contains fascinating transcripts of these conversations.) Also noteworthy is the fact that two of the groups that had at least one member with the correct answer went on to select a different answer, which again speaks against the unrestricted validity of the 'truth wins' model.[16]

More recently, Hugo Mercier and colleagues further investigated group problem-solving and interactive argumentation in a variety of experiments (for an overview, see Mercier, 2018, section on 'Reasoning in discussion'). In Trouche et al., 2014, the goal was to probe the role of confidence in group problem-solving. It had been suggested (Koriat, 2012) that confidence, rather than truth or accuracy, is what explains the apparent success of group problem-solving: it is the member with the highest confidence in her solution who will convince others, not the member(s) with the correct solution. On this interpretation, it is only insofar as there might be a correlation between having the

---

[16] Such cases are very relevant for our purposes in that they seem to suggest that, at least sometimes, the group setting may lead to a poorer deductive performance (at least for the individuals who did have the correct response initially but whose group then unanimously went on to adopt an incorrect response). Unfortunately, the article does not contain transcripts of the discussions in these groups, but we may conjecture that confidence factors played a role (the individual with the correct answer was not a particularly confident person, and/or was overpowered by a particularly dominant person with an incorrect response).

correct answer and confidence that 'truth wins.'[17] So Mercier and colleagues set out to test the 'confidence explanation,' pitching it against the 'argument explanation.'

The task participants had to solve was an intellective reasoning task, a problem formulated by computer scientist Hector Levesque (1986):

Paul is looking at Linda and Linda is looking at Patrick. Paul is married but Patrick is not. Is a person who is married looking at a person who is not married?

Participants were then given three options to choose from: Yes/No/Cannot be determined. Effectively, this is a deductive reasoning task: given the premises (Paul is looking at Linda and Linda is looking at Patrick; Paul is married but Patrick is not), does the conclusion, 'A person who is married is looking at a person who is not married' follow? The correct response is 'Yes,' at least on the assumption that Linda is either married or not married (i.e. that the two options exhaust the realm of possibilities), but typically only a small subset of participants in individual conditions gives this answer (around 20 percent in the Trouche et al. study). The majority of responses are 'Cannot be determined,' as reasoners presumably view the fact that they are ignorant of Linda's marital status as precluding any conclusion from being drawn.[18]

As in the third condition of Moshman & Geil, 1998, the experimenters first tracked individual responses to the problem (including reasons offered: only correct answers with accompanying correct reasons were coded as correct), and then divided participants into groups. The results of Experiment 3 in Trouche et al., 2014 again confirm the strength of interactive problem-solving in deductive tasks, though the increase in deductively correct responses was not as dramatic as in Moshman & Geil, 1998: 22 percent of correct responses in the individual condition vs. 63 percent of correct responses for participants in the interactive condition (fourteen of the twenty-five groups). Of the fourteen groups who achieved the correct response, eleven had at least one member who had obtained the correct answer in the individual setting;[19] in other words,

---

[17] Koriat, 2012 argues that in the case of perceptual or even general knowledge questions, the outcome of group discussion can be emulated by aggregating the individual judgments of the group members weighed by their confidence.

[18] This problem is interesting because it does not seem to trigger belief projection effects such as the ones described in the previous section. Instead, the failure to identify the correct response here seems to stem from difficulties related to disjunctive reasoning/reasoning by cases; what a reasoner must do is consider the two options (Linda being married and Linda not being married), and notice that in both cases the conclusion follows. (Note that reasoning by cases is a very important strategy for mathematical proof.) I am not aware of any deductive reasoning experiments specifically testing the effects of belief bias in group reasoning; this is unfortunate, as ideally we would like to probe whether the group setting has a similar effect on e.g. syllogistic tasks as it has for the Wason selection task and the 'married' problem.

[19] One group had a member who had obtained the correct answer 'Yes,' but then the group settled on 'Cannot be determined.' However, the reason the group provided was that the categories

three groups were able to arrive at the correct answer by 'working together,' even though none of the members had the correct answer initially. Moreover, Trouche et al. did not find the strong effect of confidence predicted by Koriat, 2012, and indeed found their results to confirm the 'argument explanation.'[20]

The (presumed) beneficial epistemic and cognitive effects of collaborative discourse and argumentation have attracted much attention from educational psychologists and educators (Nussbaum, 2008; Kuhn & Crowell, 2011), but studies specifically on deductive reasoning are not very numerous.[21] The available results, in particular from the two studies just discussed, do indicate superiority of group problem-solving for deductive tasks (which is to be expected, given the intellective nature of these tasks and the general observation that groups tend to do better in intellective tasks), though one may wonder whether this homogeneous picture is not at least in part a result of publication bias (i.e., perhaps studies that do not identify improved performance in group settings are simply not published). It is also important to notice that group problem-solving involving argumentative interaction seems to require considerably more time than individual problem-solving, so the improved performance does not come entirely for free, so to speak. Moreover, there are issues pertaining to scaling up the number of members in these groups: beyond a certain point, additional members in fact hinder rather than facilitate the process (Mercier, 2018).

8.4   Conclusion

In sum, the general picture emerging is one of human reasoners failing miserably at deductive reasoning in individual settings, but improving significantly in deductive performance when reasoning in groups, in particular when adopting an interactive, argumentative approach (Mercier & Sperber, 2017).[22] Results

'married' and 'not married' do not exhaust the realm of possibilities, and this is indeed an assumption for the 'Yes' solution to emerge as the correct one, as noted above. This group was excluded from the analysis. (See footnote 3 of Trouche et al., 2014.)

[20] "[I]n some groups a member who had found the correct answer individually was able to convince her peers who had the wrong answer despite the fact that she was not the most confident group member, or even that she was less confident than the average of the others. This means that when the most confident member did not have the right answer and that another member did, the former never managed to sway the group" (Trouche et al., 2014, p. 1964).

[21] But see also Chapter 6 of Laughlin, 2011 on letters-to-numbers problems, which can be viewed as essentially a deductive task similar to e.g. Sudoku.

[22] An alternative model, which has many proponents, is a different 'wisdom of the crowds' story where varying opinions must be aggregated while remaining independent, thus excluding occurrences of reason exchange. This approach has venerable origins in results like Condorcet's jury theorem; its proponents highlight the potential for countering well-known pitfalls of group reasoning such as groupthink (Solomon, 2006). However, there is no evidence that I am aware of suggesting that aggregation works better than argumentation specifically for deductive reasoning tasks, and the results of the experiments discussed here speak clearly against this model.

showing that groups where no one has the correct answer individually can still achieve the correct answer after deliberation lend support to the epistemic value of exchanging reasons. Taken as a whole, these results are consistent with the dialogical conception of deduction defended here, but a number of important questions remain. What is it about group interaction that accounts for the improved performance? How does the group setting relate to the three main characteristics of deductive reasoning described in Chapters 1 and 4? Can the group setting have a debiasing effect, especially with respect to belief projection? In the next chapter, I discuss these and other questions, and examine empirical evidence for the presumed dialogical nature of the three main characteristics of deductive reasoning.

9   The Ontogeny of Deductive Reasoning

9.1   Introduction

In Chapter 8, we saw that belief projection is a very strong cognitive tendency in humans, one that must to some extent be overridden for the purposes of deductive reasoning. But besides belief projection, another 'fundamental computational bias' of human cognition is what Keith Stanovich (2003) refers to as the tendency to socialize abstract problems. Relying on Hilton, 1995, he remarks:

> Hilton (1995) argues that people treat even decontextualized and depersonalized situations as conversational exchanges with an active interlocutor – "that no utterance is depersonalized, all messages have a source, and that reasoning and inference processes typically operate on socially communicated information" (p. 267). In short, people tend to treat even depersonalized communications as quasi-personal linguistic encounters in a social context. As in our previous discussion of the automatic recruitment of prior knowledge, this too is a type of automatic use of stored information. (Stanovich, 2003, p. 302)

Moreover, in line with a number of influential authors (such as Grice, Levinson, Sperber and Wilson, and Tomasello), Stanovich notes that the 'default' mode of communication is *cooperative communication*, as captured for example by Gricean conversational maxims. This may become an impediment in the case of abstract cognitive tasks such as deductive problems, given that, as aptly observed by Jonathan Adler, "abstraction is uncooperative" (Adler, 1984). (What it means to say that deduction in particular is uncooperative will be discussed in more detail below.) In other words, this is yet another reason (besides belief projection) why participants seem to perform poorly in deductive reasoning experiments (in individual settings, at least), as well as other reasoning experiments (e.g. those on the conjunction fallacy/ Linda problem): they project a specific conversational structure onto the task that leads to a misrepresentation of what exactly is expected of them in that particular situation.

Given these observations, one way to elicit deductive reasoning might be to incentivize reasoners to adopt strategies so as to block the tendency to socialize abstract problems. This is arguably the 'classical' approach in education and schooling: to 're-program' the mind with abstract, non-personalized, decontextualized modes of thinking (which involve a whole suite of cognitive strategies).[1] However, this approach remains inherently limited, given that decontextualized modes of thinking are computationally costly for the agent, and that more spontaneous, contextualized modes of thinking remain active and thus must be constantly suppressed and overridden.

By contrast, a potentially more promising approach, which will be explored in this chapter, is to suitably contextualize/personalize deductive reasoning instead of decontextualizing it. If the dialogical account of deductive reasoning defended here is correct, then deduction corresponds to rather contrived forms of dialogue that are very much at odds with the essentially cooperative conversational structures that permeate much of human linguistic interactions. What is required to nudge reasoners towards deductive reasoning is to enact/simulate these somewhat unusual dialogical conditions: a 'language game' where one participant will seek to convince the other participant of a given claim; the second participant will not easily be convinced and thus will present counterexamples and objections. The prediction is that, on this contextualization, reasoners will more readily adopt modes of thinking that come closer to the deductive canons. In other words, if features of the historical development of the deductive method (i.e., semi-adversarial debates) can be reenacted by means of dialogical cues, leading to improved deductive performance, then we might say that there is a sense in which 'ontogeny recapitulates history' (as conjectured in Chapter 2).

In this chapter, I discuss empirical evidence supporting this prediction and offer suggestions for future work. I focus on the three main features of deductive reasoning that have been with us since Chapter 1 – necessary truth-preservation, belief-bracketing, and perspicuity – and discuss the evidence indicating that specific dialogical cues may nudge reasoners towards deductive reasoning by eliciting reasoning modes that adhere to the three key properties of deductive reasoning. In other words, this chapter focuses on the emergence of deductive reasoning at the ontogenetic level, emphasizing the crucial role of teaching and training. This is a process that can be optimized if deduction is introduced to students by means of specific dialogical situations (a dialogical scaffolding). In the final section, I also discuss the notion of internalization in more detail, relying in particular on Vygotsky, 1978.

---

[1] "Indeed, many developmental theorists, as have influential cognitive psychologists (e.g., Kahneman & Tversky 1982), emphasize how schooling teaches children to decouple reasoning from the pragmatic inferences of language comprehension" (Stanovich, 2003, p. 320).

9.2   Necessary Truth-Preservation: Adversariality

Let us now return to the idea of belief projection, discussed in Chapter 8, and the claim that, in reasoning experiments, what participants tend to do is concoct their preferred model (to borrow a term from the literature on non-monotonic reasoning) of the premises. However, given the observation that participants will often project a conversational structure onto the experimental task (as argued in Adler, 1984 and Hilton, 1995), then it is plausible to expect that many participants will in fact not only take their own beliefs into account but also what they presume to be in the experimenter's mind when designing the experiment. Indeed, in most 'mundane,' cooperative conversations, what seems to occur is that interlocutors communicate in order to coordinate on a jointly preferred model of the available information and discursive commitments, in the spirit of David Lewis' conversational scorekeeping (Lewis, 1979). In other words, in most everyday conversations, people attempt to guess what the intended model of their interlocutors might be, which essentially amounts to a cooperative stance.[2] In turn, in experiments, participants may take the experimenter to be the relevant interlocutor, and reason on the basis of their beliefs as well as on the basis of what they take to be the experimenter's intentions. It is because we make (cooperative) assumptions of all kinds that the 'logic' of these conversations is thoroughly non-monotonic and does not respect necessary truth-preservation.

Interestingly, even in the highly regimented context of mathematical deductive proofs, the tendency to focus on a few relevant models/examples is also observed: for example, when asked to prove a mathematical statement, many students respond by checking examples rather than producing a general proof (Gilmore et al., 2018, pp. 157–158). This is arguably a manifestation of the same tendency to focus on a small number of salient models.

This is, however, in conflict with what a participant in a deductive dialogue should do: making implicit assumptions and jumping to conclusions is incompatible with deductive, monotonic reasoning. Given that it so accurately captures the 'adversarial' nature of deduction, let me here repeat a passage by cognitive scientist Keith Stenning already quoted in Chapter 4:

What *follows* in deduction is anything that is true in *all* interpretations of the premises – that is the definition of logically valid inference. Our job, as speaker or hearer of a discourse that purports to be a deduction, is to test the drawing of inferences to

---

[2] "In conversation hearers try to arrive at the speaker's 'intended' model of their utterances. We jump to all sorts of conclusions about this model on the basis of assuming mutual habits of communication and mutual beliefs about the topic at hand ... We generally jump correctly to the intended model, ignoring many models logically compatible with what was actually said ... Jumping to conclusions is a staple of co-operative communication, but it is bad logical form" (Stenning, 2002, p. 138).

destruction, to ensure that what is inferred is true in *all* models of the premises, not just the intended one. It is in this technical sense that logic models adversarial discourse. We may actually be socially co-operating in testing a deduction for validity, and certainly we have to co-operate a great deal to be sure that we are assuming the same things about the range of interpretations which are intended, but there is a core of seeking out all possible assignments of things, not simply finding one intended one. (Stenning, 2002, p. 138)

If deductive reasoning is 'adversarial' in this specific sense, then in order to elicit deductive reasoning, one avenue to be explored is the enactment of an explicitly adversarial conversational situation, which would allow the reasoner to 'turn off' temporarily her default cooperative conversational habits. With this idea in mind, Stenning (in collaboration with Theodora Achourioti) ran a study on syllogistic problems with a creative experimental manipulation: beside a control group who tackled the problems with no context (as in most experiments in the literature), another group was told to imagine that they were in a betting situation:

A nefarious character called Harry-the-Snake is at the fairground offering bets on syllogistic conclusions. You always have the choice of refusing the bets Harry offers, but if you think the conclusion he proposes does not follow from his premises (i.e., is invalid), then you should choose to bet against him. If you do so choose, then you must also construct a counterexample to his conclusion. (Achourioti et al., 2014, p. 9)

The researchers were particularly interested in participants' ability to identify arguments without valid deductive conclusions, as it is known from the literature that participants tend to identify valid arguments as valid more reliably than they identify invalid arguments as invalid. In the terminology adopted in Dutilh Novaes & Veluwenkamp, 2017, they overgenerate (deem invalid arguments as valid) more often than they undergenerate (deem valid arguments as invalid) with respect to the deductive canons. In the Harry-the-Snake condition, failing to identify an argument as invalid represents a missed opportunity to win a bet against Harry, but at the same time betting against Harry entails the cognitively costly task of having to provide a counterexample.

Crucially, the betting scenario (coupled with the colorful description of Harry as a suspicious figure) should disable default cooperative modes of conversational engagement. The prediction was that, instead of formulating a plausible model of the premises and checking whether the conclusion is true in the model, participants would be motivated to consider a much wider range of models for the premises, while looking for one model that would count as a counterexample (premises true, conclusion false). In this setting, a participant should neither be reasoning with her own preferred model, nor with what she takes her interlocutor's intended model to be; instead, she is pragmatically nudged towards countermodel reasoning, where the 'good' model of the premises is not the one that accords with her prior beliefs, but rather a model that verifies the premises but falsifies the conclusion, so as to win the bet.

The results confirmed the experimenters' predictions: in the Harry condition, participants correctly identified invalid syllogisms (with accompanying counterexamples) in 74 percent of the cases – a very significant improvement over the dismal 37 percent of accuracy in the conventional task. Accuracy in identifying valid syllogisms was a bit lower, at 66 percent, but still well above chance. (Perhaps participants were overly eager to bet against Harry and win?) Equally significant is the observation that, while performance is improved, participants seem to find the Harry condition more demanding than the conventional one, taking up to three times longer to complete the task: "Countermodel reasoning is hard work" (Achourioti et al., 2014, p. 10). Apparently, they are being asked to do something that is quite different from what they are used to doing in more mundane situations.

In sum, Achourioti and Stenning used a betting scenario to emulate the kind of 'adversariality' that is required for deductive reasoning: to prompt participants to reason towards an 'uncooperative' model where the premises are true but the conclusion is not (i.e., if there is such a model; obviously, there is at least one for each invalid syllogism). Seen thus, a betting scenario is particularly suitable for emulating adversariality.[3] These results suggest again that deductive reasoning is something that humans *can* do, if given the right cues, but in the absence of these cues they simply fall back on cooperative, non-monotonic conversational structures.

I am not aware of any other experimental studies relying on adversarial background conditions for deductive reasoning; moreover, Achourioti and Stenning's study itself was rather small-scale (and never reported in detail, other than the description of its outlines available in Achourioti et al., 2014). So, more research is required to investigate the presumed connection between adversariality and deductive reasoning before more substantive conclusions can be drawn. But these encouraging preliminary results strongly suggest that the link between deductive reasoning and adversariality deserves further investigation.

There is, however, an ongoing 'natural experiment' in the social sciences that, while not pertaining specifically to deductive reasoning, seems to point in a similar direction: the protocol of *adversarial collaboration*, as advocated by, among others, Daniel Kahneman (Mellers et al., 2001). This is a protocol for two (or more) researchers who disagree on a specific matter – for example, they entertain competing hypotheses about given phenomena/experimental findings – to set out to investigate the issue jointly, while maintaining their initial conflicting convictions. The parties agree on tests to be run or experiments to be conducted which may deliver decisive evidence one way or another. The

---

[3] Notice also that betting is a key concept in a number of other accounts of rationality, e.g. Dutch book arguments in Bayesian accounts of rationality.

concept of adversarial collaboration is also motivated by concerns of insuffi-
cient transparency in the empirical sciences (e.g. researchers who formulate
a 'hypothesis' after collecting the data, when their initial hypothesis is not
borne out by the data collected); but at heart it is based on the idea that people
who disagree with each other, and are thus 'adversaries' to this extent, will be
able to contemplate aspects of the problem that the other side will fail to
contemplate in virtue of confirmation bias, tunnel vision, and other cognitive
limitations.

It is noteworthy that even the vocabulary used to refer to the different parties in
adversarial collaborations very much resembles the one adopted here: in Matzke
et al., 2015, for example, the terms 'proponent' and 'skeptic' are used to refer to
the different stances in the debate. Indeed, there is a neat analogy here between
adversariality in deductive reasoning and adversariality in the empirical sciences
(thus understood). The empirical data gathered are the counterpart of premises: in
an individual setting or in a multi-agent but strictly collaborative setting, belief
projection will kick in and most likely lead to the adoption of a (potentially
unique) model of the premises or an interpretation of the data that confirms prior
beliefs. In an adversarial setting, by contrast, a wider range of models/interpret-
ations must be considered, and conflicting beliefs by the different parties keep
individual belief projection to some extent in check. Adversarial collaboration is
thus a 'real-life experiment' illustrating the debiasing power of a certain amount
of 'adversariality,' here corresponding to epistemic disagreement, an 'old' idea
famously defended by John Stuart Mill (1999).

9.3   Bracketing Belief: Fantasy and the 'Hypothetical Other'

In Chapter 8, I discussed the effects of belief projection on the ability to reason
from starting points with which one disagrees without letting one's doxastic
state interfere in the reasoning process – a fundamental aspect of deductive
skills.[4] This is a general phenomenon that affects reasoners with different levels
of schooling, as predicted if belief projection is indeed a 'fundamental computational bias.' Moreover, there's something rather 'anti-Gricean' about suppos-
ing/assuming, especially in a conversational context, something one does not in
fact believe; it seems to go against ideals of truthfulness in conversation.

Formal schooling has the potential to mitigate this spontaneous cognitive
tendency, at least to some extent: ordinary formal schooling typically exposes
reasoners to the practice of putting aside one's beliefs with respect to the
contents of the available information for the purposes of reasoning. A school
context fosters the kind of dialogical interaction where one interlocutor (the
teacher) puts forward claims that the other interlocutor (the student) must

[4] Parts of this section appeared in Dutilh Novaes, 2013b.

accept as true in order to reason with – e.g. the formulation of an arithmetic problem. It is thus not surprising that schooling facilitates the emergence of what can be described as an 'analytic orientation' (more on which below), which finds its pinnacle in debating practices where a debater can argue for a given thesis entirely independently of her own doxastic position towards it.

To further probe these conjectures, an approach that naturally suggests itself is to investigate (deductive) reasoning skills in reasoners with different levels of schooling. Indeed, as Heinrich et al. (2010) have eloquently argued, given that the great majority of studies in the behavioral sciences are based on samples drawn from WEIRD (Western, educated, industrialized, rich, and democratic) societies, addressing questions of human nature on the basis of data drawn from this particularly thin, and rather unusual, slice of humanity seems methodologically suspicious. In practice, unfortunately, there is a scarcity of reasoning studies with populations having low educational levels (for reviews, see Counihan, 2008, chapters 1 and 3, and Harris, 2000, chapter 5).

The seminal work on reasoning with non-WEIRD populations is Luria, 1976, a study conducted in the 1930s with unschooled peasants in remote parts of what was then the Soviet Union (Uzbekistan). Alexander Luria, who was to become a very influential figure in a number of subfields within psychology (he is known as one of the fathers of neuropsychology for his work on brain-injured victims of World War II), embraced and further developed Vygotsky's ideas, according to whom thinking and reasoning are deeply influenced by cultural, social, and historical factors. "[Luria and Vygotsky] speculated that the radical changes in the lifestyle of the peasants, notably their increased access to education and their incorporation into Stalin's agricultural collectives, should produce dramatic cognitive changes" (Harris, 2000, p. 95). In his study, Luria conducted experiments with two groups of participants: one group composed of illiterate peasants with no schooling and working in a traditional, non-technological economy; and the other group having recently received one or two years of basic education and been involved in collective farming.

The results were striking. Both groups performed close to deductive normative responses in simple reasoning tasks whose premises referred to contents they were familiar with, but the first group 'failed miserably' in reasoning tasks with unfamiliar content. The second group, however, with only a modicum of formal education, performed much closer to the normative canons of deduction, even with unfamiliar content. In fact, participants in the first group often seemed not to understand what exactly was expected of them with the unfamiliar content tasks: Why were they being asked to answer questions about things they could not possibly know anything about? Here is one illustrative exchange (also quoted in Chapter 1):

Experimenter: In the Far North, where there is snow, all bears are white. Novaya Zemlya is in the Far North and there is always snow there. What color are the bears there?

Subject: I don't know what color the bears are there, I never saw them . . . E: But what do you think? S: Once I saw a bear in a museum, that's all. E: But on the basis of what I said, what color do you think the bears are there? S: Either one-colored or two-colored . . . [ponders for a long time]. To judge from the place, they should be white. You say that there is a lot of snow there, but we have never been there! (Luria, 1976, p. 111)

In contrast, participants with just a few (recent) years of schooling had no issues reasoning with unfamiliar content. Luria's results remained unpublished until 1976, for political reasons. For the same reasons, he could not pursue his program of cross-cultural investigation of reasoning (but went on to produce seminal work in other important fields). It was only in the 1970s that Michael Cole and Sylvia Scribner (Cole et al., 1971; Scribner, 1977; Scribner & Cole, 1981) reinitiated a cross-cultural research program on reasoning, this time investigating unschooled groups in Africa. Their results were very similar to Luria's. On the basis of these results, Scribner (1977) hypothesized the existence of two possible 'orientations' towards a reasoning task: an empirical one and an analytic one. According to Scribner (in the words of Harris),

In the absence of schooling, [participants] adopt an "empirical orientation": they use their own experience to supplement, to distort, or even to reject the premises supplied by the interviewer; they reason instead on the basis of their empirical experience. After two or three years of schooling, they adopt what might be called a "theoretical" or "analytic" orientation instead: they focus on the claims encapsulated in the premises of the problem even when those premises do not fit into their everyday experience and they confine their reasoning to what follows from those premises. (Harris, 2000, pp. 98–99)

In other words, Scribner claimed that unschooled participants tend to stay close to their own beliefs and experiences, whereas schooled participants more easily put their beliefs and experiences aside even if the premises conflicted with their convictions (in other words, overriding belief projection). In the spirit of Vygotsky and Luria's original ideas, Scribner concluded that schooling has the potential to give rise to an analytic orientation in the reasoner, who would otherwise be confined to an empirical orientation.[5]

More recently, Scribner's conclusions have been further investigated by Paul Harris and collaborators. They conducted a number of experiments with young children (Dias & Harris, 1988; Dias & Harris, 1990), as well as unschooled adults in the northeast of Brazil (Dias et al., 2005). They found that it is not only through schooling that reasoners are able to override their own beliefs in a reasoning task; by modifying the formulation of the task materials, children

---

[5] These observations may smack of a problematic colonial attitude towards 'primitive people.' (I owe this point to David Ludwig.) While this issue deserves more space than I can dedicate to it here, let me just note that, on my account at least, the presupposition that the 'analytic orientation' is superior to the 'empirical orientation' is vehemently rejected. If anything, it is the 'analytic orientation' that constitutes a cognitive oddity, as does deductive reasoning.

and unschooled adults can be prompted to take the premises as if they were true and to reason on their presumed truth, even when the premises conflict with their beliefs or are unknown to them.

As described by Harris (2000, chapter 5), pretense play situations, for example, may prompt a (young) reasoner to put aside her factual knowledge and to focus on the pretense truth of some statements. Indeed, Harris and colleagues obtained results much closer to the deductively normative responses by formulating reasoning tasks in terms of make-believe storytelling and pretense play for children.[6] They found that even the intonation used by the experimenter had a significant impact (if the experimenter adopted a 'storytelling' intonation, children were more willing to reason on the basis of the premises provided). With unschooled adults, they obtained a similar effect by postulating that the premises in the experiment were about a 'different planet,' which in practice prompted participants to suppress or put aside their factual beliefs about the actual world (Dias et al., 2005).

More recently, Marian Counihan (2008) presented experimental results with participants having varying but low educational levels in South Africa. Her investigation explored some often neglected aspects of the experimental setup, in particular its semantic and pragmatic components. How do unschooled participants interpret the task proposed to them by the experimenter? Which semantic interpretation do they attribute to the premises? Many seem, for example, to interpret the 'All' in categorical sentences ('All bears are white') as allowing for exceptions, giving it instead a generic reading.[7] Counihan found that participants with low educational levels deviated more strongly from the normative responses of traditional logic in syllogistic tasks than in conditional tasks. Another important finding in Counihan, 2008 is that schooled reasoners who have been away from the school environment for many years, having since returned to activities such as agriculture or herding, often give typical 'unschooled' responses in experiments. This suggests that the effects of schooling on reasoning become less pronounced over time, once the reasoner is no longer at school; 'default' modes of thinking eventually settle in again.

However, as already noted, overriding belief projection when reasoning is challenging even for highly schooled reasoners; they also tend to approach reasoning tasks in a contextualized way, taking into account prior beliefs. Simply telling participants to take premises as if they were true, as in the study reported in Sá et al., 1999 (see Chapter 8), does not seem to produce

---

[6] See also Markovits et al., 1996 for an investigation of the effects of fantasy settings on reasoning. When conditional statements were embedded in a fantasy context, elementary school children were more likely to inhibit prior beliefs than when the inferences were presented in a reality context.

[7] Stenning and Yule, 1997 also observed non-logical interpretations of the quantifiers among highly educated (WEIRD) participants.

any significant effects. So what kind of manipulation might allow reasoners to suppress or at least mitigate this tendency?

In line with the discussions on belief-bracketing in previous chapters, a natural suggestion would be to encourage reasoners to draw conclusions from someone else's beliefs and commitments rather than their own. In particular, when discussing reductio ad absurdum arguments in Chapter 4, I conjectured that enacting a dialogical situation where one person commits to the initial assumption (to be refuted later) and another person then leads the initial assumption to absurdity is likely to increase a reasoner's understanding of what is going on with a reductio argument. This is so because the strangeness of making an initial assumption that goes against one's entrenched beliefs (*contro le mie normali vedute*, as one of the participants in the Antonini & Mariotti, 2008 study put it) is no longer present. Might taking someone else's perspective when reasoning help counter belief-projection tendencies more generally?

The authors of a recent study set out to investigate precisely this hypothesis: whether "asking reasoners to consider a problem from another person's perspective can reduce or eliminate the effect of beliefs on judgements" (Beatty & Thompson, 2012, p. 2). They formulated an experiment where participants evaluated four different hypothetical (fictional) scientific scenarios, each containing a description of a researcher, a hypothesis, a piece of evidence, and four possible conclusions. In other words, rather than trying to elicit impersonal decontextualization, what this experimental setup does, much as in the Harry-the-Snake condition described above, is enact a different social contextualization intended to 'turn off' temporarily default forms of contextualization based on belief projection and cooperative conversational structures. Participants then evaluated the evidence provided twice, once from the researcher's perspective and again from their own perspective. Participants received the following instructions:

On the following pages you will be asked to read and evaluate four experiments from two perspectives. First, you will be asked to select the conclusion that follows logically from the evidence provided from the perspective of the experimenter, putting aside your own knowledge and beliefs. In other words, what should the experimenter conclude based on the evidence? Second, you are asked to choose the conclusion that follows from your perspective. In other words, what are you prepared to conclude based on the evidence? (Beatty & Thompson, 2012, pp. 5–6)

Participants had undergone a pretest where their beliefs about several general propositions were assessed, so that the degree to which their beliefs affected their responses to the evidence evaluation test just described could be measured more rigorously. The crucial question was: Will their responses in the researcher's perspective condition be less affected by their own background beliefs, or will there be no noticeable difference between the two conditions? (Beatty and Thompson also introduced high-authority/low-authority conditions in their descriptions of the fictional experimenters, but this manipulation had no significant effect.) Notice, however, that the problems participants were presented with were not deductive problems strictly speaking; they were statistical problems (the article describes only one such problem), and participants were asked to determine whether the evidence (i) supported the initial hypothesis, (ii) supported the opposite of the initial hypothesis, (iii) had no relationship with the hypothesis, or (iv) did not warrant any conclusion to be drawn.

While there was an overall effect of belief (as to be expected), there was also a significant interaction between belief and perspective, such that the effect of belief was larger from the participant's perspective than from the researcher's perspective. Indeed, the belief effect was significant from the participant's perspective but only marginally so from the researcher's perspective. The authors concluded that the perspective manipulation was effective in reducing reliance on beliefs, thus supporting the initial hypothesis that shift in perspective evokes analytic reasoning. Notice, though, that the reduction of belief projection, even in the researcher's perspective condition, was still relatively modest: 24 percent in terms of absolute differences (Beatty & Thompson, 2012, p. 15). But this result is not overly surprising, considering the strength of our belief-projection tendencies and the limitations of our perspective-taking capacities (Butterfill & Apperly, 2013; Spaulding, 2016). Shifting one's perspective to another person's perspective is bound to happen only partially, despite our best efforts (as anyone who has been involved in challenging emotional discussions with spouses, offspring, etc. surely knows).

Even if somewhat modest, these results do suggest that perspective-shifting might well be one of the most effective manipulations in terms of promoting reasoning with starting points that go against the reasoner's own background beliefs. Simply telling her to disregard these beliefs is clearly not very effective; activating the human tendency to socialize/contextualize problems, in particular to put themselves in someone else's position, might lead to better results: "people may be unwilling to modify their own belief systems based on presented arguments, but may be more willing to accept that belief updating is appropriate for a 'hypothetical other'" (Ball & Thompson, 2018, p. 32). But naturally, there is only so much that we may conclude from one such study; it is to be hoped that other studies relying on perspective-shift conditions will be conducted, with a wider range of task materials (including more strictly deductive problems).

To sum up, two manipulations have been found to be effective in mitigating the tendency towards belief projection (while not overriding it completely) with respect to premises: positing a fictional/fantasy background context (including 'another planet,' as in the Dias et al., 2005 study with adults) and positing a hypothetical 'other.' In particular, the latter manipulation is strongly related to dialogical practices, as being able to ascertain what follows from one's interlocutor's discursive commitments is an essential skill in many dialogical situations (in particular, practices of 'giving and asking for reasons'; Brandom, 1994). Relatedly, there is evidence suggesting that we are better at evaluating the quality of other people's arguments than at producing good arguments ourselves (or evaluating the quality of our own arguments; Mercier & Sperber, 2017; Mercier, 2018), which again suggests that perspective shift can be a powerful counterbalance to belief projection.

Indeed, it is presumably the real-time perspective shift that takes place in actual situations of deliberation/discussion (such as in the group experiments discussed in Chapter 8) – that is, by listening to someone else's arguments, one can actually 'see' things from their perspective to some extent – that accounts for the possibility of going beyond one's initial convictions when approaching a problem. When reasoning alone, a reasoner can at least try to simulate a similar kind of perspective shift by attempting to adopt the perspective of a hypothetical other.

9.4   Perspicuity: Explaining to Others

Of the three key features of deduction posited in Chapter 1, perspicuity is the least peculiar, cognitively as well as pragmatically speaking. Precisely because it represents the cooperative component of deductive reasoning, it speaks to default cooperative conversational structures in ways that the other two features do not. Producing persuasive arguments and explanations is part and parcel of everyday interactions for most humans: it allows for social coordination and the exchange of epistemic resources. True enough, within regimented contexts of deduction, perspicuity acquires a rather specific shape, in the limit cases only allowing for inferential steps that are explicitly codified within a given formal system. But the general idea of a dialogue that proceeds in a stepwise manner such that all steps are clear and convincing for its intended audience is perfectly in the spirit of the 'default' cooperative conversational structures described earlier.

Perhaps because it does not seem to pose great challenges for reasoners, this specific feature of deduction has not been (to my knowledge, at least) systematically (experimentally) investigated. Moreover, most reasoning experiments focus on argument evaluation, whereas competence with respect to perspicuity pertains primarily to the production side of the equation (although proof comprehension is also a challenge, as mathematics educators know). Furthermore, experimenters typically use very simple, one-step arguments as task materials (syllogisms, modus ponens, modus tollens), which again do not address the core skill of concatenating simple inferential steps into a more complex argument. So, where might we look for empirical evidence pertaining to perspicuity?

Here, our best shot is to turn to the literature in mathematics education on how students learn to produce and understand mathematical proofs. It is widely recognized that students tend to experience difficulties with the technique of mathematical proofs, but it is not clear exactly why (Gilmore et al., 2018, chapter 9). Educators have thus experimented with a number of interventions in order to facilitate mastery of this essential skill for high-level mathematics, with different degrees of success. Crucially, measuring the outcomes of the interventions is not a trivial task, as these are not experimental situations in a controlled setting. Often, what we have is mostly anecdotal evidence from the practices of educators on which methods do or do not work for certain learning goals. But with this caveat in place, these discussions are clearly relevant for our purposes here, as some of the interventions reflect aspects of dialogical conceptions of mathematical proof – in particular, the idea that a mathematical proof is an instrument to persuade and explain rather than a sterile exercise only intended to show to the teacher that the student has understood the problem.

An influential 'dialogical' approach to teaching the technique of mathematical proof dates back to the early twentieth century: the so-called Moore method (Jones, 1977). The method is named after its creator, the mathematician Robert Lee Moore (1882–1974). He devised a method to teach proof skills where students are given theorems to prove and are expected to find a solution for themselves, with very little guidance from the instructor. When a student claims that they can prove a given theorem, they are asked to go to the blackboard and present the proof. The other students then adopt a critical attitude towards the proposed proof so as to ensure that it is correct and convincing. When a flaw appears in a proof, students spend some time trying to find an example to show that it can't be 'patched up,' i.e., a counterexample to the argument. (This classroom dynamic in fact enacts the 'proofs and refutations' dialectic described by Lakatos. Moore can thus be described as a Lakatosian *avant la lettre*, given that he developed the method some fifty years before Lakatos' first writings on the topic.) Incidentally, for Moore, the competition among peers to be the first to prove a given result or to spot the mistake in a proposed proof was an important component of the method (which echoes the discussion on adversariality earlier in this chapter).

The Moore method has had and continues to have ardent supporters,[8] including in recent years under different names such as 'inquiry-based learning.' (Moore himself was a rather problematic character, in particular owing to

---

[8] See this website dedicated to his legacy: http://legacyrlmoore.org/index.html.

his racist convictions and behavior, so many educators felt the need to distance themselves from his persona; Haberler et al., 2018). According to anecdotal evidence, the Moore method is exceptionally good for producing research mathematicians (which is not surprising, given that it enacts a research context in the classroom situation), but less suitable for struggling students. More generally, the efficacy of inquiry-based learning in different fields is a contested matter (see Kirschner et al., 2006 for a negative assessment and Hmelo-Silver et al., 2007 for a reply to Kirschner et al.), but there is some robust evidence for its efficacy for college-level instruction in mathematics (Kogan & Laursen, 2014).

However, these general findings still do not address the specific question we are interested in now, namely whether a dialogical setting facilitates deductive performance on the perspicuity dimension. Recall that, on the present account, perspicuity corresponds to the openly *cooperative* dimension of deductive reasoning (whereas necessary truth-preservation corresponds to its adversarial dimension), as it pertains to the goal of producing an explanatory, persuasive argument that proceeds by individually transparent inferential steps, so as to transfer the relevant epistemic insights to its intended audience. So, we need to look for approaches that, unlike Moore's original approach, emphasize cooperation instead of competition among peers. One such approach is *peer instruction*, originally developed by physicist Eric Mazur for physics instruction in the 1990s (Mazur, 1997), but now used in different areas, including philosophy and logic (Butchart et al., 2009).

Specifically for mathematics, an influential tradition is the so-called Grenoble School, which emphasizes enacting scientific debates in classroom situations (Alibert & Thomas, 1991). This approach stresses the communicative role of a proof as an instrument for scientific debates among peers. As described by Daniel Alibert, one of the core members of the Grenoble School,

> The context in which students meet proofs in mathematics may greatly influence their perception of the value of proof. By establishing an environment in which students may see and experience first-hand what is necessary for them to convince others, of the truth or falsehood of propositions, proof becomes an instrument of personal value which they will be happier to use in future. (Alibert & Thomas, 1991, p. 230)

However, another member of the Grenoble School, Nicolas Balacheff, has also argued that creating a social-dialogical classroom situation may not be sufficient for the emergence of 'mathematical debate' properly speaking. In Balacheff, 1991, he reports on a study with 13-/14-year-old pupils (thus younger than the university students that Alibert was considering), where students were asked to write a message for other students of the same grade, giving them enough information to solve a given problem. Students worked in small groups of three or four and wrote their messages on large sheets of paper, which were then displayed on a wall of the classroom and further discussed. What Balacheff and colleagues observed was that, rather than adopting the appropriate 'rules of engagement' for mathematical proof, students fell back onto modes of dialogical interaction more familiar to them, in particular by producing convincing but not very rigorous arguments that did not meet minimal standards to be considered mathematical proofs.

What Balacheff's study shows is a point that has been stressed multiple times throughout this book, namely that the specific dialogues that correspond to mathematical proofs (and deductive arguments more generally) are quite far removed from more mundane, familiar forms of dialogical interaction. The specific rules for deductive dialogues must be taught explicitly, especially as they deviate considerably from a reasoner's everyday repertoire of dialogical interactions. Nevertheless, taken as a whole, the findings described in this section suggest that suitably contextualizing the practice of mathematical proof as an instrument for communication among peers, rather than a sterile, formalistic exercise of applying some arbitrary rules when solving a problem merely to satisfy the expectations of a teacher, does facilitate the relevant learning processes. In particular, when combined with the 'adversarial' component of focusing on indefeasible, necessarily truth-preserving arguments, emphasis on communication among peers facilitates the emergence of proper 'mathematical debates.'

9.5   Internalization

So far we've looked into forms of dialogical scaffolding that may facilitate the learning process for deductive skills. But, naturally, fully-fledged deductive competence requires that the reasoner be able to deploy these skills also in mono-agent situations. The key notion that allows for the transition from explicitly multi-agent situations to mono-agent reasoning is that of *internalization*, and internalization of Skeptic in particular. Is there support for the hypothesis that internalization plays a relevant role in these processes? A number of general findings on internalization, inner speech, and related topics do lend further support to the notion of internalization of a specific interlocutor, namely the fictive Skeptic.

That thought is essentially a form of inner dialogue with oneself is an idea with a long, venerable past. Plato famously developed it in detail in a number of dialogues, in particular the *Theaetetus*, the *Sophist*, and the *Hippias Major* (see Duncombe, 2016). More recently, and more relevant for us now, the concept of inner speech features as one of the cornerstones of Vygotsky's sociocultural theory of cognition (Vygotsky, 1931; John-Steiner, 2007). The crucial contribution of internal dialogical speech for human cognition is now widely recognized and studied by psychologists and cognitive scientists (Alderson-Day &

Fernyhough, 2015) as well as cognitive linguists (Pascual & Oakley, 2017). Against this background, the hypothesis of an internalized interlocutor such as Skeptic is in fact quite plausible, but still requires further corroboration.

As noted before, the idea of internalization of Skeptic proposed here is heavily influenced by the Vygotskian notion of internalization, which for Vygotsky is a general phenomenon underpinning the emergence of individual higher cognition in its full scale (not only with respect to deductive reasoning specifically). Here is an apt summary of Vygotsky's notion of internalization:

> Internalization, Vygotsky explains, is not a matter of merely transplanting a social activity onto an inner plane, for the internalized practice is transfigured in the act of internalization. Nevertheless, the developmental roots of the higher mental functions lie in the mastery of social practices: "genetically, social relations, real relations of people, stand behind all the higher functions and their relations . . . [T]he mental nature of man represents the totality of social relations internalized." (Vygotsky 1931, p. 106). (Bakhurst, 2007, p. 54)

The process of internalization consists in a series of transformations (here in Vygotsky's own words):

(a) *An operation that initially represents an external activity is reconstructed and begins to occur internally.* Of particular importance to the development of higher mental processes is the transformation of sign-using activity, the history and characteristics of which are illustrated by the development of practical intelligence, voluntary attention, and memory.

(b) *An interpersonal process is transformed into an intrapersonal one.* Every function in the child's cultural development appears twice: first, on the social level, and later, on the individual level; first, *between* people (*interpsychological*), and then *inside* the child (*intrapsychological*). This applies equally to voluntary attention, to logical memory, and to the formation of concepts. All the higher functions originate as actual relations between human individuals.

(c) *The transformation of an interpersonal process into an intrapersonal one is the result of a long series of developmental events.* The process being transformed continues to exist and to change as an external form of activity for a long time before definitively turning inward. For many functions, the stage of external signs lasts forever, that is, it is their final stage of development. Other functions develop further and gradually become inner functions. However, they take on the character of inner processes only as a result of a prolonged development. Their transfer inward is linked with changes in the laws governing their activity; they are incorporated into a new system with its own laws. (Vygotsky, 1978, pp. 56–57)

Vygotsky's notion of internalization has been influential in a number of fields, including education studies, developmental psychology, and cultural psychology. (It has also been either ignored or outright rejected in many circles where the hypothesis of human cognition being significantly shaped by culture does not enjoy the best of reputations, e.g. much of traditional cognitive science.) But while it is a fruitful idea in terms of further developments and explanatory power, it has also been criticized as not sufficiently precise (in particular, in that the exact mechanisms for internalization are only gestured towards rather than properly described) and as relying on an inadequate spatial metaphor (internal vs. external; Zittoun & Gillespie, 2015). However, rather than abandoning the notion completely, a number of authors have taken it upon themselves to further develop and clarify Vygotskian internalization; these enriched versions of the concept have given rise to a number of valuable research programs (Zittoun & Gillespie, 2015).

For our purposes, the notion of internalization thus described is instrumental in explaining why students tend to struggle when learning the technique of deductive proofs and arguments (in mathematics as well as elsewhere). Rather than first being introduced to the 'language game of deduction' in a social setting – the practice of producing arguments intended to be explanatory and persuasive for a given intended audience of 'skeptics,' and following fairly rigid conventions as to what counts as a legitimate move in these dialogues – students are immediately expected to perform the internal, intrapersonal process of reasoning deductively without having properly mastered the corresponding external, interpersonal process of engaging in these specialized dialogues. Instead, following the Vygotskian insight on the presumed correct order of development of 'higher' faculties, one must first become familiar with the relevant social practices to then be able to simulate them as a sole reasoner. In other words, after the experience of interacting with real Skeptics, a reasoner will be in a position to simulate such dialogues without the presence of actual Skeptics.

Naturally, the details of how exactly this process of internalization occurs must still be examined in more detail. One study that addresses the process of internalization of Skeptic (though, of course, the authors do not describe it in these exact terms) is the work by Mark Hodds and colleagues on self-explanation training to increase students' proof comprehension (Hodds et al., 2014). The training consists in teaching students to ask themselves questions about proofs that are very similar to the questions that Skeptic asks: Do I understand the ideas used in this inferential step? Do I understand the general idea of the proof? Does the information provided in the proof contradict my beliefs on the topic thus far? (This may prompt a search for counterexamples.) Students are even instructed to provide answers to these questions out loud, as if engaging in a real, oral dialogue, thus enacting the fictive interaction of the written form. The results indicate that this approach substantially improves proof comprehension, thus suggesting that enacting a dialogical version of the proof and engaging in dialogue with oneself – channeling one's inner Skeptic, as it were – has significant cognitive impact.

186 Deduction and Cognition

There is also what can be described as anecdotal evidence on the internalization of Skeptic. Over the years, I have discussed the idea of an internalized Skeptic with a number of practicing mathematicians/logicians. Many of them agree that the Prover–Skeptic interplay seems to capture a fundamental aspect of the phenomenology of producing mathematical proofs (as they experience it). They report that, when approaching a conjecture, they first start out in the position of Prover, trying to find a proof strategy to tackle the conjecture.[9] After some time, however, if no immediate success is forthcoming, they switch roles and adopt Skeptic's perspective: they start to look for counterexamples to the conjecture so as to better understand what would be needed to prove it or else outright refute it by means of a concrete counterexample (if they find one).

There is nothing particularly surprising about these observations; if I am right in claiming that high-level mathematical instruction by and large consists in internalizing Skeptic (insofar as Skeptic's role is codified in key components of the method of mathematical proof), then this outcome is exactly what one would expect. Naturally, these informal conversations provide rather limited evidence for the hypothesis. Still, the phenomenology of proof in terms of a Prover–Skeptic interplay could well be studied empirically in a more rigorous, systematic way, perhaps using a methodology similar to the one adopted in Andersen, 2017 to study the refereeing practices of mathematicians.

9.6   Conclusion

In this chapter, I've examined empirical evidence pertaining to the hypothesis that suitably contextualizing deductive reasoning in terms of rather contrived, specific semi-adversarial dialogical situations can have a facilitating effect, insofar as it allows reasoners to temporarily 'turn off' more familiar, cooperative forms of dialogical interaction. To be clear, I do agree with a number of authors (Balacheff, 1991 in particular, but also in a sense Stanovich, 2003) that fully mastering deductive reasoning skills would require the reasoner to be able eventually to reason in an abstract, decontextualized manner; in other words, the thought here is not that the dialogical contextualization would be *sufficient* for the emergence of fully-fledged, high-level deductive reasoning. But at earlier stages of the learning process, the dialogical contextualization may well provide the kind of scaffolding required to master the (rather peculiar) language game of deduction. If this is so, and if this scaffolding reflects aspects of the historical emergence of deductive reasoning, then there is a sense in which 'ontogeny recapitulates history' for deductive reasoning.

---

[9] When inspecting a proof so as to ascertain its correctness, however, mathematicians outright adopt a Skeptic perspective, as shown, for example, in Line Andersen's work on the refereeing practices of mathematicians (Andersen, 2017), to be discussed in more detail in Chapter 11.

10   The Phylogeny of Deductive Reasoning

10.1   Introduction

In Chapter 2, I argued against the view that deductive reasoning would be a straightforward genetic adaptation. Indeed, the claim that deductive reasoning is a trait in humans emerging from processes of natural selection (i.e., by conferring fitness advantages on our ancestors possessing this trait over other individuals not possessing it) stumbles upon the uncomfortable observation that modern humans by and large do not seem to deploy deductive reasoning in any systematic way outside of niches of specialists. If the well-known experimental results discussed in Chapter 8 are to be believed, then we must conclude that people do not typically engage in deductive reasoning spontaneously, and so it seems quite far-fetched to view a trait that is scarcely present in the relevant population as an adaptation (in the sense that it will have been selected for).

Instead, I submit that deductive reasoning is more plausibly seen as emerging from cultural processes rather than from genetic evolution. Thus, contra Hugo Mercier and Dan Sperber's claim that reasoning in general corresponds to a specialized module that is part of the human genetic endowment (a product of natural selection; Mercier & Sperber, 2017), I defend the view that argumentation and reasoning in general, and deductive reasoning specifically, are in fact best conceived as 'cognitive gadgets' (Heyes, 2018) emerging from a much leaner genetically encoded 'starter kit,' in Cecilia Heyes' terminology. On the phylogenetic timescale, deductive reasoning/argumentation is very much a latecomer, appearing only some 2,500 years ago (as described in Chapters 5 and 6). Deduction is thus a recent gadget, in fact more recent than another quintessential cultural skill, literacy. But according to the dialogical hypothesis, deduction emerged as a spinoff of a presumably older cultural phenomenon, namely argumentation (as it is conceivable that, prior to literacy, argumentative styles of obtaining consensus for e.g. coordinated action were already in place; Norman, 2016).[1] Incidentally, it is interesting to note that deductive reasoning skills seem much harder to learn than literacy. This is arguably due to the fact that, more than literacy, deductive reasoning is in tension with other more spontaneous cognitive tendencies in humans, such as belief projection and cooperative conversation, which need to be constantly over-ridden if an agent is to engage in deductive reasoning.

But even if they require specific training to emerge, deductive reasoning skills will obviously build upon preexisting, genetically encoded cognitive possibilities in humans – the human genetic 'starter kit.' So, it makes sense to inquire into the evolutionary basis for deductive reasoning, i.e. which ancestral traits are presumably co-opted and redeployed so as to give rise to new, culturally shaped cognitive possibilities ultimately leading specifically to deductive reasoning. Again, the comparison with literacy is illuminating: while no one thinks that the ability to read and write is a product of genetic evolution (particularly given that it is a very recent phenomenon), a number of researchers have investigated the neuronal, evolutionary basis for the emergence of this cultural technology, for example through the concept of neuronal recycling (Dehaene, 2009). Here, we can pose similar questions with respect to deduction, while firmly maintaining that deductive reasoning is not (at least, not directly) a product of genetic evolution or natural selection.

I start with a brief discussion of what is known about the proto-deductive reasoning skills of non-human animals and the modicum of deductive competence they seem to display, so as to ascertain the extent to which we may share some of the relevant cognitive basis with other animals. I then turn to two recent influential accounts of human cognition: Mercier and Sperber's adaptationist account of reasoning and argumentation (2017) and Heyes' cognitive gadgets model (2018). The discussion of these two frameworks will allow for the formulation of some tentative hypotheses on the cognitive evolutionary basis for deductive reasoning. In the final section, I turn to the neural basis for deductive reasoning, and briefly review the findings of neuroimaging studies that also seem to confirm that deductive reasoning does not correspond to a clearly circum-scribed cognitive system. This lends further support to a cultural account of the emergence of deduction, and thus to the dialogical hypothesis.

Admittedly, the claims in this chapter are more speculative than the ones discussed in the previous two chapters. My goals here are modest: I seek to establish that Heyes' gadgets framework is likely to deliver a more fruitful, more evolutionarily plausible account of the emergence of (deductive) argu-mentation than Mercier and Sperber's adaptationist story, as it seems to offer

---

[1] Naturally, claims on the development of argumentation prior to literacy are bound to remain speculative, given the lack of material documentation. Some further evidence can be gathered from argumentative practices in small-scale societies, such as in the seminal work by Edwin Hutchins on argumentative practices in the Trobriand Islands (Hutchins, 1980).

a better fit with the developmental, pedagogical, and longitudinal effects described in Chapter 9. A full account of the evolutionary emergence of argumentation remains a topic for future work.

10.2   Deductive Reasoning in Non-human Animals

Deductive (logical) reasoning in non-human animals is an age-old preoccupation among philosophers. Indeed, fundamental philosophical issues on the nature of logical/deductive reasoning arise if we can attribute this mode of thinking to non-human animals. For example, if non-linguistic animals display some degree of deductive competence, then perhaps deductive reasoning is not intrinsically a linguistic phenomenon after all. A much-discussed exemplar is known as 'Chrysippus' dog,' as the Stoic thinker allegedly attributed the ability to perform disjunctive syllogism to dogs. Sextus Empiricus describes the argument as follows:

And according to Chrysippus, who shows special interest in irrational animals, the dog even shares in the far-famed 'Dialectic.' This person, at any rate, declares that the dog makes use of the fifth complex indemonstrable syllogism when, on arriving at a spot where three ways meet, after smelling at the two roads by which the quarry did not pass, he rushes off at once by the third without stopping to smell. For, says the old writer, the dog implicitly reasons thus: "The creature went either by this road, or by that, or by the other: but it did not go by this road or that, therefore he went the other way." (Sextus Empiricus, 1966, pp. 164–165)

While often discussed in different periods, in the second half of the twentieth century Chrysippus' dog attracted renewed interest in the context of defenses of relevant logic. Thus described, the dog seems to abide by the principle of classical disjunction; this seems to pose a challenge for the proponents of relevant logic, but one which relevant logicians think they can respond to (Garfield, 1990). However, beyond the question of which specific 'logic' Chrysippus' dog might be said to be following, there is the more fundamental question of whether the dog is following logic at all, i.e. whether it is truly sharing "in the far-famed 'Dialectic'" when displaying this behavior.[2] It has been argued that the 'disjunctive' behavior of the dog can be equally well explained in terms of probabilistic reasoning over cognitive maps (Rescorla, 2009), thus undermining the presumed evidentiary support of this behavior for the thesis that the dog is reasoning logically/deductively. Moreover, work on reasoning by exclusion in human infants also suggests that, while seemingly

---

[2] In fact, another fundamental question is whether dogs in general do display the behavior described in Sextus' passage at all. On the basis of experimental work, it has been argued that they do, though for dogs, too, social cues (or absence thereof) seem to have a significant effect on 'logical' behavior (Erdőhegyi et al., 2007). Great apes and corvids have also been shown to display behavior that is compatible with reasoning from exclusion (Andrews, 2015, p. 108).

displaying deductive behavior in simple disjunctive tasks, with a more complex experimental setup children under 3 years do not in fact display the behavior that would be expected if they were applying disjunctive reasoning (Mody & Carey, 2016). From this observation, the authors conclude, "a non-deductive approach may be behind the successful performance of nonhuman animals and human infants" in reasoning by exclusion.

In addition to reasoning by exclusion, another principle that has been extensively investigated in non-human animals is transitive inference (Allen, 2006; Lazareva, 2012). This is the kind of inference where, from a transitive relation between items A and B,[3] and the same relation between items B and C, we may conclude that the same holds between A and C ('Andy is taller than Bart, and Bart is taller than Charlie; so Andy must be taller than Charlie'). Transitive-like behavior has been identified in virtually all the animal species that have been tested so far, including rats, pigeons, crows, monkeys, and fish (Andrews, 2015, p. 108), with the curious exception of honey bees (Lazareva, 2012). This suggests that something like transitive inference is a widespread cognitive tendency across species, and thus, presumably, a phylogenetically ancient component. However, here too, there is no consensus as to whether these instances of transitive-like behavior in different animals should be seen as instances of *reasoning* properly speaking, or whether they are best attributed to simpler mechanisms of associative conditioning and reinforcement. Indeed, the available evidence simply does not offer enough information to adjudicate between the two models (Lazareva, 2012). Moreover, the usual worries pertaining to the ecological validity of results obtained in the laboratory also apply to the experimental paradigms that have been used so far to study transitive inference (Allen, 2006).

Researchers have also identified reasoning patterns where non-human animals show little to no competence. In particular, as reviewed in Yamazaki, 2004, the formation of equivalence relations, which is an essential component of e.g. syllogistic reasoning, is a skill that appears to be largely absent in non-human animals (with a few notable exceptions, such as a sea lion named Rio; Schusterman & Kastak, 1993). So, even if there is something like 'animal logic' (Andrews, 2015, section 4.2.6), its scope and range appear to be quite limited.

In sum, many non-human animals have been shown to display behavior that is compatible with reasoning principles such as reasoning by exclusion and transitive inference, which prima facie may suggest the presence of a modicum of deductive competence in these animals. However, when seemingly displaying deductive reasoning/behavior, these animals may well in fact be doing something else that happens to coincide in specific cases with the deductively

---

[3] Obviously, not all relations are transitive, so one cognitively demanding task for the animal is to discriminate between transitive and non-transitive relations.

predicted outcomes/responses.[4] The bottom line is thus that apparent displays of deductive/logical behavior must be cautiously interpreted; usually, there will be equally compelling alternative explanations for the behavior that rely on less complex cognitive mechanisms such as teleosemantic (Millikan, 2006), probabilistic (Rescorla, 2009), causal (Bermúdez, 2006), or associative (Allen, 2006) mechanisms.

Nevertheless, even if (rudimentary) principles of deductive reasoning cannot be confidently attributed to non-human animals – in view of the equally plausible non-deductive alternative accounts and the absence of conclusive empirical evidence in either direction – it is still relevant for our purposes to note that some of the cognitive substratum that human reasoners presumably co-opt when reasoning deductively may well be shared with other animal lineages (either because they are phylogenetically ancient or because they represent instances of convergence due to environmental pressure). In particular, inference by exclusion and inference by transitivity appear to be cognitive abilities shared with a plethora of animal species. But, of course, this is still a far cry from fully-fledged deductive reasoning, so further investigation into the evolutionary cognitive antecedents of deductive reasoning, including cognitive features that may be uniquely human, is still needed.[5] To this end, let us start with the genus reasoning, of which deductive reasoning is a species, by turning to a recent influential evolutionary account of human reasoning.

---

[4] The same observation applies to humans. For example, in experiments, participants typically display very high levels (above 90 percent) of deductively correct responses with simple instances of modus ponens; but does this necessarily mean that they are reasoning deductively, or are they in fact adopting a different reasoning strategy that simply converges in outcome with deductive reasoning in these simple cases? Consider the results on so-called suppression tasks, where additional premises are brought in after participants have responded to simple instances of modus ponens. In these experiments, a large number of participants retract the conclusion previously drawn, even if the additional premise is itself a conditional proposition. In the seminal study of suppression tasks with modus ponens (Byrne, 1989), while the simple modus ponens argument, 'If she has an essay to finish, she will stay late in the library. She has an essay to finish' elicited almost unanimous endorsement (96 percent) of the deductively correct conclusion, 'she will stay in the library,' the addition of a conditional premise, 'If the library is open, then she will stay late in the library,' swayed a significant number of participants to suppress the deductively valid conclusion: only 38 percent then concluded that 'she will stay late in the library' follows from the three premises. If participants were really following the precepts for deductive modus ponens, then this discrepancy would not have been observed, which suggests that all along they are most likely applying what might be described as defeasible modus ponens.

[5] Given the conception of reasoning as closely tied to argumentative practices adopted here, the possibility of proto-argumentative practices in non-human animals also becomes relevant. If argumentation is strictly defined, i.e. as exchange of reasons, it does not seem to be present in any recognizable way among non-human animals, including among our closest living relatives such as chimpanzees and bonobos (despite the fact that these species display high levels of social complexity). However, practices of social coordination through vocalization – for example, 'travel hoos' in chimpanzees (Sievers & Gruber, 2016) – might well be viewed as phylogenetic antecedents of more complex forms of argumentation.

10.3   Mercier and Sperber on the Evolution of Reasoning

In recent years, Mercier and Sperber have been developing an account of reasoning that was originally described as 'the argumentative theory of reasoning' (Mercier & Sperber, 2011) but is now described as 'the interactionist theory of reasoning': "reason, we maintain, is first and foremost a social competence" (Mercier & Sperber, 2017, p. 11).[6] This account is contrasted with what they refer to as intellectualist views, according to which reason and reasoning are phenomena primarily pertaining to the individual thinking subject, as capacities that enable her to achieve greater knowledge and make better decisions through purely individualistic processes. In view of the various biases that human cognition is prone to (see Chapter 8), they argue convincingly that the intellectualist account of reasoning is deeply misguided. Instead, reason is the faculty that enables us to engage in the practice of 'giving and asking for reasons' (Brandom, 1994), a practice that is arguably central to human sociality:

> By giving reasons to explain and justify yourself, you do several things. You influence the way people read your mind, judge your behavior, and speak of you. You commit yourself by implicitly acknowledging the normative force of the reasons you invoke: you encourage others to expect your future behavior to be guided by similar reasons (and to hold you accountable if it is not). You also indicate that you are likely to evaluate the behavior of others by reasons similar to those you invoke to justify yourself. Finally, you engage in a conversation where others may accept your justifications, question them, and invoke reasons of their own, a conversation that should help you coordinate with them and from which shared norms actually may progressively emerge. (Mercier & Sperber, 2017, pp. 185–186)

In line with their previous joint work, and with Sperber's longstanding research interests, they adopt an evolutionary perspective to address the question of the function(s) of reason.[7] The perspective they adopt is, however, not merely evolutionary: it is also *adaptationist*,[8] like most of the work done under the heading of evolutionary psychology. Schematically, an adaptationist explanation proceeds by observing a trait in an organism, postulating that it must be an adaptation, and indeed an *optimal solution* (not merely a satisficing one), to the function(s) it is supposed to be a response to, and then formulating an account that presents itself as the best explanation for the purported adaptiveness and optimality of the trait, given the purported function(s) attributed to it.

---

[6] This section is a shortened version of my critical notice of Mercier & Sperber, 2017, which appeared in a book symposium in the journal *Mind & Language* (Dutilh Novaes, 2018b).

[7] "The main function of reason is social. Why resort to an evolutionary approach? Because this is the only approach that explains the fact that complex inheritable traits of living things tend to produce beneficial effects. Outside of an evolutionary perspective, it is quite unclear why human reason, or anything else for that matter, should have any function at all" (Mercier & Sperber, 2017, p. 176).

[8] See Lewens, 2009 for different versions of adaptationism.

Mercier and Sperber posit without hesitation that reason, as they understand it, must be an adaptation. "Reason is an adaptation to the hypersocial niche humans have built for themselves" (Mercier & Sperber, 2017, p. 330). The hypothesis that reason may be a product of non-selective forces in evolution (e.g. an exaptation), or perhaps not a product of genetic evolution at all, is not given much consideration. The gist of their argument seems to be: reason must be an adaptation, but if conceived as having the function of supporting the cognitive processes of the lone reasoner, it does not seem to perform this function very well.[9] So, there must be a different function that reason is in fact responding to, given that it cannot be anything other than an adaptation.

Prima facie, to argue for the adaptive nature of reason seems like a tall order in view of the numerous empirical findings suggesting that human reason is 'biased and lazy':

> Human reason is both biased and lazy. Biased because it overwhelmingly finds justifications and arguments that support the reasoner's point of view, lazy because reason makes little effort to assess the quality of the justifications and arguments it produces. (Mercier & Sperber, 2017, p. 9)

But Mercier and Sperber go on to argue that these two features are in fact *advantageous* for the function of reason as socially conceived:

> In our interactionist account, reason's bias and laziness aren't flaws; they are features that help reason fulfill its function. People are biased to find reasons that support their point of view because this is how they can justify their actions and convince others to share their beliefs. (Mercier & Sperber, 2017, p. 331)

At the individual level, the claim seems to be that being very certain of one's own beliefs and to a large extent insensitive to contrary evidence will make people better arguers, because they are likely to convey a greater degree of conviction to others in argumentative situations; they will thus be more likely to convince others. As for laziness, the principle of least effort would dictate that the reasons to be produced should be only as good as required by the situation. When facing a gullible interlocutor, why spend precious cognitive resources in formulating arguments that are unnecessarily strong? And so Mercier and Sperber draw a Panglossian conclusion: it is actually all for the best (Mercier & Sperber, 2017, p. 264).

---

[9] "Failures of reasoning are lazily explained by various interfering factors and by weaknesses of reason itself. Again, this doesn't make much evolutionary sense. A genuine adaptation is adaptive: a genuine function functions" (Mercier & Sperber, 2017, p. 331). But how do we know that reason is a genuine adaptation? What seems to be going on is that Mercier and Sperber (tacitly) rely on what Lewens, 2009 describes as 'strong heuristic adaptationism': the assumption that "only by beginning to think of traits as adaptations can we uncover their true status, whatever that status may be."

But is it really the case that myside bias and laziness thus described constitute an optimal solution for the social, argumentative function of reasoning? One prediction that seems to follow from these considerations is that people who are more prone to myside bias would be better at convincing others than people who can see more clearly the different sides of a question. Granted, disturbing recent events in world politics seem to suggest that uttering lies and pseudo-arguments often enough and loudly enough, with a great amount of conviction, does seem to work as a strategy to sway large numbers of voters. But it seems equally plausible that, perhaps in less heated, less polarized situations, the more convincing arguers are those who can anticipate the audience's responses and tailor their arguments to the audience's needs. Mercier and Sperber do raise this possibility (2017, p. 222), recognizing that a venerable tradition in rhetoric and dialectic emphasizes the importance of seeing the different sides of a question, including arguments and counterarguments, in order to argue convincingly for a given position.

Their answer to this objection is that it would be pointlessly costly to take the other side's perspective in order to anticipate possible objections. Given the interactive nature of dialogue, justifications and arguments are refined with the interlocutors' feedback, thus giving rise to a *division of cognitive labor* (2017, p. 236). However, the notion of division of cognitive labor introduces a group/ collective perspective that does not seem to sit well with the overall goals of their project.[10] Indeed, from the group perspective, a combination of myside bias and sensible laziness may well be an optimal solution to how we organize our social and cognitive lives, as it may give rise to an efficient division of labor. (Such a model has been described as 'Mandevillian intelligence': individual vices leading to collective virtue; Smart, 2018). However, this is not an adequate response to the objection that, from the individual-level perspective, myside bias in particular may not be an optimal solution at all, perhaps not even a satisficing one, for the purposes of argumentation. Recall that the tendency towards belief projection discussed in Chapter 7 – which is fundamentally the same as myside bias – was described by Keith Stanovich as essentially adaptive in the sense of representing a good tradeoff between cognitive simplicity and accuracy. So, the claim here is not that myside bias/belief projection is not adaptive at all, but rather that it is not adaptive specifically *for the purposes of argumentation*.

---

[10] "Group-level selection favors the pursuit of collective benefits over that of individual benefits. Reason as we have described it is, by contrast, a mechanism for the pursuit of individual benefits. An individual stands to benefit from having her justifications accepted by others and from producing arguments that influence others. She also stands to benefit from evaluating objectively the justifications and arguments presented by others and from accepting or rejecting them on the basis of such an evaluation. These benefits are achieved in social interaction, but they are individual benefits all the same" (Mercier & Sperber, 2017, p. 333). It is not clear, though, how these benefits should translate into differential/relative fitness.

Naturally, whether people more prone to myside bias are better at convincing others is a question that could in principle be investigated experimentally. As it stands, however, Mercier and Sperber have not convincingly established that myside bias is an adaptive feature *for the individual qua arguer*, and indeed more adaptive than not having this trait. Even if the relevant evolutionary environment will not have resembled the highly regimented contexts in which anticipating your interlocutor's objections is clearly useful – courts of law, scientific argumentation, debating – it seems quite plausible that being attuned to your intended audience in an argumentative situation would be a more adaptive trait than the stubborn dogmatism of myside bias. That this is so is reinforced by the idea (which Mercier and Sperber seem to endorse; 2017, p. 98) that human mind-reading capacities are an adaptive trait for humans; myside bias is ultimately a form of mind-reading failure.

In conclusion, many features of Mercier and Sperber's proposal on the nature of reasoning in general are aligned with my account of the nature of deductive reasoning specifically: both emphasize the dialogical, interactionist nature of reasoning understood as emerging from argumentative practices of giving and asking for reasons to explain and justify one's claims. But while they defend an evolutionary, adaptive account of reasoning in general, I defend an account of deductive reasoning that emphasizes its cultural basis, as not directly emerging from the genetically encoded cognitive makeup of humans. Our two accounts might still be compatible if I accepted their evolutionary account of reasoning in general (as arising from argumentative practices, which in turn are a product of straightforward natural selection processes) and supplemented it with a cultural account of deductive reasoning specifically, building upon the evolutionary basis for reasoning in general. However, their evolutionary account of reasoning in general is not truly convincing, as I have argued. So, a different story of how the genetically encoded human cognitive endowment gives rise to the possibility of deductive reasoning is still needed. To this end, I now turn to a recent proposal by another influential cognitive scientist, Cecilia Heyes.

10.4   Heyes on Cultural Gadgets

Alongside the claim that reasoning is an adaptation in humans, Mercier and Sperber (2017) postulate a complex modular structure for human cognition as genetically encoded. This does not entail a complete disregard for the cultural enhancements that also shape specific practices of higher cognition. But, for them, the genetic human starter kit prior to these cultural enhancements is already quite substantive, containing a variety of specialized modules (including one that produces intuitive, metarepresentational conclusions about reasons – and indeed *only* about reasons). In contrast, Heyes postulates a very lean starter kit, and then goes on to describe in detail how a number of key features of human cognition arise through cultural evolution from her minimalistic starter kit. These are the *cognitive gadgets*, the cultural enhancements that constitute human cognition as we know it (i.e., insofar as it is distinct from cognition in other animals):[11]

New gadgets emerge, not by genetic mutation, but by innovations in cognitive development; they are specialised cognitive mechanisms built by general cognitive mechanisms using information from the sociocultural environment. Innovations are passed on to subsequent generations, not by DNA replication, but through social learning: people with a new cognitive mechanism pass it on to others through social interaction. And some of the new mechanisms, like literacy, have spread through human populations, while others have died out, because the holders had more students, not just more babies. (Heyes, 2019, p. 1)

Heyes then applies the framework to four case studies, four 'gadgets' in her terminology: selective social learning, imitation, mind reading, and language. Her proposal is all the more innovative precisely because these four features of human socio-cognition are often viewed as quintessential cases of straightforward genetic adaptation (e.g. 'the language instinct'; Pinker, 1994). But the fact that she focuses on these nearly universal features of human socio-cognition does not mean that the cognitive gadgets framework cannot be applied to less pervasive cognitive skills such as deductive reasoning.[12] In fact, Heyes often cites literacy as an archetypal cognitive gadget, which, although quite widespread among many human cultures, is obviously not a human universal (not in terms of actual occurrence, at least; presumably, all typically developing humans can acquire literacy if given the right kind of exposure/training). Moreover, sensitivity to cross-cultural variation in how minds work is a central component of the whole approach.

So, with these observations in place, we can now investigate whether the concept of cognitive gadgets and the details of Heyes' proposal can help us make sense of the cognitive roots of deductive reasoning. We will do so by focusing on the question of how, from Heyes' minimal starter kit, cultural practices of argumentation could have emerged, which in turn provide the substratum for the development of reasoning. The three main components of Heyes' genetic starter kit – that is, features that are distinctive to humans when compared to other species – are thus described (I comment briefly on each of them below):

Genetic evolution has not given us programs for the development of powerful domain-specific cognitive mechanisms, such as mindreading and language, but it has made us (i)

---

[11] "The bulk of our behaviour is controlled by mechanisms we share with other animals but cognitive gadgets are what make human minds and human lives so very odd" (Heyes, 2019).

[12] There is a programmatic reason why Heyes focuses on these four 'gadgets': one of her main goals is to provide a detailed account of the very mechanisms of cultural learning that she claims are so crucial for what is distinctive about human cognition (the 'mills' of the human mind, as she puts it). So, it is natural for her to focus on these very basic building blocks of human cognition (which, although basic, are still gadgets, not instincts).

friendlier than our primate ancestors; (ii) enhanced our attentional biases towards other agents; and (iii) expanded our capacities for domain-general learning and executive control. These are the "Small Ordinary" gene-based changes that enable developing humans to upload "Big Special" cognitive mechanisms – cognitive gadgets – from their culture-soaked environments. (Heyes 2019, p. 4)

(i) According to Heyes, "there is evidence that modern humans are more socially tolerant (less aggressive to conspecifics) and more socially motivated (more inclined to seek and value social rewards) than our primate ancestors, and that these propensities are due to genetic evolution." One piece of evidence adduced is the 'craniofacial feminization' of humans in the last 200,000 years, which suggests a reduction in androgen activity related to a decrease in the propensity to initiate and elicit aggression from conspecifics. Relatedly, we appear to be more socially motivated than our primate ancestors: we seek and value social rewards such as praise and agreement. This is a quantitative change in disposition which, as Heyes argues, has a profound impact on human cognition because it makes us more prone to act as teachers and mentors not only to our own offspring.

(ii) We are not only more tolerant of our conspecifics than our primate ancestors; we in fact positively seek contact with other humans constantly. This is what is meant by 'attentional bias towards other agents'; given a wide range of options, humans tend to interact with other humans rather than with other portions of the environment. This is evidenced by, for example, the preference that newborns show for voices and faces or face-like shapes. This is crucial, as it means that human infants (and in fact humans of all ages) are more teachable than other animals, because their attention is more easily controlled by knowledgeable adults/peers.

(iii) The more clearly cognitive (as opposed to social) components of Heyes' starter kit for human cognition are mechanisms for enhanced associative learning (enhanced if compared to other animals; associative learning itself is phylogenetically very widespread, as also suggested by the findings discussed in Section 10.2) and for executive functions, which include inhibitory control, working memory, and cognitive flexibility. While the cognitive boost afforded by these mechanisms in terms of tracking causal connections and making predictions is uncontroversial, Heyes argues that these features also have an impact on our capacities to teach and to engage in group decision-making.

Given the social/dialogical account of deduction defended here, the components of Heyes' genetic starter kit can quite naturally be viewed as implicated in the cognitive substratum that allows for deductive reasoning to emerge (both as a social practice and as a cognitive skill). Recall that the missing link we are looking for at this point is how argumentative practices of giving and asking for reasons may emerge, from an evolutionary perspective. Mercier and Sperber's account in terms of genetic adaptation and modules was found wanting (as argued in more detail in Dutilh Novaes, 2018b), so perhaps the more minimalistic starter kit hypothesized by Heyes will deliver a more satisfactory explanation.

Let us pause for a moment and reflect on argumentative practices in very general terms. Crucially, engaging in argumentation, understood as the exchange of reasons, is a specific response to group living and to the inevitable situations of conflict and disagreement that emerge (though incidence of conflict and disagreement may vary in function of how hierarchical a society is). Importantly, argumentation is a response that differs from other common strategies for conflict management, in particular flight or fight strategies.[13] In argumentation, the parties experiencing disagreement do not *flee*, as they purposefully seek to engage with each other to discuss their differences rather than simply disengaging and walking away (perhaps because the cost of losing these social connections would be too high). But they do not *fight* either, at least not physically, and instead seek to resolve their differences by less aggressive means.

The possibility for this in-between response to conflict is consistent with Heyes' starter kit: we do not flee, because we cherish human contact and we value social rewards. But we do not fight, because we have a high level (compared to other primate species, at least) of social tolerance towards conspecifics; instead, we seek less confrontational modes of conflict management. Attentional bias towards other humans in turn ensures the likelihood of a dialogical engagement being initiated and maintained; it makes it more likely that the disagreeing parties actually pay attention to each other (and listen to each other's reasons).

To be clear, the claim is not that the only natural response to dissent and conflict emerging in group situations given Heyes' hypothesized starter kit is to engage in argumentation; actually, this would be vastly descriptively inadequate, as humans in fact more often than not do seem to engage in either flight or fight. Moreover, there are many situations in which engaging in argumentation does not seem the most rational option from a cost–benefit perspective (Paglieri & Castelfranchi, 2010). Rather, the claim is simply that Heyes' starter kit makes the in-between response to conflict that is engaging in argumentation at least *possible/viable*, and perhaps even attractive in a number of situations. In other words, the specific picture of human sociality that emerges from Heyes' starter kit is precisely one where argumentative practices may emerge: a fair amount of friendliness towards conspecifics, a tendency to seek social rewards

---

[13] To be sure, there is a wide range of conflict-avoidance strategies found in non-human animals, so in-between responses are not unique to humans.

such as signs of respect and appreciation from peers, and a tendency to pay attention to conspecifics, in particular their voices and faces, which in turn facilitates the initiation and maintenance of dialogical engagements.

The third, cognitive cluster of components in Heyes' starter kit, pertaining to associative learning and executive functions, should also be implicated in the emergence of argumentation (and specifically of *deductive* argumentation). In Heyes' account, associative learning gives rise to the ability to draw and recognize causal connections between phenomena, and this ability is, of course, a central component of argumentation insofar as it involves reasons and explanations being offered to support claims. (A: 'It is going to rain soon.' B: 'Why do you think that?' A: 'Because I see very dark clouds coming our way.') As for executive functions, working memory and cognitive flexibility obviously contribute to keeping track of complex networks of discursive commitments by different parties in an argumentative situation. Lastly, inhibitory control is presumably crucially required for deductive reasoning specifically, given that, as argued in Chapters 8 and 9, deductive reasoning is at odds with more spontaneous cognitive tendencies such as belief projection, which thus must be inhibited when an agent is engaging specifically in deduction.

The components discussed so far have been shown to be necessary for the emergence of practices of argumentation, but are they *sufficient*? Most likely not; the economical starter kit is still too minimalistic to fully explain the cognitive basis for argumentation. But insofar as the starter kit allows for the development of some fundamental cognitive gadgets, these basic cognitive gadgets can in turn become building blocks for other, more specific cognitive gadgets higher up the ladder, so to speak. Consider the very cognitive gadgets discussed in detail in Heyes, 2018; a number of them also seem directly relevant for the emergence of argumentative skills, so let us now turn to them. (I do not comment on imitation, as its relevance for argumentative practices is much less substantial than the other three.)

Language. That argumentative practices must rely extensively on linguistic skills is almost a truism. (But see Norman, 2016 on how sophisticated language may not be a prerequisite for argumentation, at least not for what might be described as proto-argumentation.) While exchanging reasons may at least in principle take place with other communicative means (e.g. with gestures), it is undeniable that, as a matter of fact, most of the phenomena that fall under the scope of argumentation do take place within language, either spoken or written. Heyes' claims on the status of language as a cognitive gadget are more cautious than her claims concerning her other three case studies, but for my purposes nothing much hinges on the status of (spoken) language as an instinct or as a gadget. At the risk of stating the obvious, I simply note here the relevance of linguistic abilities for more sophisticated practices of argumentation, and so whichever mechanisms underpin linguistic abilities in humans will almost trivially be part of the cognitive basis for argumentation.

Selective Social Learning. According to Heyes, selective social learning is selective on two main dimensions: 'when' – greater influence in unknown environments/situations – and 'who' – greater influence by older or more knowledgeable conspecifics. Now, if we take argumentative practices to be based on skills that must be learned socially (much as e.g. counting routines), then mechanisms for selective learning must be in place, in particular regarding who is de facto to be copied. This is all the more pressing if argumentation is indeed a skill to be developed by exposure and training rather than a natural inclination in humans,[14] given that young learners must ensure they copy the right people. (Sadly, as of late, prominent figures in world politics have been terrible role models for good argumentative practices.)[15] Moreover, if we consider deductive argumentation and deductive reasoning more specifically, then the importance of selective social learning is even more acutely felt. If, as I claim, deductive argumentation/reasoning belongs to niches of specialists and to specific contexts, a learner must attend to the specificities of these situations (including relations of epistemic authority) in order to master the technique successfully.

Mind Reading. Of the four fundamental gadgets analyzed by Heyes, mind reading seems to be the one most directly implicated in argumentative practices. It is on this point that I disagree quite fundamentally with Mercier and Sperber's characterization of myside bias as a feature of argumentation, not a bug. (As argued above, it might be a feature if one considers an agent's cognitive economy more broadly – belief projection – but it is particularly counterproductive for argumentation specifically.) Indeed, a good arguer is above all a good conversationalist, someone who is sensitive to the viewpoint of her interlocutors and who adjusts her style of dialogical engagement depending on whom she is talking to (Cohen, 2016). Persuasive arguments are first and foremost those that are tailored to their intended audience. And thus, mind-reading capacities broadly understood, such as sensitivity and responsiveness to the standpoints of others, are clearly essential to engage in fruitful argumentation. (The fact that we are much less competent at mind reading than we take ourselves to be [Spaulding, 2016] further explains why successful argumentation is such a demanding practice.)

---

[14] The jury is still out on this specific question. Mercier defends the view that humans are natural-born arguers (Mercier et al., 2016), even if these natural dispositions can benefit from specific external circumstances and certain kinds of training.

[15] In fact, this very observation seems to militate against the view that argumentative skills should naturally emerge as a result of our genetic encoding.

When it comes to deductive reasoning as understood here, mind reading remains of paramount importance, perhaps even more so than for argumentation more generally: the audience-relativity of a good deductive argument in terms of levels of granularity (i.e. what counts as sufficiently perspicuous is relative to contexts) requires sensitivity to the epistemic standpoint of the intended audience. Moreover, if bracketing belief is best understood as attributing a certain position to a hypothetical other (as argued in Chapter 9), then, again, mind-reading abilities must be activated for the difficult task of putting aside one's own beliefs for the purposes of reasoning from premises one does not endorse (see Section 10.5 for findings on neural connections between perspective-taking and reasoning).

To conclude, in this section I briefly reviewed some of the key components of the account of human cognition as by and large a product of cultural evolution (contra nativists of various stripes, who view the bulk of human cognition as genetically encoded) proposed by Heyes. I then applied the framework to a specific kind of socio-cognitive practice, argumentation. I argued that the cognitive gadgets account has the resources to explain the emergence of argumentation as one among different strategies for conflict management; this means that Mercier and Sperber's adaptationist account, discussed in Section 10.3, is not the only viable evolutionary account of the emergence of argumentation available. And because Heyes' account is firmly grounded in the concept of cultural learning and cultural processes giving rise to new cognitive skills, if it can be deployed successfully to explain how argumentative practices might have arisen, then we have at least the beginnings of a cultural account of the evolution of argumentation and reasoning, and of deductive argumentation and reasoning specifically. To be sure, at this point this is a sketch rather than a fully developed proposal; more work is required here. But it does offer some clues as to what the cognitive and social prerequisites for the emergence of argumentation might be: a friendly disposition towards conspecifics; openness to engaging in dialogical interactions with them; associative learning mechanisms giving rise to the identification of causal connections; and sensitivity to what might or might not come across as persuasive to one's interlocutor (and thus some degree of mind-reading abilities).

Admittedly, one very important aspect of the overall dialogical account of deduction defended here that does not seem to be directly derivable from Heyes' cognitive gadgets framework is the component of *adversariality*. Perhaps this is because adversariality is the least quintessentially *human* component of the whole account, but rather a fact of life for organisms of all sorts that must compete with others for their survival. (Recall that the cognitive gadgets framework avowedly focuses on what is distinctively *human* in human cognition, while not denying that there is much that we share with other animals.) Still, how to integrate the adversarial component into the cognitive gadgets framework is an interesting theoretical challenge, especially in view of the fact that the competing account discussed previously, namely Mercier and Sperber's account of argumentation skills as ensuring individual benefits, has built-in adversariality from the start.

10.5   Deduction in the Brain

While the focus so far has been on Heyes' account of how social and cultural phenomena shape human minds, the general point of the significance of culture for human cognition has been defended and developed by a number of authors (Vygotsky, 1978; Hutchins, 2011; Tomasello, 1999; Menary, 2013; Menary & Gillett, 2017; Heinrich, 2015). A term that is often used to describe the processes in question is *enculturation* (interestingly, a term that Heyes does not seem to use), which is aptly described in the following passage:

Phylogenetically, enculturation is the result of the co-evolution of human organisms and their socio-culturally structured cognitive niche. It is rendered possible by evolved cerebral and extra-cerebral bodily learning mechanisms that make human organisms apt to acquire culturally inherited cognitive practices. In addition, cultural learning allows for the intergenerational transmission of relevant knowledge and skills. Ontogenetically, enculturation is associated with neural plasticity and the development of new motor routines and action schemas. It relies on scaffolded learning that structures novice–teacher interactions. (Fabry, 2018, p. 1)

What the different enculturation accounts have in common is the idea that many distinctively human features continued to develop even after the emergence of modern humans (anatomically/genetically speaking), owing to cultural innovations not reflected in genetic changes, even if there can be some amount of co-evolution of genes and cultural practices (e.g. cooking) within the species. They also share a commitment to the idea of *neural plasticity*, which can be understood as structural (actual changes to the physical structure of the brain) or functional (certain parts of the brain can be deployed for different functions). Another key notion in many of these proposals is that of *neural reuse* (Anderson, 2010) or *neuronal recycling* (Dehaene, 2009), i.e. processes through which phylogenetically older forms of cognition are redeployed (or retrained) to service more recent cultural innovations. The different proposals do diverge in some of their details, for example in what they take to constitute the genetic starter kit, and the extent to which cognitive plasticity is constrained by the structural properties and functional biases that define the possibility space for plastic changes in the brain.

For our purposes, the neural reuse/neuronal recycling idea introduces the possibility of connecting the present discussion to the interesting body of work on 'deduction in the brain,' i.e. the neural basis for deductive reasoning (Goel,

2007; Prado et al., 2011; Goel & Waechter, 2018). Even if deduction is not an instinct or an innate capacity in humans, it may still give rise to distinctive patterns of brain activation, as the process of enculturation that corresponds to learning how to reason deductively may have specific effects in terms of brain activity. Moreover, through patterns of brain localization, we may gain some insight into the phylogenetically earlier forms of cognition that are redeployed for deductive reasoning. The study of deduction in the brain can thus also offer further elements for the investigation of the cognitive roots of deduction, even within a thoroughly cultural account of deductive reasoning.

Neuroimaging studies have been used to investigate deduction reasoning for over two decades. The main finding seems to be that there is no unitary system ('module') for deductive reasoning in the brain (unlike reading/writing, which seems to elicit more predictable, localized, and consistent patterns of brain activation; Dehaene, 2009), as the brain network activated for deductive reasoning is highly heterogeneous. Different brain areas are recruited depending on a number of parameters of the deductive problem an agent is engaging with, such as type of argument (syllogisms, transitive inferences, conditionals, etc.), presence of unbelievable sentences, presence or absence of content, level of familiarity with content, and emotional valence of content, among others (Goel & Waechter, 2018). The evidence thus points towards "a fractionated system that is dynamically configured in response to certain task and environmental cues" (Goel, 2007, p. 440).

The heterogeneity of the brain network implicated in deductive reasoning suggests that deductive reasoning does not correspond to a unified, neuronally well-circumscribed cognitive process. Instead, it corresponds to a plethora of different cognitive activities whose unity is arguably a theoretical construct rather than a clearly discernible and well-defined cognitive mechanism or module. This observation seems to lend support to one of the central claims of the present investigation, namely that deduction is a term of art corresponding to practices belonging to niches of specialists, rather than a basic building block of human cognition.

There are, however, some interesting discernible patterns emerging from the neuroimaging results. For example, the left inferior parietal lobe (IPL) has been found to be consistently implicated in reasoning (not only deductive reasoning; Wendelken, 2015), while it is also known to be strongly related to perspective-taking (Arora et al., 2015). This finding seems to offer further support to the dialogical conception of deductive reasoning defended here (and, more generally, to a dialogical/interactionist conception of reasoning *tout court*), given the centrality of perspective-taking for this conception. It also suggests that one of the phylogenetically earlier forms of cognition apparently redeployed for deductive reasoning, namely perspective-taking, is firmly grounded in human socio-cognitive skills. In other words, these results suggest that, also in the brain, deduction is primarily a social phenomenon.

10.6   Conclusion

In this chapter, I adopted a phylogenetic timescale perspective to investigate the cognitive roots of deduction. I started by examining the evidence for the presence of (precursors of) deductive reasoning in non-human animals. While behaviors consistent with inference by exclusion and transitive inference have been observed in a number of non-human animals, we cannot confidently conclude that these animals are de facto reasoning according to the corresponding logical, deductive principles. Indeed, non-deductive, non-logical explanations of these behaviors fare equally well (if not better) than the attribution of a modicum of deductive competence to these species. I then went on to focus specifically on humans, and discussed a recent influential proposal for the evolutionary origins of reasoning in general: Mercier and Sperber's interactionist account of reasoning. While agreeing with them in many respects, I argued that their claim that reasoning is best seen as a genetic adaptation corresponding to a specialized module is in fact quite implausible. Instead, I sketched and defended an account of reasoning in general, and of deductive reasoning in particular, as a result of processes of cultural evolution, based on Heyes' cognitive gadgets framework. Finally, I briefly surveyed some of the findings on the neural basis for deductive reasoning, which has been found to be highly heterogeneous and fractionated. I argued that these findings lend further support to the present account of deductive reasoning insofar as they suggest that there is no such thing as a neutrally localized 'module for deduction' in the brain.

11   A Dialogical Account of Proofs
in Mathematical Practice

11.1   Introduction

In this final chapter, the dialogical framework developed so far, in particular in terms of the Prover–Skeptic dialogues, is applied to contemporary mathematical practices (Ancient Greek mathematics is briefly discussed in Chapter 5). The philosophy of mathematical practice is currently a well-regarded (though still not entirely mainstream) subfield in philosophy of mathematics. The starting point is the observation that what mathematicians de facto do qua mathematicians (how they make discoveries, how they communicate and justify their findings, the social structure underlying mathematical practice, etc.) is a legitimate object for philosophical analysis. While more traditional philosophy of mathematics addresses abstract questions such as the ontological status of mathematical objects (e.g. numbers), the nature of mathematical truth, and the foundations of mathematics, the philosophy of mathematical practice attends to the 'human factor' and focuses on descriptive as well as normative questions pertaining to these practices. The idea is that, by attending to such practices, we may gain a deeper *philosophical* understanding of what mathematics really is, which in turn allows for new perspectives on traditional philosophical questions (Mancosu, 2008; van Bendegem, 2018). Moreover, the observation that, in mathematical practice, informal proofs rather than formal derivations take pride of place has led to research on the connections between argumentation theory and proofs and arguments in mathematical practice (Aberdein & Dove, 2013) – naturally, a topic directly relevant for the present purposes.

In this chapter, I apply the Prover–Skeptic framework to a number of salient aspects of mathematical practice, and argue that it offers an attractive account of (a significant portion of) what mathematicians do. It is, again, the unifying potential of the dialogical hypothesis that has explanatory power, as a number of apparently disparate aspects of mathematical practice can be shown to be manifestations of a common underlying dialogical structure. Mathematics educators have long been interested in dialogical approaches to teaching mathematics (see Chapter 9), but to my knowledge the only other thoroughly *philosophical* dialogical account of mathematical practice (though in close connection with education) is the one developed by Paul Ernest (1994). Nevertheless, dialectical/dialogical ideas permeate much of the research at the intersection between argumentation theory and the philosophy of mathematical practice (e.g. Krabbe, 2008), and the present discussion is also indebted to this body of research.

I start with the question of what kinds of entities mathematical proofs are; this allows me to clarify the exact subject matter of this chapter. I then turn to real-life Provers and Skeptics in mathematical practice, looking at their patterns of interaction such as peer review, online cooperation, and 'adversarial collaboration,' and discuss three case studies analyzed from a Prover–Skeptic perspective. In Section 11.4, I focus on the multifaceted character of practices of mathematical proofs, discussing the different functions attributed to proofs, and recent developments that seem to challenge the classical notion of mathematical proof (and thus the Prover–Skeptic model), such as probabilistic and computational proofs.

11.2   What Kinds of Entities Are Mathematical Proofs?

Let us start with an abstract, quasi-esoteric question: What are mathematical proofs, really? What kinds of entities are they? In other words, before embarking on an analysis of proofs in mathematical practice, let me specify which objects I take myself to be talking about in this chapter.

According to a prima facie plausible view, proofs are abstract entities distinct from their actual presentations in specific media such as speech or writing. The legendary mathematician Paul Erdős spoke of 'The Book' in which God maintained the perfect proofs waiting to be discovered by us mere mortals. Naturally, this was a humorous remark by the atheist Erdős,[1] but it suggests the idea that proofs themselves, not only the mathematical objects they talk about, have some sort of freestanding existence independent of human agency. Presumably, the 'human' proofs expressed in speech and writing would then be instantiations of these ideal entities, something like Platonic forms imperfectly instantiated in the physical world. This is, of course, a rather implausible view for metaphysical and epistemological reasons, but it raises the question: If this is not what proofs are, what are they?

Similarly, proofs can be viewed as conceptual, intensional entities (the question of whether they are created or discovered can be set aside). On this conception, what individuates a proof are its key idea and the inferential connections therein; specific presentations, for example, with different

---

[1] It inspired, however, an actual 'human' book in this spirit (Aigner & Ziegler, 1999), a project with which Erdős was involved at the very end of his life.

levels of detail, are then versions of the same proof rather than different proofs themselves. While prima facie intuitive, this view is complicated by difficulties in determining when two proof presentations are in fact versions of the same proof, understood as a conceptual entity. Take Georg Cantor's diagonal argument proving the uncountability of the real numbers; it can be formulated as a reductio argument or as a direct proof. While the basic idea of diagonalization is present in both, they have different inferential profiles; are they then the same proof or not? Despite such difficulties, I suspect that the view that proofs correspond to conceptual, intensional entities is widely (albeit perhaps tacitly) held by practicing mathematicians.

However, there are compelling cognitive and philosophical reasons against this view (other than issues pertaining to effective criteria of individuation). In recent decades, philosophers and cognitive scientists have emphasized the relevance of embodiment and concrete aspects of mathematical practices. Features such as gestures (Greiffenhagen, 2008), physical metaphors (Lakoff & Nunez, 2000), and notations (Dutilh Novaes, 2012a) have been shown to have significant impact on how mathematical practices are shaped. These observations suggest that a more suitable level of analysis is rather that of *proof presentation* in specific media such as speech and writing (and combinations thereof, including diagrams). To be clear, the claim is not that, purely on metaphysical grounds, what a proof *really is* corresponds to its presentation in a physical medium. Rather, the point is chiefly a methodological one: given the features of mathematical practices we are interested in here, it is sensible to take proofs in their concreteness as our objects of analysis. (Actually, I don't think there are independent, purely metaphysical facts that determine univocally what proofs *really are*.)

Another reason to consider proof presentations as the relevant ontological entities for the present analysis pertains to the functions of proofs (see Section 11.4.1), in particular the functions of communication, explanation, and persuasion. For a proof to be persuasive and/or explanatory, it must be formulated with the appropriate level of granularity (detail) for its intended audience (Schiller, 2013). Proofs intended for professional mathematicians in journals are usually very succinct, just stating the basic idea, on the assumption that the intended audience will be able to reconstruct the proof (should they wish to). By contrast, proofs aimed at students will typically be more detailed, as the succinct proofs for professional mathematicians would fail in their roles of persuasion and explanation for the less experienced audience. The distinguished mathematician Paul Halmos puts this point eloquently in his famous essay 'How to write mathematics':

When you decide to write something, ask yourself who it is that you want to reach. Are you writing a diary note to be read by yourself only, a letter to a friend, a research announcement for specialists, or a textbook for undergraduates? The problems are much the same in any case; what varies is the amount of motivation you need to put in, the extent of informality you may allow yourself, the fussiness of the detail that is necessary, and the number of times things have to be repeated. All writing is influenced by the audience, but, given the audience, an author's problem is to communicate with it as best he can. (Halmos, 1970, p. 126)

Indeed, as discussed by Don Fallis (2003), proofs intended for professional mathematicians are often 'gappy' in that some relevant inferential steps are not made explicit. This is prima facie a puzzling phenomenon, at least from the point of view of what Fallis dubs the 'Cartesian story,' according to which a mathematical proposition must be "deduced from true and known principles by the continuous and uninterrupted action of a mind that has a clear vision of each step in the process"[2] (Descartes, *Rules for the Direction of the Mind*, quoted in Fallis, 2003, p. 46). And yet, inferential gaps are routinely tolerated in the presentation of mathematical proofs.

By contrast, from a dialogical perspective, these gaps are unproblematic, and in fact anticipated: a proof is typically formulated with the right level of detail, the right granularity and inferential decomposition, *for the specific audience to whom it is directed*. In fact, too much detail would be counterproductive for a proof understood as a communicative device, as it would make the argument tedious (a violation of the Gricean maxim of quantity, perhaps). In her work on the refereeing practices of mathematicians, Line Andersen (2018) specifically addressed the issue of 'acceptable gaps.' She identified two methods of validation used by referees: validation by comparison (against the background of the mathematician's own prior convictions) and line-by-line validation. In particular, line-by-line validation is required when the result presented, or the technique used, is somehow surprising or non-standard. Naturally, in validation by comparison, gaps are tolerated to a much greater extent. (More on refereeing practices in mathematics in Section 11.3.1.)

A related issue is the relation between informal proofs and formal derivations. According to an influential view, defended in particular by Jody Azzouni (2004), an informal mathematical proof, such as the ones we encounter in mathematical journals or textbooks, is correct only insofar as it corresponds to, or 'indicates' in Azzouni's terminology, a formal derivation. This view emerged from the axiomatic, foundational projects that appeared at the turn of the nineteenth to the twentieth century (Awodey & Reck, 2002; see Chapter 7), which have been very fruitful in a number of senses, but which ultimately failed to reduce all of

---

[2] A similar view, which was/is influential in recent philosophy of logic and mathematics, is Frege's ideal of 'gap-free' proofs, developed in the *Begriffsschrift*.

mathematical practice and knowledge to the study of formal systems. A number of philosophical arguments against the view that proofs correspond to formal derivations have been formulated in the literature, such as that there are too many different associated formal derivations corresponding to each informal proof (Tanswell, 2015), and that "the level of detail required by certain types of formalization may actually interfere with the recognition of larger-scale structures in proofs upon which their explanatory potential depends" (Detlefsen, 2008, p. 28).

Naturally, the view that proofs should be considered at the level of proof presentation (at least for the present purposes) also faces issues pertaining to criteria of individuation. Do mere typographical distinctions between two proof presentations (say, one written in LaTex, the other in Word) count as two different proofs? We certainly wouldn't want to go this far.[3] But even different but formally equivalent notations (say, standard notation for propositional/ predicate logic vs. Polish notation) may have significantly different cognitive effects (Dutilh Novaes, 2012a), so these criteria of identity must be quite fine-grained and discriminating (even if they should not discriminate on the basis of typographical differences alone, for example).

Thus, informal proofs, or informal proof presentations, to be exact, emerge as ontologically autonomous entities whose existence does not depend on underlying conceptual entities or formal derivations (though they do depend on the producers and receivers of discourse). They are best seen as a species of the genus 'discourse,' linguistic entities embedded in the human practices of mathematicians (Dutilh Novaes, 2019). (Naturally, this is very much a claim one would expect to find in this book, given its dialogical main hypothesis.) It is these informal proofs that will be the object of analysis in this chapter.[4]

11.3   Provers and Skeptics in Mathematical Practice

Throughout this book, the two fictive (idealized) characters Prover and Skeptic have played an important role. We will now see that they are not only fictive characters; they are also instantiated by flesh-and-blood mathematicians in their practices. Indeed, mathematicians regularly enact the 'moves' attributed to Prover and Skeptic in Chapters 3 and 4, as we will see now.

---

[3] As a matter of fact, these are distinctions that mathematicians do take into account when evaluating a new proof (even if they should not), as revealed by the episode of Thomas Royen's proof of the Gaussian Correlation Inequality, which was initially not taken seriously (among other reasons) because it was written in Word (Wolchover, 2017).

[4] This introduces a potential methodological complication, namely that many of the sources I rely on for this chapter may in fact have a different conception of proofs as entities, i.e. not at the level of proof presentation. I acknowledge the risk of misalignment here, but it does not strike me as substantially affecting the analysis to follow.

I start by reviewing some aspects of practices of peer review in mathematics, as referees are the most obvious real-life instantiations of Skeptic. I then turn to collaboration in mathematics, arguing that forms of adversarial collaboration (a concept discussed in Chapter 9) are also present in mathematical practices. I close with a comparative analysis of three case studies, namely the receptions of Kurt Gödel's incompleteness theorems (1930), Edward Nelson's failed proof of the inconsistency of Peano Arithmetic (2011), and Shinichi Mochizuki's purported proof of the ABC conjecture (2012 and ongoing).

11.3.1   Peer Review

The peer review system in general has been extensively studied in recent years, in particular for the biomedical sciences.[5] However, peer review in mathematics remains largely unexplored terrain, with only a handful of studies (such as Geist et al., 2010; Frans & Kosolosky, 2014; Andersen, 2017, 2018). In this section, I rely on these studies to discuss peer review practices in mathematics in relation to the Prover–Skeptic model.

Two features in mathematical peer review stand out as diverging from other fields: a mathematical paper is typically refereed by only one expert, and the process is typically not double-anonymous, as the referee usually knows the identity of the author (but not the converse).[6] When commissioning a referee report, a journal editor expects (tacitly, as no explicit instructions are normally given) the referee to take three main aspects into account when evaluating the results, known as 'Littlewood's precepts' (Geist et al., 2010): Is it correct? Is it new? Is it interesting?[7] All three aspects are taken to be important, possibly to different degrees, depending on the reputation of the journal. A severely incorrect proof is in principle disqualified immediately, and so the issues of novelty and interest do not even arise. Surprisingly though, it seems that many mathematicians do not take it to be the responsibility of the referee to check for the correctness of the proof: they take it to be the author's job rather than the referee's (Geist et al., 2010).

How does a referee evaluate the correctness of a proof? It seems that factors such as the reputation of the author and their level of seniority have a decisive impact on how rigorously a proof is scrutinized: typically, the more junior the author (say, a Ph.D. student), or if they have a reputation of being 'careless'

---

[5] Geist et al., 2010 provides a number of references to studies of peer review in the biomedical sciences.

[6] Another related feature of mathematical academic publishing and peer review is that papers are usually made available as preprints through arXiv in non-anonymous form.

[7] This may be a misattribution, as different sources attribute the three questions to G. H. Hardy (Halmos, 1985).

with details, the more scrutiny the proof will receive (Geist et al., 2010, section 5.6). Andersen (2018, section 3) identifies two strategies adopted by referees:

[T]he referee does two types of things when she checks the proof in broad outline against what she knows: She checks whether each subresult of the proof seems reasonable in light of what she knows and, at least for most of the subresults, whether it seems reasonable that this type of result can be proved in this type of way, with this type of tools. If so, she will usually not go on to check the subproof line by line. We may thus speak of two types of proof validation. We call them Type 1 validation, or validation by comparison, and Type 2 validation, or line-by-line validation.

It appears thus that the line-by-line check that an ideal Skeptic is supposed to undertake when presented with a proof is not a procedure uniformly adopted by mathematicians when they referee a paper; alongside factors related to content, the reputation or seniority of the paper's author plays a role in the choice of strategy. (And yet, anecdotal evidence suggests that mathematicians often take quite a long time to referee a paper; proof-checking is simply a very laborious and time-consuming task.) The fact that referees do not always engage in line-by-line validation is prima facie puzzling, and might be seen as an argument against the Prover–Skeptic model. However, recall that the main goal for Skeptic is to become convinced of the truth of the conclusion given the truth of the premises, and this effect can occur also with Type 1 validation as described by Andersen. In fact, what these observations suggest is that, when refereeing a paper, a referee is in fact engaging in a specific conversation with a specific interlocutor, the Prover in question; the referee adjusts the level of scrutiny that she considers adequate for the specific content and Prover in question.

The fact that a Prover must formulate a proof with the level of detail appropriate for its intended audience has been noted many times previously in this book; we now see that responsiveness to specific interlocutors is also a property of Skeptic engagement in these refereeing practices (justly or not, as it may give rise to forms of epistemic injustice; Rittberg et al., 2018). In fact, a referee is not only interested in whether she herself finds the proof convincing; she also checks for 'checkability' for/by the relevant mathematical community:

The interviews suggest that a referee checks a proof for "checkability" by the relevant experts, so when she checks the proof for correctness in the way described above, she also takes into account whether others would be able to check the proof for correctness in the same type of way. Hence, she does not only comment on the parts that she cannot follow herself, but also on parts that she believes will be hard for others to follow unless more information is provided. In doing so, she appears to be guided by the criterion that a large majority of the experts in the specialized field should be able to validate the proof within a reasonable amount of time. (Andersen, 2018, section 5)

In other words, when acting as a Skeptic (looking for mistakes or counterexamples to specific steps in the proof; asking for further clarification for steps that are not sufficiently perspicuous), a referee is not only taking into consideration her own doxastic reactions to the proof; her job is to help Prover to formulate a proof that will be understood by the members of the particular mathematical (sub-)community for which it is intended. The proof should thus be as *transferable* as possible, to use Kenny Easwaran's terminology (2009), while not becoming redundant and tedious for the intended audience: it must have the right amount of inferential decomposition for that audience (Paseau, 2016). The referee thus "speaks with the voice of the subcommunity" (Andersen, 2018, section 6).

But perhaps the most striking point of convergence of the Prover–Skeptic model with refereeing practices in mathematics is the observation that the review process itself is very much like a dialogue between a Prover (the author of the paper) and a Skeptic (the referee). As described by Andersen (commenting specifically on the Prover–Skeptic model):

> Contained in the published proof are the author's responses to the responses of this voice [the referee's voice representing the subcommunity] to the author. In this sense, the proof can be said to consist in a dialogue between the relevant community and the author ... [This] suggests that we speak, as we do above, of a published mathematical proof as a piece of discourse *with* the relevant audience, not only as a piece of discourse aimed at that audience. (Andersen, 2018, section 6)

In other words, traces of the interaction, and thus the 'voice' of the referee/ Skeptic, are still to be found in the end result insofar as the author has responded to requests for further clarification voiced by the referee for specific steps of the proof. The peer review process, which corresponds to a Prover–Skeptic dialogue between the author of the paper and the referee, fundamentally affects what published proofs look like.

As for the other two aspects that referees are expected to pay attention to, the novelty and the interestingness of the results, they are less obviously captured by the Prover–Skeptic model (as the model primarily addresses structure rather than content). However, they follow quite straightforwardly from Gricean principles of relevance: don't say what has already been said (novelty); and make sure your contribution to the conversation advances it in relevant ways (interestingness). Moreover, Skeptic may decide not to engage in the dialogue at all if, once the conclusion to be proved and the premises have been stated, he anticipates that the proof that Prover is about to formulate is trivial or not novel. This move would correspond to a referee who does not even bother to check the details of a proof because what it proves does not seem novel or interesting (and thus, presumably, rejects the paper).

But given these observations, how reliable is refereeing in mathematics? The fact that papers are typically examined by only one referee, and that not all referees perform the line-by-line check that a diligent Skeptic ought to perform, should give us pause. Nevertheless, it has been argued that mathematical refereeing is pretty reliable after all (Andersen, 2017), in particular in that there appears to be more inter-reviewer agreement in the case of mathematics than in the empirical sciences (Geist et al., 2010) (presumably, something that is ensured by higher intersubjective agreement on the general principles underlying the relevant methods). Furthermore, post-publication informal peer review ensures that published work continues to be scrutinized by the Skeptics of the relevant community (Andersen, 2017), so publication is not the end of the 'conversation.'

In sum, peer review practices in mathematics lend strong support to the (descriptive and prescriptive) adequacy of the Prover–Skeptic model, as referees are by and large expected to engage as a Skeptic does in our fictive dialogues. The review process itself is very much like a dialogue between a Prover and a Skeptic, and the end result, the published proof, will contain the voices of both (though, of course, predominantly that of Prover).

11.3.2   Collaboration in Mathematics

Is mathematics a collaborative endeavor? To a layperson, producing mathematical knowledge may appear to be essentially an individual process, especially when compared to the empirical sciences, where research is organized in teams and laboratories. By contrast, a mathematician would mostly work alone, cracking puzzles and only occasionally consulting with colleagues. True enough, the structure of *certification* for mathematical knowledge, described in Sections 11.3.1 and 11.4.1, is a complex social phenomenon, but this is not incompatible with a picture of production of mathematical knowledge being essentially an individual process.

As a contrastive claim, it is probably fair to say that production of knowledge in mathematics is more individual-based than in a number of other fields of inquiry. It is also probably true that a significant number of mathematicians still prefer to work mostly by themselves – Andrew Wiles being a prominent recent example. Nevertheless, collaboration in mathematics is a widespread phenomenon, which has attracted more attention in the last ten years with the advent of massive online collaborations on the crowdsourcing model such as the Polymath project (Gowers & Nielsen, 2009).[8] Indeed, it has been argued that these new technologies are fundamentally changing mathematical practice toward a 'social machine' model (Martin & Pease, 2013), but massive collaboration in mathematics predates the age of the Internet. A famous earlier example was the Bourbaki group in France, a project which began in the 1930s and which continued to produce groundbreaking mathematics for decades (Atiyah, 2007). Another well-known collaborative

---

[8] Mathematicians also often collaborate in small groups, often resulting in team-authored papers.

project in mathematics is the classification of the finite simple groups, a theorem stating that every finite simple group belongs to one of four broad classes. The proof of the theorem consists of several hundred journal articles, produced by over 100 mathematicians over a period of decades (roughly 1955–2004) (Aschbacher, 2004). Alongside these more systematic collaborative projects, numerous online fora provide the background for informal collaboration, such as MathOverflow, a question-and-answer website where users can ask questions, submit answers, and rate both (users get merit points for their activities).

Obviously, massive collaboration will require massive amounts of dialogical interaction among mathematicians, either face-to-face (as for the classification of finite simple groups; Steingart, 2012) or online (as in Polymath or MathOverflow). These dialogues have been fruitfully studied from the perspective of dialectic and argumentation theory (Corneli et al., 2017), which again lends support to a dialogical conception of mathematical practice. True enough, these dialogues do not always correspond neatly to Prover–Skeptic dialogues, in particular in that they often start with a question or a request for help, which are very different starting points from that of a Prover–Skeptic dialogue. Nevertheless, once a candidate proof or argument is put forward, those involved in the interaction will presumably behave as Skeptics, looking for possible flaws or steps in the proof which remain obscure. (Naturally, this is an empirical hypothesis that could be studied systematically with the large databases of interactions from Polymath and MathOverflow.) Indeed, it is also by not being easily convinced that a mathematician can collaborate with her peers, as well described in a memorable quote from Imre Lakatos' *Proofs and Refutations* (see Chapter 3 for a detailed discussion of Lakatos' views):

SIGMA: Then not only do refutations act as fermenting agents for proof-analysis, but proof-analysis may act as a fermenting agent for refutations! What an unholy alliance between seeming enemies! (Lakatos, 1976, p. 48)

The observant reader may recall that we've previously encountered the concept of *adversarial collaboration* (Chapter 9), which has been proposed as a protocol to conduct research in the social sciences (Mellers et al., 2001). To recapitulate, this is a protocol for two (or more) researchers who disagree on a specific matter – e.g. competing hypotheses about given phenomena or experimental findings – to set out to investigate the issue jointly, while maintaining their initial conflicting convictions. The parties agree on tests to be run or experiments to be conducted, which might deliver decisive evidence one way or another. An arbiter may also be involved, typically another scientist who is 'neutral' on the question at hand.[9]

---

[9] It is an interesting question what would correspond to the role of 'arbiter' in the case of mathematics. Journal editors might be candidates for the position, but the analogy is far from perfect.

While in the social/empirical sciences adversarial collaboration is a recent concept (at least its explicit conceptualization), if the Lakatosian picture of mathematics as proceeding by means of proofs and refutations is accurate, then adversarial collaboration has been central to mathematical practice for centuries (or even millennia, if we go back to the Ancient Greek origins of mathematical proof, discussed in Chapter 5). Indeed, at the very heart of the Prover–Skeptic model is the idea of a complex interplay between adversariality and cooperation (Chapter 3), where the parties collaborate precisely by being adversarial in the specific sense of disagreeing with each other and/or not being easily convinced by the position of their interlocutors. In practice, adversarial collaboration in mathematics occurs, for example, when a mathematician helps a peer improve a particular result by finding a flaw in the argument, thus giving her the opportunity to fix it, in either formal or informal peer review. When Wiles submitted his 200-page proof of Fermat's Last Theorem to the journal *Inventiones Mathematicae*, the editor split up the proof among six referees, one of whom was Nick Katz. What ensued was a typical instance of Prover–Skeptic adversarial/collaborative interaction:

For two months, Katz and a French colleague, Luc Illusie, scrutinized every logical step in Katz's section of the proof. From time to time, they would come across a line of reasoning they couldn't follow. Katz would email Wiles, who would provide a fix. But in late August, Wiles offered an explanation that didn't satisfy the two reviewers. And when Wiles took a closer look, he saw that Katz had found a crack in the mathematical scaffolding. At first, a repair seemed straightforward. But as Wiles picked at the crack, pieces of the structure began falling away. (Brown, 2015)

As we now know, this was in fact a serious error, which took Wiles a full year to fix (importantly, not on his own but in collaboration with Richard Taylor). He had not found the problem while working on the proof by himself; it took the external perspective of two Skeptics, Katz and Illusie, for the issue to be spotted. Katz and Illusie were obviously collaborating with Wiles in producing a more solid proof, but they did so by 'adversarially' challenging the original proof.

What makes adversarial collaboration in mathematics thus understood particularly fruitful and manageable is a key property of deductive proofs, *transferability*:

[T]he basic idea is that a proof must be such that a relevant expert will become convinced of the truth of the conclusion of the proof just by consideration of each of the steps in the proof. With non-transferable proofs, something extra beyond just the steps in the proof is needed . . . (Easwaran, 2009, p. 343)

The notion of transferability is very naturally understood in terms of the dialogical Prover–Skeptic model: Skeptic represents the 'relevant expert' who will become convinced of the truth of the conclusion (conditional on the truth of premises) just by considering each step of the proof as formulated by

Prover (provided the proof has no serious flaws, of course). Transferability therefore relates to the line-by-line checking of a proof termed Type 2 validation in Andersen, 2018. As this kind of transparency is viewed as a central component in a (classical) mathematical proof, adversarial collaboration thus understood is more easily implemented than in most other fields.[10]

Indeed, the more transferable a proof is, the easier it is for a Skeptic to find possible mistakes and loopholes. So Prover also collaborates with Skeptic (and thus with herself, indirectly) when producing a transparent proof, where all details are spelled out with the adequate level of inferential decomposition, even if it makes the proof more vulnerable to Skeptic's 'attacks.' In the next section, I discuss three case studies, three (purported) proofs with different levels of transferability, that result in different outcomes for the process of adversarial collaboration and proof certification.

For now, the conclusion is that mathematics is indeed a highly collaborative enterprise, and perhaps more so in recent decades with the advent of new technologies that facilitate collaboration. Mathematical collaboration takes different forms: mathematicians may collaborate 'cooperatively' by joining forces to work on a problem together (e.g. the classification of the finite simple groups, or the Polymath problems), but they may also collaborate 'adversarially' by deliberately looking for flaws in a colleague's work. A referee has the official assignment to collaborate in an adversarial manner, but this happens also informally as mathematicians scrutinize each other's proofs as part of their regular activities (informal peer review).

11.3.3   Three Case Studies

In this section, I discuss three case studies, which together illustrate adversarial collaboration in action in mathematics. These are: Gödel's proofs of the incompleteness theorems in 1930, Nelson's failed proof of the inconsistency of Peano Arithmetic (PA) in 2011, and the saga, ongoing since 2012, of Mochizuki's purported proof of the ABC conjecture. In the first two cases, the relevant proofs were highly transferable, and thus the process of adversarial collaboration could run smoothly. In the last one, the lack of transferability of the proof has created the strange situation of a proof 'in limbo,' which has neither been certified nor refuted in the seven years since it was first announced.

In September 1930, Gödel made the first public announcement of his incompleteness results. In the first instance, he had proved only the first incompleteness theorem: in any consistent formal system F within which a certain amount of arithmetic can be carried out, there are statements in the language of F which

---

[10] A counterpart of transferability in other fields of inquiry is the *principle of publicity*, according to which scientific methods should be public and fully transparent to peers (Piccinini, 2003).

can neither be proved nor disproved in F. From the first theorem, the second incompleteness theorem (that such a formal system F cannot prove that the system itself is consistent, assuming it is indeed consistent) was then proved independently by Gödel himself and by John von Neumann. In fact, von Neumann was one of the few who immediately understood the new results; he may have been the first to see the far-reaching consequences it had. In particular, while Gödel was still cautious regarding the impact of his results for Hilbert's Program, von Neumann immediately drew the conclusion that the implications would be tremendous.

But most mathematicians were initially so taken aback by Gödel's results that they were convinced a mistake would be found somewhere in the proof; many of them then set out to find it. As described in Mancosu, 2010, the news of Gödel's results spread quickly, but, in the absence of the Internet or other fast means of dissemination, most people did not have immediate access to the article where the results were presented, and so could not attend to its details. For example, before inspecting the proof, the Polish mathematician (and avant-garde artist) Leon Chwistek suspected that the proof would be based on misunderstandings. However, once he read the article, he stood corrected:

In my last letter I have raised some doubts concerning Dr Gödel's work that have completely disappeared after a more attentive study of the problem. I had at first thought that there was a tacit introduction of non-predicative functions which makes the use of a rigorous symbolical procedure impossible and I even feared the possibility of an antinomy. Now I see that this is out of the question. The method is truly wonderful and it fits pure type theory thoroughly. (Letter to Kaufmann, cited in Mancosu, 2010, p. 44)

In a nutshell, Gödel's proof was highly transferable: it had the right level of inferential decomposition and contained clear descriptions of the key ideas. The process of 'adversarial collaboration' between Prover and Skeptics could run smoothly in this case: all 'relevant experts' became convinced of its correctness upon close inspection, despite the counterintuitive results it proved (given that Hilbertian optimism was still widespread).

Fast-forward eight decades: on September 26, 2011, Edward Nelson, a highly respected professor of mathematics at Princeton, announced on the FOM (Foundations of Mathematics) mailing list that he had a proof of the inconsistency of PA. (The fact that he was well regarded is a fundamental aspect of the story. Outrageous results are announced by 'crackpot' mathemat-icians on a daily basis [Hodges, 1998], but for the most part the mathematical community pays no attention to them.) He offered two formulations of the proof: one in book form and one in short-summary form. From the start, many mathematicians were convinced that there had to be a mistake in the proof, just as had been the case initially with Gödel. (Real-life Skeptics do take such prior beliefs into account.) External evidence strongly suggests that PA is consistent, in particular in that so many robust mathematical results would have to be revised if PA were inconsistent (not to mention a number of proofs of the consistency of arithmetic in alternative systems, such as Gentzen's; Siders, 2013).

It did not take long before a loophole in Nelson's purported proof was found. Fields medalist Terence Tao first voiced his reservations on the Google+ thread opened by mathematical physicist John Baez on the topic.[11] At the same time, Daniel Tausk, a mathematician at the University of São Paulo, had identified the same mistake in Nelson's argument, and alerted Nelson to the problem in private communication. Judging from his replies (which can be read in the FOM archive),[12] Nelson did not immediately understand the objection, but within a few days a consensus had emerged that the mistake identified by Tao and Tausk was irreparable.[13] Then, on October 1, Nelson acknowledged the fatal nature of the error and publicly withdrew the claim of having a proof of the inconsistency of PA. In less than a week, the case was closed.

Naturally, the technological conditions that allow for mathematical results to spread quickly and to be discussed in real time online were essential for the speed with which Nelson's purported proof was found to be beyond repair. However, an important feature of the (failed) proof was its clarity and precision. Asked about how he identified the mistake in the proof, Tao wrote:[14]

Actually, Nelson's proof was relatively easy to understand, in part because he took the trouble to write out a short outline which makes clear the general strategy of proof while omitting most of the technical details (though it was ambiguous at one very crucial juncture) ... Aside from this one ambiguity, though, the outline was quite clear. Certainly there have been other manuscripts claiming major results that were much more difficult to adjudicate because they were written so badly that there were multiple ambiguities or inaccuracies in the exposition, and any high-level perspective on the argument was obscured.

Technically, we can't say that Nelson's flawed proof was highly transferable (in Easwaran's sense), because it did *not* convince the relevant experts of the truth of the conclusion, since they spotted an error. But it was highly transferable in the sense that Nelson had been a cooperative Prover when providing both an outline of the main strategy and a detailed description of the steps of the proof, thus greatly facilitating the work of Skeptics such as Tao and Tausk. In this

---

[11] Interestingly, mathematicians were quite active on the social media platform launched by Google, Google+, which was discontinued in 2019 as a commercial failure. Since Google+ shut down, a number of mathematicians are now active on Twitter.

[12] https://cs.nyu.edu/pipermail/fom/2011-September/subject.html#15816

[13] The mistake was based on the false assumption that the hierarchy of subtheories built for the proof maps neatly onto the hierarchy of the Kolmogorov complexity of each of these subtheories.

[14] http://m-phi.blogspot.com/2011/10/inconsistency-of-pa-and-consensus-in.html (I was the author of this blog post, which provides the basis for the analysis here.)

respect, it belongs to the same class as Gödel's proof regarding clarity and transparency.

Roughly one year later, another earth-shattering announcement was made: the distinguished mathematician Shinichi Mochizuki (Kyoto University) claimed to have proved the ABC conjecture. The conjecture concerns a very simple equation, $a + b = c$, where a, b, and c are positive integers. It pertains to the product of all the prime numbers that divide any of the three integers, and states that there are finitely many cases where this product will fall below a certain threshold.[15] Like Fermat's Last Theorem, the ABC conjecture is easy to understand but exceedingly hard to prove. It is not only significant in itself, but it also implies a number of other important mathematical statements, such as Catalan's conjecture and Fermat's Last Theorem. So, a proof of the ABC conjecture, which has been described as "the most important unsolved problem in Diophantine analysis" (Goldfeld, 1996), would constitute a major breakthrough in mathematics.

Mochizuki is a highly regarded mathematician who had been working in nearly complete isolation for about ten years developing ideas on elliptic curves, in what he calls inter-universal Teichmüller theory (IUTeich for short). In August 2012, Mochizuki uploaded four very long papers presenting this novel framework; one of the results that follow from it (or so he claims) is the ABC conjecture. This was exciting news, but soon after, the mathematical community came to realize with disappointment that the proof was impenetrable; it depended on a whole mathematical world, as it were, that no one other than Mochizuki was familiar with. What's more, Mochizuki did not make access to this new world particularly easy, as he refused to travel outside Japan to explain IUTeich to mathematicians elsewhere; in a sense, he did not fulfill his duty as a Prover to make his proof easily accessible to the relevant Skeptics. Instead, a number of specialists traveled to Japan to speak to him, and a conference in Oxford was organized in 2015 dedicated to IUTeich (Mochizuki participated via video conference).

Typically, when a new proof of a high-profile result is announced, the process of certifying or refuting it happens within a reasonable amount of time. (One exception is Thomas Hales' proof of Kepler's conjecture: after a long period of examination by multiple referees, the journal editor could only go as far as stating that he was "99% sure" that the proof was correct.) The case of Mochizuki's purported proof of the ABC is perplexing, because it has been in

---

[15] More precisely: "The *abc* conjecture involves an even simpler equation: $a + b = c$; and affirms that for positive integers a, b, and c with no common prime divisors, if $\varepsilon > 0$ and $c > \mathrm{rad}(abc)^{1+\varepsilon}$, then $a + b = c$ has only *finitely* many solutions. The radical, rad(*abc*), denotes the product of the distinct prime divisors of the number *abc*. What is mysterious about this conjecture is the connection drawn between two very simple arithmetical operations: addition, $a + b$, and multiplication, *abc*" (Roberts, 2019).

220 Deduction and Cognition

limbo for many years (Castelvecchi, 2015). For years, only a handful of specialists, all belonging to Mochizuki's inner circle, were certain of its correctness, but nobody had been able to locate an error in the proof, so it had not been refuted either. As mathematician Matthew Emerton noted, "no expert who claims to understand the arguments has succeeded in explaining them to any of the (very many) experts who remain mystified" (quoted in Klarreich, 2018).

In March 2018, mathematicians Peter Scholze and Jakob Stix went to Japan to discuss with Mochizuki what they thought was a fatal error in the proof, in Corollary 3.12. They are both mathematicians of considerable stature: Scholze received the Fields Medal in 2018, and Stix is a leading authority on Mochizuki's own main area of research, anabelian geometry. So, their concerns were not to be taken lightly.[16] Despite everyone's best efforts, however, the stalemate continues: Mochizuki couldn't convince Scholze and Stix that his proof was correct,[17] and they could not convince him that what they take to be an error in the proof is indeed an error (Klarreich, 2018). In other words, it is still not clear whether the proof has an error or whether Mochizuki simply needs to explain his reasoning further.

What can the Prover–Skeptic model say about this saga? One important question is whether the Prover, Mochizuki, and the Skeptics of the relevant mathematical subcommunity have each fulfilled their functional duties as Prover and Skeptic.[18] On the one hand, Mochizuki seems not to have produced an argument that is perspicuous and convincing, instead relying on an obscure new theory, IUTeich; he further refuses to formulate the proof in terms that are more familiar to the mathematical community. He has thus arguably failed his duties as a Prover.[19] On the other hand, Mochizuki himself thinks that most mathematicians are not being diligent Skeptics, as they are not doing the work required to become acquainted with his new theory (he attributes to his colleague Go Yamashita the estimation that it would take roughly six months to become acquainted with the theory by studying it systematically from the beginning; Mochizuki, 2014). There is, in sum, a disagreement regarding the optimal division of labor between Prover and Skeptic (Tanswell, 2017, p. 192) and thus regarding who is failing to fulfill their duties.[20]

---

[16] See Roberts, 2019 for an accessible discussion of some of the mathematical details, as well as an insightful analysis of some of the social aspects involved in the controversy.

[17] Their own account of the purported error can be found in Scholze & Stix, 2018.

[18] See Tanswell, 2017, section 5.8 for an analysis of the ABC conjecture controversy in virtue-theoretic terms.

[19] "It only constitutes a proof if I can readily convince my audience, i.e. other mathematicians, that something is true. Moreover, if I claim to have proved something, it is my responsibility to convince others I've done so; it's not their responsibility to try to understand it (although it would be very nice of them to try)" (O'Neill, 2012).

[20] It may be argued that there is an asymmetry in that it is common practice for mathematicians presenting new results to relate them in illuminating ways to prior mathematical knowledge. This is something that Mochizuki has by and large refused to do.

Moreover, there is disagreement on who counts as a 'relevant expert' who must be able to understand the proof. In Easwaran's definition of transferable proofs, this is a key notion: to be transferable, "a proof must be such that a *relevant expert* will become convinced of the truth of the conclusion of the proof just by consideration of each of the steps in the proof" (Easwaran, 2009, p. 343, emphasis added). Mochizuki thinks that only those who have studied IUTeich in depth count as relevant experts who should become convinced by the proof; according to him, all such experts have indeed become fully convinced by it so far (Tanswell, 2017, p. 191). (In fact, he thinks that the proof has received much more critical scrutiny than the usual level of refereeing for a mathematical journal.) By contrast, most other mathematicians seem to think that the relevant experts here are researchers working on arithmetic geometry in general, not just those initiated in IUTeich; these remain "mystified," according to Emerton (see quote above). So, from the perspective of the mathematical community at large, Mochizuki's proof is not transferable; from Mochizuki's own perspective, his proof *is* transferable, as the small group of 'relevant experts' who have inspected it have become fully convinced. (One wonders whether Scholze and Stix count as relevant experts for Mochizuki.)

At the time of writing (May 2020), the most important development since the extensive discussion in Roberts, 2019 has been the controversial acceptance for publication of the relevant papers in a journal published by Mochizuki's home institute, while many experts seem to think that the presumed flaws identified by Scholze and Stix have not been properly addressed (Castelvecchi, 2020). The story will continue to unfold (especially because, in mathematics, a journal's seal of approval is often not the end of the peer review process), but it is already one of the most fascinating episodes in the history of mathematical proof, as a rare instance of adversarial collaboration between Prover and Skeptics breaking down.

11.4 Proofs as a Multifaceted Phenomenon

As a contribution to the philosophy of mathematical practice, the Prover–Skeptic model seeks to explain a number of interesting (occasionally puzzling) features of practices of proofs in one coherent story. However, a crucial aspect of the practice of mathematical proofs is that it in fact corresponds to a very diverse collection of practices – a *motley*, as Wittgenstein puts it (Wittgenstein, 1978, III, §46) – rather than to a uniform class of phenomena. So the philosopher of mathematical practice interested in proofs is confronted with the challenge of doing justice to the multifaceted nature of its explanandum, while at the same time identifying some commonalities and patterns in these practices so as to articulate an intelligible philosophical account at a suitable level of generality. Clear-cut 'necessary and sufficient conditions' for something to count as a proof cannot be formulated, but a number of paradig-matic cases (which themselves might constitute a rather diverse collection) may well serve as a legitimate starting point.

In this section, I grapple with the diversity vs. explanatory unity tension; my goal in this chapter (as with the whole book, in fact) is to capture a wide class of phenomena typically associated with the concept of mathematical proof, while recognizing that my Prover–Skeptic model will likely fail to encompass a number of important exemplars (see in particular the section on probabilistic and computational proofs below). The Prover–Skeptic model is not an essen-tialist account; it is rather a bottom-up attempt to describe some pervasive patterns in these practices while not claiming to be fully encompassing.

11.4.1   The Functions of Mathematical Proofs

As a motley of practices, mathematical proofs have many functions/roles within mathematical practices (broadly construed), something that is recog-nized by a number of practicing mathematicians (Auslander, 2008).[21] So far in this book, the two functions that have been emphasized are *persuasion* and *explanation*, but we must also address a number of other functions attributed to proofs in mathematics (some of which do not fit neatly within the Prover–Skeptic model). In particular, different functions may belong to different contexts (e.g. teaching vs. research), but even within one and the same context there may well be different roles that proofs are expected to fulfill.

A traditional view, which still has currency, at least among philosophers, is that the main and perhaps even sole function of a proof is to establish the truth of a mathematical statement (or that the conclusion follows from the premises, and so its truth is conditional on the truth of the premises).[22] Now, if establish-ing truths were all that mathematics is about, then mathematicians would be content with being told by an oracle or God whether a particular statement is true or not. But as noted by mathematician John Franks (cited in Auslander, 2008, p. 62), "who would be satisfied if God were to announce that the Riemann hypothesis is true, but deny us the proof?" Crucially, mathematicians also seek to obtain *understanding* (Thurston, 1994). Lakatos (1976) famously

---

[21] The responses (Atiyah, 1994) to an influential article by Arthur Jaffe and Frank Quinn on the significance of proofs in mathematics (Jaffe & Quinn, 1993) offer a good illustration of these different views.

[22] The mathematician Keith Devlin provocatively describes this conception as the 'right wing' conception of proof, as opposed to a 'left wing' one: "What is a proof? The question has two answers. The right wing ('right-or-wrong,' 'rule-of-law') definition is that a proof is a logically correct argument that establishes the truth of a given statement. The left wing answer (fuzzy, democratic, and human centered) is that a proof is an argument that convinces a typical mathematician of the truth of a given statement" (Devlin, 2003). He goes on to argue that the 'left wing' answer is the one that actually fits mathematical practice.

argued that establishing the truth of a statement is a complete misconception of the goal of a mathematical proof, especially as, on his view, one never comes to a definitive end point in the process of proofs and refutations. But one need not go as far as Lakatos in claiming that establishing the truth of mathematical statements is not *at all* one of the goals of proofs to recognize that there are a number of other, equally important roles for proofs in the practices of mathematicians.

While any list of the functions of proofs in mathematics is bound to be incomplete, we discern a number of regularities in the lists available in the literature. For Camilla Gilmore and colleagues (2018, section 9.1), the following main roles for proofs are identified: to verify the truth of a statement/theorem; to explain why the theorem is true; to introduce new ideas and techniques; and to systematize results into a coherent theory of definitions and other results. Paul Auslander (2008) highlights the following functions/roles: proof as certification within the relevant mathematical community; proof as explanation; proof as exploration leading to new insights, techniques or ideas; and proofs as justification of definitions. Michael De Villiers (1999) discerns verification, explanation, systematization, discovery, intellectual challenge, and communication as the roles of proofs. Reuben Hersh (1993) emphasizes convincing and explaining as the main function of proofs, as does John Dawson (2006), for whom a proof's "purpose is to convince those who endeavor to follow it that a certain mathematical statement is true (and, ideally, to explain *why* it is true)" (p. 270). J. A. Robinson also emphasizes the roles of convincing and explaining (as discussed in Detlefsen, 2008). On Paul Ernest's (1994) dialogical conception, proofs are viewed as a critical component of the general 'conversation' that is mathematics, and thus essentially as communicative, discursive entities. Yehuda Rav (1999) stresses the creative dimension of proofs in giving rise to new methods, tools, strategies and concepts; the same holds for Lakatos (Tanswell, 2018). We thus obtain the following list of (partially interrelated) roles for proofs in mathematical practices (in the context of research), identified and recognized by mathematicians themselves and by those who think about mathematical practice, such as philosophers and educators.

Proof as Verification. This is the traditional view as described above: "How do mathematicians know that mathematical propositions are true? The standard answer is that a mathematician knows that a proposition is true because she knows a proof of that proposition" (Fallis, 2003, p. 45). This is certainly one of the functions attributed to proofs by mathematicians: if there is a correct proof of a theorem, and if the premises are true, then the theorem will be true. Thus formulated, the view does not invoke the social fabric of mathematics and is at odds with a number of important features of the relevant practices. Indeed, verification is only the beginning of a much more complex story describing the multiple roles of proofs in mathematical practice.

Proof as (Ground for) Certification.   Because mathematics is a social practice, individual attributions of truth to given theorems in the presence of proofs need to be coordinated within the relevant community. In particular, this is indispensable because it is obviously not feasible for an individual mathematician to examine carefully every proof of every theorem that is interesting/relevant to her. Instead, the institutional structure of mathematics is such that when a proof becomes certified by the relevant community (a process involving different aspects), mathematicians can assume the theorem that it proves to be acceptable without having to run through the proof themselves (though when using the result in their own research or teaching, it is a reasonable expectation that they understand the basic features of the proof; Auslander, 2008, p. 65; Andersen, 2018). Joseph Auslander offers a compelling description of the crucial role of certification via proofs in mathematical practice:

We accept that a purported result is correct when we hear that it has been proved by a mathematician we trust and "validated" by experts in the author's mathematical specialty. This is the case even if we haven't read the proof, or more frequently when we don't have the background to follow the proof. As an extreme, perhaps hackneyed, example, mathematicians accept Wiles' proof of Fermat's last theorem because number theorists have "certified" it to be correct . . . [Certification] is an indication that we are part of a community whose members trust one another. In fact, mathematics could not be a coherent discipline, as opposed to a random collection of techniques and results, without the process of certification. (Auslander, 2008, p. 64)

But when does a proof count as certified? Simply having been published in a professional journal might not be good enough, as referees are obviously fallible beings themselves and so mistakes inevitably slip by. (Very refreshingly, Auslander himself comes out as having been one such 'careless referee' on one occasion; Auslander, 2008, p. 105). And so, in some circumstances at least, the bar must be higher. As noted by Todd CadwalladerOlsker, "the Clay Mathematics Institute, which offers a one million dollar prize for a proof of any one of seven mathematical conjectures, stipulates that any proof must be published and accepted by the community of mathematicians for two years before a prize will be awarded" (2011, p. 37). The two-year period is an interesting criterion, as it reflects the recognition that finding mistakes in a proof may take some time (even for high-visibility results that attract a lot of attention from 'Skeptics' in the community). Indeed, proofs continue to be scrutinized even after they have been published in a journal, in a process of informal peer review (Andersen, 2018). However, in practice, once a proof has been published in a well-regarded journal, it is typically presumed to be correct unless there are compelling reasons to believe otherwise. Matthew Inglis calls this the 'negative view' of mathematical proofs: "A mathematical argument which purports to establish a result is said to be a mathematical proof if no one who has considered the argument has found a serious problem with it yet" (Inglis, 2018). A paper published in a serious journal will have been inspected by at least one Skeptic, the referee.

In Prover–Skeptic terms, we may say that a proof has been certified if it has been examined by a sufficient number of suitable Skeptics and none of them has found errors in it. Of course, what counts as a 'sufficient number' and a 'suitable Skeptic' is to some extent a contextual matter. Inevitably, high-profile results by distinguished mathematicians will receive more attention from Skeptics, and thus will be certified to a higher degree, if no mistakes are found, than an unremarkable result published in an obscure journal. Presumably, the stakes are also higher because more people will rely on these 'famous' results in their own work. Certification can thus be conceived as a matter of degree (perhaps similar to robustness and replication in empirical research): the more competent experts have scrutinized a proof and not found any significant mistakes, the more certified it is.

Summing up, while certification is obviously related to verification (the latter can be said to be contained in the former), certification is a much more complex, social process and a unifying force for mathematics as a discipline.

Proof for Communication and Persuasion.   An elementary and yet important observation is that proofs are a crucial instrument for mathematicians to communicate with one another: a proof is a piece of discourse, as argued in Section 11.2. To be clear, proofs are certainly not the *only* way mathematicians communicate, but they occupy a special position in the constellation of mathematical discourse.[23] Ernest puts this point eloquently:

Mathematical proofs or other proposals are offered to the appropriate mathematical community as part of a continuing dialogue. They are addressed to an audience, and they are tendered in the expectation of reply, be it acceptance or critique. Such replies may play a part in the development and formulation of new mathematical knowledge. However, such replies, when given by the gatekeepers of institutionalized mathematical knowledge (e.g., PhD examiners, conference referees, journal editors) play the essential warranting role in the acceptance (or rejection) of candidates presented as new mathematical knowledge. This conversation constitutes the social acceptance mechanism for mathematical knowledge [i.e. certification]. (Ernest, 1994, p. 43)

---

[23] Thurston, 1994 describes a number of ways in which communication in mathematics is not optimal, while noting that, within each subfield/subcommunity of mathematicians, communication works surprisingly well. It is as if each subfield of mathematics had its own specific language not understood by outsiders.

For proofs to play this role, one of the main perlocutionary effects of these speech acts must be that of *persuasion*. As stressed many times throughout this book, a proof is meant to convince its intended audience of the truth of its conclusion (given the presumed truth of its premises), and this feature is indispensable for its certification function. A proof that is 'correct' in some suitable, objective sense, but which fails to be persuasive (e.g. Mochizuki's purported proof of the ABC conjecture, if indeed it turns out to be correct) is simply not suitable to put in motion the process of certification described above, and thus fails miserably as a communicative device (though the communicative dimension of proofs arguably goes beyond mere persuasion).

Naturally, persuasion is at the heart of the Prover–Skeptic account of proofs developed here. The whole point of the exercise is for Prover to convince Skeptic of the truth of the conclusion (given the presumed truth of the premises). But the kind of persuasion in question cannot be based on mere deception (which wouldn't work on a skilled Skeptic anyway); Skeptic must become convinced of the conclusion because he truly understands the proof as a whole and recognizes the correctness of each step. This is why the persuasion in question is more aptly described as *explanatory* persuasion; so let us now turn to explanation, yet another role frequently attributed to proofs.

Proof as Explanation.   It is a common observation (e.g. see passage by Dawson quoted above) that, ideally, a proof should indicate not only *that* its conclusion is true (given the truth of the premises) but also *why* it is true. This expectation is usually formulated in terms of the desideratum that a proof be *explanatory*. Explanatoriness is typically not seen as a necessary condition for a mathematical argument to be considered a proper proof, but, all things being equal, it is considered a highly desirable property in a proof.

The explanatoriness of mathematical proofs has given rise to a lively debate in philosophy of mathematics (Mancosu & Pincock, 2012; Mancosu, 2011). It is a matter of contention what exactly the property of explanatoriness in a proof *is*: realist accounts defend that there really is 'something' in the relevant mathematical entities that is captured by the proof (Steiner, 1978; Colyvan, 2010), whereas pragmatic accounts focus on concrete 'human' aspects of the proof situation, such as its intended audience (Heinzmann, 2006; Paseau, 2010; Dutilh Novaes, 2018a). But that proofs are expected to perform an explanatory role is widely accepted by mathematicians, philosophers of mathematics, and mathematics educators (Hanna et al., 2010), as this simply reflects the importance of *understanding* in mathematical practice.[24] An explanatory proof is precisely one that is more likely to generate understanding (Inglis & Mejía-Ramos, 2019).

---

[24] In recent years, the concept of understanding has received more attention within epistemology and philosophy of science (Grimm et al., 2017).

On the dialogical conception of proofs developed here, explanatoriness comes out as a very natural desideratum for proofs. An explanation is plausibly conceived as a triad involving the producer, the explanation itself, and the receiver, which in this case are Prover, the proof, and Skeptic, respectively. It is thus a *relational* property: a proof is explanatory *for a given audience* rather than explanatory in absolute terms (Paseau, 2010; Dutilh Novaes, 2018a). Moreover, recall that one of the moves for Skeptic in the Prover–Skeptic dialogues described in previous chapters is to ask for further clarification when a particular inferential step is not sufficiently clear: 'Why does this follow?' By asking appropriate why-questions, Skeptic may help Prover produce a proof that is overall more explanatory, enhancing our understanding of why the theorem in question holds (given truth of premises).

Proof as Driver of Innovation.   The functions described so far – verification, certification, persuasion, and explanation – are all closely related. Another important function of proofs, however, points in a different direction: proofs as sources for new ideas, concepts, techniques, etc. (There may be interesting connections between explanation and innovation in proofs, but I will not pursue this idea here for reasons of space.) Strikingly, there are a number of interesting cases in the history of mathematics of 'proofs' that failed to prove what they were meant to prove initially (as they had some fatal flaw, and/or the 'theorem proved' turned out not to be true), but where new techniques, ideas, definitions, problems, etc. were introduced that later turned out to lead to a number of important further results. Some examples are Gerolamo Saccheri's 'proof' of Euclid's fifth postulate, where Saccheri believed he had deduced absurdities from assuming the postulate to be false, and instead discovered non-Euclidean geometry without realizing it; and Henri Poincaré's work on the three-body problem, which, despite receiving wide appraisal initially, was later viewed as fatally flawed, and yet gave rise to chaos theory.[25] In these cases, the epistemic value of the proofs transcended the (failed) attempt to establish the truth of a mathematical statement. According to Rav,

Proofs are for the mathematician what experimental procedures are for the experimental scientist: in studying them one learns of new ideas, new concepts, new strategies – devices which can be assimilated for one's own research and be further developed. (Rav, 1999, p. 20)

Admittedly, this particular function of mathematical proofs is not well captured in the Prover–Skeptic model, even though it is certainly an important role for proofs in mathematics. This is because the Prover–Skeptic model mostly offers

---

[25] There are many more such examples, some of which are mentioned in a Twitter thread in response to my request for examples of such flawed proofs: https://twitter.com/cdutilhnovaes/status/1140264575482388480.

a local perspective on individual proofs, whereas the innovative potential of proofs stands out in particular against the background of mathematical knowledge as a whole. Moreover, the model focuses on structural aspects of the Prover–Skeptic interaction rather than on content, and is thus not sensitive to content-related features of a proof.

Proof as Systematization.   Finally, another important role attributed to proofs is to 'bring together' elements that turn out to be related but which had so far not been connected by mathematicians. Interestingly, systematization is a feature of proofs that Kitcher associates with explanatoriness; for Philip Kitcher, "an explanatory proof in pure mathematics is one that is part of a small collection of argument patterns that allows the derivation of the mathematical claims that we accept" (Mancosu & Pincock, 2012, p. 15). Notice that Kitcher's focus is not on an individual argument for a single theorem, but rather on clusters of arguments for multiple, related statements. This is a global (as opposed to e.g. Steiner's local) conception of the explanatoriness of proofs. In fact, proofs may foster unification and systematization of mathematical knowledge in at least two ways: by exposing connections between different mathematical concepts (sometimes even from very different mathematical fields)[26] in one and the same proof, and by instantiating argument patterns that are used in a number of different proofs.

This, too, is a function of mathematical proofs that the Prover–Skeptic model does not address explicitly, again because it primarily offers a local perspective. As the model focuses on individual proofs (corresponding to specific dialogues), it does not have much to say about clusters of arguments. Moreover, as noted above, it does not address the contentual components of proofs. As with proofs as driver of innovation, rather than downplaying the importance of this role so as to avoid objections to the Prover–Skeptic model, the intellectually honest response here is to acknowledge the significance of these two roles while recognizing that they fall outside the reach of the model (at least on its current formulation; it is conceivable that the model could be generalized and expanded so as to cover these two roles as well).

11.4.2 *Computational and Probabilistic Proofs*

One of the most significant developments in mathematical practices pertaining to proofs in the last decades has been the increasing significance of computers and computational methods. While, with hindsight, Hilbert's Program at the dawn of the twentieth century was already an attempt to implement a computational approach to proofs, it is only in recent decades that digital

---

[26] As noted in Auslander, 2008, p. 67, well-known occurrences of this kind of unification are combinations of algebra and topology, and of combinatorics and number theory.

computers became routinely used for the formulation of mathematical proofs. A watershed in these developments was the much-discussed computer-assisted solution of the four-color problem proposed by Kenneth Appel and Wolfgang Haken in 1977. In an influential paper published shortly thereafter, Thomas Tymoczko (1979) discussed the philosophical significance of the Appel–Haken solution, going as far as to state that, "if we accept the 4CT as a theorem, we are committed to changing the sense of 'theorem,' or, more to the point, to changing the sense of the underlying concept of 'proof'" (Tymoczko, 1979, p. 58). Donald MacKenzie (1999) also sees the history of the four-color theorem as revealing the negotiability and plasticity of the very concept of mathematical proof.

Since then, the use of computational methods in mathematical proofs has only increased, with a huge literature on automated proof-checkers, automated theorem-provers, and, more recently, a whole new research program in mathematics, homotopy type theory, which has as its starting point the idea that proofs should be formulated directly in formalized form, with the help of the automated proof assistant Coq (Univalent Foundations Program, 2013). Some other well-known computer-assisted proofs are Hales' 1998 proof of the Kepler conjecture, and the solution to the Pythagorean triples problem by Marijn Heule and collaborators (in 2016), which corresponds to an astounding 200 terabytes.[27]

What do these new developments represent for the dialogical conception of proofs defended here? Do they entail that the 'classical,' Euclidean deductive conception, which is what the Prover–Skeptic model is intended to capture, no longer holds? Or do they entail something even more radical, namely the 'death of proof' in mathematics, as controversially suggested by *Scientific American* staff writer John Horgan (1993)? In a recent post for *Scientific American* (Horgan et al., 2020), three professional mathematicians revisited Horgan's claim, and concluded that the rumors of proof's death have been greatly exaggerated: while computational methods have become more pervasive within mathematical practices, 'classical' proofs continue to be central to these practices, and in fact a number of groundbreaking results have recently been proved classically/deductively. In the words of mathematician Scott Aaronson,

there's been no fundamental change to mathematics that deserves such a dramatic title ['The Death of Proof']. Proof-based math remains quite healthy, with (e.g.) a solution to

---

[27] A terminological clarification: I use 'computer-assisted proofs' to refer to proofs some of whose steps are carried out by computer calculation. In the limit case, *all* steps in a proof are carried out by a computer, in which case we may say that the proof is purely computational. This seems like a distinction of degree rather than of kind, but these two types of proofs may well raise different philosophical questions. Despite possible differences, for reasons of space I treat them together, mostly focusing on computer-assisted proofs.

the Poincaré conjecture since your article came out [Horgan, 1993], as well as to the Erdős discrepancy problem, the Kadison–Singer conjecture, Catalan's conjecture, bounded gaps in primes, testing primality in deterministic polynomial time, etc. – just to pick a few examples from the tiny subset of areas that I know anything about.

Despite the healthy state of deductive proofs in mathematics, computer-assisted and computational proofs are not the only new development challenging the classical conception of proof; probabilistic and zero-knowledge proofs (proofs that convey no additional knowledge other than that the conclusion is true) are two prominent examples of novel non-standard approaches. In this section, I discuss computer-assisted and probabilistic proofs in particular, and what they represent for a classical, deductive conception of mathematical proofs and the Prover–Skeptic model. They each diverge from the model in different ways.

A significant number of mathematicians still profoundly dislike computer-assisted proofs, arguably largely because these proofs do not look or feel like the Prover–Skeptic dialogues they are used to. What exactly is 'wrong' with them? Do these mathematicians not trust the calculations performed by computers? Do they think these calculations are misleading in that they 'prove' something false? The issue seems not to lie in the truth or falsity of the relevant theorems, but rather in the lack of perspicuity/transparency of these proofs. As candidly described by mathematician John H. Conway, "I don't like them, because you sort of don't feel you understand what's going on" (quoted in Chang, 2004). Seen thus, the situation is not much different from learning about the truth of a mathematical statement from God or an oracle: without the accompanying proof, we do not really know *why* or *how* it is true. The computer would be a mere 'black box' spitting out results without providing insight or ensuring accountability. (This issue is now even more acute with the advent of machine learning techniques in computer science.)

In a similar vein, Tymoczko (1979) emphasizes the lack of surveyability of these proofs, and since he takes surveyability to be a key component of the classical conception, he concludes that these proofs represent a significant departure from the latter. Michael Detlefsen (2008) in turn argues that Tymoczko's characterization of the 'classical conception' is incorrect, and thus that the solution to the four-color problem is not as much in conflict with the classical notion as Tymoczko claims.

Be that as it may, it is clear that computational and computer-assisted proofs pose a challenge for the Prover–Skeptic account. One of the key components of deductive arguments such as mathematical proofs on this account is *perspicuity*, which is closely related to surveyability (though perhaps a proof can be sufficiently perspicuous for the Skeptic in question without being fully surveyable). And thus, computational and computer-assisted proofs do not straightforwardly correspond to canonical Prover–Skeptic dialogues, insofar as their inferential steps are not explicitly, transparently presented to the audience. They are also lacking on the explanatory dimension, as presumably they do not elicit the kind of understanding that classical deductive proofs are expected to elicit. In sum, they may well establish the truth of their conclusion beyond reasonable doubt, but they lack transparency and explanatoriness.

The challenge posed by probabilistic proofs is of a different nature. Here the canonical example is the Miller–Rabin primality test, which is used to determine whether a given number is a prime number or not (Rabin, 1980). Until the development of this test, the available methods for determining primality had impractical upper bounds, so a more manageable primality test would be a significant breakthrough. This breakthrough came in 1976:

Gary Miller and Michael Rabin introduced a new twist into our subject by producing (in 1976) a *probabilistic proof* of a mathematical theorem. They studied how to prove whether a certain large number p is prime, by devising an iterative procedure with the property that each application of the algorithm increases the probability that the number is prime (or else shows that it is not). So, with enough iterations, one could make the probability as close to 1 as desired. But their method could never be used to achieve mathematical certainty (unless the answer was negative). (Kranz, 2011, pp. 16–17)

These probabilistic proofs cannot achieve 'mathematical certainty,' at least as traditionally conceived, but Rabin argues that the probability of them being incorrect is actually smaller than the probability of most classical proofs being incorrect, given the possibility of mistakes cropping up especially in very long proofs. Fallis (1997, 2002) further argues that, from an epistemological point of view, probabilistic proofs are not that different from classical, deductive proofs. Easwaran provides a helpful summary of Fallis' position:

In a series of papers, Don Fallis points out that although mathematicians are generally unwilling to accept merely probabilistic proofs, they do accept proofs that are incomplete, long and complicated, or partly carried out by computers. He argues that there are no epistemic grounds on which probabilistic proofs can be rejected while these other proofs are accepted. (Easwaran, 2009, p. 341)

Easwaran then argues that there is in fact a property that classical deductive proofs possess and that probabilistic proofs, the Miller–Rabin primality test in particular, lack: transferability.

With non-transferable proofs, something extra beyond just the steps in the proof is needed – in the case of probabilistic proofs, this extra component is a knowledge of the process by which the proof was generated, and in particular that the supposedly random steps really were random. (Easwaran, 2009, p. 343)

A probabilistic proof is not transferable in this sense, because it is Prover who picks the supposedly random steps and claims that they were random, something that cannot be verified by Skeptic. Indeed, for all Skeptic knows,

Prover has cherry-picked the supposedly random steps, or the supposedly random witness of a universal claim (Easwaran, 2009, p. 357). (Recall that, as discussed in Chapter 3, in game-theoretical, dialogical accounts of the universal quantifier, to prove a universal statement by means of a randomly chosen witness, the witness has to be chosen not by Prover but by *Skeptic* – or the corresponding character: opponent, Nature, etc.)

The conclusion is thus that computer-assisted/computational proofs as well as probabilistic proofs do not naturally fall under the Prover–Skeptic model: they fail to produce the kind of explanatory persuasion that these dialogues are supposed to give rise to (though they may be sufficiently convincing in other respects). What must we conclude from this mismatch?[28] Is the Prover–Skeptic model defective in view of these new types of proofs? Or are these proofs not to be considered as proper proofs? The fact that there is still considerable discontent with these types of proofs among mathematicians suggests that the classical, deductive conception, which is what the Prover–Skeptic model is meant to capture, is still the dominant paradigm. But the situation may well change within the next decades or centuries, just as practices and standards of proof have already changed significantly over the last 2.5 millennia (Kranz, 2011).

Mathematical proof is not an ahistorical, atemporal concept; rather, it is an open-textured concept that continues to evolve as the practices of mathematicians change over time.[29] This is not a problem for the Prover–Skeptic model as such, as the goal is not to capture a purportedly atemporal 'essence' of what mathematical proofs 'really are.' Rather, the model intends to capture a historically influential, for now still pervasive conception of mathematical proof and the underlying practices. If these practices change substantially in the next decades or centuries, then the model will become mostly of historical interest; for now, however, it still seems to have considerable explanatory power in accounting for mathematical practices, as argued in this chapter.

11.5   Conclusion

In this chapter, deductive proofs in mathematical practice have been analyzed from the perspective of the Prover–Skeptic model. I've argued that, in mathematical practice, these are not only fictive characters: they are instantiated by real-life mathematicians. This is particularly clear in peer review practices and in various forms of collaboration in mathematics. But I've also highlighted some of the limitations of the model, in that it does not naturally capture two of the main functions frequently associated with proofs (proof as driver of

---

[28] By contrast, notice that a 'new' type of proof, so-called interactive proof systems, shares a multi-agent, interactive notion of proof with the Prover–Skeptic model (Goldwasser et al., 1989).

[29] See Tanswell, 2018 on the open-textured nature of mathematical concepts.

innovation and as systematization), and in that recent developments in 'non-standard' proof techniques seem at odds with the Prover–Skeptic model. I've argued that, since the model is not intended as an essentialist account of what proofs really are, the fact that some aspects of mathematical practice do not fit the broad story does not count as decisive evidence against the model. Overall, the model still accommodates very large portions of mathematical practice, offering a unified account of various activities that mathematicians engage in.

Conclusions

Throughout this book, deduction has been examined and discussed from many angles and perspectives. However, one question has remained conspicuously unaddressed until now: Is deduction a correct, reliable method for reasoning? In other words, is deduction *justified* (Dummett, 1978)?

This investigation has focused extensively on the social conditions and factors influencing the emergence of deduction, both historically and ontogenetically. It is thus reasonable to ask whether it offers a *social constructivist* account of deduction, which in turn has implications for the justification problem. Indeed, on at least some versions of social constructivism, the very question of the correctness of deductive reasoning as a scientific method, understood in absolute terms, is seen as misguided. There would be no external, absolute measure of correctness for a scientific method, as the social practices of scientists alone determine what counts as correct. To paraphrase Bruno Latour and Steve Woolgar's remark on the objectivity of scientific facts, the correctness of a scientific method would be "the consequence of scientific work rather than its cause" (1986, p. 182).

Is the account presented here indeed a version of social constructivism, thus joining the camp of authors such as Paul Ernest (1997) and Julian Cole (2015), who have defended social constructivism for mathematics? To address this question, we must first consider the well-established distinction between strong and weak versions of social constructivism. On strong social constructivism, there is no objective truth or matter of fact outside of the relevant practices and social conditions. By contrast, weak social constructivism holds that, were the relevant social conditions different, *beliefs and practices* (scientific or otherwise) would be different, but not the facts as such. In other words, strong social constructivism entails ontological claims, whereas weak social constructivism entails descriptive claims about doxastic states and cognitive practices. Weak social constructivism is often taken to be true but philosophically uninteresting, whereas strong social constructivism would be an interesting but wildly implausible view (Khalifa, 2010).

The present account of deduction undoubtedly qualifies as social constructivist in the weak sense. I have emphasized numerous times the importance of contingent social factors for the emergence of deductive argumentation and reasoning, both historically (in particular, the polemic sociopolitical background of Athenian democracy) and ontogenetically (the social and cognitive scaffolding that facilitates mastery of deductive reasoning skills). Does this mean that my story is philosophically uninteresting, as suggested by Khalifa, 2010 about weak social constructivism in general? I think not, as I will argue now.

There is a staggering number of 'truths' that a knower may want to discover in the world (assuming, for now, that there are mind-independent facts); but given time and capacity limitations, not all truths will be worth investigating or become salient to a given knower. The number of grains of sand on Ipanema beach at any given time is presumably an objective fact which one may acquire knowledge of; but it is highly implausible that there should ever be a set of circumstances prompting a knower to expend time and energy to investigate this issue, given its utter irrelevance for human matters. Thus, inquiry (scientific or otherwise) must necessarily be *selective*, focusing on aspects of reality that are deemed most important. This point is eloquently made by Kitcher, 2001, and is to some extent present in discussions on pragmatic encroachment (Fantl & McGrath, 2009). What makes a certain concept or content *salient* to the knower, such that she comes to hold beliefs about that concept or content, is to a great extent determined by non-epistemic, practical, contingent factors, in particular (but not exclusively) social circumstances.

Something similar holds for *methods of inquiry*. While the range of methods of inquiry may not be as large as that for facts/truths, there are still a number of options (associative learning, induction, abduction, deduction, analogical reasoning, Bayesian probabilities, etc.). I take it that it is of philosophical (not 'merely' historical or sociological) significance *how* a given community of inquirers has come to adopt a particular method of inquiry. Moreover, I maintain that a number of contingent social factors will influence method development and selection. Attending to these social factors is particularly important for methods that have become so influential within a given tradition that one may easily forget that tortuous historical paths and contingencies led to the emergence and establishment of the method in question.

Throughout this book, I have argued that the emergence and establishment of deduction as a canonical approach to arguing and reasoning in science and mathematics in Europe (and perhaps in other traditions, too, either under the influence of European developments or as independent discoveries) is causally related to (though not uniquely determined by) a number of social factors. Specific social conditions, especially the polemical background in Ancient Greece, made the usefulness of *incontrovertible arguments* particularly salient, thus providing an impulse for the initial development of the deductive method. My aim was thus to engage in what Netz, 1999 describes as 'cognitive history.'

To my mind, such an investigation is philosophically (not only historically) significant for a number of reasons, most importantly because current instantiations of the concept and practices of deduction still carry traces of earlier instantiations – in particular *dialogical* components; these must be taken into account for a thorough philosophical understanding of deduction. Moreover, by outlining the contingent factors involved in its emergence, we may obtain a better appreciation of how much of a cognitive oddity deduction really is. Deductive canons and practices seem to have emerged independently only a few times in history (perhaps even only once, in Ancient Greece), which means that they are not 'cultural attractors' in the way that, e.g. practices of counting are (Sperber, 1996). This has implications, for example, for empirical research on human cognition: the psychology of reasoning tradition spent decades "looking for logic in all the wrong places" (Counihan, 2008), something that could have been avoided had the researchers in this tradition had a better grasp of the historical background of deduction.

However, highlighting contingencies in the development of deduction does not necessarily entail the relativistic claim that deductive reasoning is just as good (or bad!) as any other method of reasoning or argumentation. It is not by chance that deduction came to occupy such a prominent position in (European) science and mathematics, as it has much to show for itself: it affords a higher degree of certainty for a conclusion (given the truth of the premises) than reasoning methods that do not guarantee truth-preservation; it allows for the mitigation of cognitive biases by forcing the reasoner to take *all* the models of the premises into account, not only her preferred ones, and more generally by requiring that her prior beliefs be set aside momentarily (see Chapter 9). These are desirable properties for a method of reasoning in the context of scientific (including mathematical) inquiry, but are basically out of place in more mundane situations.

In fact, the present account of deduction is neutral with respect to the question of whether the deductive method was *discovered or invented* (i.e. socially constructed). In other words, the genealogical narrative presented here is compatible with the view that the deductive method is objectively correct but had to be discovered by diligent minds. The fact that contingent social factors played a role in the history of this (putative) discovery would not make it less objectively correct, in a mind- and practice-independent way. This means that the present account is social constructivist in a weak but not in a strong sense. (To be sure, it is *also* compatible with a strong social constructivist account of deduction, which, however, is not decisively established by the findings presented here.) Indeed, this is the reason why it is often said that weak social constructivism is philosophically uninteresting: it "is compatible both with scientific realism and other forms of scientific antirealism" (Khalifa, 2010, p. 47).

In short, this investigation does not establish conclusively whether deduction is, objectively and absolutely speaking, a correct method for reasoning or not (let alone if it is the *only* correct method for reasoning). If strong social constructivism is true for deduction, then the question does not even make sense. In turn, if strong social constructivism is false for deduction, and for canons of reasoning more generally, then the substantive question of which modes of reasoning (possibly more than one) are correct, either across the board or for specific situations/applications, remains. But I am not sure it can ever be resolved, as it is not clear what kind of evidence could be adduced for the different positions and what might ground normative claims of correctness, other than quasi-pragmatic considerations on whether these different methods deliver what different inquirers expect of them, given their goals.

It may be objected that I have written a whole book on the topic and yet failed to address a most fundamental philosophical question, namely that of the justification of deduction (Dummett, 1978). What I have done instead is to focus on deduction insofar as it is instantiated and embedded in actual human practices, thus giving it a human face, as it were – in particular, in terms of the fictive characters Prover and Skeptic. One possible interpretation of my investigation is that it *dissolves*, rather than solves (in Wittgenstein's terms), the problem of the justification of deduction as traditionally construed by emphasizing the 'human factor' behind the abstract concept. Indeed, I have reframed the justification question in functionalist terms, which then becomes the question(s) of *why*, *when*, *where*, and *how* human reasoners feel inclined toward and are able to rely on something like deductive reasoning and argumentation. To my mind, thanks to the unifying power of the dialogical hypothesis, this book has offered compelling, novel answers to these questions. Above all, I hope readers will come out of it with a richer, more nuanced conception of deduction, even if many questions still remain, and some new questions have emerged.

References

Aberdein, A. (2009). Mathematics and argumentation. *Foundations of Science*, 14, 1–8.

Aberdein, A., & Dove, I. (2013). *The Argument of Mathematics*. Dordrecht: Springer.

Achourioti, T., Fugard, A. J., & Stenning, K. (2014). The empirical study of norms is just what we are missing. *Frontiers in Psychology*, 5, 1159.

Adler, J. E. (1984). Abstraction is uncooperative. *Journal for the Theory of Social Behaviour*, 14, 165–181.

Aigner, M., & Ziegler, G. (1999). *Proofs from THE BOOK*. Berlin: Springer.

Alderson-Day, B., & Fernyhough, C. (2015). Inner speech: Development, cognitive functions, phenomenology, and neurobiology. *Psychological Bulletin*, 141, 931–965.

Alibert, D., & Thomas, M. (1991). Research on mathematical proof. In D. Tall (ed.), *Advanced Mathematical Thinking* (pp. 215–230). New York, NY: Kluwer.

Allen, C. (2006). Transitive inference in animals: Reasoning or conditioned associations? In S. Hurley & M. Nudds (eds.), *Rational Animals?* (pp. 175–186). Oxford: Oxford University Press.

Andersen, L. E. (2018). Acceptable gaps in mathematical proofs. *Synthese*, 197, 233–247.

(2017). On the nature and role of peer review in mathematics. *Accountability in Research*, 24, 177–192.

(2017). Social Epistemology and Mathematical Practice: Dependence, Peer Review, and Joint Commitments. Ph.D. thesis, University of Aarhus.

Anderson, M. L. (2010). Neural reuse: A fundamental organizational principle of the brain. *Behavioral and Brain Sciences*, 33, 245–313.

Andrade-Lotero, A., & Dutilh Novaes, C. (2012). Validity, the squeezing argument and alternative semantic systems. *Journal of Philosophical Logic*, 41, 387–418.

Andrews, G. (2010). Belief-based and analytic processing in transitive inference depends on premise integration difficulty. *Memory and Cognition*, 38, 928–940.

Andrews, K. (2015). *The Animal Mind*. London: Routledge.

Antonini, S., & Mariotti, M. A. (2008). Indirect proof: What is specific to this way of proving? *ZDM – The International Journal on Mathematics Education*, 40, 401–412.

Aristotle. (2009). *Prior Analytics I* (translated by G. Striker). Oxford: Clarendon Press.

Arora, A., Weiss, B., Schurz, M., Aichhorn, M., Wieshofer, R., & Perner, J. (2015). Left inferior-parietal lobe activity in perspective tasks: Identity statements. *Frontiers in Human Neuroscience*, 9, 360.

Aschbacher, M. (2004). The status of the classification of the finite simple groups. *Notices of the American Mathematical Society*, 51, 736–740.

Ashworth, E. (2016). The post-medieval period. In C. Dutilh Novaes & S. Read (eds.), *The Cambridge Companion to Medieval Logic* (pp. 166–191). Cambridge: Cambridge University Press.

(2011). The scope of logic: Soto and Fonseca on dialectic and informal arguments. In M. Cameron & J. Marenbon (eds.), *Methods and Methodologies: Aristotelian Logic East and West, 500–1500* (pp. 127–145). Leiden: Brill.

Atiyah, M. (2007). Commentary: Bourbaki, *A Secret Society of Mathematicians* and *The Artist and the Mathematician* – A book review. *Notices of the AMS*, 54, 1150–1152.

(1994). Responses to: A. Jaffe and F. Quinn, "Theoretical mathematics: toward a cultural synthesis of mathematics and theoretical physics." *Bulletin of the American Mathematical Society*, 30, 178–207.

Auslander, J. (2008). On the roles of proof in mathematics. In B. Gold & R. Simons (eds.), *Proof and Other Dilemmas: Mathematics and Philosophy* (pp. 61–77). Washington, DC: Mathematical Association of America.

Awodey, S., & Reck, E. (2002). Completeness and categoricity. Part I: Nineteenth-century axiomatics to twentieth-century metalogic. *History and Philosophy of Logic*, 23, 1–30.

Azzouni, J. (2004). The derivation-indicator view of mathematical practice. *Philosophia Mathematica*, 12, 81–106.

Bakhurst, D. (2007). Vygotsky's demons. In H. Daniels, M. Cole, & J. Wertsch (eds.), *The Cambridge Companion to Vygotsky* (pp. 50–76). Cambridge: Cambridge University Press.

Balacheff, N. (1991). The benefits and limits of social interaction: The case of mathematical proof. In A. Bishop (ed.), *Mathematical Knowledge: Its Growth through Teaching* (pp. 175–192). Dordrecht: Kluwer.

Ball, L., & Thompson, V. (2018). Belief bias and reasoning. In L. Ball & V. Thompson (eds.), *International Handbook of Thinking and Reasoning* (pp. 16–36). New York, NY: Routledge.

Barnes, J. (2008). Introduction: Logic and language. In K. Algra, J. Barnes, J. Mansveld, & M. Schofield (eds.), *The Cambridge History of Hellenistic Philosophy* (pp. 65–76). Cambridge: Cambridge University Press.

(2007). *Truth, Etc.* Oxford: Oxford University Press.

(1969). Aristotle's theory of demonstration. *Phronesis*, 14, 123–152.

Bazán, B., Wippel, J., Fransen, G., & Jacquart, D. (1985). *Les questions disputées et les questions quodlibétiques dans les facultés de théologie, de droit et de médecine*. Turnhout: Brepols.

Beall, J. (2007). Truth and paradox: A philosophical sketch. In D. Jacquette (ed.), *Philosophy of Logic* (pp. 325–410). Amsterdam: Elsevier.

Beall, J., & Restall, G. (2006). *Logical Pluralism*. Oxford: Oxford University Press.

Beatty, E. L., & Thompson, V. (2012). Effects of perspective and belief on analytic reasoning in a scientific reasoning task. *Thinking & Reasoning*, 18, 441–460.

Beiser, F. (2011). *The German Historicist Tradition*. Oxford: Oxford University Press.

Benson, H. (1995). The dissolution of the problem of the elenchus. *Oxford Studies in Ancient Philosophy*, 13, 45–112.

Bermúdez, J. (2006). Animal reasoning and proto-logic. In S. Hurley & M. Nudds (eds.), *Rational Animals?* (pp. 127–138). Oxford: Oxford University Press.

Betti, A., & van den Berg, H. (2014). Modelling the history of ideas. *British Journal for the History of Philosophy*, 22, 812–835.

Bex, F., & Verheij, B. (2013). Legal stories and the process of proof. *Artificial Intelligence and Law*, 21, 253–278.

Bocheński, J. (1961). *A History of Formal Logic*. South Bend, IN: University of Notre Dame Press.

Boghossian, P. (2008). *Content and Justification: Philosophical Papers*. Oxford: Oxford University Press.

Bassler, O. B. (2006). The surveyability of mathematical proof: A historical perspective. *Synthese*, 148, 99–133.

Brandenburger, A., & Nalebuff, B. (1996). *Co-Opetition: A Revolution Mindset that Combines Competition and Cooperation*. New York, NY: Crown.

Brandom, R. (1994). *Making It Explicit: Reasoning, Representing, and Discursive Commitment*. Cambridge, MA: Harvard University Press.

Brown, P. (2015). How math's most famous proof nearly broke. *Nautilus*, May 28, https://medium.com/nautilus-magazine/how-maths-most-famous-proof-nearly-broke-f05cef973cb1

Bueno, O., & Shalkowski, S. A. (2009). Modalism and logical pluralism. *Mind*, 118, 295–321.

Buridan, J. (2001). *Summulae de dialectica* (translated by G. Klima). New Haven, CT: Yale University Press.

Burnyeat, M. F. (2000). Plato on why mathematics is good for the soul. In T. Smiley (ed.), *Mathematics and Necessity: Essays in the History of Philosophy* (pp. 1–81). Oxford: Oxford University Press.

Buroker, J. (2014). Port-Royal logic. In E. Zalta (ed.), *Stanford Encyclopedia of Philosophy*, https://plato.stanford.edu/entries/port-royal-logic/

Burris, S., & Legris, J. (2015). The algebra of logic tradition. In E. Zalta (ed.), *Stanford Encyclopedia of Philosophy*, https://plato.stanford.edu/entries/algebra-logic-tradition/

Butchart, S., Handfield, T., & Restall, G. (2009). Using peer instruction to teach philosophy, logic and critical thinking. *Teaching Philosophy*, 32, 1–40.

Butterfill, S., & Apperly, I. (2013). How to construct a minimal theory of mind. *Mind & Language*, 28, 606–637.

Byrne, R. (2018). Counterfactual reasoning and imagination. In L. Ball, & V. Thompson (eds.), *The Routledge International Handbook of Thinking and Reasoning* (pp. 71–87). New York, NY: Routledge.

(1989). Suppressing valid inferences with conditionals. *Cognition*, 31, 61–83.

CadwalladerOlsker, T. (2011). What do we mean by mathematical proof? *Journal of Humanistic Mathematics*, 1, 33–60.

Caret, C., & Hjortland, O. (2015). Logical consequence: Its nature, structure, and application. In C. Caret & O. Hjortland (eds.), *Foundations of Logical Consequence* (pp. 3–29). Oxford: Oxford University Press.

Carroll, L. (1895). What the Tortoise said to Achilles. *Mind*, 104, 691–693.

Carter, J. (2019). Exploring the fruitfulness of diagrams in mathematics. *Synthese*, 196, 4011–4032.

Carus, A. (2008). *Carnap and Twentieth-Century Thought: Explication as Enlightenment*. Cambridge: Cambridge University Press.

Castagnoli, L. (2010). *Ancient Self-Refutation: The Logic and History of the Self-Refutation Argument from Democritus to Augustine*. Cambridge: Cambridge University Press.

Castelnérac, B. (2015). Impossibility in the *Prior Analytics* and Plato's dialectic. *History and Philosophy of Logic*, 36, 303–320.

Castelnérac, B., & Marion, M. (2013). Antilogic. *The Baltic International Yearbook of Cognition, Logic and Communication*, 8, 1–31.

(2009). Arguing for inconsistency: Dialectical games in the academy. In G. Primiero (ed.), *Acts of Knowledge: History, Philosophy and Logic* (pp. 37–76). London: College Publications.

Castelvecchi, D. (2020). Mathematical proof that rocked number theory will be published. *Nature*, 580, 177.

(2015). The impenetrable proof. *Nature*, 526, 178–181.

Chang, K. (2004). In math, computers don't lie. Or do they? *New York Times*, April 6, www.nytimes.com/2004/04/06/science/in-math-computers-don-t-lie-or-do-they.html

Charette, F. (2012). The logical Greek versus the imaginative Oriental: On the historiography of 'non-Western' mathematics during the period 1820–1920. In K. Chemla (ed.), *The History of Mathematical Proof in Ancient Traditions* (pp. 274–292). Cambridge: Cambridge University Press.

Chemla, K. (2012). *The History of Mathematical Proof in Ancient Traditions*. Cambridge: Cambridge University Press.

(2012a). Reading proofs in Chinese commentaries: Algebraic proofs in an algorithmic context. In K. Chemla (ed.), *The History of Mathematical Proof in Ancient Traditions* (pp. 423–486). Cambridge: Cambridge University Press.

Clerbout, N., Gorisse, M., & Rahman, S. (2011). Context-sensitivity in Jain philosophy: A dialogical study of Siddharṣigaṇi's *Commentary on the Handbook of Logic*. *Journal of Philosophical Logic*, 40, 633–662.

Cohen, D. H. (2016). Argumentative virtues as conduits for reason's causal efficacy: Why the practice of giving reasons requires that we practice hearing reasons. *Topoi*, 38, 711–718.

Cohen, M. R., & Nagel, E. (1934). *An Introduction to Logic and Scientific Method*. London: Routledge and Kegan.

Cole, M., Gay, J., Glick, J. A., & Sharp, D. W. (1971). *The Cultural Context of Learning and Thinking*. New York, NY: Basic Books.

Cole, J. C. (2015). Social construction, mathematics, and the collective imposition of function onto reality. *Erkenntnis*, 80, 1101–1124.

Colyvan, M. (2010). There is no easy road to nominalism. *Mind*, 119, 285–306.

Cooper, W. S. (2003). *The Evolution of Reason: Logic as a Branch of Biology*. Cambridge: Cambridge University Press.

Corcoran, J. (2003). Aristotle's *Prior Analytics* and Boole's *Laws of Thought*. *History and Philosophy of Logic*, 24, 261–288.

Corneli, J., Martin, U., Murray-Rust, D., & Pease, A. (2017). Towards mathematical AI via a model of the content and process of mathematical question and answer dialogues. In H. Geuvers, M. England, O. Hasan, F. Rabe, & O. Teschke (eds.),

CICM 2017: Intelligent Computer Mathematics (pp. 132–146). New York, NY: Springer.

Counihan, M. (2008). Looking for Logic in All the Wrong Places: An Investigation of Language, Literacy and Logic in Reasoning. Ph.D. dissertation, ILLC-University of Amsterdam.

D'Agostino, M., & Floridi, L. (2009). The enduring scandal of deduction. *Synthese*, 167, 271–315.

Dawson, Jr, J. W. (2006). Why do mathematicians re-prove theorems? *Philosophia Mathematica*, 14, 269–286.

De Jong, W., & Betti, A. (2010). The classical model of science: A millennia-old model of scientific rationality. *Synthese*, 174, 185–203.

De Neys, W. (2014). Conflict detection, dual processes, and logical intuitions: Some clarifications. *Thinking & Reasoning*, 20, 169–187.

De Strycker, E. (1932). Le syllogisme chez Platon (suite et fin). *Revue néo-scolastique de philosophie*, 34, 218–239.

De Villiers, M. D. (1999). *Rethinking Proof with the Geometer's Sketch-Pad*. Emeryville, CA: Key Curriculum Press.

Dehaene, S. (2009). *Reading in the Brain: The Science and Evolution of a Human Invention*. New York, NY: Viking.

Descartes, R. (1988). Rules for the direction of our native intelligence. In *Selected Philosophical Writings* (pp. 1–19). Cambridge: Cambridge University Press.

    (1985). Principles of philosophy. In *The Philosophical Writings of Descartes, Vol. 1* (pp. 177–292). Cambridge: Cambridge University Press.

Detlefsen, M. (2008). Proof: Its nature and significance. In B. Gold & R. Simons (eds.), *Proof and Other Dilemmas: Mathematics and Philosophy* (pp. 3–32). Washington, DC: Mathematical Association of America.

Devlin, K. (2003). When is a proof? *Devlin's Angle*, Mathematical Association of America, www.maa.org/external_archive/devlin/devlin_06_03.html

Dias, M., & Harris, P. (1990). The influence of the imagination on reasoning by young children. *British Journal of Developmental Psychology*, 8, 305–318.

    (1988). The effect of make-believe play on deductive reasoning. *British Journal of Developmental Psychology*, 6, 207–221.

Dias, M., Roazzi, A., & Harris, P. L. (2005). Reasoning from unfamiliar premises: A study with unschooled adults. *Psychological Science*, 16, 550–554.

Dod, B. (1982). Aristoteles Latinus. In N. Kretzmann, A. Kenny, & J. Pinborg (eds.), *The Cambridge History of Later Medieval Philosophy* (pp. 45–79). Cambridge: Cambridge University Press.

Dogramaci, S. (2015). Communist conventions for deductive reasoning. *Nous*, 49, 776–799.

Douven, I. (2011). Abduction. In E. Zalta (ed.), *Stanford Encyclopedia of Philosophy*, http://plato.stanford.edu/entries/abduction/

Dufour, M. (2013). Arguing around mathematical proofs. In A. Aberdein & I. J. Dove (eds.), *The Argument of Mathematics* (pp. 61–76). Dordrecht: Springer.

Dummett, M. (1978). The justification of deduction. In *Truth and Other Enigmas* (pp. 290–318). Cambridge, MA: Harvard University Press.

Duncombe, M. (2016). Thought as internal speech in Plato and Aristotle. *Logical Analysis and History of Philosophy*, 19, 105–125.

(2014). Irreflexivity and Aristotle's *syllogismos*. *Philosophical Quarterly*, 64, 434–452.

Duncombe, M., & Dutilh Novaes, C. (2016). Dialectic and logic in Aristotle and his tradition. *History and Philosophy of Logic*, 37, 1–8.

Dutilh Novaes, C. (2019). The beauty (?) of mathematical proofs. In A. Aberdein & M. Inglis (eds.), *Advances in Experimental Philosophy of Logic and Mathematics* (pp. 63–93). London: Bloomsbury Academic.

(2018a). A dialogical conception of explanation in mathematical proofs. In P. Ernest (ed.), *The Philosophy of Mathematics Education Today* (pp. 81–98). Cham: Springer.

(2018b). The enduring enigma of reasoning. *Mind & Language*, 33, 513–524.

(2017a). The syllogism as defined by Aristotle, Ockham, and Buridan. In J. Pelletier & M. Roques (eds.), *The Language of Thought in Late Medieval Philosophy* (pp. 217–231). Berlin: Springer.

(2017b). What is logic? *Aeon*, January 12, https://aeon.co/essays/the-rise-and-fall-and-rise-of-logic

(2016a). Medieval theories of consequence. In E. Zalta (ed.), *Stanford Encyclopedia of Philosophy*, http://plato.stanford.edu/entries/consequence-medieval/

(2016b). Reductio ad absurdum from a dialogical perspective. *Philosophical Studies*, 173, 2605–2628.

(2015a). A dialogical, multi-agent account of the normativity of logic. *Dialectica* 69, 587–609.

(2015b). Conceptual genealogy for analytic philosophy. In J. Bell, A. Cutrofello, & P. Livingston (eds.), *Beyond the Analytic–Continental Divide: Pluralist Philosophy in the Twenty-First Century*. London: Routledge.

(2015c). The formal and the formalized: The cases of syllogistic and supposition theory. *Kriterion*, 131, 253–270.

(2013a). The Ockham–Burley dispute. In A. Conti (ed.), *A Companion to Walter Burley* (pp. 49–86). Leiden: Brill.

(2013b). A dialogical account of deductive reasoning as a case study for how culture shapes cognition. *Journal of Cognition and Culture*, 13, 459–482.

(2012a). *Formal Languages in Logic: A Philosophical and Cognitive Analysis*. Cambridge: Cambridge University Press.

(2012b). Reassessing logical hylomorphism and the demarcation of logical constants. *Synthese*, 185, 387–410.

(2012c). Form and matter in later Latin medieval logic: The cases of *suppositio* and *consequentia*. *Journal of the History of Philosophy*, 50, 339–364.

Dutilh Novaes, C., & French, R. (2018). Paradoxes and structural rules from a dialogical perspective. *Philosophical Issues*, 28, 29–158.

Dutilh Novaes, C., & Read, S. (2016). *The Cambridge Companion to Medieval Logic*. Cambridge: Cambridge University Press.

Dutilh Novaes, C., & Veluwenkamp, H. (2017). Reasoning biases, non-monotonic logics, and belief revision. *Theoria*, 83, 29–52.

Easwaran, K. (2015). Rebutting and undercutting in mathematics. *Philosophical Perspectives*, 29, 146–162.

(2009). Probabilistic proofs and transferability. *Philosophia Mathematica*, 17, 341–362.

Egan, K. (1997). *The Educated Mind*. Chicago, IL: University of Chicago Press.

Einarson, B. (1936). On certain mathematical terms in Aristotle's logic: Part I. *American Journal of Philology*, 57, 33–54.

Elio, R. (2002). *Common Sense, Reasoning, and Rationality*. Oxford: Oxford University Press.

Elqayam, S. (2018). The new paradigm in psychology of reasoning. In L. Ball & V. Thompson (eds.), *The Routledge International Handbook of Thinking and Reasoning* (pp. 130–150). New York, NY: Routledge.

El-Rouayheb, K. (2016). Arabic logic after Avicenna. In C. Dutilh Novaes & S. Read (eds.), *The Cambridge Companion to Medieval Logic* (pp. 67–93). Cambridge: Cambridge University Press.

Empiricus, Sextus (1966). Outlines of Pyrrhonism. In J. Saunders (ed.), *Greek and Roman Philosophy after Aristotle* (pp. 152–182). New York, NY: The Free Press.

Erdőhegyi, Á., Topál, J., Vrányi, Z., & Miklósi, Á. (2007). Dog-logic: Inferential reasoning in a two-way choice task and its restricted use. *Animal Behavior*, 74, 725–737.

Ernest, P. (1997). *Social Constructivism as a Philosophy of Mathematics*. New York, NY: State University of New York Press.

    (1994). The dialogical nature of mathematics. In *Mathematics, Education and Philosophy: An International Perspective* (pp. 33–48). London: Falmer Press.

Etchemendy, J. (1990). *The Concept of Logical Consequence*. Cambridge, MA: Harvard University Press.

    (1983). The doctrine of logic as form. *Linguistics and Philosophy*, 6, 319–34.

Evans, J. S. (2016). Belief bias in deductive reasoning. In R. F. Pohl (ed.), *Cognitive Illusions: Intriguing Phenomena in Judgement, Thinking and Memory*, 2nd edn. (pp. 165–184). London: Routledge.

    (2002). Logic and human reasoning: An assessment of the deduction paradigm. *Psychological Bulletin*, 128, 978–996.

    (1989). *Bias in Human Reasoning: Causes and Consequences*. Hillsdale, NJ: Erlbaum.

Evans, J. S., & Curtis-Holmes, J. (2005). Rapid responding increases belief bias: Evidence for the dual-process theory of reasoning. *Thinking & Reasoning*, 11, 382–389.

Evans, J. S., & Stanovich, K. E. (2013). Dual-process theories of higher cognition: Advancing the debate. *Perspectives on Psychological Science*, 8, 223–241.

Evans, J. S., Barston, J. L., & Pollard, P. (1983). On the conflict between logic and belief in syllogistic reasoning. *Memory & Cognition*, 11, 295–306.

Evans, J. S., Handley, S. J., & Harper, C. N. (2001). Necessity, possibility and belief: A study of syllogistic reasoning. *Quarterly Journal of Experimental Psychology*, 54, 935–958.

Evans, J. S., Handley, S. J., Harper, C. N., & Johnson-Laird, P. (1999). Reasoning about necessity and possibility: A test of the mental model theory of deduction. *Journal of Experimental Psychology: Learning, Memory, & Cognition*, 25, 1495–1513.

Evans, J. S., Newstead, S., Allen, J., & Pollard, P. (1994). Debiasing by instruction: The case of belief-bias. *European Journal of Cognitive Psychology*, 6, 263–285.

Fabry, R. (2018). Enculturation and narrative practices. *Phenomenology and the Cognitive Sciences*, 17, 911–937.

Fallis, D. (2003). Intentional gaps in mathematical proofs. *Synthese*, 134, 45–69.

    (2002). What do mathematicians want? Probabilistic proofs and the epistemic goals of mathematicians. *Logique et analyse*, 45, 1–16.

    (1997). The epistemic status of probabilistic proof. *The Journal of Philosophy*, 94, 165–186.

Fantl, J., & McGrath, M. (2009). *Knowledge in an Uncertain World*. Oxford: Oxford University Press.

Field, H. (2008). *Saving Truth from Paradox*. Oxford: Oxford University Press.

Fink, J. (2012). Introduction. In *The Development of Dialectic from Plato to Aristotle* (pp. 1–23). Cambridge: Cambridge University Press.

Fisher, M. A. (1989). Phases and phase diagrams: Gibbs' legacy today. In G. Mostow & D. Caldi (eds.), *Proceedings of the Gibbs Symposium: Yale University, May 15–17*. Providence, RI: American Mathematical Society.

Fjellstad, A. (2016). Naive modus ponens and failure of transitivity. *Journal of Philosophical Logic*, 45, 65–72.

Frankish, K. (2010). Dual-process and dual-system theories of reasoning. *Philosophy Compass*, 5, 914–926.

Frans, J., & Kosolosky, L. (2014). Revisiting the reliability of published mathematical proofs: Where do we go next? *Theoria*, 29, 345–60.

Fraser, C. (2018). Mohist canons. In E. Zalta (ed.), *Stanford Encyclopedia of Philosophy*, https://plato.stanford.edu/entries/mohist-canons/

    (2015). School of names. In E. Zalta (ed.), *Stanford Encyclopedia of Philosophy*, https://plato.stanford.edu/entries/school-names/

    (2013). Distinctions, judgment, and reasoning in Classical Chinese thought. *History and Philosophy of Logic*, 34, 1–24.

Frederick, S. (2005). Cognitive reflection and decision making. *Journal of Economic Perspectives*, 19, 25–42.

Frege, G. (1967). *Basic Laws of Arithmetic*. Berkeley, CA: University of California Press.

    (1967). Begriffsschrift, a formula language, modeled upon that of arithmetic, for pure thought. In J. van Heijenoort (ed.), *From Frege to Gödel: A Source Book in Mathematical Logic* (pp. 1–82). Cambridge, MA: Harvard University Press.

French, R. (2019). A dialogical route to logical pluralism. *Synthese*, 2019, 1–21.

    (2015). Prover–Skeptic games and logical pluralism. In T. Brochhagen, F. Roelofsen, & N. Theiler (eds.), *Proceedings of the 20th Amsterdam Colloquium* (pp. 128–136). Amsterdam: ILLC.

Ganeri, J. (2003). Ancient Indian logic as a theory of case-based reasoning. *Journal of Indian Philosophy*, 31, 33–45.

    (2001). Introduction: Indian Logic and the Colonization of Reason. In J. Ganeri (ed.), *Indian Logic: A Reader* (pp. 1–25). London: Routledge.

Garfield, J. L. (1990). The dog: Relevance and rationality. In J. Dunn & A. Gupta (eds.), *Truth or Consequences: Essays in Honour of Nuel Belnap* (pp. 97–109). Dordrecht: Kluwer Academic Publishers.

Geist, C., Löwe, B., & van Kerkhove, B. (2010). Peer review and knowledge by testimony in mathematics. In B. Löwe, & T. Müller (eds.), *PhiMSAMP. Philosophy of Mathematics: Sociological Aspects and Mathematical Practice* (pp. 155–178). London: College Publications.

Gentzen, G. (1969). Investigations into logical deduction. In *The Collected Papers of Gerhard Gentzen* (pp. 68–131). Amsterdam: North-Holland.

Geuss, R. (1994). Nietzsche and genealogy. *European Journal of Philosophy*, 2, 274–292.

Gigerenzer, G. (1996). On narrow norms and vague heuristics: A reply to Kahneman and Tversky. *Psychological Review*, 103, 592–596.

Gillon, B. (2016). Indian logic. In E. Zalta (ed.), *Stanford Encyclopedia of Philosophy*, https://plato.stanford.edu/entries/logic-india/

Gilmore, C., Gobel, S., & Inglis, M. (2018). *An Introduction to Mathematical Cognition*. New York, NY: Routledge.

Ginzburg, J. (2016). The semantics of dialogue. In M. Aloni & P. Dekker (eds.), *The Cambridge Handbook of Formal Semantics* (pp. 130–172). Cambridge: Cambridge University Press.

Glivický, P., & Kala, V. (2017). Fermat's last theorem and Catalan's conjecture in weak exponential arithmetics. *Mathematical Logic Quarterly*, 63, 162–174.

Goel, V. (2007). Anatomy of deductive reasoning. *Trends in Cognitive Science*, 11, 435–441.

Goel, V., & Waechter, R. (2018). Inductive and deductive reasoning Integrating insights from philosophy, psychology, and neuroscience. In L. Ball & V. Thompson (eds.), *The Routledge International Handbook of Thinking and Reasoning*. London: Routledge.

Goldfeld, D. (1996). Beyond the last theorem. *Math Horizons*, 4, 26–34.

Goldwasser, S., Micali, S., & Rackoff, C. (1989). The knowledge complexity of interactive proof systems. *SIAM Journal on Computing*, 18, 186–208.

Gould, S. J. (1977). *Ontogeny and Phylogeny*. Cambridge, MA: Harvard University Press.

Gowers, T., & Nielsen, M. (2009). Massively collaborative mathematics. *Nature*, 461, 879–881.

Greiffenhagen, C. (2008). Video analysis of mathematical practice? Different attempts to 'open up' mathematics for sociological investigation. *Forum: Qualitative Social Research*, 9, 32.

Grimm, S., Baumberger, C., & Ammon, S. (2017). *Explaining Understanding: New Perspectives from Epistemology and Philosophy of Science*. London: Routledge.

Haberler, Z., Laursen, S. L., & Hayward, C. N. (2018). What's in a name? Framing struggles of a mathematics education reform community. *International Journal of Research in Undergraduate Mathematics Education*, 4, 415–441.

Hahn, U., & Oaksford, M. (2008). A normative theory of argument strength. *Informal Logic*, 26, 1–24.

Halmos, P. R. (1985). *I Want to Be A Mathematician: An Automathography*. New York, NY: Springer.

(1970). How to write mathematics. *L'enseignement mathématique*, 16, 123–152.

Hanna, G., Jahnke, H. N., & Pulte, H. (2010). *Explanation and Proof in Mathematics: Philosophical and Educational Perspectives*. Berlin: Springer.

Hansen, M. (1991). *The Athenian Democracy in the Age of Demosthenes*. Oxford: Blackwell.

Harman, G. (2009). Field on the normative role of logic. *Proceedings of the Aristotelian Society*, 109, 333–335.

(1986). *Change in View*. Cambridge, MA: MIT Press.

Harris, P. L. (2000). *The Work of the Imagination*. London: Wiley-Blackwell.

Hasnawi, A., & Hodges, W. (2016). Arabic logic up to Avicenna. In C. Dutilh Novaes & S. Read (eds.), *The Cambridge Companion to Medieval Logic* (pp. 45–66). Cambridge: Cambridge University Press.

Hasse, D. (2014). Influence of Arabic and Islamic philosophy on the Latin West. In E. Zalta (ed.), *Stanford Encyclopedia of Philosophy*, https://plato.stanford.edu/entries/arabic-islamic-influence/

Hatfield, G. (1997). The workings of the intellect: Mind and psychology. In P. Easton (ed.), *Logic and the Workings of the Mind: The Logic of Ideas and Faculty Psychology in Early Modern Philosophy* (pp. 21–45). Atascadero, CA: Ridgeview Publishing.

Heath, T. (1908). *The Thirteen Books of Euclid's Elements*. Cambridge: Cambridge University Press.

Hegel, G. (1991). *Elements of the Philosophy of Right*. Cambridge: Cambridge University Press.

Heinzmann, G. (2006). Naturalizing dialogic pragmatics. In J. van Benthem, G. Heinzmann, M. Rebushi, & H. Visser (eds.), *The Age of Alternative Logics: Assessing Philosophy of Logic and Mathematics Today* (pp. 285–279). Berlin: Springer.

Hempel, C., & Oppenheim, P. (1948). Studies in the logic of explanation. *Philosophy of Science*, 15, 135–175.

Henkin, L. (1961). Some remarks on infinitely long formulas. In International Mathematical Union (ed.), *Infinitistic Methods (Proceedings of the Symposium on Foundations of Mathematics, Warsaw, 2–9 September 1959)* (pp. 167–183). Oxford: Pergamon.

Henrich, J. (2015). *The Secret of our Success*. Princeton, NJ: Princeton University Press.

Henrich, J., Heine, S. J., & Norenzayan, A. (2010). The weirdest people in the world? *Behavioral and Brain Sciences*, 33, 61–83.

Hersh, R. (1993). Proving is convincing and explaining. *Educational Studies in Mathematics*, 24, 389–399.

Heyes, C. (2019). Précis of *Cognitive Gadgets: The Cultural Evolution of Thinking*. *Behavioral and Brain Sciences*, 42, e169.

(2018). *Cognitive Gadgets: The Cultural Evolution of Thinking*. Cambridge, MA: Harvard University Press.

Hilton, D. J. (1995). The social context of reasoning: Conversational inference and rational judgment. *Psychological Bulletin*, 118, 248–271.

Hintikka, J. (1996). *The Principles of Mathematics Revisited*. Cambridge: Cambridge University Press.

(1995). Commentary on Allen. *Proceedings of the Boston Area Colloquium of Ancient Philosophy*, 11, 206–215.

(1973). *Logic, Language-Games and Information: Kantian Themes in the Philosophy of Logic*. Oxford: Clarendon Press.

Hintikka, J., & Sandu, G. (1997). Game-theoretical semantics. In J. van Benthem, & A. ter Meulen (eds.), *Handbook of Logic and Language* (pp. 361–410). Amsterdam: Elsevier.

Hmelo-Silver, C. E., Duncan, R. G., & Chinn, C. A. (2007). Scaffolding and achievement in problem-based and inquiry learning: A response to Kirschner, Sweller, and Clark (2006). *Educational Psychologist*, 42, 99–107.

Hodds, M., Alcock, L., & Inglis, M. (2014). Self-explanation training improves proof comprehension. *Journal for Research in Mathematics Education*, 45, 62–101.

Hodges, W. (2018). Proofs as cognitive or computational: Ibn Sīnā's innovations. *Philosophy and Technology*, 31, 131–153.

    (2017). Ibn Sina on reduction ad absurdum. *Review of Symbolic Logic*, 10, 583–601.

    (2013). Logic and games. In E. Zalta (ed.), *Stanford Encyclopedia of Philosophy*, http://plato.stanford.edu/entries/logic-games/

    (2009). Traditional logic, modern logic and natural language. *Journal of Philosophical Logic*, 38, 589.

    (2001). Dialogue foundations: A sceptical look. *Proceedings of the Aristotelian Society*, Supp. Vol. 75, 17–32.

    (1998). An editor recalls some hopeless papers. *Bulletin of Symbolic Logic*, 4, 1–16.

Horgan, J. (1993). The death of proof? *Scientific American*, 269, 93–103.

Horgan, J., S. Aaronson, P. Woit, & K. Dahlke (2020). OK, maybe proofs aren't dying after all. Scientific American blog, March 7, https://blogs.scientificamerican.com /cross-check/okay-maybe-proofs-arent-dying-after-all/

Hundleby, C. (forthcoming). Feminist perspectives on argumentation. In E. Zalta (ed.), *Stanford Encyclopedia of Philosophy*.

Hutchins, E. (2011). Enculturating the supersized mind. *Philosophical Studies*, 152, 437–446.

    (1980). *Culture and Inference: A Trobriand Case Study*. Cambridge, MA: Harvard University Press.

Inglis, M. (2018). The negative view of proof. Wiki Mathematics Education, https://m aths4maryams.org/mathed/wp-content/uploads/2018/09/WikiLetter-6.pdf

Inglis, M., & Mejía-Ramos, J. (2019). Functional explanation in mathematics. *Synthese*, 2019, 1–24.

Irani, T. (2017). *Plato on the Value of Philosophy*. Cambridge: Cambridge University Press.

Jaffe, A., & Quinn, F. (1993). Theoretical mathematics: Towards a cultural synthesis of mathematics and theoretical physics. *Bulletin of the American Mathematical Society*, 29, 1–13.

Jago, M. (2013). The content of deduction. *Journal of Philosophical Logic*, 42, 317–334.

Jaskowski, S. (1967). On the rules of supposition in formal logic. In S. McCall (ed.), *Polish Logic 1920–1939* (pp. 232–258). Oxford: Oxford University Press.

Johnson-Laird, P. (2008). Mental models and deductive reasoning. In L. Rips (ed.), *Reasoning: Studies in Human Inference and Its Foundations* (pp. 206–222). Cambridge: Cambridge University Press.

John-Steiner, V. (2007). Vygotsky on thinking and speaking. In H. Daniels, M. Cole, & J. Wertsch (eds.), *The Cambridge Companion to Vygotsky* (pp. 136–152). Cambridge: Cambridge University press.

Jones, F. (1977). The Moore method. *The American Mathematical Monthly*, 84, 273–278.

Kant, I. (1998). *Critique of Pure Reason* (edited by P. Guyer & A. Wood). Cambridge: Cambridge University Press.

Kapp, E. (1975). Syllogistic. In J. Barnes, M. Schofield, & R. Sorabji (eds.), *Articles on Aristotle* (pp. 1–35). London: Duckworth.

Keefe, R. (2014). What logical pluralism cannot be. *Synthese*, 191, 1375–1390.

Keiff, L. (2009). Dialogical logic. In E. Zalta (ed.), *Stanford Encyclopedia of Philosophy*, http://plato.stanford.edu/entries/logic-dialogical/

Khalifa, K. (2010). Social constructivism and the aims of science. *Social Epistemology*, 24, 45–61.

Kirschner, P., Sweller, J., & Clark, R. (2006). Why minimal guidance during instruction does not work: An analysis of the failure of constructivist, discovery, problem-based, experiential, and inquiry-based teaching. *Educational Psychologist*, 41, 75–86.

Kitcher, P. (2001). *Science, Truth, and Democracy*. Oxford: Oxford University Press.

Klarreich, E. (2018). Titans of mathematics clash over epic proof of ABC conjecture. *Quanta*, September 20, www.quantamagazine.org/titans-of-mathematics-clash-over-epic-proof-of-abc-conjecture-20180920/

Klement, K. (2002). When is genetic reasoning not fallacious? *Argumentation*, 16, 383–400.

Klima, G. (2006). Syncategoremata. In K. Brown (ed.), *Encyclopedia of Language and Linguistics, Vol. xii* (pp. 353–356). Oxford: Elsevier.

Knorr, W. (1989). The Philonian method of cube duplication. In W. Knorr (ed.), *Textual Studies in Ancient and Medieval Geometry* (pp. 41–61). Boston, MA: Birkhäuser.

Koetsier, T. (1991). *The Philosophy of Mathematics of Imre Lakatos, a Historical Approach*. Amsterdam: Elsevier.

Kogan, M., & Laursen, S. L. (2014). Assessing long-term effects of inquiry-based learning: A case study from college mathematics. *Innovative Higher Education*, 39, 183–199.

Kolata, G. (1986). Prime tests and keeping proofs secret. *Science*, 233, 938–939.

Koons, R. (2013). Defeasible reasoning. In E. Zalta (ed.), *Stanford Encyclopedia of Philosophy*, http://plato.stanford.edu/entries/reasoning-defeasible/

Koriat, A. (2012). When are two heads better than one and why? *Science*, 336, 360–362.

Kouri Kissel, T., & Shapiro, S. (2020). Logical pluralism and normativity. *Inquiry: An Interdisciplinary Journal of Philosophy*, 63, 389–410.

Krabbe, E. (2008). Strategic maneuvering in mathematical proofs. *Argumentation* 22, 453–468.

(2006). Dialogue logic. In D. Gabbay & J. Woods (eds.), *Handbook of History of Logic. Volume 7* (pp. 665–704). Amsterdam: Elsevier.

(2001). Dialogue logic revisited. *Proceedings of the Aristotelian Society*, Supp. Vol. 75, 33–49.

Krämer, S. (2003). Writing, notational iconicity, calculus: On writing as a cultural technique. *Modern Languages Notes (German Issue)*, 118, 518–537.

Kranz, S. (2011). *The Proof Is in the Pudding: The Changing Nature of Mathematical Proof*. New York, NY: Springer.

Kuhn, D., & Crowell, A. (2011). Dialogic argumentation as a vehicle for developing young adolescents' thinking. *Psychological Science*, 22, 545–552.

Lakatos, I. (1976). *Proofs and Refutations: The Logic of Mathematical Discovery*. Cambridge: Cambridge University Press.

Lakoff, G., & Nunez, R. (2000). *Where Mathematics Comes From*. New York, NY: Basic Books.

Larvor, B. (2001). What is dialectical philosophy of mathematics? *Philosophia Mathematica*, 9, 212–229.

Latour, B., & Woolgar, S. (1986). *Laboratory Life: The Construction of Scientific Facts*. Princeton, NJ: Princeton University Press.

Laughlin, P. R. (2011). *Group Problem Solving*. Princeton, NJ: Princeton University Press.

Lazareva, O. (2012). Transitive inference in nonhuman animals. In E. Wasserman & T. Zentall (eds.), *The Oxford Handbook of Comparative Cognition* (pp. 718–735). Oxford: Oxford University Press.

Leron, U. (1985). A direct approach to indirect proofs. *Educational Studies in Mathematics*, 16, 321–325.

Lesher, J. (2002). Parmenidean elenchos. In G. Scott (ed.), *Does Socrates Have a Method?* (pp. 19–35). University Park, PA: Pennsylvania State University Press.

Levesque, H. J. (1986). Making believers out of computers. *Artificial Intelligence*, 30, 81–108.

Lewens, T. (2009). Seven types of adaptationism. *Biology and Philosophy*, 24, 161–182.

Lewis, D. (1979). Scorekeeping in a language game. *Journal of Philosophical Logic*, 8, 339–359.

Liberman, K. (2007). *Dialectical Practice in Tibetan Philosophical Culture: An Ethnomethodological Inquiry into Formal Reasoning*. London: Rowman & Littlefield.

Lloyd, G. (2013). Reasoning and culture in a historical perspective. *Journal of Cognition and Culture*, 13, 437–457.

(2012). The plurality of Greek 'mathematics.' In K. Chemla (ed.), *The History of Mathematical Proof in Ancient Traditions* (pp. 294–310). Cambridge: Cambridge University Press.

(1996). *Adversaries and Authorities: Investigations Into Ancient Greek and Chinese Science*. Cambridge: Cambridge University Press.

(1996). Science in Antiquity: The Greek and Chinese cases and their relevance to the problem of culture and cognition. In D. Olson & N. Torrance (eds.), *Modes of Thought: Explorations in Culture and Cognition* (pp. 15–33). Cambridge: Cambridge University Press.

(1990). *Demystifying Mentalities*. Cambridge: Cambridge University Press.

Lorenzen, P. (1960). Logik und agon. International Congress of Philosophy (ed.), *Atti del XII Congresso Internazionale di Filosofia, 4* (pp. 187–194). Florence: Sansoni Editore.

Lorenzen, P., & Lorenz, K. (1978). *Dialogische Logik*. Darmstadt: Wissenschafstliche Buchgesellschaft.

Luria, A. R. (1976). *Cognitive Development: Its Social and Cultural Foundations*. Cambridge, MA: Harvard University Press.

Macbeth, D. (2012). Diagrammatic reasoning in Frege's Begriffsschrift. *Synthese*, 186, 289–314.

MacFarlane, J. (2004). In what sense (if any) is logic normative for thought? Draft of presentation at Central Division APA 2004, http://johnmacfarlane.net/normativity_of_logic.pdf

(2000). What Does It Mean To Say That Logic Is Formal? Ph.D. dissertation, University of Pittsburgh.

MacKenzie, D. (2001). *Mechanizing Proof; Computing, Risk, and Trust.* Cambridge, MA: MIT Press.

(1999). Slaying the Kraken: The sociohistory of a mathematical proof. *Social Studies of Science*, 29, 7–60.

MacKenzie, J. (1989). Reasoning and logic. *Synthese*, 79, 99–117.

Maddy, P. (2002). A naturalistic look at logic. *Proceedings and Addresses of the American Philosophical Association*, 76, 61–90.

Malink, M. (2015). The beginnings of formal logic: Deduction in Aristotle's *Topics* vs. *Prior Analytics. Phronesis*, 60, 267–309.

(2014). Deduction in *Sophistici Elenchi* 6. In M. Lee (ed.), *Strategies of Argument: Essays in Ancient Ethics, Epistemology, and Logic* (pp. 149–174). Oxford: Oxford University Press.

Mancosu, P. (2011). Explanation in mathematics. In E. Zalta (ed.), *Stanford Encyclopedia of Philosophy*, https://plato.stanford.edu/entries/mathematics-explanation/

(2010). Between Vienna and Berlin: The immediate reception of Gödel's incompleteness theorems. *History and Philosophy of Logic*, 20, 33–45.

(2008). *The Philosophy of Mathematical Practice.* Oxford: Oxford University Press.

Mancosu, P., & Pincock, C. (2012). *Mathematical Explanation.* Oxford Bibliographies. Oxford: Oxford University Press.

Marion, M. (2011). Wittgenstein on surveyability of proofs. In M. McGinn & O. Kuusela (eds.), *The Oxford Handbook of Wittgenstein* (pp. 138–161). Oxford: Oxford University Press.

(2009). Why play logical games? In O. Majer, A. Pietarinen, & T. Tulenheimo (eds.), *Games: Unifying Logic, Language, and Philosophy* (pp. 3–26). Berlin: Springer.

(2006). Hintikka on Wittgenstein: From language-games to game semantics. *Acta Philosophica Fennica*, 78, 255–274.

Marion, M., & Rückert, H. (2016). Aristotle on universal quantification: A study from the point of view of game semantics. *History and Philosophy of Logic*, 37, 201–229.

Markovits, H., & Nantel, G. (1989). The belief-bias effect in the production and evaluation of logical conclusions. *Memory and Cognition*, 17, 11–17.

Markovits, H., Venet, M., Janveau-Brennan, G., Malfait, N., Pion, N., & Vadeboncoeur, I. (1996). Reasoning in young children: Fantasy and information retrieval. *Child Development*, 67, 2857–2872.

Martin, U., & Pease, A. (2013). Mathematical practice, crowdsourcing, and social machines. In J. Carette, D. Aspinall, C. Lange, P. Sojka, & W. Windsteiger (eds.), *CICM 2013: Intelligent Computer Mathematics* (pp. 98–119). New York, NY: Springer.

Matilal, B. (1998). *The Character of Logic in India.* Albany, NY: State University of New York Press.

Matzke, D., Nieuwenhuis, S., van Rijn, H., Slagter, H. A., van der Molen, M. W., & Wagenmakers, E.-J. (2015). The effect of horizontal eye movements on free recall:

A preregistered adversarial collaboration. *Journal of Experimental Psychology: General*, 144, e1–e15.

Mazur, E. (1997). *Peer Instruction: A User's Manual*. Upper Saddle River, NJ: Prentice Hall.

Mellers, B., Hertwig, R., & Kahneman, D. (2001). Do frequency representations eliminate conjunction effects? An exercise in adversarial collaboration. *Psychological Science*, 12, 269–275.

Menary, R. (2007). Writing as thinking. *Language Sciences*, 29, 621–632.

Menary, M., & Gillett, A. (2017). Embodying culture. In J. Kiverstein (ed.), *The Routledge Handbook of Philosophy of the Social Mind* (pp. 72–87). London: Routledge.

Menary, R. (2013). Cognitive integration, enculturated cognition and the socially extended mind. *Cognitive Systems Research*, 25/26, 26–34.

Mercier, H. (2018). Reasoning and argumentation. In L. Ball & V. Thompson (eds.), *The Routledge International Handbook of Thinking and Reasoning* (pp. 401–414). New York, NY: Routledge.

Mercier, H., & Sperber, D. (2017). *The Enigma of Reason*. Cambridge, MA: Harvard University Press.

(2011). Why do humans reason? Arguments for an argumentative theory. *Behavioral and Brain Sciences*, 34, 57–74.

Mercier, H., Trouche, E., Boudry, M., & Paglieri, F. (2016). Natural born arguers: An evolutionary perspective on critical thinking education. *Educational Psychologist*, 52, 1–16.

Merton, R. (1942) *The Sociology of Science: Theoretical and Empirical Investigations*. Chicago, IL: University of Chicago Press.

Mill, J. S. (1999). *On Liberty*. Peterborough: Broadview Press.

Miller, L. (1984) Islamic Disputation Theory: A Study of the Development of Dialectic in Islam from the Tenth through the Fourteenth Centuries. Ph.D. dissertation, Princeton University.

Millikan, R. G. (2006). Styles of rationality. In S. Hurley & M. Nudds (eds.), *Rational Animals?* (pp. 117–126). Oxford: Oxford University Press.

Minio-Paluello, L. (1962). *Aristoteles Latinus: Analytica Priora*. Leiden: Brill.

Mochizuki, S. (2014). On the verification of inter-universal Teichmüller theory: A progress report (as of December 2014), www.kurims.kyoto-u.ac.jp/~motizuki/IUTeich%20Verification%20Report%202014-12.pdf

Mody, S., & Carey, S. (2016). The emergence of reasoning by the disjunctive syllogism in early childhood. *Cognition*, 154, 40–48.

Moore, C., & Mertens, S. (2011). *The Nature of Computation*. Oxford: Oxford University Press.

Moshman, D., & Geil, M. (1998). Collaborative reasoning: Evidence for collective rationality. *Thinking and Reasoning*, 4, 231–248.

Moss, J. (2007). The doctor and the pastry chef: Pleasure and persuasion in Plato's *Gorgias*. *Ancient Philosophy*, 27, 229–249.

Moulton, J. (1983). A paradigm of philosophy: The adversary method. In S. Harding & M. B. Hintikka (eds.), *Discovering Reality* (pp. 149–164). Dordrecht: Kluwer.

Mueller, I. (1974). Greek mathematics and Greek logic. In J. Corcoran (ed.), *Ancient Logic and Its Modern Interpretations* (pp. 35–70). Dordrecht: Reidel.

Mugnai, M. (2010). Logic and mathematics in the seventeenth century. *History and Philosophy of Logic*, 31, 297–314.

Musgrave, A., & Pigden, C. (2016). Imre Lakatos. In E. Zalta (ed.), *Stanford Encyclopedia of Philosophy*, https://plato.stanford.edu/archives/win2016/entries/lakatos/

Nauta, L. (2009). *In Defense of Common Sense: Lorenzo Valla's Humanist Critique of Scholastic Philosophy*. Cambridge, MA: Harvard University Press.

Nehamas, A. (1990). Eristic, antilogic, sophistic, dialectic: Plato's demarcation of philosophy from sophistry. *History of Philosophy Quarterly*, 7, 3–16.

Netz, R. (2003). Introduction: The history of early mathematics – ways of re-writing. *Science in Context*, 16, 275–286.

(1999). *The Shaping of Deduction in Greek Mathematics: A Study in Cognitive History*. Cambridge: Cambridge University Press.

Newstead, S., Handley, S. J., & Buck, E. (1999). Falsifying mental models: Testing the predictions of theories of syllogistic reasoning. *Memory & Cognition*, 27, 344–354.

Nichols, M. (2009). *Socrates on Friendship and Community: Reflections on Plato's Symposium, Phaedrus, and Lysis*. Cambridge: Cambridge University Press.

Nickerson, R. S. (1998). Confirmation bias: A ubiquitous phenomenon in many guises. *Review of General Psychology*, 2, 175–220.

Nietzsche, F. (2007). *On the Genealogy of Morality*. Cambridge: Cambridge University Press.

Norman, A. (2016). Why we reason: Intention-alignment and the genesis of human rationality. *Biology and Philosophy*, 31, 685–704.

Normore, C. (1993). The necessity in deduction: Cartesian inference and its medieval background. *Synthese*, 96, 437–454.

Norris, S. P., & Ennis, R. H. (1989). *Evaluating Critical Thinking*. Pacific Grove, CA: Midwest Publications.

Notomi, N. (2014). The Sophists. In J. Warren, & F. Sheffield (eds.), *The Routledge Companion to Ancient Philosophy* (pp. 94–110). New York, NY: Routledge.

Novikoff, A. (2013). *The Medieval Culture of Disputation: Pedagogy, Practice, and Performance*. Philadelphia, PA: University of Pennsylvania Press.

Nussbaum, E. M. (2008). Collaborative discourse, argumentation, and learning: Preface and literature review. *Contemporary Educational Psychology*, 33, 345–359.

Nye, A. (1990). *Words of Power*. New York, NY: Routledge.

Oakhill, J., & Johnson-Laird, P. (1985). The effect of belief on the production of syllogistic conclusions. *Quarterly Journal of Experimental Psychology*, 37, 553–569.

Oaksford, M., & Chater, N. (2002). Commonsense reasoning, logic and human rationality. In R. Elio (ed.), *Common Sense, Reasoning and Rationality* (pp. 174–214). Oxford: Oxford University Press.

(1994). A rational analysis of the selection task as optimal data selection. *Psychological Review*, 101, 608–631.

(1991). Against logicist cognitive science. *Mind & Language*, 6, 1–38.

Ockham, William of. (1974). *Summa logicae*. St. Bonaventure, NY: The Franciscan Institute.

Oetke, C. (1996). Ancient Indian logic as a theory of nonmonotonic reasoning. *Journal of Indian Philosophy*, 24, 447–539.

O'Neill, C. (2012). The ABC conjecture has not been proved. *Mathbabe* blog post, https://mathbabe.org/2012/11/14/the-abc-conjecture-has-not-been-proved/

Paglieri, F., & Castelfranchi, C. (2010). Why argue? Towards a cost–benefit analysis of argumentation. *Argument & Computation*, 1, 71–91.

Panaccio, C. (2004). *Ockham on Concepts*. Aldershot: Ashgate.

Pascual, E., & Oakley, T. (2017). Fictive interaction. In B. Dancygier (ed.), *The Cambridge Handbook of Cognitive Linguistics* (pp. 347–360). Cambridge: Cambridge University Press.

Paseau, A. (2016). What's the point of complete rigour? *Mind*, 125, 177–207.

(2010). Proofs of the compactness theorem. *History and Philosophy of Logic*, 31, 73–98.

Pease, A., Lawrence, J., Budzynska, K., Corneli, J., & Reed, C. (2017). Lakatos-style collaborative mathematics through dialectical, structured and abstract argumentation. *Artificial Intelligence*, 246, 181–219.

Peckhaus, V. (2009). The mathematical origins of nineteenth-century algebra of logic. In L. Haaparanta (ed.), *The Development of Modern Logic* (pp. 159–195). Oxford: Oxford University Press.

Pelletier, J. (1999). A brief history of natural deduction. *History and Philosophy of Logic*, 20, 1–31.

Perelman, C., & Olbrechts-Tyteca, L. (1969). *The New Rhetoric: A Treatise on Argumentation* (translated by J. Wilkinson & P. Weaver). Notre Dame, IN: University of Notre Dame Press.

Phillips, S. (2017). Fallacies and defeaters in early Navya Nyaya. In J. Tuske (ed.), *Indian Epistemology and Metaphysics* (pp. 33–52). London: Bloomsbury Academic.

Piccinini, G. (2003). Epistemic divergence and the publicity of scientific methods. *Studies in History and Philosophy of Science Part A*, 34, 597–612.

Pinker, S. (1994). *The Language Instinct*. New York, NY: Harper Collins.

Plato (2010). *Meno and Phaedo*. Cambridge: Cambridge University Press.

Plumwood, V. (1993). The politics of reason: Towards a feminist logic. *Australasian Journal of Philosophy*, 71, 436–462.

Poincaré, H. (1946). *The Foundations of Science*. Lancaster: The Science Press.

Pollock, J. (1987). Defeasible reasoning. *Cognitive Science*, 11, 481–518.

(1974). *Knowledge and Justification*. Princeton, NJ: Princeton University Press.

Prado, J., Chadha, A., & Booth, J. R. (2011). The brain network for deductive reasoning: A quantitative meta-analysis of 28 neuroimaging studies. *Journal of Cognitive Neuroscience*, 23, 3483–3497.

Prawitz, D. (2005). Logical consequence from a constructive point of view. In S. Shapiro (ed.), *The Oxford Handbook of Philosophy of Mathematics and Logic* (pp. 671–695). Oxford: Oxford University Press.

Priest, G. (2018). *The Fifth Corner of Four: An Essay on Buddhist Metaphysics and the Catuskoti*. Oxford: Oxford University Press.

Prior, A. (1960). The runabout inference ticket. *Analysis*, 21, 38–39.

Quine, W. V. (1974). *The Roots of Reference*. Chicago, IL: Open Court.

Rabin, M. (1980). Probabilistic algorithm for testing primality. *Journal of Number Theory*, 12, 128–138.

Rahman, S., Klev, A., McConaughey, Z., & Clerbout, N. (2018). *Immanent Reasoning or Equality in Action*. Cham: Springer.

Rav, Y. (1999). Why do we prove theorems? *Philosophia Mathematica*, 7, 5–41.

Read, S. (1994). Formal and material consequence. *Journal of Philosophical Logic*, 23, 247–265.

——— (1988). *Relevant Logic: A Philosophical Examination of Inference*. Oxford: Blackwell.

Rescorla, M. (2009). Chrysippus' dog as a case study in non-linguistic cognition. In R. Lurz (ed.), *The Philosophy of Animal Minds* (pp. 52–71). Cambridge: Cambridge University Press.

Rescorla, M. (2009). Epistemic and dialectical regress. *Australasian Journal of Philosophy*, 87, 43–60.

Restall, G. (2005). Multiple conclusions. In P. Hajek, L. Valdez-Villanueva, & D. Westerståhl (eds.), *Proceedings of the Twelfth International Congress on Logic, Methodology and Philosophy of Science*. London: King's College Publications.

——— (2004). Logical pluralism and the preservation of warrant. In S. Rahman, J. Symons, D. M. Gabbay, & J. P. van Bendegem (eds.), *Logic, Epistemology, and the Unity of Science* (pp. 163–173). Dordrecht: Springer.

Rittberg, C., Tanswell, F., & Van Bendegem, J. (2018). Epistemic injustice in mathematics. *Synthese*, 2018, 1–30.

Robert, A., & Schwarzenberger, R. (1991). Research in teaching and learning mathematics at an advanced level. In D. Tall (ed.), *Advanced Mathematical Thinking* (pp. 127–139). New York, NY: Kluwer.

Roberts, D. (2019). A crisis of identification: On Mochizuki's proof of the ABC conjecture. *Inference: International Review of Science*, 4, https://inference-review.com/article/a-crisis-of-identification

Rosenblatt, L. (2017). Naive validity, internalization, and substructural approaches to paradox. *Ergo*, 4, 93–120.

Rota, G. C. (1997). The phenomenology of mathematical proof. *Synthese*, 111, 183–196.

Russell, B., & Whitehead, A. (1910–13). *Principia Mathematica*. Cambridge: Cambridge University Press.

Russell, G. (2013). Logical pluralism. In E. Zalta (ed.), *Stanford Encyclopedia of Philosophy*, https://plato.stanford.edu/entries/logical-pluralism/

Sørensen, M. H., & Urzyczyn, P. (2006). *Lectures on the Curry–Howard Isomorphism*. New York, NY: Elsevier.

Sá, W., West, R. F., & Stanovich, K. E. (1999). The domain specificity and generality of belief bias: Searching for a generalizable critical thinking skill. *Journal of Educational Psychology*, 91, 497–510.

Saito, K., & Sidoli, N. (2012). Diagrams and arguments in ancient Greek mathematics: lessons drawn from comparisons of the manuscript diagrams with those in modern critical editions. In K. Chemla (ed.), *The History of Mathematical Proof in Ancient Traditions* (pp. 135–162). Cambridge: Cambridge University Press.

Schechter, J. (2013). Could evolution explain our reliability about logic? *Oxford Studies in Epistemology*, 4, 214–239.

Schiller, M. R. (2013). Granularity analysis for mathematical proofs. *Topics in Cognitive Science*, 5, 251–269.

Schliesser, E. (2019). Synthetic philosophy. *Biology & Philosophy*, 34, 1–9.

Schmandt-Besserat, D. (1996). *How Writing Came About*. Austin, TX: University of Texas Press.

Scholze, P., & Stix, J. (2018). Why *abc* is still a conjecture, www.kurims.kyoto-u.ac.jp /~motizuki/SS2018-08.pdf

Schotch, P., Brown, B., & Jennings, R. (2009). *On Preserving: Essays on Preservationism and Paraconsistent Logic*. Toronto: University of Toronto Press.

Schroeder-Heister, P. (2016). Open problems in proof-theoretic semantics. In T. Piecha & P. Schroeder-Heister, *Advances in Proof-Theoretic Semantics* (pp. 253–283). Cham: Springer.

(2012). Paradoxes and structural rules. In C. Dutilh Novaes & O. Hjortland, *Insolubles and Consequences* (pp. 203–211). London: College Publications.

(2012). The categorical and the hypothetical: a critique of some fundamental assumptions of standard semantics. *Synthese*, 187, 925–942.

Schusterman, R. J., & Kastak, D. (1993). A California sea lion (Zalophus californianus) is capable of forming equivalence relations. *Psychological Record*, 43, 823–839.

Scotto di Luzio, P. (2000). Logical systems and formality. In M. Anderson, P. Cheng, & V. Haarslev, *Theory and Application of Diagrams. Diagrams 2000* (pp. 117–132). Berlin: Springer.

Scribner, S. (1977). Modes of thinking and ways of speaking: Culture and logic reconsidered. In P. N. Johnson-Laird & P. C. Wason (eds.), *Thinking: Readings in Cognitive Science* (pp. 483–500). New York, NY: Cambridge University Press.

Scribner, S., & Cole, M. (1981). *The Psychology of Literacy*. Cambridge, MA: Harvard University Press.

Sen, A. (2005). *The Argumentative Indian*. Harmondsworth: Allen Lane.

Sequoyah-Grayson, S. (2008). The scandal of deduction. *Journal of Philosophical Logic*, 37, 67–94.

Shapiro, L. (2016). The very idea of a substructural approach to paradox. *Synthese*, 2016, 1–20.

(2015). *Varieties of Logic*. New York, NY: Oxford University Press.

(2005). Logical consequence, proof theory, and model theory. In S. Shapiro (ed.), *The Oxford Handbook of Philosophy of Mathematics and Logic* (pp. 651–670). Oxford: Oxford University Press.

Shoham, Y. (1987). A semantical approach to nonmonotonic logic. In J. McDermott (ed.), *Proceedings of the Tenth International Conference on Artificial Intelligence* (pp. 227–250). Los Altos, CA: Morgan Kaufmann.

Shorey, P. (1924). The origin of the syllogism. *Classical Philology*, 19, 1–19.

Siders, A. (2013). Gentzen's consistency proof without heightlines. *Archive for Mathematical Logic*, 52, 449–468.

Sidoli, N. (2018). Uses of construction in problems and theorems in Euclid's Elements I–VI. *Archive for History of Exact Sciences*, 72, 403–452.

Sievers, C., & Gruber, T. (2016). Reference in human and non-human primate communication: What does it take to refer? *Animal Cognition*, 19, 759–768.

Smart, P. (2018). Mandevillian intelligence: From individual vice to collective virtue. In J. Carter, A. Clark, J. Kallestrup, S. Palermos, & D. Pritchard (eds.), *Socially-Extended Epistemology* (pp. 253–274). Oxford: Oxford University Press.

Smiley, T. (1988). Conceptions of consequence. In E. Craig (ed.), *The Routledge Encyclopedia of Philosophy* (pp. 599–603). London: Routledge.

Smith, P. (2011). Squeezing arguments. *Analysis*, 71, 22–30.

Smith, R. (1997). *Aristotle's Topics: Books* I *and* VIII. Oxford: Oxford University Press.

(1994). Dialectic and the syllogism. *Ancient Philosophy*, 14, 133–151.

(1978). The mathematical origins of Aristotle's Syllogistic. *Archive for History of Exact Sciences*, 19, 201–209.

Solomon, E. (1976). *Indian Dialectics: Methods of Philosophical Discussion*. Ahmedabad: B. J. Institute of Learning and Research.

Solomon, M. (2006). Groupthink versus the wisdom of crowds. *Southern Journal of Philosophy*, 44, 28–42.

Sorabji, R. (2004). *The Philosophy of the Commentators, 200–600* AD, *Vol. 3: Logic and Metaphysic*. London: Bloomsbury.

Spaulding, S. (2016). Mind misreading. *Philosophical Issues*, 26, 422–440.

Sperber, D. (1996). *Explaining Culture: A Naturalistic Approach*. Oxford: Blackwell.

Spinoza, B. (1985). Ethics. In *The Collected Writings of Spinoza, Vol. 1* (edited and translated by E. Curley). Princeton, NJ: Princeton University Press.

Spruyt, J., & Dutilh Novaes, C. (2015). Those funny words: Medieval theories of syncategorematic terms. In M. Cameron & R. Stainton (eds.), *Linguistic Content: New Essays on the History of Philosophy of Language* (pp. 100–120). Oxford: Oxford University Press.

Solmsen, F. (1951). Aristotle's syllogism and its Platonic background. *The Philosophical Review*, 60, 563–571.

Stanovich, K. E. (2012). On the distinction between rationality and intelligence: Implications for understanding individual differences in reasoning. In K. J. Holyoak & R. G. Morrison (eds.), *The Oxford Handbook of Thinking and Reasoning* (pp. 433–455). Oxford: Oxford University Press.

(2003). The fundamental computational biases of human cognition: Heuristics that (sometimes) impair decision making and problem solving. In J. Davidson & R. J. Sternberg (eds.), *The Psychology of Problem Solving* (pp. 291–342). Cambridge: Cambridge University Press.

(1999). *Who Is Rational? Studies of Individual Differences in Reasoning*. Mahwah, NJ: Erlbaum.

Stanovich, K. E., & West, R. F. (2008). On the relative independence of thinking biases and cognitive ability. *Personality Processes and Individual Differences*, 94, 672–695.

Steinberger, F. (2017). Frege and Carnap on the normativity of logic. *Synthese*, 194, 143–162.

(2017). The normative status of logic. In E. Zalta (ed.), *Stanford Encyclopedia of Philosophy*, https://plato.stanford.edu/entries/logic-normative/

(2016). Explosion and the normativity of logic. *Mind*, 125, 385–419.

Steiner, M. (1978). Mathematical explanation. *Philosophical Studies*, 34, 135–151.

Steingart, A. (2012). A group theory of group theory: Collaborative mathematics and the 'uninvention' of a 1,000-page proof. *Social Studies of Science*, 42, 185–213.

Steinkrüger, P. (2015). Aristotle's assertoric syllogistic and modern relevance logic. *Synthese*, 192, 1413–1444.

Stenning, K. (2002). *Seeing Reason: Image and Language in Learning to Think*. Oxford: Oxford University Press.

Stenning, K., & van Lambalgen, M. (2008). *Human Reasoning and Cognitive Science*. Cambridge, MA: MIT Press.

Stenning, K., & Yule, P. (1997). Image and language in human reasoning: A syllogistic illustration. *Cognitive Psychology*, 34, 109–159.

Sterelny, K. (2012). *The Evolved Apprentice*. Cambridge, MA: MIT Press.

Street, A. (2013). Arabic and Islamic philosophy of language and logic. In E. Zalta (ed.), *Stanford Encyclopedia of Philosophy*, https://plato.stanford.edu/entries/arabic-islamic-language/

Striker, G. (2009). *Aristotle's Prior Analytics Book I: Translated with an Introduction and Commentary*. Oxford: Oxford University Press.

Strobino, R. (2018). Ibn Sina's logic. In E. Zalta (ed.), *Stanford Encyclopedia of Philosophy*, https://plato.stanford.edu/entries/ibn-sina-logic/

Stupple, E. J., Ball, L. J., Evans, J. S., & Kamal-Smith, E. (2011). When logic and belief collide: Individual differences in reasoning times support a selective processing model. *Journal of Cognitive Psychology*, 23, 931–941.

Sunstein, C. R. (2002). The law of group polarization. *Journal of Political Philosophy*, 10, 175–195.

Sweeney, E. (2008). Literary forms of medieval philosophy. In E. Zalta (ed.), *Stanford Encyclopedia of Philosophy*, https://plato.stanford.edu/entries/medieval-literary/

Szabó, A. (1978). *The Beginnings of Greek Mathematics*. Dordrecht: Reidel.

Taber, J. (2004). Is Indian logic nonmonotonic? *Philosophy East and West*, 54, 143–170.

Tanswell, F. (2020). Go forth and multiply! On actions, instructions and imperatives in mathematical proofs. Manuscript.

(2018). Conceptual engineering for mathematical concepts. *Inquiry*, 61, 881–913.

(2017). Proof, Rigour and Informality: A Virtue Account of Mathematical Knowledge. Ph.D. thesis, University of St Andrews.

(2015). A problem with the dependence of informal proofs on formal proofs. *Philosophia Mathematica*, 23, 295–310.

Tarnopolsky, C. (2010). *Prudes, Perverts, and Tyrants: Plato's "Gorgias" and the Politics of Shame*. Princeton, NJ: Princeton University Press.

Tarski, A. (2002). On the concept of following logically. *History and Philosophy of Logic*, 23, 155–196.

Taylor, R., & Wiles, A. (1995). Ring theoretic properties of certain Hecke algebras. *Annals of Mathematics*, 141, 553–572.

Thom, P. (2016). Robert Kilwardby's disputational logic. *History and Philosophy of Logic*, 37, 230–243.

(2016). The syllogism and its transformations. In C. Dutilh Novaes & S. Read (eds.), *The Cambridge Companion to Medieval Logic* (pp. 290–315). Cambridge: Cambridge University Press.

Thompson, V., Striemer, C. L., Reikoff, R., Gunter, R. W., & Campbell, J. D. (2003). Syllogistic reasoning time: Disconfirmation disconfirmed. *Psychonomic Bulletin & Review*, 10, 184–189.

Thomsen Thörnqvist, C. (2014). *'Anonymus Aurelianensis III' in Aristotelis Analytica Priora: Critical Edition, Introduction, Notes, and Indexes*. Leiden: Brill.

Thurston, W. (1994). On proof and progress in mathematics. *Bulletin of the American Mathematical Society*, 30, 161–177.

Tolley, C. (2012). Bolzano and Kant on the nature of logic. *History and Philosophy of Logic*, 33, 307–327.

Tomasello, M. (2014). *A Natural History of Human Thinking*. Cambridge, MA: Harvard University Press.

(1999). *The Cultural Origins of Human Cognition*. Cambridge, MA: Harvard University Press.

Torrens, D., Thompson, V., & Cramer, K. M. (1999). Individual differences and the belief bias effect: Mental models, logical necessity, and abstract reasoning. *Thinking & Reasoning*, 5, 1–28.

Trafford, J. (2017). *Meaning in Dialogue*. Berlin: Springer.

Trippas, D., Thompson, V., & Handley, S. J. (2017). When fast logic meets slow belief: Evidence for a parallel-processing model of belief bias. *Memory & Cognition*, 45, 539–552.

Trouche, E., Sander, E., & Mercier, H. (2014). Arguments, more than confidence, explain the good performance of reasoning groups. *Journal of Experimental Psychology: General*, 143, 1958–1971.

Tymoczko, T. (1979). The four-color problem and its philosophical significance. *The Journal of Philosophy*, 76, 57–83.

Uckelman, S. L., Alama, J., & Knoks, A. (2014). A curious dialogical logic and its composition problem. *Journal of Philosophical Logic*, 43, 1065–1100.

Unguru, S. (1975). On the need to rewrite the history of Greek mathematics. *Archive for History of Exact Sciences*, 15, 67–114.

Univalent Foundations Program (2013). *Homotopy Type Theory: Univalent Foundations of Mathematics*. Princeton, NJ: Institute for Advanced Study, https://homotopytype theory.org/book

Van Bendegem, J. (2018). The who and what of the philosophy of mathematical practices. In P. Ernest (ed.), *The Philosophy of Mathematics Education Today* (pp. 39–60). Cham: Springer.

Vlastos, G. (1982). The Socratic elenchus. *The Journal of Philosophy*, 79, 711–714.

Vygotsky, L. S. (1978). *Mind in Society: The Development of Higher Psychological Processes* (edited by M. Cole, V. John-Steiner, S. Scribner, & E. Souberman). Cambridge, MA: Harvard University Press.

(1931). History of the development of the higher mental functions. In *The Collected Works of L. S. Vygotsky, Vol. 4* (pp. 1–251). New York, NY: Plenum Press.

Walton, D., & Krabbe, E. (1995). *Commitment in Dialogue*. Albany, NY: State University of New York Press.

Wayner, P. (2009). *Disappearing Cryptography: Information Hiding: Steganography and Watermarking*, 3rd edn. Burlington, MA: Morgan Kaufmann.

Wendelken, C. (2015). Meta-analysis: how does posterior parietal cortex contribute to reasoning? *Frontiers in Human Neuroscience*, 8, 1042.

Wilkins, M. C. (1928). The effect of changed material on the ability to do formal syllogistic reasoning. *Archives of Psychology*, 16, 5–83.

Wilpert, P. (1956/57). Aristoteles und die Dialektik. *Kant-Studien*, 48, 247–257.

Wilson, D., & Sperber, D. (1981). On Grice's theory of conversation. In P. Werth (ed.), *Conversation and Discourse* (pp. 155–178). London: Croom Helm.

Wittgenstein, L. (1978). *Remarks on the Foundations of Mathematics*, 3rd edn. Oxford: Blackwell.

    (1953). *Philosophical Investigations*. Oxford: Blackwell.

Wolchover, N. (2017). A long-sought proof, found and almost lost. *Quanta Magazine*, March 28, www.quantamagazine.org/statistician-proves-gaussian-correlation-inequality-20170328/

Wolfsdorf, D. (2013). Socratic philosophizing. In J. Bussanich & N. Smith (eds.), *The Bloomsbury Companion to Socrates* (pp. 34–67). London: Bloomsbury.

Yamazaki, Y. (2004). Logical and illogical behavior in animals. *Japanese Psychological Research*, 46, 195–206.

Zardini, E. (2008). A model of tolerance. *Studia Logica*, 90, 337–368.

Zittoun, T., & Gillespie, A. (2015). Internalization: How culture becomes mind. *Culture & Psychology*, 21, 477–491.

Zollman, K., Bergstrom, C., & Huttegger, S. (2013). Between cheap and costly signals: The evolution of partially honest communication. *Proceedings of the Royal Society B*, 280, 1–8.

Index

Aaronson, Scott, 229–230
ABC conjecture, 219–220
abductive reasoning, 29
Abelard, Peter, 138–139
Achourioti, Theodora, 172, 173
Adler, Jonathan, 169
adversarial collaboration, 173–174
adversariality, 54–59
  in Ancient Greek dialectic, 104–106
  cognitive gadgets and, 201–202
  deductive reasoning and, analogy
    between, 174
  in dialogical logic, 54–55
  feminist critique of, 58–59
  in Game-Theoretical Semantics, 54–55
  logical pluralism and, 83
  necessary truth-preservation and, 62–63
  ontogeny of deductive reasoning and,
    171–174
    collaboration between, 173–174
agonist origins, of logic, 39
Akṣapāda Gautama, 124
Albert the Great, 133
Alibert, Daniel, 182–183
analogy
  between adversariality and deductive
    reasoning, 174
  in Ancient Greek dialectic, 129
Ancient Greece. *See also* Athenian democracy
    period
  mathematics in, 93–98
    axiomatic-deductive method, 4, 90, 94
    certainty as feature of, 94
    Euclidean turn in, 95
    generality as feature of, 94
    proofs as element of, 94
    in Prover–Skeptic dialogues, 97
    sociopolitical contexts for, 94, 95–97
Ancient Greek dialectic, 42–43, 98–106
  adversariality in, 104–106
  analogy in, 129
  Aristotle and, 98–100. *See also syllogismos*

Chinese classical thought compared to, 128
classical Indian thought compared to,
  125, 126
cooperation in, 104–106
elenchus in, 101–104, 110–111
  reductio ad absurdum arguments
    compared to, 103
  general background for, 98–101
  Plato and, 98–100
  reductio ad absurdum arguments, 103
Andersen, Line, 208, 211
antilogic, 100
Apollonius, 94
Apology (Plato), 92, 99
Aquinas. *See* Thomas Aquinas
Arabic medieval logic, 140–143
  during Abbasid Caliphate, 140
  assent in, conception compared to, 141–142
  Avicenna and, 139, 141–143
  conception in, assent compared to, 141–142
  disputations in, 143
  falsafa tradition and, 140–143
  al-Kindī and, 140
  Peripatetics and, 140–141
Archimedes, 94
arguments. *See also* deductive argumentation;
    reductio ad absurdum arguments
  definitional scope of, 3
  inferences as distinct from, 3
Aristotle, 131. *See also syllogismos*
  Organon, 140–141
  Posterior Analytics, 4, 8, 19, 109–118
  Prior Analytics, 68, 109–118
  scientific method theory, 19
  Sophistical Refutations, 99, 100
  syllogistic, 3
  theory of demonstration, 67
  Topics, 30–31, 99, 100, 106
associative learning, 197–198, 199
Athenian democracy period, 30
  golden age of, 92
  main political bodies during, 91–92

For EU product safety concerns, contact us at Calle de José Abascal, 56–1°, 28003 Madrid, Spain or eugpsr@cambridge.org.

www.ingramcontent.com/pod-product-compliance
Ingram Content Group UK Ltd.
Pitfield, Milton Keynes, MK11 3LW, UK
UKHW020307140625
459647UK00006B/74

.